JEAN-JACQUES ROUSSEAU

PORTRAIT PAINTED BY ALLAN RAMSAY OF ROUSSEAU
DURING HIS STAY IN ENGLAND (1766)

JEAN-JACQUES
ROUSSEAU

A CRITICAL STUDY OF HIS
LIFE AND WRITINGS

BY

F. C. GREEN

Professor of French Literature at the
University of Edinburgh, and late Fellow of
Magdalene College, Cambridge

BARNES & NOBLE, Inc.
NEW YORK
PUBLISHERS & BOOKSELLERS SINCE 1873

First published, 1955
by Cambridge University Press

This edition reprinted, 1970
by Barnes & Noble, Inc. through special arrangement
with Cambridge University Press

SBN 389 01173 8

Printed in the United States of America

PREFACE

John Morley's admirable *Rousseau* (1873) has never really had a successor in this country, whilst the most recent complete study, in French, of Rousseau's life, personality and work is still that written by Louis Ducros in 1918. Inevitably, both are now out of date owing to the mass of new Rousseau documents published in the last forty years, notably in the vast *Correspondance Générale* (1924–34) and in the *Annales de la Société Jean-Jacques Rousseau* (1905–). As a result, we have several excellent biographies, numerous studies or monographs devoted to special aspects of Rousseau's thought, but no critical survey of his life and writings based on an appreciation of all the material now available. In an attempt to fill this gap I have written the present study, hoping that it will appeal not only to students of French literature and civilisation but also to readers whose interests range over a wider field.

I gladly seize this opportunity of thanking the Leverhulme Research Fellowships and the University of Edinburgh, whose grants have enabled me to consult material in Switzerland and in France. I wish also to express my gratitude to Mlle Rosselet, Chief Librarian of Neuchâtel and Custodian of the Rousseau MSS. deposited there. Her unfailing kindness and expert advice greatly helped me in my researches. Finally I desire to thank the Board of Trustees of the National Galleries of Scotland for permission to reproduce Ramsay's famous portrait of Jean-Jacques Rousseau.

Pending the appearance of a definitive edition of Rousseau's works, the latest is still that published in 1865 by Hachette and out of print. Luckily, there are recent and excellent editions of the major writings.

F. C. G.

CONTENTS

NOTE ON ABBREVIATIONS

Works to which frequent reference is made are abbreviated thus:

Ann.   *Annales de la Société Jean-Jacques Rousseau.* Geneva, 1905– .

C.G.   *Correspondance Générale de Jean-Jacques Rousseau.* Colin, Paris, 1924–34, 20 vols.

Conf.   *Les Confessions de Jean-Jacques Rousseau.* Bibl. de la Pléiade, 1950.

E.G.   *Emile, ou de l'Education.* Garnier, Paris, 1939.

H.   *Oeuvres complètes.* Hachette, Paris, 1865.

NH.   *La Nouvelle Héloïse.* Ed. by Daniel Mornet. Hachette, Paris, 1925.

R.   *Les Rêveries du promeneur solitaire.* Ed. by Marcel Raymond. Lille, Giard; Geneva, Droz, 1948.

V.   *The Political Writings of Jean-Jacques Rousseau.* Ed. by C. E. Vaughan. Cambridge University Press, 1915.

CHAPTER I

THE LOCUST YEARS
SUMMER 1712–SUMMER 1731

Ce qu'on dit de soi est toujours poésie. RENAN

THE lives of great men may not always remind us that 'we can make our lives sublime'. But they do often remind us that our psychological existence is a tricky process of adjustment and readjustment in which our individual self and our social self are continuously trying to achieve a working partnership. For most of us, the most difficult phase of this operation has been virtually completed by late adolescence. By then, the individual self, exposed since early childhood to the moulding influences of family, school and Church, has acquired the habit of conforming, almost unthinkingly, to its social obligations. For others, however, who lack such an environment, life is apt to be a prolonged battle relieved by periods of unstable, illusory calm. Or again, if these environmental influences assume a too repressive form, they defeat their object, opening a cleft between our individual self and our social self; in short, expanding and fortifying our ego. We are all, of course, familiar with the psychological process I have described and, in the light of that knowledge, we pass judgment on our fellows. Yet its complexity and true significance are never more clearly perceived than when exteriorised in the soul-history of an original personality; for example, in the *Confessions* of Jean-Jacques Rousseau.

Born at Geneva on 28 June 1712, Rousseau lost his mother nine days afterwards. She was thirty-nine. Suzanne Bernard, about whom we know little, was connected through her paternal grandfather with the upper class of Genevan *bourgeoisie* which comprised affluent business-men, professors and ministers. Her father, who died at thirty-seven, was twice haled before the Consistory on a charge of 'fornication'. And Suzanne herself appeared before the same august body, once for having encouraged the visits of a married man and again for having attended a theatre at the Fair in disguise. These, however, were nothing more than the escapades of a spirited, pretty girl of twenty-two from whom, as the niece of the respected and venerable Pastor Bernard, public opinion demanded a very high standard of behaviour.

No word of this, obviously, ever reached the ears of Jean-Jacques who heard from his father, Isaac Rousseau, only of Suzanne's gentleness, beauty and virtue. One of his earliest recollections illuminates a common but pathetic situation: the very natural yet foolish attempt of a bereaved husband to melt the bright armour of his child's insensibility. So when in the evening Isaac used to say: 'Jean-Jacques, parlons de ta mère', the small boy would gaily reply: 'Hé bien, mon père, nous allons donc pleurer.'[1] Isaac remarried in 1726, but when he died, writes his son, forty years after losing his first wife, her name was on his lips. Poetry or fact? History shows that Isaac could not have been very uxorious since, in 1705, he left Suzanne to go to Constantinople where he worked as a watchmaker until September 1711. Why he did so is not known. E. Ritter, on sound evidence, rejects the story that Isaac was involved in the political troubles of that period and suggests that he had quarrelled over money matters with his mother-in-law, who had never approved Suzanne's choice of a husband.[2] This seems plausible for it would explain why they married so late, Isaac being thirty-two and his wife thirty-three. Incidentally, Jean-Jacques had a brother, François, born probably in 1702. He was apprenticed at twenty to a watchmaker whom he deserted about two years later. What happened to him subsequently is a mystery. However, shortly after receiving his own legitim, Jean-Jacques drew up a memoir claiming also the half of their mother's dowry belonging to François, on the presumption that the latter had died at Freiburg in Baden.[3]

Isaac Rousseau came of French stock, a Protestant ancestor

---

[1] *Conf.* 7: 'Jean-Jacques, let's talk about your mother.'...'All right, father, then we are going to cry.'
[2] In his excellent 'La Famille et la jeunesse de J.-J. Rousseau', in *Ann.* xvi.
[3] *C.G.* i, no. 38 (1739?).

having emigrated in the sixteenth century from France to
Geneva. But, although bourgeois, his people were small beer
compared to the Bernards. The Rousseau family, if never
politically active, was suspect to the Genevan authorities. Isaac
as a young man gave up watchmaking for a time to become a
dancing-master in partnership with a certain David Noiret who
was accused of impiety. And in 1701 he was convicted of having
challenged to a duel one of the many Englishmen who used to
visit Geneva. In October 1722 he was charged with the more
serious offence of having struck on the cheek with his sword a
Captain Gautier during a quarrel arising from trespass. To
escape a fine and three months in gaol Isaac slipped across the
Genevan boundary to Nyon. Jean-Jacques, as a loyal son, asserts
that his father was the victim of class prejudice since Gautier,
described as a liar and coward, had relatives in the government.
He defends also Isaac's view that, by Genevan law, accuser and
accused should have been treated alike pending a trial. It is
clear, however, that there was no miscarriage of justice. But
the paternal version of the affair left an indelible trace on the
mind of young Jean-Jacques.

It is not easy to form a clear, objective picture of young
Rousseau's upbringing. He himself claims that no royal infant
was more lovingly protected against bad influences. Naturally
sweet-tempered and docile, he enjoyed, we are told, a happy
childhood under the care of Isaac's sister, Suzanne, from whom
Jean-Jacques acquired his passion for music. There were, in fact,
three aunts, 'all good and virtuous', especially Theodora who
was piously inclined and fond of psalm-singing. But, as Ritter
discovered, Theodora, who married an engineer called Gabriel
Bernard, was publicly reprimanded for having scandalously
anticipated her marriage; and all three sisters had incurred the
displeasure of the Consistory for playing cards on Sunday in their
front garden. One has to be, indeed, a wise child to know the
truth about one's relatives. Later, Jean-Jacques grew to dislike
Aunt Theodora whom he suspected of snobbery. Presumably,
in church-going Geneva, the boy's religious education was not
neglected. At his father's bench he acquired the rudiments
usually taught at school and also a passion or the interminable

French romances of the seventeenth century. Over these they used to linger until, surprised by dawn, Isaac hustled his son to bed, exclaiming ruefully: 'Je suis plus enfant que toi.'[1] Indeed, Rousseau once told Malesherbes that at the age of eight, he knew these novels by heart.[2] Their effect, we learn from the *Confessions*, was to develop his imagination and sensibility long before his reason, thus imparting to his mind a very special orientation. 'Je n'avais rien conçu; j'avais tout senti.'[3] This dangerous method, as Rousseau correctly describes it, gave him a precocious knowledge of the passions and sentiments as well as a completely unreal picture of life which experience never quite effaced.

Fortunately, says Jean-Jacques, there were more serious books on his father's bench, drawn from Pastor Bernard's library. These, we are assured, the boy of nine read aloud to Isaac Rousseau and from them derived a taste unique in one of his tender years. Unique is the word, as the titles indicate: Lesueur's *Histoire de l'église et de l'empire*, Plutarch's *Hommes illustres* (in Amyot's charming but unfaithful translation), Bossuet's *Discours sur l'histoire universelle* not to mention others: Ovid's *Metamorphoses* and the works of Molière, La Bruyère and Fontenelle. Yet I wonder if we can trust Rousseau's memory on this point. Certainly not in regard to Lesueur whose *Histoire* did not appear until 1730. And, of all the authors mentioned, he is the one whom Jean-Jacques is most certain he read at nine and remembered, in 1728, at a most opportune moment. For it was thanks to Lesueur, he asserts, whose history was an arsenal of useful facts, that the Turin priests did not have it all their own way in their theological arguments with that remarkable catechumen, Jean-Jacques. One need not, of course, question Rousseau's sincerity. Everyone knows how easy it is, gazing down the long avenue of the past, to make mistakes in chronology.

His passion for Plutarch, however, might well go back to 1720 because Amyot's translucent prose could be understood by an intelligent boy of eight. Besides, his father loved to talk

---

[1] *Conf.* 8: 'I am more of a child than you are!'
[2] *C.G.* vii, no. 1883 (4 Jan. 1762).
[3] *Conf.* 8: 'I had conceived nothing; I had felt everything.'

about Plutarch's heroes and their austere, republican virtues. And Jean-Jacques without doubt approached this author in a spirit of hero-worship reinforced by Isaac's homilies on the rights and liberties originally symbolised in the proud title, 'citoyen de Genève'. Through this mirage his son viewed the ancient republics described by Plutarch and it was the source of many illusions. Indeed, according to M. Oltramare, all the important themes embodied in Rousseau's 'system' derive, not from the famous 'conversion' on the road to Vincennes, but from Plutarch, the link between the proletarian philosophers of early Greece and the Genevan eighteenth-century moralist. When the French monarchy was beginning to decline, says M. Oltramare, Rousseau was completely saturated with these ancient doctrines which, just as much as the emotions of his 'ulcerated heart', turned him at a critical moment against the social state.[1] This is a very attractive and plausible theory, but it does not explain why a whole generation of eighteenth-century schoolboys whose staple pabulum was the Greek and Roman classics produced only one Jean-Jacques Rousseau.

Isaac Rousseau's eclipse in October 1722, winked at by the police, broke up the little household in the rue de Coutance. François was apprenticed and Jean-Jacques, it seems, went to his maternal uncle Bernard who had a son called Abraham. Here, once again, Rousseau's memory deceived him for it was in 1724, not as he imagined in 1722, that he and Abraham became the pupils at Bossey of Pastor Lambercier. In the *Confessions* we read that the two years Jean-Jacques spent in that little village somewhat tempered his 'Roman toughness' and made him a child again. But vigilant researchers have disclosed that this period lasted only a few months. He was at Bossey in August 1724 and back in Geneva before the end of the winter of 1724–5. Jean-Jacques was not, moreover, eight as he asserts, but nearly twelve, a fact which is not unimportant, as we shall observe.

The narrative of his brief sojourn at Bossey consists, quite naturally, of scattered perceptions and sensations. Of the instruction imparted by Lambercier he remembers nothing save

[1] 'Plutarque dans Rousseau', in *Mélanges d'histoire littéraire et de philosophie offerts à M. Bernard Bouvier* (Genève, 1920).

that although he learned little, the pastor's method must have been excellent since it left only pleasant memories. Trifling incidents, however, stand out with increasing prominence on the far horizon of boyhood: the furnishings of Lambercier's study, the fly that settled on Rousseau's hand as he recited his lesson, the swallow that darted through the room, the raspberry canes peeping in at the back window, the charming little epic of the newly planted walnut tree and of the subtle aqueduct contrived by Jean-Jacques and his cousin to divert its waters to their rival willow. Here Rousseau's narrative style reveals the alertness, grace and humour of an original *conteur*.

But we leave this sunny climate when the author enters what he calls the dark and dirty labyrinth of his confessions to dwell upon an experience which a modern psychologist would regard as less unique than it seemed to Jean-Jacques. It concerns the sensation, akin to sexual pleasure, which he derived from the smackings administered by the pastor's sister. Mlle Lambercier, like a sensible woman, delegated this task to her brother on observing the effect produced by her castigations. Yet, according to Jean-Jacques, they exercised a determining and lasting influence on his sexual life. Most probably a psychiatrist would say that he displayed belated symptoms of infantile 'anal erotism' the object of which, however, was always an individual of the opposite sex. One was the enigmatic little Mlle Goton who, on Rousseau's return to Geneva, resumed the punishment discontinued by Mlle Lambercier. That these childish phantasies persisted until adolescence is shown by the following incident which occurred in Turin. Jean-Jacques, then sixteen, was roving the streets looking, as he says, for a Mlle Goton. One day, the wretched lad conceived a sudden impulse to exhibit his bare posterior to some women scouring clothes at a well. A few laughed, others shouted and Jean-Jacques, hotly pursued by a tall man with a bushy moustache and a long sabre, took to his heels. Trapped in a blind alley, he begged for mercy, claiming to be a young foreigner of princely rank but mentally deranged who had escaped from home to avoid incarceration. Somehow his cock and bull story was accepted and he was let off with a caution. But some days later, Jean-Jacques ran into this terrible person who advised 'His Highness' not to try the same game again, jeeringly mimicking the 'prince's' whinings. The shock of this fright appears to have had a salutary effect, for we hear no more of these antics. Rousseau tells us, however, that the original tare manifested itself in another way: in a masochistic desire to 'lie at the feet of an imperious mistress, to obey her commands and ask her forgiveness'.[1] This novel type of love-making, he remarks dryly, seldom led to spectacular conquests. To finish with an unpleasant topic, it seems clear that what psychologists call the autoerotic stage was prolonged in Rousseau beyond infancy. But we can surely dismiss the far-fetched theory of M. Martin-Chauffier that it later passed into a heterosexual phase.[2]

It might be more useful to note that the corporal punishment Jean-Jacques received at Bossey was a novel experience. At home, he had been worshipped but not, he hastily adds, spoilt. Another equally memorable whacking from Uncle Bernard pro-duced a quite different impression. Wrongly accused of having broken a comb and despite his passionate denials, Jean-Jacques along with his cousin Abraham, convicted of another offence, was royally chastised. Thus he conceived his first notion of injustice. The *Confessions* present a vivid image of the young martyrs sitting up in bed, interrupting their weeping to scream a hundred times: 'Carnifex! Carnifex!' From that moment, says Rousseau, occurred a marked and progressive deterioration in his behaviour and general character. The idea of injustice was now ineradicably planted in his consciousness. And, ever after-wards, the knowledge or the spectacle of any unjust action aroused him to a state of ungovernable fury.

At thirteen, the sketchy instruction received by Jean-Jacques came to an end, including the lessons in algebra, trigonometry and drawing he shared with Abraham, who was to be an engineer

---

[1] *Conf.* 17. 'Etre aux genoux d'une maîtresse impérieuse, obéir à ses ordres, avoir des pardons à lui demander.'

[2] *Conf.* 763. Discussing the Turin incident, M. Martin-Chauffier says that the motive of this exhibition was to redeem the crime of having cost his mother's life: Jean-Jacques sought unconsciously to replace her by inverting his sex. But Rous-seau explodes this pseudo-Freudian notion by telling us his motive: it was to obtain a revival of the pleasurable sensations procured by Mlle Goton.

like his father. The latter emigrated to America but there is no truth in Rousseau's statement that his uncle designed the plans for the town of Charleston. He is mistaken also in thinking that two or three years elapsed between his return from Bossey and the decision, reached only after long deliberation, to place him in the office of a *greffier* or notary public named Masseron. He got rid of Jean-Jacques very quickly, irately complaining that Bernard had sold him a pup, or rather a donkey. Uncle Gabriel, indeed, appears to have described the youngster as a prodigy of learning: Masseron and his staff insisted, on the other hand, that Rousseau was no good for anything but watchmaking.[1]

The truth is that, at thirteen, he was singularly ill-equipped for even the humblest post leading to a professional career. Yet, in the absence of any systematic instruction, his passion for reading had given Jean-Jacques a remarkable fund of what schoolmasters used to call general intelligence. What of his education in the larger sense of the term? Except for cousin Abraham, he seems to have consorted only with adults and indeed used to feel sorry for the schoolboys he saw at Bossey who did not enjoy his freedom. His only contacts with these poor captives were the scuffles in which the 'paladin' Jean-Jacques defended his weaker cousin. And what little we know about his home life does not suggest an environment apt to foster the early habits which form a sense of social obligation. As if to counteract such an impression, Rousseau insists that he must have been a docile, timid child always governed by the voice of reason and brought up in an atmosphere of kindness and justice. On the other hand he thinks he was probably 'ardent, fier, in-domptable dans les passions', though honesty compels him to admit that this is pure conjecture: 'je ne me sens pas capable de démêler, de suivre la moindre trace de ce qui se passait alors en moi.'[2] To judge by his subsequent behaviour Jean-Jacques was the type of youngster now described as a potential delinquent: one who has not, in short, enjoyed the advantages of a normal up-bringing. But we must allow the facts to evolve their own pattern.

[1] *Conf.* 30.
[2] *Conf.* 19: 'ardent, proud, untameable in my passions. . . . I feel incapable of distinguishing, of following up the slightest trace of what went on inside me then.'

On 26 April 1725 Rousseau was apprenticed for five years to a master engraver, Abel Ducommun who was, by the way, only twenty. For the rest we must rely on the *Confessions* which portray him as a violent, tyrannical boor who, in the space of three years, transformed a sensitive and eager lad into a furtive little liar and petty thief. Ducommun, we are told, tarnished the brightness of Rousseau's boyhood and very quickly blunted his lively and loving spirit, whereas under a different master, he would have grown to like his craft. Yet, one suspects that Ducommun had good reason to be enraged at an apprentice who broke into his office, abstracted his materials and ruined his best tools by engraving medals for an imaginary order of chivalry. The fact is that Jean-Jacques was now, for the first time, subjected to a disciplined mode of life which he detested. Moreover, proud of his book-learning, he found it intolerable to be classed with his unlettered mates and to be obliged to leave the table whilst Ducommun and his journeymen enjoyed the more attractive dishes. Deprived of his former liberty, he reacted by wasting his master's time in private ploys of his own invention. In retrospect, Jean-Jacques viewed this period as one of moral degeneration during which he rapidly exchanged his good habits and gentle tastes for those of his corrupt fellow apprentices. Suborned by a journeyman to steal and sell asparagus belonging to the latter's mother, Jean-Jacques soon became expert at pilfering on his own account, though only eatables and never money. Soundly and frequently whipped, he grew taciturn, moody and unapproachable. An avid reader, he sold his shirts to borrow books from the lending library of old Mme La Tribu, devouring a great deal of rubbish yet with the instinctive shame or *pudeur* of youth, refusing the smutty works she sometimes leeringly pressed upon him. It is ironical to reflect that Rousseau who was so often to be branded as an immoralist, never read an obscene book until he was thirty and then only by accident and with revulsion.

The Jean-Jacques of fifty-three dwells pityingly on the image of the forlorn urchin of thirteen who sought in the world of cheap fiction an escape from the harsh tyranny of Ducommun and the society of his brutal companions. To this, he later ascribed that love of solitude which his enemies wrongly called misanthropy. Wrongly, because it sprang from an excess of sensibility, from the yearning of a tender, loving soul driven to seek in books what he could not find in his uncongenial environment: the love and sympathy of kindred spirits. It transpires, however, that Jean-Jacques was by no means a complete recluse for, on Sundays, he used to go with the other apprentices on their jaunts outside the city walls. We learn that on two occasions they returned too late and found the gates closed. That meant sleeping outside town followed by a painful interview with Ducommun. One Sunday, according to Rousseau, a malicious officer of the guard deliberately ordered the drawbridge to be raised half an hour before the usual time. As he saw the terrible horns ascending, Rousseau was seized by a strange intuition. They symbolised, he thought, a turning point in his destiny. In an access of despair and grief, he threw himself on his face, biting the turf to the huge amusement of his companions. Then, turning on his heel, Jean-Jacques swore never to go back to Ducommun but to seek his fortune outside Geneva.

We have no way of verifying his dramatic story. It is plain, however, that three years of rigid discipline had failed to inculcate in Rousseau those habits which in a normal domestic environment are usually acquired at an earlier age. The root cause of his misery at Ducommun's was not, I think, his employer's severity but the latter's failure to discern the uniqueness of Jean-Jacques. By flattering the lad's excessive *amour-propre*, Ducommun could easily have won his affection and admiration as did later the wise abbé Gaime. Instead, he treated him exactly as an apprentice, more idle and perhaps more recalcitrant than the average. Indeed, he had promised Jean-Jacques a really memorable lambasting on his next offence. But this the latter was resolved to avoid. What the 'terrible horns' really symbolised, therefore, was the culprit's refusal to accept the painful consequences of his conduct, a fundamental trait of Rousseau's character. Time and again, in the *Confessions*, the admissions prompted by sincerity are half retracted in a phrase dictated by his ineradicable *amour-propre*. And how truly Jean-

Jacques remarks, alluding to the events of these formative years: 'pour me connaître dans mon âge avancé, il faut m'avoir bien connu dans ma jeunesse.'[1]

Apologising for such 'puerile' details, Rousseau points out that his readers were never promised the spectacle of a 'great personage' but only a true portrait. Yet what guarantee have we that he was capable of etching an objective self-portrait? Here one might profitably consider a passage contained in the original MS. of the first four books of his *Confessions*: 'En me livrant à la fois au souvenir de l'impression reçue et au sentiment présent, je peindrai doublement l'état de mon âme, savoir au moment où l'événement m'est arrivé et au moment où je l'ai décrit.'[2] This claim is based on an error which has been exposed by modern psychology. It is an illusion to suppose, like Rousseau, that we can hold simultaneously in the consciousness two separate, clear-cut images: that of our immediate psychic state and the exact recollection of a past state of soul. And it so happens that the *Confessions* furnish, at this point, a typical illustration of this psychological error and its effects. In 1765, when he composed these pages about his youth, Jean-Jacques was obsessed by the fixed idea that the public, because of his love of solitude, regarded him as a misanthrope. Had not the perfidious Diderot, in one of his plays, maliciously coined the maxim, expressly aimed at Jean-Jacques, that only a wicked man lives alone? In this state of soul the latter tried to re-create his psychological existence at Ducommun's with the inevitable result that the present retroactively influenced his memory-images. And so we have the picture, not only of the idle apprentice who reads at his work-bench or when running errands —which is perfectly normal—but also of a lonely, misunderstood adolescent, naturally affectionate and gregarious, yet clinging to the solitude of his ivory tower so as to escape the harsh reality of an intolerable milieu. In short, Rousseau does

---

[1] *Conf.* 171: 'to know me in my riper years, it is necessary to have known me well in my youth.'

[2] *Conf.* 756: 'By surrendering myself simultaneously to the memory of the impression received and to my actual feeling, I shall paint a double picture of my state of soul, viz. at the moment the event occurred and at the moment I described it.'

not present a 'double' picture but one in which the impressions of childhood are subtly coloured and distorted by the psychic state of the adult who tries to seize and immobilise their original quality.

The Benjamin, from earliest childhood, of a sentimental father, Jean-Jacques never seems to have realised that the 'virtuous citizen' on whose work-bench Plutarch, Grotius and Tacitus were mixed up with the tools of his craft,[1] was singularly ill-equipped to teach his son those habits which, in their ensemble, constitute a sense of social obligation. From Isaac he heard plenty about his rights as a citizen of Geneva, but one wonders how much he heard about his duties. For example, Rousseau thought it quite natural, apparently, that his father should leave for Nyon unaccompanied by his sons. He remarried there four years later shortly after sending Jean-Jacques as apprentice to Ducommun, having thus, it would seem, fulfilled his paternal obligations. The boys would follow in father's footsteps. Yet Rousseau always implies that he had been brought up with different expectations and indeed he was first sent to work as pupil to a notary, Masseron. His father's decision, therefore, must have come as a disagreeable shock and it would seem that his violent hatred of Ducommun camouflaged his hatred of employers in general and of the social organisation which they represent. In short, Rousseau unconsciously made Ducommun and his kind the scapegoats of his disappointed hopes. This attitude, as we shall see, became a habit: in his lifetime Jean-Jacques embarked upon and abandoned twelve different trades. But the original cause of this instability may be fairly traced to his early upbringing.

On turning his back on Geneva he was invaded by a lively sense of freedom and happiness. The world lay before him and some day the world, he resolved, must take notice of Jean-Jacques Rousseau. Beautiful visions presented themselves, of castles inhabited by tender, high-born ladies whose noble brothers would vie for his friendship. He did, in fact, haunt the courtyards of several *châteaux*, singing beneath their windows. But no blessed damosel leaned out from her casement to beckon

---

[1] *V.* i, 131. *Dédicace* to the *Discours sur l'inégalité.*

him inside. Rousseau did, however, receive hospitality from various farmers of his acquaintance which suggests that he and his companions had often passed that way. It is difficult to say whether Rousseau, now that he had burnt his boats, knew what he was going to do next. His first action was to inform Abraham who obediently arrived bringing money and the gift of a little sword greatly coveted by his cousin. Yet Abraham, observes Jean-Jacques reproachfully, made no effort to dissuade him from his resolution or to share it because his uncle and aunt disapproved of their son's friendship with a common apprentice. Abraham, as Rousseau had no doubt intended, informed Uncle Gabriel, who set forth in pursuit of his nephew, followed some days later by Isaac Rousseau.

Meanwhile, after wandering aimlessly in the region, Jean-Jacques called on a M. de Pontverre, the *curé* of Confignon, a little village barely four miles from Geneva. This priest was well known to the Genevan pastors as an active proselytizer. De Pontverre gave the boy an excellent meal, chatted about the heresy of Calvin and directed Jean-Jacques to a devout lady, recently converted to the true faith, the baronne de Warens. Need one say that Rousseau could have floored De Pontverre with a few well chosen arguments from his vast store of theological learning? But a guest has certain obligations and the *curé*'s Frangy wine was exquisite. 'Je sentais ma supériorité; je ne voulais pas l'en accabler pour prix de son hospitalité.'[1] It appears, therefore, that Rousseau, even at fifty-three, was still unaware of the old man's technique. For De Pontverre, an expert at his job, knew perfectly well what the effect would be of Mme de Warens's charms on an impressionable youth. Yet Rousseau naïvely pictures the *curé* as a senile fanatic, good-hearted to be sure, but lamentably failing in his duty which was to have sent the lad back to his family. De Pontverre was, on the contrary, an experienced recruiting sergeant in the service of Rome with a long record of successes.

Jean-Jacques first met Mme de Warens at Annecy on Palm Sunday, 1728. It was in a little passage behind her house leading

---

[1] *Conf.* 45: 'I felt my superiority; I did not wish to crush him with it as the reward of his hospitality.'

to the Church of the Cordeliers. 'Que ne puis-je', he exclaims, 'entourer d'un balustre d'or cette heureuse place! Que n'y puis-je attirer les hommages de toute la terre!'[1] Exactly fifty years later to a day, Rousseau composed, in honour of her memory, the tenth and last and never completed *Promenade* of his *Rêveries du promeneur solitaire*. In 1728 Mme de Warens was nearly twenty-nine, Jean-Jacques almost seventeen. Expecting to meet and old and desiccated *dévote*, he was ravished and amazed to look into the blue eyes of a young woman with ash-blond hair and a softly modulated voice. As no doubt old De Pontverre had foreseen, Rousseau became from that moment the adoring slave of this dream princess. Yet the *curé* was nearly betrayed by the lady's natural kindness and pity which almost impelled her to send the boy home to his father, even at the risk of losing her main source of income. For Mme de Warens's house at Annecy was a kind of collecting-station, subsidised by the Church, a halt on the road followed by catechumens on their way to conversion and abjuration.

M. de Conzié, comte des Charmettes, who knew her well, has left a brief outline of Mme de Warens's history in a letter written to a friend in 1786.[2] His impressions of her character and appearance tally, on the whole, with those of Rousseau as presented in the *Confessions*. Later biographers, notably Mugnier, De Montet and Ritter, have produced additional information without, however, substantially altering De Conzié's portrait.[3] At fourteen, Louise-Françoise-Eléonore de la Tour, then an orphan, married Sébastien-Isaac de Loys who was for five years owner and seigneur of Warens. Hence the title 'baronne' retained by his wife after her husband had lost it with the estate. As a girl she came under the influence of François Magny, an adept of German Pietism who was for some months her guardian. A wealthy heiress, Mme de Warens was a born speculator and soon ruined herself and her husband by

---

[1] *Conf.* 47: 'Oh that I could surround that blessed spot with a balustrade of gold! Oh that I might attract to it the homage of the whole earth!'

[2] *C.G.* I, no. 127 (to M. de Mellarède).

[3] A. de Montet, *Mme de Warens et le Pays de Vaud* (Paris, 1891); M. Mugnier, *Mme de Warens et J.-J. Rousseau* (Paris, 1891); E. Ritter, 'La Famille et la jeunesse de J.-J. Rousseau', in *Ann.* XVI.

her grandiose industrial ventures. After thirteen years of marriage, she vanished from her home overnight, in July 1726, and turned up at Evian where the pious Victor-Amadeus II, King of Sardinia, was in residence. One day, as the monarch and his courtiers were entering church they were suddenly accosted by Mme de Warens who threw herself at the feet of M. de Bernex, Bishop of Annecy, seizing his robe and shouting: *In manus tuas, Domine, commendo spiritum meum*! The king, impressed by the fervour of this interesting penitent, had her placed in the neighbouring convent of the Sisters of the Visitation where she abjured and shortly afterwards donated her property, such as it was, to her husband. The latter, in February 1727, obtained a divorce. The king granted the new convert a pension of 1500 francs which the Church supplemented with another thousand. As this was then a comfortable sum, the gossips said Mme de Warens had made a good bargain at a difficult moment. Others believed her conversion to be genuine. She herself told De Conzié that for two years she was much troubled in her conscience. Yet, as Ritter shrewdly observes, from the point of view of a Pietist, there could have been no great difference between Catholicism and Calvinism, an interesting fact which probably explains Rousseau's bewilderment when Mme de Warens, although faithfully observing the ritual of her adopted Church, used to express certain views on religion that embarrassed her confessor. De Conzié thinks the conversion was a *coup de tête*, yet casts no doubts on the lady's good faith.

He saw Mme de Warens at various intervals in her chequered life and speaks warmly of her attainments, charm and intelligence. Pretty rather than beautiful, with a complexion of roses and cream, she had an infectious, tinkling laugh and everyone was captivated by her transparent kindness. Her manner towards Jean-Jacques, De Conzié observes, was that of a tender, indulgent *Maman* whilst he addressed her with deference, even submissiveness. Chockful of energy, Mme de Warens's great ambition was to make a fortune with one of her numerous, ingenious schemes most of which failed merely because she lacked the requisite capital. Havelock Ellis saw her as a restless woman of remarkable intelligence yet perhaps somewhat hysterical. On the other hand, her voluminous business correspondence reveals a keen, tenacious and not over-scrupulous person, in short, the typical, persuasive company promoter ever on the verge of bankruptcy. She had the temperament of a born gambler, really loving the excitement of the game even more than the money. More than likely, in her private relationships, Mme de Warens was, as Rousseau claims, straightforward and incapable of rancour. But, in the desperate period between 1745 and her death, these qualities are conspicuously absent. To Jean-Jacques, *Maman* was a bundle of contradictions. Perhaps, he remarks ironically, Nature ought to have made her less complicated, but he must show her as she was. One suspects, however, that there were pages in the book of Mme de Warens's life which her protégé was not allowed to see because of his youthful inexperience and indiscretion. How much did he know, for instance, of her activities as an agent of the Sardinian government? He portrays her generally as the credulous dupe of cranks, spongers and charlatans, yet admires the dynamic energy and acumen which she lavished on her wild-cat ventures. The truth is that Mme de Warens prefigures a twentieth-century type: the independent woman whose career lies outside marriage, in the exciting world of speculation and intrigue. I have no doubt that as an agent, she tried to play a double game, knowing she was under observation and fearing exposure. All this was incomprehensible to Rousseau whose notions of feminine character were derived from the romances of a bygone age. Often, he noticed, Mme de Warens fell into a reverie, brooding over her plans. 'Hé bien! je la laissai rêver, je me taisais, je la contemplais et j'étais le plus heureux des hommes.'[1] She retired, in short, into that private world, her real world where there was no place for Jean-Jacques. But, like most women of her type, she knew how to relax and then her *Petit* found the Mme de Warens he understood, ready for fun and games or even for long talks about books although, he implies, her literary tastes had largely been superseded by other interests. Bayle, Saint-Evremond, La Bruyère, the authors of her girlhood, were still her favourites.

---

[1] *Conf.* 105: 'Well! I let her dream; I kept silent; I watched her and was the happiest of men.'

But there was nothing old-fashioned about her knowledge of the world and that, Rousseau sensibly observes, is what he most needed as a corrective to his 'idées chimériques'.

To complete this portrait of a remarkable woman, it is necessary to anticipate events. Probably in the autumn of 1733, perturbed by the advances made to Jean-Jacques by the mother of one of his music pupils, and still more by his obvious ignorance of their purpose, Mme de Warens decided that the time had come to initiate him into the mysteries of sex. She therefore appointed a rendezvous in the garden and with impressive solemnity warned him of the dangers consequent upon promiscuous associations with women. Then, in language of the utmost gravity and decency, she made her proposal, insisting that he must take a week to consider his reply. The *Confessions* reflect the complexity of Rousseau's emotions. He was young, ardent and imaginative yet had never thought of his benefactress save with filial tenderness. Intuition urged him to refuse, but curiosity, desire and a spurious sense of obligation prevailed. Too late he realised that his intuition had been terribly right. 'J'étais comme si j'avais commis un inceste.'[1]

Reviewing this scabrous episode, Rousseau insists that Mme de Warens's conduct was actuated by pure and altruistic motives. That is not absolutely impossible. Life is so strange and no man, however rich or varied be his experience, is vouchsafed more than a tiny glimpse of its immense complexity. Yet, in accepting the favours of *Maman*, Rousseau knew that for some years she had been sexually intimate with her amanuensis, Claude Anet, a serious, taciturn young man six years older than Jean-Jacques, who liked and admired him greatly. Probably in 1732, wounded by an insulting remark uttered in anger by his mistress, Anet tried to poison himself with laudanum. It was during the emotional reconciliation which followed, that Jean-Jacques first realised the true nature of their intimacy, which continued until Anet's death in March 1734. For some months, therefore, Jean-Jacques was a reluctant partner in a *ménage à trois*. Yet this fact, he insists, in no way degraded Mme de Warens in his eyes because she was a woman to whom the

[1] *Conf.* 193: 'I felt as if I had been guilty of incest.'

ordinary standards of feminine morality could not be applied. She was, he explains, a sexually frigid type who nevertheless loved her male friends most tenderly. And since they attached an absurd importance to physical possession it seemed to her equally absurd to refuse them anything that might strengthen the bonds of friendship. Now this may be a faithful interpretation of Mme de Warens's promiscuous sexual habits. More probably, however, it reflects an unconscious attempt by Jean-Jacques to soothe his *amour-propre*, grievously wounded, in 1737, by Mme de Warens's preference for the more virile Winzenried de Courtilles. Rousseau seems, nevertheless, to have convinced Dr Otto Adler,[1] who defines Mme de Warens as the type of 'kalte Freundin'. But why assume that she was necessarily undersexed? True, her ruling passion was speculation, and had always been so since her marriage. Yet it is by no means unusual for such women to offer themselves the indulgence of keeping a young man, or as we should say, a 'gigolo'. Later, when bad times came, Mme de Warens could no longer afford an idle and useless 'gigolo', however charming or talented, and, realising that despite all her efforts Jean-Jacques was never likely to earn his keep she was regretfully obliged to put business before pleasure. In any case, Rousseau's continual anxiety about his health and about her financial situation, his habit of waking her in the small hours to discuss these worries must have imposed an intolerable strain on Mme de Warens's indulgence and natural kindness. That she fully appreciated his tender solicitude is beyond doubt. But as a practical woman she must often have reflected that 'handsome is as handsome does'; that, in brief, if *Petit* really wanted to help her, he had only to stick to the post she had found him in the Survey Office at Chambéry instead of quitting it after a few months in order to give music lessons. Clearly, by 1737, she regarded him as a broken reed and turned for solid comfort to a new young man, the more reliable Winzenried. From that moment, as we shall observe, Rousseau's high opinion of her character began to decline and with it his profound love and gratitude. Her subsequent misfortunes, her 'avilissement' or degradation, saddened but did not surprise

[1] *Geschlecht und Gesundheit* (Berlin, 1908), ch. III.

Jean-Jacques. Were they not prefigured in that fatal error of judgment which induced her to prefer a Winzenried to a Jean-Jacques Rousseau? But for that, how different life would have been for both of them in that earthly paradise symbolised by the words, 'Les Charmettes'!

After the failure of her agricultural enterprises in the valley of Les Charmettes, near Chambéry, Mme de Warens embarked on a series of equally unfortunate industrial ventures. At the same time she was tormented by the fear of losing her pension. On her death at Chambéry in 1762, she was quite destitute. Rousseau did not learn the sad news for some months, from De Conzié, who tells us that for some time Mme de Warens had kept house for a wealthy old gentleman. As the latter was unaware of her poverty he left her nothing on his death. In losing him she was therefore reduced to beggary and subsisted on the charity of neighbours. De Conzié severely condemns Rousseau for deserting his benefactress; for preferring, he says, the interests of a washerwoman like Thérèse Levasseur to those of a lady more worthy of his respect. Yet this harsh judgement is based on the ignorance of certain pertinent facts. Mme de Warens tacitly broke with Rousseau when she replaced him by Winzenried. Jean-Jacques, in August 1754, accompanied by Thérèse, visited Mme de Warens at Grange-Canal, near Geneva and tried to persuade her to live with them. Not surprisingly, she rejected his somewhat indelicate offer but accepted some small financial help. Rousseau, to do him justice, confesses that he should have left all and followed *Maman*. On account of his new attachment he did not yield, however, to this impulse. Moreover, he adds, because of his inability to help her, their former friendship had suffered. So he wept for Mme de Warens but did not follow her.

De tous les remords que j'ai sentis en ma vie, voilà le plus vif et le plus permanent. Je méritai par là les châtiments terribles qui depuis n'ont cessé de m'accabler; puissent-ils avoir expié mon ingratitude! Elle fut dans ma conduite; mais elle a trop déchiré mon cœur pour que jamais ce cœur ait été celui d'un ingrat.[1]

[1] *Conf.* 384: 'Of all the remorse I have felt in my life this was the sharpest and most permanent. I deserved by my conduct the terrible punishment which has since

We must now, however, return to the spring of 1728, when Jean-Jacques left Annecy for the hospice maintained at Turin for catechumens by the *Arciconfraternita dello Spirito Santo* where aspirants were prepared for conversion and received into the Roman communion. It was not Mme de Warens but an interested and officious individual called Sabran who approached the bishop and obtained funds for the journey. It took not seven but twenty days to reach Turin and, en route, Sabran and his wife stripped their young companion of everything but his clothes and little sword. Jean-Jacques was too happy to care. He was young, healthy, full of confidence, gloriously happy, a state of soul admirably communicated in the following words: 'J'étais dans ce court, mais précieux moment de la vie où sa plénitude expansive étend pour ainsi dire notre être par toutes nos sensations, et embellit à nos yeux la nature entière du charme de notre existence.'[1] He entered the sinister portals of the Hospice of the Holy Ghost on 12 April 1728.

Meanwhile, what efforts had been made by his family to catch up with the truant? Uncle Gabriel let nearly a week pass before setting out and then got no farther than Confignon. Isaac Rousseau, ten days after his son's flight, left Nyon for Annecy and, having presumably interviewed Mme de Warens, went home. On 30 March he signed a promise to pay Ducommun twenty-five crowns if the fugitive did not return in four months. Rousseau, to account for this lack of paternal zeal, suggests that his father was unconsciously influenced by the fact that during the absence of both sons he enjoyed the usufruct of their mother's dowry. Isaac's conduct, Jean-Jacques claims, taught him a great moral lesson, perhaps the only valuable maxim he ever acquired. It is to avoid situations which place our duty in conflict with our interest. Otherwise, however sincerely we love virtue we may commit, involuntarily, a wicked act whilst still remaining good: a variant of the Jesuitical sophism which was

continually overwhelmed me. May it have atoned for my ingratitude! This revealed itself in my conduct, but has torn my heart too much for it to have ever been the heart of an ingrate.'

[1] *Conf.* 56: 'I was in that brief yet precious moment of life when its expansive plenitude extends our being, so to speak, through all our sensations and embellishes with the charm of our existence our whole vision of Nature.'

anathema to Pascal. It crops up frequently in Rousseau's more subjective writings. Although he had no love for the Jesuits, he derived great comfort from the Casuist doctrine that where there is purity of intention there can be no wickedness. 'Toute la moralité de la vie humaine est dans l'intention de l'homme', he wrote to Mme d'Houdetot.[1] And, like Rousseau himself, his hero Saint-Preux may be very often capable of an involuntary fault though his heart is incapable of harbouring a wicked design. 'That is what distinguishes the frail man from the wicked man.'[2]

In considering Rousseau's account of his sojourn at the Hospice, we must note what he says in the *Rêveries du promeneur solitaire* about how he composed the *Confessions*. Writing from memory, he often forgot or but vaguely recalled what had actually happened. And, in such cases, says Rousseau:

I related the things I had forgotten as it seemed to me they must have been, as perhaps, in fact, they had been, never contrary to my memory of what they had been. Sometimes I invested the truth with alien charms; but never did I substitute lies in order to palliate my vices or to arrogate virtues to myself.[3]

We may assume, therefore, that Rousseau, in telling of his abjuration, never deliberately lied. Yet, in re-creating the tattered fresco of remembered experience, he frequently inserted 'what must have been'. As a result, we have the impression of a most reluctant catechumen who grappled with his examiners for a month before the final capitulation. In all, we are told in the *Confessions*, he spent two months as a prisoner in the hospice. Now part of Rousseau's story is flatly contradicted by the records of that institution. They show that he entered on 12 April 1728 and was rebaptised—which is unusual in the case

---

[1] *C.G.* III, p. 364 (*Lettres morales*): 'The whole morality of human life is in man's intention.'

[2] *N.H.* VI, Lettre 8: 'C'est ce qui distingue l'homme fragile du méchant homme.'

[3] *R.* 68: 'Je disais les choses que j'avais oubliées comme il me semblait qu'elles avaient dû être, comme elles avaient été peut-être en effet, jamais au contraire de ce que je me rappelais qu'elles avaient été. Je prêtais quelquefois à la vérité des charmes étrangers, mais jamais je n'ai mis le mensonge à la place pour pallier mes vices, ou pour m'arroger des vertus.'

of a Protestant—on 22 April. There is no record either of his abjuration or of his departure. E. Ritter surmises, however, that Jean-Jacques abjured on 21 April and, because he was a difficult subject requiring further indoctrination, remained until June.[1] More recently, E. Gaillard concludes that Rousseau abjured on 22 April and left, after rebaptism, on the following day.[2] I think we must face the fact that, lacking documentary evidence, we do not know exactly when Jean-Jacques, after having abjured, cleared out of the hospice and suggest, tentatively, that since he had very little money and did not know the town, he may have asked for and been granted bed and board for a time at the hospice in order to find his bearings in Turin and acquire a smattering of Italian. After all, why assume that his hosts were inhuman? On the other hand, it is equally possible that their argumentative convert outstayed his welcome and was then, as he complains, thrust out into the street to fend for himself.

If *amour-propre* and belated regret blurred certain recollections of the hospice, others, on the contrary, survived the corroding effect of time. Confronted by the spectacle of human life in its most repellent aspects, this sensitive and intelligent adolescent acquired impressions which left an indelible trace in his consciousness. Small wonder, therefore, that he felt impelled to stress, some thirty years later, in his *Emile*, the danger inherent in a too precocious knowledge of sexual matters, for in the hospice sexual vice in its most hideous, abnormal forms, was brutally thrust upon him: homosexuality, onanism and exhibitionism. But what revolted him even more, we are told, was the memory of his subsequent interview with a priest to whom he complained; the latter's refusal to credit the boy's innocence; the unctuous attempt to gloss over these foul realities and to pretend that they were not, after all, so very unnatural. Here, of course, we have no means of verifying Rousseau's terrible indictment. That the 'Moor' whose vile overtures revolted Jean-Jacques really existed is, however, quite certain: his name figures in the register as Abram Ruben of Aleppo, baptised the day after Rousseau, but retained for a week. Like most of the other catechu-

---

[1] *Ann.* xvi, 162 *seq.*   [2] *Ann.* xxxii, 'Jean-Jacques Rousseau à Turin'.

mens, he was apparently a professional convert. In describing his former companions, Jean-Jacques coins some new and striking epithets:

mes camarades d'instruction et qui semblaient plutôt des archers du diable que des aspirants à se faire enfants de Dieu...nos sœurs les catéchumènes...étaient bien les plus grandes salopes et les plus vilaines coureuses qui jamais aient empuanté le bercail du Seigneur.[1]

One cannot but admire, incidentally, the self-restraint observed by one gifted with such a rare talent for vituperation in his subsequent replies to the abuse hurled at him by Voltaire and other equally ill-mannered adversaries.

Probably until the end of July 1728 Rousseau tramped the streets of Turin in search of work, helped by the wife of a poor tradesman who lodged him for a sou a day. He was sustained, however, by the incurable optimism, the eager curiosity of youth and, above all, by his incorrigible craving for romance. We glimpse him mingling with the crowd at the royal Mass, dazzled by the splendour of music such as he had never heard; earning an odd coin by his old craft of engraving; haunted always by visions of some dream-princess worthy of his homage. She materialised, finally, as Mme Basile, the pretty young wife of a shop-keeper in whose absence she was jealously guarded by a surly clerk. Touched by the boy's plight, she gave him some articles to engrave and listened to his sad tale, unaware of the havoc she had wrought in Rousseau's inflammable soul. But this romance was nipped in the bud with the return of the suspicious Basile who rudely ejected the juvenile Romeo. Like all Rousseau's frustrated passions, however, it blossomed with the years into the memory of a profoundly beautiful sentimental experience though, in reality, the sole reward of his adoration was a respect-ful kiss lightly bestowed on the lady's fingertips. It was not to this princess but to his blowsy landlady that Rousseau owed the post he found, in August, as lackey to Mme de Vercellis, a widowed countess afflicted with cancer. She died three months later without remembering him in her will, an oversight quite

---

[1] *Conf.* 59: '...my fellow-pupils, who seemed like Devil's constables rather than aspirants to the honour of becoming God's children...our sister catechumens... were certainly the biggest sluts and the most disgusting trollops who ever defiled the fold of the Lord.'

unjustly attributed by Jean-Jacques to her lack of natural sensibility and the intrigues of her servants.[1]

But this period of Rousseau's life was to be for ever graven in
his memory by a much more serious incident. At the inventory
of Mme de Vercellis's belongings, someone missed a bit of red
and silver ribbon that had arrested the magpie glance of
Rousseau; he had stolen it, and it was found in his possession.
Pressed for an explanation, he stammered, blushed then said he
had got it from a servant-girl Marion to whom, indeed, he had
meant to give the ribbon. In Marion's presence he boldly
repeated his lying accusation, despite her earnest appeals to his
better nature. Both were dismissed by the comte de la Roque,
nephew of Mme de Vercellis, with the remark that the conscience
of the guilty one would avenge the innocent. And, says Jean-
Jacques, never was a prophecy more terribly and integrally fulfilled. To the end of his life he was intermittently haunted by
visions of Marion's possible fate. Indeed, it is clear from a page
in Rousseau's last work, the *Rêveries*, that time had never closed
this festering sore in his conscience. Yet here, as in the *Confessions*, the quality of his self-reproach is adulterated by
dialectic. We look in vain for any sign of what the old schoolmen
called *contrition*, real sorrow for sin. No. Jean-Jacques lied from
vanity, from the fear, which he dreaded more than death, of
being humiliated in the presence of people whose good opinion
he valued. In falsely accusing Marion, his intention was not
evil, because evil could not exist in his nature. On the contrary,
in a strange way, it was his very affection for Marion which
procured her undoing.[2] Had De la Roque interviewed him
privately, exhorting him gently to tell the truth, Jean-Jacques
would have made a clean breast of the whole affair. I wonder.

During the five or six weeks following Rousseau's departure
from Mme de Vercellis's occurred the incident at the well and
the flight from the tall man with the long sabre and the big
moustache. Rousseau himself ascribes his agitated psycho-

---

[1] E. Gaillard (*Ann.* xxxii) has established the useful chronological fact that
Mme de Vercellis died on 20 December 1728. He proves also that the 'clever' and
'insinuating' couple accused by Rousseau of intriguing against him were called
not Lorenzi, but Lorenzini and were old, trusted stewards.

[2] *Conf.* 84.

logical state at this period to the effects of puberty in an adolescent whose only erotic memories were associated with Mlle Goton and Mlle Lambercier. Luckily, during that critical phase, he came under the influence of a Savoyard, the abbé Gaime whose acquaintance he had made at Mme de Vercellis's. This wise and good priest gave the lad precious advice. He taught Rousseau to view himself and society in proper perspective. An experienced judge of human nature, Gaime seems to have rightly diagnosed the cause of Rousseau's spiritual distemper. Therefore, instead of vainly attempting to stamp out his egotism, he gently showed him the illusory character of his present ambitions. He pointed out to Jean-Jacques that it requires more true virtue and moral strength to fulfil the little daily obligations of social life than to perform heroic deeds; it is also infinitely harder to win the esteem of men than their admiration. The secret of education, as Anatole France once wisely observed, lies in the art of exciting curiosity and, above all, of satisfying it at the moment of its ripeness. Gaime possessed this art. His maxims, carefully timed, sank into an eagerly receptive mind. We know how keenly sensible Rousseau was of his debt to Gaime, who is in part the original of the *Vicaire savoyard.*

Apparently, however, although Gaime's teachings halted that inclination to vice which, says Rousseau, was fostered by idleness and lack of vocation, they had no retrospective effect. Thus, whilst telling us of the visit he paid to De la Roque, it does not occur to Jean-Jacques that here was an admirable opportunity to purge his conscience by exonerating poor Marion. Instead, he recalls only his bitter chagrin on learning that the new post found for him by the count was merely that of lackey to the venerable comte de Gouvon, equerry to the queen and head of the House of Solar. Now, the Marion incident raises a question which has always intrigued me. Jean-Jacques was a fresh convert to Catholicism. It is improbable that he did not occasionally go to confession. If so, either he hid the fact that he had broken the ninth commandment, or else disobeyed the order which his confessor must have given him to tell De la Roque the truth. But, most probably, Rousseau had forgotten the whole affair.

The idea which had obsessed Jean-Jacques at Mme de Vercellis's persisted during his nine months in the service of the Comte de Gouvon. It may be crystallised in one phrase: 'je n'étais pas à ma place.'[1] But whereas the Lorenzini, observing this fact, had assiduously concealed it from their mistress, the Gouvon family seemed, on the contrary, to recognise the unique intelligence and talents of their lackey. Note, for instance, the minor sensation created at table when, during an argument about the meaning of the family motto *Tel fiert qui ne tue pas*, Jean-Jacques, consulted by the kindly old count, explains that *fiert* is the present indicative of the archaic verb *férir*, to strike. That, says Rousseau, was one of those brief but delicious moments which restores the natural order of things by avenging depreciated merit for the insults of fortune.[2] Delicious, because it won him an interested glance from the count's proud granddaughter, Mlle de Breil, hitherto maddeningly unresponsive to the discreet overtures of the timid, infatuated flunkey. That Rousseau was distinguished from the other servants is evident from the fact that the abbé de Gouvon taught him Latin and sometimes employed him as a secretary. Whether, as Jean-Jacques asserts, he was being groomed for a more permanent and confidential post in the Gouvon family, it is hard to say. If so, he missed a great opportunity by his irrational, ungrateful conduct. Meeting one day a former fellow-apprentice named Bâcle, he began to neglect his duties for the society of that jovial individual. When reprimanded, Jean-Jacques sulked and, on learning that Bâcle was about to set out for Geneva on foot, resolved to accompany him. Dismissed for insolence, he rudely brushed aside the kind offers of De Gouvon's nephew to intercede on his behalf and, in great fettle, marched off with Bâcle. They carried a small pneumatic fountain, *une fontaine de Hiéron*, which they fondly imagined would prove a gold-mine. It did indeed excite curiosity at the various inns where they lodged but no one felt inclined to pay his penny for the peepshow. Nearing Annecy, eager to get rid of his friend, Rousseau treated him coldly. But Bâcle, who was no fool, needed no such hint and made for Geneva. Jean-Jacques, trembling with anxiety, went

---

[1] *Conf.* 81: 'I was not in my rightful place.' [2] *Conf.* 93.

to see Mme de Warens and threw himself at her feet. She received him kindly, yet with no surprise. Providence had sent him back to her and she would not desert him. People, she remarked, could say what they liked, which suggests that her doings were a fertile topic of public gossip and speculation.

Young Rousseau, at last, had found the home for which he had longed and in a perfect setting. For the first time since Bossey, he woke up to see green leaves and fields outside his window. So, ever afterwards, he will remember Mme de Warens against a background of flowers and verdure: 'Ses charmes et ceux du printemps se confondaient à mes yeux. Mon cœur, jusqu'alors comprimé, se trouvait plus au large dans cet espace, et mes soupirs s'exhalaient plus librement parmi ces vergers.'[1] The days flitted by in an atmosphere of serene happiness, crowded with trivial yet exciting incidents. Soon Mme de Warens was his *Maman* and he her *Petit*; for Jean-Jacques, with his frustrated craving for maternal love and caresses, was still a child. On this point he insists. And but for Mme de Warens, their original, perfect relationship would never have altered. She would have always have been for him a young and pretty mamma, a beloved sister or a delightful, loving friend. Never, as Rousseau later reaffirms, was he really in love with her. We need not doubt his word.

Now, it is very easy to form an over-simplified and perhaps false impression of this phase in Rousseau's psychological existence. To the objective spectator, Jean-Jacques figures as the classic 'bel ami' kept by a woman ten years his senior. And, indeed, it is undeniable that he was housed, fed and clothed by his benefactress for almost thirteen years, a situation which he appears to have accepted as a matter of course. Though keenly sensible of her precarious financial position, his attitude was that if Mme de Warens did not spend her money on *Petit*, it would have trickled inevitably into the pockets of the sharks who exploited her credulity and generosity. One must remember that in his eyes she was, for all their intimacy, la baronne de

---

[1] *Conf.* 103: 'In my eyes her charms were confused with those of springtime. My heart, till then constricted, had more room to expand in that spacious milieu and my sighs found a freer outlet amongst those orchards.'

Warens, a point which De Conzié noted. And, if she lived in a chronic state of debt, this very fact in the eyes of a completely penniless youngster was a sign of affluence, especially since Mme de Warens always kept open house and a generous table. He never discerned, I feel sure, the unpleasant implications of his own situation as the protégé of Mme de Warens and that is odd in one so passionately obsessed by the idea of independence. But one must not forget, on the other hand, that at least until the momentous interview in the garden at Chambéry, Rousseau pictured himself as a petted adopted son. Besides, he was by no means an idle parasite, for *Maman*, an accomplished herbalist, kept him busy, he says, with all sorts of uninteresting jobs: copying recipes, sorting and macerating herbs for her weird elixirs.

In one of his most exquisite pages, Rousseau has distilled the fragrant essence of his sensations and emotions during his sojourn at Annecy in 1729. Strolling one evening in the country-side while Mme de Warens is at vespers, it gradually dawns upon him that this period of supreme felicity cannot long endure. To escape the intolerable thought, launching out on the wings of imagination towards the distant future, he conceives the blessed vision of a happiness more durable, unclouded by fears of a separation.

Cela donnait à ma rêverie [he writes] une tristesse qui n'avait pourtant rien de sombre, et qu'un espoir flatteur tempérait. Le son des cloches, qui m'a toujours singulièrement affecté, le chant des oiseaux, la beauté du jour, la douceur du paysage, les maisons éparses et champêtres dans lesquelles je plaçais en idée notre commune demeure; tout cela me frappait tellement d'une impression vive, tendre, triste et touchante, que je me vis comme en extase transporté dans cet heureux temps et dans cet heureux séjour où mon cœur, possédant toute la félicité qui pouvait lui plaire, la goûtait dans des ravissements inexprimables, sans songer même à la volupté des sens.[1]

---

[1] *Conf.* 105: 'That imparted to my reverie a sadness with no trace, however, of sombreness, and tempered by flattering hopes. The sound of the bells, which has always strangely affected me, the song of the birds, the beauty of the day, the sweetness of the landscape, the scattered rustic houses wherein imagination situated our common abode—all this evoked in me an impression so vivid, so tender, sad and moving that I saw myself, as in an ecstasy, transported to that happy time and place where my heart, possessing all the felicity it could desire, enjoyed it with inexpressible rapture, with not a thought of sensual voluptuousness.'

The strange thing is that his dream actually materialised although, as Jean-Jacques sadly records, it lasted not a lifetime, but only a moment. Prefigured in that first experience of frustrated happiness, he suggests, was the design of his whole existence. That he himself and not fate alone, had a share in the weaving of this pattern is something that Rousseau never would admit. Yet the facts tell a different story.

The De Warens household comprised, besides Jean-Jacques, a cook, a gardener, the enigmatic Claude Anet and a maid, Anne-Marie Merceret, a pretty girl from Fribourg. It resembled a caravanserai, since its châtelaine was obliged to entertain a constant stream of callers drawn from various social categories. She found time, however, to observe her protégé, sounding him on his tastes and attainments, discussing plans for his future. She formed, thinks Rousseau, an exaggerated notion of his abilities. Indeed, he was unfitted for any post demanding the most elementary qualifications. From the abbé de Gouvon he had acquired a smattering of Latin, a fair command of Italian and a taste for literature. After leaving Geneva, he had lost his former passion for reading. But in Mme de Warens's modest library he discovered Saint-Evremond, the *Spectator*, Pufendorf, Voltaire's *La Henriade*. Gouvon, moreover, had taught him to read with more discernment and to reflect upon style and construction. It was at this stage that *Maman*, without informing Jean-Jacques of her ulterior motive, introduced him to one of her friends, Paul Bernard d'Aubonne, a colonel of militia, a Bernese and, from all accounts, a somewhat shady character. D'Aubonne, having discreetly examined Rousseau, said that the lad, for all his apparent brightness, was unintelligent, woefully ignorant if not silly. It might be possible to make a village *curé* of him, but certainly nothing more ambitious.

It is amusing to note how keenly Rousseau, nearly forty years afterwards and at the height of his fame, still resents D'Aubonne's verdict and what pains he takes to account for it. Incidentally, his delicate essay in self-analysis affords a precious insight into Rousseau's mental habits. He stylises in a brilliant metaphor the violent conflict between emotion and ideation which characterised his efforts to interpret and communicate his experience.

Rousseau asks us to view his consciousness as a stage, like that of the Italian opera, in the process of scene-shifting. First we observe a painful disorder produced by the intermingling of different sets. Gradually, however, just as we think the whole business will end in chaos, there emerges from the confusion a ravishing spectacle. Such is the process that takes place in Rousseau's mind during his attempts at literary composition. This is amply confirmed by the various manuscript drafts of his works not one of which was ever ready for the press until it had been amended and transcribed four or five times. No doubt all intellectual effort is accompanied to some extent by the state of tension, of anxious expectation so well described by Jean-Jacques. In his case, however, the strain was singularly acute because of his highly emotional temperament. It was almost, he remarks significantly, as if heart and mind belonged to two separate individuals. 'Le sentiment, plus prompt que l'éclair, vient remplir mon âme; mais au lieu de m'éclairer, il me brûle et m'éblouit. Je sens tout et je ne vois rien. Je suis emporté mais stupide; il faut que je sois de sang-froid pour penser.'[1] Rousseau implies that emotion cannot be reduced to ideation and thus, precociously, raises a problem which was not to engage the serious attention of psychologists until the close of last century, with the researches of Paulhan, Dewey and, of course, Bergson.

Mme de Warens, on the advice of D'Aubonne, enrolled Jean-Jacques as a boarder in the Lazarist seminary at Annecy directed by le Père Gros, but after two months he was sent home. His conduct was exemplary yet they found him an unsatisfactory pupil. The fact is that Rousseau, never having received any systematic instruction could only learn when the mood seized him, in his own time and in his own way. Gros was a kindly principal and gave the lad special attention. Jean-Jacques, on the other hand, detested his Latin master:

Il avait des cheveux plats, gras et noirs, un visage de pain d'épice, une voix de buffle, un regard de chat-huant, des crins de sanglier au

---

[1] *Conf.* 111: 'Feeling invades my soul like a flash of lightning; but instead of illuminating, it burns and dazzles me. I feel everything; I see nothing. I am exalted but stupid; in order to think I must be cool and collected.'

lieu de barbe; son sourire était sardonique; ses membres jouaient comme les poulies d'un mannequin; j'ai oublié son odieux nom; mais sa figure effrayante et douceureuse m'est bien restée, et j'ai peine à me la rappeler sans frémir.[1]

He adored the gentle abbé Gâtier who respected, one gathers, the susceptibilities of this backward adolescent. In all good faith, Rousseau portrays Gâtier as a sensitive young priest who, having mistaken his vocation, was later imprisoned and defrocked for seducing one of his parishioners. It appears that this is a pure legend which secured, however, for Gâtier a niche in *Emile*, whose *Vicaire savoyard* was created from memories of Gaime and Gâtier. Evidently, Rousseau had now become for *Maman* something of a problem. At the seminary he had spent much of his time studying a volume of cantatas by Clérimbault, one of her gifts. Now convinced that music was his true vocation, Rousseau pestered her to send him as a pupil to the choir school attached to the Cathedral of Notre-Dame at Annecy where Merceret's father was organist. So, for about six months, until April 1730, Rousseau studied under a kind master and good composer named Lemaistre who was unfortunately subject to epileptic fits and periodic bouts of heavy drinking. Enchanted with his new life, Jean-Jacques was a docile and eager pupil, swelling with pride when he waited, holding his little flageolet, for the sign to play his little piece. Basking in the warmth of *Maman*'s smiles he felt immune in this sanctuary from the unwholesome, unsettling influences that had led him astray in Turin.

But one February evening in 1730, a stranger asked to see Lemaistre. This disturbing individual, to whom clung an exciting aroma of Bohemianism, announced himself as Venture de Villeneuve, a musician from Paris. Despite his shabby attire he had the raffish, assured air of a man of the world. His casual, *nil mirari* attitude gave Lemaistre the impression that here was a conceited amateur, but his first performance was a brilliant

---

[1] *Conf.* 115–16: 'He had sleek, greasy black hair, a gingerbread face, the voice of a buffalo, the look of a screech-owl and a beard like the bristles of a wild boar. His smile was sardonic; his limbs jerked like the joints of a manikin; I have forgotten his odious name but his terrifying, sickly-sweet expression has certainly stayed in my memory and I can hardly recall it without a shudder.'

success. The ladies of Annecy sang the praises of Venture, and Jean-Jacques thought him marvellous. The experienced Mme de Warens sized him up immediately as an adventurer and bad company for *Petit*. Lemaistre, whose naturally gentle temper was soured by tippling, quarrelled violently with the Chapter and suddenly resolved to desert his post, leaving his superiors in the lurch, for Easter was at hand. Mme de Warens, partly out of kindness, partly for private reasons, ordered Jean-Jacques to accompany the absconding choirmaster to Lyons. The secret departure was carefully planned, and the first stage of the journey successfully negotiated thanks to Rousseau's ingenuity. But soon the hue and cry was up and poor Lemaistre's trunk with all his goods and musical compositions was seized by the bishop's order. In a narrow street at Lyons, the wretched man fell down writhing in an epileptic fit whilst the panic-stricken Rousseau screamed for help. Bystanders rushed up, to whom he gave the victim's address, then quietly vanished down an alley with never a backward glance. At the time, Jean-Jacques confesses he felt no remorse. He had accompanied Lemaistre to Lyons and there was really nothing more he could do. There was no point in following his friend to the hotel which would only have involved the latter in needless expense. Only later—we do not know how much later—did Rousseau experience the sharp pangs of remorse for this inhuman desertion of a comrade in distress. In the *Confessions* he does not spare himself: 'Grâce au ciel, j'ai fini ce troisième aveu pénible. S'il m'en restait beaucoup de pareils à faire, j'abandonnerais le travail que j'ai commencé.'[1]

Here Lemaistre disappears from Rousseau's story. He himself made for Annecy only to find that Mme de Warens had vanished, leaving no address, accompanied by the faithful Anet. It is now known that, after calling at Lyons, she left for Paris on a secret mission for the King of Sardinia. Returning to Lyons in July, she visited again an old friend, Mlle du Châtelet, a *pensionnaire* at the Couvent des Chazeaux. In August we find her at Chambéry whence, after a brief stay, Mme de Warens proceeded to

---

[1] *Conf.* 127: 'Thank Heaven, I have finished this third painful confession! If I had many more of a similar kind to make I should abandon the task I have begun.'

Turin. Here, early in September, her employer, Victor-Amadeus II abdicated in favour of Charles Emmanuel, a fact which belies, as L. Courtois has pointed out, Rousseau's assertion that *Maman* went to Paris in connexion with this palace revolution.[1] It is not clear why he claims that Mme de Warens sent him off with Lemaistre so as to protect her ewe-lamb from the big bad wolf Venture, unless indeed, she expected him to stay for some time with the choirmaster as pupil and companion. More probably, immersed in her own affairs, she simply forgot everything else. Jean-Jacques now went to live with his hero, Venture, who was greatly in demand at social functions. His neglected fellow-lodger was therefore thrown back on the society of the maid, Merceret and her friends, one of whom, Esther Giraud, an ill-favoured wench, so exasperated Rousseau by her playful attentions that he was often tempted to spit in her 'sour, black, snuff-besmeared mug',[2] a crude and typically juvenile outburst which suggests that Jean-Jacques, at eighteen, was still an unlicked cub.

One gorgeous July morning, sauntering in the cool, leafy shade of a little valley beside a brook Rousseau had his first unforgettable romance. Recorded thirty-six years later at Wootton, in the grey atmosphere of the English Midlands, the elements of that flawless experience presented themselves to Jean-Jacques in their virginal freshness. As if it were yesterday, he heard the gay laughter of two charming young girls, Mlle de Graffenried and Mlle Galley, whose horses refused to cross the stream. Gallantly, because Jean-Jacques had a weakness for *demoiselles*, especially well-laundered *demoiselles*, he came to the rescue, plunging knee-deep into the water. Thereupon, he was gaily impressed as a cavalier for the rest of the day, on an excursion to the Graffenried country-house at Thônes, excited by the news that the young lady's mother was not in residence. Every detail of that heavenly day was for ever printed in Rousseau's memory: the pillion-ride with his arms clasped round Mlle de Graffenried's waist; the rustic meal in a farm-house kitchen; the cherries he gathered for dessert; the kiss timidly

[1] *Ann.* xv, 17.
[2] *Conf.* 131: 'son museau, sec et noir, barbouillé de tabac d'Espagne.'

pressed on Mlle Galley's hand in the absence of her companion; the sweet emotions aroused by a tender friendship which later inspired the creator of *La Nouvelle Héloïse*.

That evening, Jean-Jacques found Venture's smart and equivocal witticisms vaguely repellent. He mooned round Mlle Galley's house, which revealed no sign of life. But the girls had suggested, as go-between, the despised Mlle Giraud to whom, perforce, Jean-Jacques entrusted a letter for Mlle de Graffenried. In due course came a reply which the ecstatic lover smothered with kisses. How long their correspondence lasted we do not know except that Rousseau, to judge from a letter sent to Mlle Giraud from Neuchâtel two years later, was still badly smitten.[1] He appears to have softened towards Esther Giraud despite her 'leveret's eyes' and sallow complexion. This lady, who was not thirty-seven but only twenty-eight, obviously took a maternal interest in Rousseau's spiritual welfare since, in reply to her good advice and anxious inquiries, he reassures her as to his staunch Catholicism. She was, like the two *demoiselles*, a convert. It was Mlle Giraud who now persuaded Merceret to go home to Fribourg and proposed Jean-Jacques as escort. They set out on foot at her expense but as Jean-Jacques crudely remarks, if she expected any tangible return for her money she was deceived even though, *en route*, they shared the same room, Merceret being a timid girl. Her father, who had left his post as organist at Annecy did not, oddly enough, greet his daughter's companion with enthusiasm. Now here, reflects Jean-Jacques, was an opportunity designed by Providence. He could easily have married this girl thus ending his days peacefully in Fribourg as an organist. Instead, two days later, he set out for Lausanne, spurred on by the vagabond, restless urge which had lain dormant since Turin. On the way to Fribourg, however, Rousseau had visited his father at Nyon where Isaac, now remarried, welcomed the prodigal with open arms and sage advice. But he did not persuade him to stay having formed, apparently, a wrong impression of Merceret. Jean-Jacques would have died of grief, we are told, if he had failed to perform this filial duty. Nevertheless, on his return from Fribourg, he bypassed Nyon.

[1] *C.G.* I, no. 3.

Under the assumed name of Vaussore de Venture, boldly representing himself at Lausanne as a Parisian musician, Rousseau obtained credit from a kind innkeeper, Perrotet, who promised to find him pupils. Now here, says Jean-Jacques, was one of those moments of inconceivable craziness during which he was no longer himself. But time and again in the *Confessions* he records similar moments, always with the same alibi of the dual personality. In the Middle Ages it was called *démonomanie*. On this occasion, Rousseau's familiar imp, who bears a strong resemblance to Venture de Villeneuve, suggested to his victim the following mad scheme. Warmly received in the house of a professor of law, Treytorrens, who loved music, Jean-Jacques though ignorant of composition offered to score a concert piece to be played by his host's friends. In a fortnight the opus was ready for execution, which happens to be the *mot juste*. To gild the lily, Rousseau impudently added a minuet-air taught him by Venture. Those who imagine that Jean-Jacques had no sense of humour should read his superb account of this appalling fiasco:

On fait silence. Je me mets gravement à battre la mesure; on commence....Non, depuis qu'il existe des opéras français, de la vie on n'ouït un semblable charivari. Quoi qu'on eût pu penser de mon prétendu talent, l'effet fut pire que tout ce qu'on semblait attendre. Les musiciens étouffaient de rire; les auditeurs ouvraient de grands yeux, et auraient bien voulu fermer les oreilles; mais il n'y avait pas moyen. Mes bourreaux de symphonistes, qui voulaient s'égayer, raclaient à percer le tympan d'un quinze-vingt. J'eus la constance d'aller toujours mon train, suant, il est vrai, à grosses gouttes, mais retenu par la honte, n'osant m'enfuir et tout planter là. Pour ma consolation, j'entendais autour de moi les assistants se dire à leur oreille, ou plutôt à la mienne, l'un: Il n'y a rien là de supportable; un autre: Quelle musique enragée! un autre: Quel diable de sabbat![1]

---

[1] *Conf.* 146: 'Silence fell. Gravely I began to beat time; the performance commenced....No, since French opera existed, never was there such a caterwauling. Whatever they might have thought of my pretended talent, the effect was worse than anything they could have expected. The musicians choked with laughter; the audience opened startled eyes and would gladly have stopped their ears but that was impossible. My tormentors, the musicians, who were bent on fun, sawed horribly enough to have split the ear-drums of a deaf man. I had the courage to keep on at my job, sweating blood, it is true, but prevented by shame from bolting and leaving them all in the lurch. Just to console me, I heard the auditors whispering to each other, or rather to me: "It is intolerable!" or, "What crazy music!" or "What a witches' Sabbath!".'

It is, of course, rank pedantry to question the veracity of Rousseau's delightful story. But why was there no rehearsal? Unless, as I suspect, no one was ever really taken in by Rousseau at all and he was the victim of an excellent practical joke. Anyhow, it made him the talk of the town especially when, in an agony of shame and humiliation, he was foolish enough to confess his masquerade to one of the symphonists. Most of his pupils vanished and, but for occasional letters from the two *demoiselles*, he was quite neglected. A letter to his father written from Neuchâtel in November 1731 reveals his poverty and dejection. It reveals also, contrary to what is stated in the *Confessions*, that Isaac Rousseau had disowned his son who humbly confesses his 'crimes' and implores forgiveness and financial aid. Of this Rousseau says nothing in his memoirs but clearly the 'crimes' alluded to in his letter were his flight from Geneva and his apostasy.

Jean-Jacques remained until April 1731 at Neuchâtel where he found a few pupils. Mme de Warens was much in his thoughts but he felt reluctant to inquire about her whereabouts, partly, he says, through fear of compromising her, partly lest he might hear ill of *Maman*. From Lausanne, he made an excursion to her native place, lodging at the Hôtel de la Clef. At first sight Jean-Jacques fell in love with Vevey and its enchanting surroundings and many years later he chose it as the only possible setting for *La Nouvelle Héloïse*. But he adds, hurriedly, that the Vaudois bear no resemblance to his charming creations, Julie, Claire and Saint-Preux. From Lausanne, too, he used to walk out to the little church of Assens where Catholics and Protestants worshipped on alternate Sundays.

Life at Neuchâtel was, on the whole, pleasant if uneventful. He wandered often in the neighbouring woods, 'dreaming and sighing' no doubt for love, to judge from a fragment jotted down on the copy of his letter to Isaac Rousseau.[1] Now, however much the rationalists seek to belittle the role of contingency in real life, it is still considerable, especially in the existence of those who, like Rousseau, ignore Pascal's maxim

---

[1] *C.G.* i, no. 14 (*Plan de l'idille* [sic] . . .). From the tone of this fragment I doubt if, as P.-P. Plan suggests, it can apply to Mme de Warens.

about four walls. Thus, on an April day, at the little village of
Boudry, Jean-Jacques fell in with a man of noble mien, with a
long beard, a furred head-dress and violet robe. He was an
archimandrite collecting funds for the restoration of the Holy
Sepulchre and has since been identified as Father Athanasius
Paulus, of the Order of Saints Peter and Paul of Jerusalem.
Paulus knew no French but was fluent in Italian of which
Rousseau had a working knowledge. Over a good dinner the
archimandrite invited Jean-Jacques to act as his interpreter and
secretary. The offer was quickly accepted and next day the
oddly assorted pair sallied forth on their mission, arriving at
Fribourg on 16 April 1731.

The municipal records of Fribourg confirm Rousseau's remark that his master did not achieve much here and reveal, in
fact, a curious situation. Paulus was at first well received and
was voted eight *mirlitons* with permission to collect in the town
and countryside for a month. But four days later the gift was
reduced, the permit rescinded and Paulus was invited to leave
the district. On 25 April the Senate of Berne, after hearing an
eloquent harangue from Jean-Jacques, voted ten crowns. The
records do not mention the speech but note the object of
their donation—the ransoming of Christian slaves—though at
Fribourg the collection had been for the Holy Sepulchre! The
minutes of the Council of Soleure record simply that Paulus had
asked help for the poor Christians of Palestine and that if the
Provost was satisfied with his credentials, the Treasury would
disburse the usual sum for such occasions.[1] There is no hint of
the *contretemps* described in the *Confessions* where we learn that
immediately on their arrival, the archimandrite went to pay his
respects to the French ambassador, the marquis de Bonac, who
had unfortunately been *en poste* at the Sublime Porte. The
'secretary' was not present at the interview which ended in the
sudden departure of Paulus and the detention of the 'Parisian',
Vaussore de Venture. De Bonac, a kindly man, soon extracted
a full confession from Jean-Jacques who was not allowed, however, to see the Greek monk again. Paulus obviously had a bad
reputation. As to what ensued, Rousseau's memory is at fault.

[1] *Ann.* xvi, 173. Text of records by E. Ritter.

He tells us that he was on excellent terms with the Embassy secretaries, one of whom, De Merveilleux, had a friend in Paris, a Swiss colonel called Godard who required a companion for his nephew, an officer cadet. Rousseau says he accepted the post and, with 100 francs and letters of recommendation, set out for Paris on foot.

But the *Correspondance* tells a different story.[1] Rousseau stayed only a few days at Soleure then left for Neuchâtel only to find that the pupils he had deserted wanted no further instruction. In despair, he applied in vain for help to his father but with more success, it appears, to the Bishop of Annecy who recommended him to M. de Bonac. It was after his second interview that Jean-Jacques was offered the post in Paris, and left for that city in June, or perhaps in the autumn; even L. Courtois declares himself baffled by the chronology of this period. Jean-Jacques reached the capital in a fortnight but not entirely by Shanks's mare. Frequently kind carriage-folk gave him lifts which he accepted with mingled feelings since they broke into his pleasant reveries.

On his march towards the splendid unknown, Jean-Jacques was flanked by two invisible deities, Mars and Pan. As 'companion' to Godard's nephew, he was to be a soldier, a cadet. Why not an officer, a general? Field-Marshal Rousseau, telescope to his eye, coolly issuing commands on a hotly disputed redoubt, careless of shot and shell? True, he was short-sighted but so was Marshal Schomberg. Besides, he knew some geometry and Uncle Gabriel was a military engineer. Soon, however, conscious of the lovely surroundings, the woods, hills and rippling streams, invaded by Astrean memories, he turned a regretful shoulder to Mars to commune with Pan, the first and most familiar of Rousseau's tutelary gods.

Paris, entered by the Faubourg St Marcel, brought swift disillusionment. Nothing ever, indeed, quite effaced that first impression of squalor, stench and din: the collapse of Rousseau's dream-castles under the impact of reality. Enlarging on the theme, he calmly observes: 'il est impossible aux hommes et

[1] C.G. I, no. 3 (to Mlle Giraud) and no. 4 (to Isaac Rousseau). See also *Ann.* XVI, 174–6.

difficile à la nature même de passer en richesse mon imagination.'[1]
Now most people, as Bergson once complained, use the term
imagination almost negatively to designate any representations
which are neither perceptions nor memories and so, indeed, does
Jean-Jacques in the passage just quoted. Yet others make his
meaning clearer. He possessed to an unusual degree that faculty
of self-hallucination which all of us have to some extent, though
it is peculiarly intense in novelists, dramatists—not necessarily good ones—and in children. In the case of Rousseau, it
never really found a satisfactory outlet in the creation of novels
or plays. On the other hand, when his environment became intolerable, he loved to converse with his *habitants*, the imaginary
denizens of his perfect dream-world. It is a typically child-like
pastime and of that Jean-Jacques was aware when he wrote:
'Although born a man in some respects, I long remained a child
and in many other respects I am one still.'[2]

The post on which he had built such fine hopes turned out to be
merely that of officer's servant, for Godard was a wealthy old
miser. Stingy, too, was the retired officer, De Surbeck, to whom
Rousseau had been warmly recommended by De la Martinière,
the ambassador's secretary. The relatives of De Merveilleux, on
the other hand, received the lad warmly but could be of no
practical help. He did learn, however, that Mme de Warens had
left Paris for an unknown destination. Now short of cash,
Rousseau set out for Lyons, on her track. From Auxerre, he
launched a Parthian shaft at skinflint Godard, a satiric poem and
the only one he ever composed.

There is a spaciousness in these early books of the *Confessions*
which goes far to explain why they are unique in their genre.
For Jean-Jacques, the open road possessed an exciting and tonic
quality, banishing anxiety, uplifting his morale by its lure of
fresh adventure, its hint of a paradise round the corner. A born
'hiker', like Gil Blas, he loved the caress of sun and breeze, the
sheer joy of physical movement, the simple glory of being

---

[1] *Conf.* 156: 'It is impossible for men and difficult for Nature herself to surpass
the exuberance of my imagination.'

[2] *Conf.* 171: 'Quoique né homme à certains égards, j'ai été longtemps enfant et
je le suis encore à beaucoup d'autres.'

young, healthy and carefree. Yet, certainly, that complete extra-vert Gil Blas never experienced in his wanderings anything remotely akin to the feelings and sensations communicated in the following lines:

> Je dispose en maître de la nature entière; mon cœur, errant d'objet en objet, s'unit, s'identifie à ceux qui le flattent, s'entoure d'images charmantes, s'enivre de sentiments délicieux. Si pour les fixer je m'amuse à les décrire en moi-même, quelle vigueur de pinceau, quelle fraîcheur de coloris, quelle énergie d'expression je leur donne! On a, dit-on, trouvé de tout cela dans mes ouvrages, quoique écrits vers le déclin de mes ans. Oh! si l'on eût vu ceux de ma première jeunesse, ceux que j'ai faits durant mes voyages, ceux que j'ai composés et que je n'ai jamais écrits!...[1]

This is of course pure *coquetterie*. For where is the writer who has never, like Jean-Jacques, ruefully contrasted achievement with virtuality forgetting that, whilst all reality is no doubt printed in 'sense and consciousness, the task of the artist only begins when he strives to decode and transcribe his 'livre intérieur', as Proust used to call it.

Having kept no diary Rousseau has but a confused recollection of his tramp from Paris to Lyons. But one incident stuck in his memory. Footsore and hungry, he asked for food at the cottage of a poor French peasant who offered him only rough barley bread and milk. Then, judging from the youth's voracious appetite that he was not an inland-revenue spy, the man lifted a trapdoor and produced good wine, a noble ham and the makings of a golden omelette. His obvious dread of the hated *rats de cave* deeply impressed Jean-Jacques, arousing in him a generous hatred of the 'barbarous publican' who battens on the substance of the laborious husbandman. Perhaps, however, an economist might have viewed the incident rather differently; as proof, for

---

[1] *Conf.* 155: 'I am lord and master of all Nature; my heart, flitting from one object to another, fuses and identifies itself with those which caress it, surrounding itself with charming images, revelling in heady, delicious sensations. If, in order to immobilise these, I describe them to myself, for fun, how vigorous my brush-work, how fresh the colours, what power of expression! Something of all this, they say, is to be found in my works though written in my declining years. Oh! if you had only seen those of my early youth, those composed during my travels, those I never wrote!...'

instance, that the visibility of a citizen's assets is an unreliable basis for assessment. But of course, Jean-Jacques was right, although for the wrong reason: the real vice of the system was the unjust distribution of those *aides* or indirect taxes which his good Samaritan was determined to evade. At about the same period Rousseau paid another visit to Lyons which was engraved in his memory by two scabrous encounters. One concerns a silk-worker, an onanist from whose loathsome advances he fled, trembling and resolved to abandon a vice to which he himself was addicted. The other adventure, narrated in the same transparent style, involved a homosexual abbé who invited the homeless wanderer to share his room. It had a comic sequel in the treatment meted out to the invert and his innocent bedfellow next morning by the women of the hostelry. Incidentally, the quick-witted Jean-Jacques thwarted the priest's evil designs by relating to him with every circumstance of disgust his experiences at the hospice of Turin.

We move to a sunnier climate with the account of Rousseau's arrival, probably in September 1731, at Lyons. He called frequently on Mlle du Châtelet who was daily expecting news of Mme de Warens whom she had recently seen. Jean-Jacques, too proud to disclose his penniless state, was meanwhile reduced to sleeping in the open air. Luckily, the weather was superb. In a passage fragrant as a medieval *aubade* we have Rousseau's impressions of one of those September nights under the stars:

Il avait fait très chaud ce jour-là, la soirée était charmante; la rosée humectait l'herbe flétrie; point de vent, une nuit tranquille; l'air était frais, sans être froid; le soleil, après son coucher, avait laissé dans le ciel des vapeurs rouges dont la réflexion rendait l'eau couleur de rose: les arbres des terrasses étaient chargés de rossignols qui se répondaient de l'un à l'autre. Je me promenais dans une sorte d'extase, livrant mes sens et mon cœur à la jouissance de tout cela, et soupirant seulement un peu du regret d'en jouir seul. Absorbé dans ma douce rêverie, je prolongeai fort avant dans la nuit ma promenade, sans m'apercevoir que j'étais las. Je m'en aperçus enfin. Je me couchai voluptueusement sur la tablette d'une espèce de niche ou de fausse porte enfoncée dans un mur de terrasse; le ciel de mon lit était formé par les têtes des arbres; un rossignol était précisément au-dessus de moi; je m'endormis à son chant; mon sommeil fut doux, mon réveil le fut davantage. Il était grand jour: mes yeux en s'ouvrant, virent l'eau, la verdure, un paysage admirable.[1]

This was his lucky day. Marching gaily down the road, lustily singing *Les Bains de Thoméry*,[2] resolved to invest his last few coins in a square meal, he was accosted by an Antonine brother who asked if he could copy music. So for a few days, fortified by copious re_ ᵗts from the convent kitchen, Jean-Jacques copied music, neatly though with many erasures. It was, in fact, unusable but the good Antonine, M. Rolichon, gave him a crown. More than solvent, for money had arrived from *Maman*, the prodigal set out for her new home, Chambéry.

The effect of her letter, says Rousseau, was to bring him down from the empyrean to solid reality, a psychological event which he examines with great interest. Mme de Warens had found him a position which would keep him near her, so that a real happiness awaited Jean-Jacques. Yet, as a result, he set out for Chambéry in a mood completely different from that of his journey from Paris to Lyons. Then his imagination was agreeably excited precisely because his situation was the reverse of agreeable. Now, with every prospect of an assured, happy future he no longer enjoyed the ineffable delights of reverie. His heart was light but nothing more. In this pleasantly sedate and rational mood he closely observed the objects of his immediate external world, carefully watching the cross-roads lest he lose his way. Obviously puzzled by this psychological change, this

[1] *Conf.* 165–6: 'It had been very hot that day; the evening was charming; the dew refreshed the wilting grass; no wind, a calm night; the air was cool but not cold; the setting sun had left in the sky an afterglow whose reflection tinted the water rose-pink: the trees on the terraces were laden with nightingales calling to each other. I strolled in a kind of ecstasy, surrendering my heart and my senses to the enjoyment of it all with only a little sigh of regret that I must enjoy it alone. Lost in my sweet reverie, I prolonged my walk till late in the night, not observing how tired I was. At last I did. I lay down voluptuously on the shelf of a kind of niche or false door let into a terrace-wall; the canopy of my bed was formed by tree-tops; a nightingale was perched right over my head; I fell asleep lulled by his song; my slumbers were sweet, my awakening sweeter still. It was broad daylight: my eyes, on opening, beheld the water, the verdure, a wonderful landscape.'
[2] A cantata by Batistin.

shift from the plane of the waking dream to that of action, of attention to life, Rousseau tries to explain it:

Ma mauvaise tête ne peut s'assujettir aux choses. Elle ne saurait embellir, elle veut créer. Les objets réels s'y peignent tout au plus tels qu'ils sont; elle ne sait parer que les objets imaginaires. Si je veux peindre le printemps, il faut que je sois en hiver; si je veux décrire un beau paysage, il faut que je sois dans des murs....[1]

A modern psychologist, no doubt, could improve on this analysis. When Rousseau set out for Lyons his future was indefinite. He could therefore dispose of it at his own sweet will since it was pregnant with every imaginable possibility. Rousseau's experience is by no means unique, because as Bergson once observed, 'our idea of the future is more fruitful than the future itself and that is why we find more charm in hope than in possession, in dreams than in reality'.[2]

The last two pages of this fourth book merit some attention because here Jean-Jacques discusses not only the purpose and general scheme of his *Confessions* but tells us how they should be approached if we are to form an accurate picture of the author's personality. In 1761, his publisher Marc-Michel Rey urged Rousseau to write his Life. The latter, whilst not entirely rejecting the proposal, suggested a smaller autobiography, *Mon Portrait*, fragments of which survive and have been published.[3] These rough notes, jotted down in 1761–2, adumbrate the principles which later formed the basic plan of the *Confessions*. They may be summarised as follows. To be sincere and true, Rousseau's self-portrait must be essentially different from the traditional literary portraits which are mere *chimères*.[4] They are, he implies, composed merely of universal human traits which any clever author can adapt to his particular subject with an effect of

---

[1] *Conf.* 168: 'Perversely, I cannot submit to facts. My mind cannot embellish actuality, it must create. It forms exact impressions of real objects—nothing more; it can only beautify imaginary objects. If I want to depict the spring, it must be winter-time; if I want to describe a beautiful landscape, I must be within four walls....'

[2] *Time and Free-will* (translation of *Les Données immediates de la Conscience*), by F. L. Pogson (London, 1910), p. 10.

[3] By Th. Dufour in *Ann.* IV (1906), 259–76.

[4] *Ann.* IV, 263.

probability. Now Rousseau proposes to use a more empirical method, presenting only the elements of his self-portrait, the notations gleaned from his self-analysis, leaving it to the reader to deduce therefrom a general impression of the person called Jean-Jacques Rousseau: 'Quand j'écris, je ne songe point à cet ensemble, je ne songe qu'à dire ce que je sais et c'est de là que résulte l'ensemble et la ressemblance du tout à son original.'[1] Moreover, he has no moral object in view. He is an observer, not a moralist; a botanist, not a doctor concerned with *materia medica*.[2] That these observations are carried out in solitude is, Rousseau claims, an additional guarantee of their veracity because a solitary man is forced to be himself, otherwise his life would be intolerable. But Jean-Jacques hastens to explain that he is a recluse only because of illness and lethargy. Otherwise, no doubt, he would behave like other people, courting public applause.

On the last page of the fourth book, he elaborates these principles and defines the scheme and object of the *Confessions*:

Je voudrais pouvoir en quelque façon rendre mon âme transparente aux yeux du lecteur, et pour cela je cherche à la lui montrer sous tous les points de vue, à l'éclairer par tous les jours, à faire en quelque sorte qu'il ne s'y passe pas un mouvement qu'il n'aperçoive, afin qu'il puisse juger par lui-même du principe qui les produit.[3]

Thus Rousseau accounts for the mass of details about his early youth which may be considered otiose. These are the elements which the reader must assemble for himself in order to form a true picture of the author's character. But here, surely, Rousseau is the victim of the fallacy that the fundamental self of the individual can be recomposed from a series of juxtaposed 'elements' or psychic states. Or may we conclude from the following

---

[1] *Ann.* IV, 265: 'When I write, I do not think of this ensemble. I think only of telling what I know and from that emerges the ensemble and the resemblance of the whole to the original.'

[2] *Ann.* IV, 262.

[3] *Conf.* 171: 'I should like to be able to make my soul, in a way, transparent to the eyes of the reader; and, to achieve this, I try to show it to him from every point of view, to illuminate it from every angle, to contrive that none of its emotions shall escape his notice so that he may judge for himself of the principle which produces them.'

passage that Rousseau, a delicate psychologist, was precociously aware of this deficiency in associationist psychology?

Comme, en général, les objets font moins d'impression en moi que leurs souvenirs, et que toutes mes idées sont en images, les premiers traits qui se sont gravés dans ma tête y sont demeurés, et ceux qui s'y sont empreints dans la suite se sont plutôt combinés avec eux qu'ils ne les ont effacés. Il y a une certaine succession d'affections et d'idées qui modifient celles qui les suivent, et qu'il faut connaître pour en bien juger. Je m'applique à bien développer partout les premières causes pour faire sentir l'enchaînement des effets.[1]

At first sight, so prone are we to view the past in the mirage projected by the present, that it is tempting to see in this passage an anticipation of Bergson's 'pure duration'. More closely examined, however, and as a whole, it clearly reveals that Rousseau, far from perceiving psychic states permeating one another or as Bergson would say 'organising themselves like the notes of a tune', perceives them as a succession each one of which determines that which follows. Such is exactly, in fact, the point of view of an associationist psychologist. Therefore, in order to form a true picture of Rousseau's personality, of his fundamental self it would be unwise to adopt the method, prescribed in the *Confessions*, of assembling or juxtaposing the self-notations furnished therein. For these are indeed *elements* and not constitutive *parts* of the author's fundamental self. To discover that, we must observe his behaviour when he is dominated by a strong emotion like love or *amour-propre* which will reflect the whole personality.

---

[1] *Conf.* 171: 'As, in general, objects make less impression on me than my memories of them, and since all my ideas assume the form of images, the first traits which imprinted themselves on my mind have remained there and those which subsequently imprinted themselves on it have rather combined with than effaced them. There is a certain succession of affective states and ideas which modify those that follow them and which must be known in order to be properly grasped. I always endeavour to develop the first causes in order to make the concatenation of effects felt.'

CHAPTER II

PARADISE LOST
AUTUMN 1731–SUMMER 1742

Affreuse illusion des choses humaines! *Les Confessions*, Livre vi

Le Verger de Madame de Warens; *Epître à M. Bordes*; *Epître à M. Parisot*; *Projet d'Education de M. de Sainte-Marie*

A LOST dimension was restored to French literature when, in the eighteenth century, writers became aesthetically conscious of the varied elements composing their natural environment. Of these pioneers, the greatest was Rousseau whose *Confessions*, in this as in other respects, strike us as unique when compared with the works of previous memorialists, even the superbly perceptive Saint-Simon. In an age when it was considered eccentric to waste ink on such trivialities, Jean-Jacques records the following impressions of his last pedestrian journey from Lyons to Chambéry through Les Echelles, Le Guiers and the Cascade de Couz:

> Bien appuyé sur le parapet, j'avançais le nez, et je restais là des heures entières, entrevoyant de temps en temps cette écume et cette eau bleue dont j'entendais le mugissement à travers les cris des corbeaux et des oiseaux de proie qui volaient de roche en roche et de broussaille en broussaille à cent toises au-dessous de moi.[1]

And, because he was twenty and oblivious of time, he spent a glorious hour collecting huge stones for the sheer joy of watching them crashing in smithereens on the rocks below.

More serious matters awaited him at Chambéry, where Mme de Warens, who greeted Jean-Jacques as if they had been parted

---

[1] *Conf.* 169: 'Bracing myself solidly against the parapet, I cautiously poked my nose over and stayed there for hours on end glimpsing the foam and blue water I heard roaring amidst the screams of the ravens and birds of prey which flew from rock to rock and from bush to bush a hundred yards below me.'

for only a day, gravely introduced him to Don Antoine Petitti, Intendant-Général to Charles Emmanuel, with the words: 'Mon enfant, vous appartenez au Roi, remerciez M. l'Intendant qui vous donne du pain.'[1] The reason for this little touch of theatre, Rousseau discovered, was that *Maman*, worried about her pension, had leased from a colleague of Petitti a dilapidated house with rotting woodwork, rats, beetles and nothing green outside the window. Jean-Jacques, though his post was only a temporary clerkship in the Survey Office, already saw himself as an Intendant des Finances. But, inevitably, he soon loathed the office, his fellow clerks, the work and above all, the fixed hours. True, the coloured survey maps inspired him with a craze for painting, short-lived like so many of Rousseau's infatuations. Painting, he realised after examining his landscapes and flower-pieces, was not his vocation, which was undoubtedly music. Soon Jean-Jacques lived only for the monthly concerts held at Mme de Warens's house and frowned upon by the local tabbies. He conducted a little orchestra composed of *Maman*'s friends: the cultured, elegant Franciscan, Père Caton; the talented organist, the abbé Palais; the dancing-master Roche and one or two select employees from the Survey Office, most of whom were mere louts. Rousseau's intense admiration for Caton is quite exceptional: in general, he describes the regular clergy as either ignorant or crapulous.

The Ordnance Survey had no chance against such rivals as music and the *demoiselles* whom Rousseau now envisaged as his future pupils. Mme de Warens, badgered daily by *Petit*, reluctantly allowed him to resign his post. For once, reality caught up with Rousseau's imagination. Surrounded by *jeunes filles en fleur*, caressed and fêted by the charming and elegantly attired *demoiselles*, De Mellarède, De Menthon, De Challes, De Charly and by a few commoners like the statuesque and Grecian grocer's daughter, Mlle Lard, the young music master basked in a climate of sunny smiles, radiant laughter and exquisite perfumes. Yet this intoxication of the senses in no way affected Rousseau's perceptive faculty and in the *Confessions*, every one

[1] *Conf.* 170: 'My child, you belong to the King: thank the Intendant who is giving you a livelihood.'

of his favourite pupils stands out from the throng, sharply defined by some individual trait, physical or moral. Here is Mlle de Mellarède who was always *en grande toilette* in the afternoon when Rousseau called:

Ses cheveux étaient d'un blond cendré: elle était très mignonne, très timide et très blanche; une voix nette, juste et flûtée, mais qui n'osait se développer. Elle avait au sein la cicatrice d'une brûlure d'eau bouillante, qu'un fichu de chenille bleue ne cachait pas extrêmement. Cette marque attirait quelquefois de ce côté mon attention, qui bientôt n'était plus pour la cicatrice.[1]

The jovial Mme Lard, as Jean-Jacques artlessly mentioned to his benefactress, used to greet him with coffee and kisses. I have already described how *Maman* reacted to these innocent revelations. From her, in the privacy of the alcove, Rousseau now received certain intimate confidences relating to her early sex life. Her first lover, it appears, was a M. de Tavel, who is depicted as a calculating, experienced seducer, a Don Juan at grips with a young woman of cold temperament, attached to her wifely duties, extremely rational and 'unassailable through the senses'. Tavel employed, therefore, the casuistry of a Tartuffe to persuade her that conjugal fidelity is a mere social prejudice and the sexual act a bagatelle, the important thing being to observe the eleventh commandment. This wicked man, however, was justly punished for his crime. Devoured by jealousy, he became convinced that his pupil, having assimilated his immoral teachings, now bestowed her favours on other men, his immediate rival being the pastor, Perret. Now, Rousseau never denies that Mme de Warens had many lovers but, for the reasons already indicated, he strenuously rejects the suggestion that she was a woman of easy virtue. She had lovers as a matter of principle and because she was a 'good sort' and fond of male society. Not for one moment will Jean-Jacques entertain the possibility that he was just another casual bedfellow. And Mme

---

[1] *Conf.* 186: 'She had ash-blond hair; she was very slender, very timid, very fair; a clear, true and fluting voice but was afraid to use it to its full compass. She had on her bosom a scar, caused by a burn from scalding water, which was not very well concealed by a blue chenille fichu. This mark sometimes drew my attention in that direction and soon, not because of the scar.'

de Warens, by insisting upon sexual intercourse, had, with the best intentions, robbed of its bloom a unique and perfect relationship. Nor, implies Rousseau, had she even achieved her original object. In her arms, he longed for a real mistress. 'Les besoins de l'amour me dévorait au sein de la jouissance.'[1]

Rousseau's animated picture of everyday life at Chambéry from 1731 to the summer of 1736 affords only tantalising glimpses of Claude Anet with whom, probably in the autumn of 1732, he began to share the favours of Mme de Warens. Jean-Jacques, though generous in his praise of Anet's industry, good sense and uprightness, conveys the impression that he was never warmly attached to the enigmatic, silent man in black. Anet, he says, conceived a sincere affection for the friend chosen by Mme de Warens, but clearly Rousseau never dared to presume on their friendship. And, though skilled in the analysis of his own troubled psychological existence, he is oddly reticent about the tragedy which occurred shortly after his arrival at Chambéry, in the winter of 1731. Anet suddenly took poison because of an insult from Mme de Warens which, it seems, had nothing to do with the newcomer, who realised only then what were their true relations. But surely, even at twenty, one does not casually dismiss a tragic event like attempted suicide as the natural result of a domestic squabble. It is more reasonable to suppose that the altercation concerned the arrival of the new favourite who knew this and felt guiltily responsible for Claude Anet's desperate act, though not sufficiently interested to probe its origins. An incident that occurred the day after Anet's death from pneumonia in March 1734 lends colour to such an interpretation and suggests that Rousseau, although twenty-two, was still, in some respects, as thoughtless and insensible as a child. Talking sadly with *Maman* about their dead friend, Jean-Jacques suddenly remembered a black coat of Anet's which he coveted and unthinkingly voiced his desire, to the great distress of Mme de Warens who averted her face and burst into tears. Without moralising on an action which Rousseau bitterly regretted, one may assume that it expressed his real and subconscious sentiments. The terrible thing about death, as Proust

----

[1] *Conf.* 215: 'The needs of love devoured me in the midst of enjoyment.'

wisely remarked, is that it nearly always, in some degree, simpli-
fies existence for those who survive. What would be really
interesting to learn is whether Jean-Jacques ever wore that
black coat.

If Rousseau inherited the dead man's wardrobe he certainly
did not inherit Anet's firm grasp of *Maman's* household affairs,
which were soon in a hopeless mess despite his plaintive appeals
for economy. Jean-Jacques was, in fact, a broken reed. He had
not yet acquired that passion for botanising which was to prove
a source of consolation in his later years and was, therefore,
unable to provide Mme de Warens with the herbs collected by
the industrious Anet for her numerous and no doubt profitable
infusions and drugs. Eventually, since she laughed at his exhortations, and watching her money pass into the hands of the
charlatans who infested the house, Rousseau adopted as his
philosophy: *Vogue la galère!* As everything he saved went to
these swindlers why not take his own share? Where the money
came from is a mystery he never solved, though there always
seemed to be plenty.

Mme de Warens certainly held a leading position in Chambéry
society. She was on excellent terms, for example, with the
marquis d'Entremont, the Sardinian ambassador. And in
October 1733, when the Champagne Regiment passed through
the town to attack Milan, she presented Jean-Jacques to the
commanding officer, le duc de la Trémouille. Two years afterwards, her house was again full of distinguished French officers
returning from Italy on the conclusion of hostilities with the
emperor. To Rousseau, excited by these heroic events and by
Brantôme's *Vies des grands capitaines*, it seemed as if the glorious
history of military France was being re-enacted before his eyes.
A new phase of his existence had now opened. Moving in polite
society under the watchful maternal eye of Mme de Warens, he
gradually shed the austere republican prejudices of his boyhood.
Maman, who had ambitious plans for her protégé, made him
take lessons in dancing, deportment and fencing but with disappointing results; for Jean-Jacques, who had long been a
martyr to corns, had acquired the ungainly habit of walking on
his heels. Besides, he was not really interested in the art of

killing and lacked the swordsman's quickness of eye. Mme de Warens did not, however, relax her efforts to prepare Jean-Jacques for a successful career, partly because she was a kind and generous woman, partly no doubt because she was beginning to cast an anxious eye on the future. One of her least crazy schemes was the establishment of a Royal Botanic Garden at Chambéry with Anet as its curator. For this project she enlisted the support of Dr Grossi, late physician-in-ordinary to Victor Amadeus. That was indeed an achievement, for everyone lived in terror of Grossi's merciless sarcasm. He formed a high opinion of Anet, but for whose death the project would have been realised.

French opera, with the mounting fame of Rameau, now began to recover its former prestige and Rousseau, convinced that music was his vocation, assiduously studied the great composer's *Traité de l'harmonie*. In June 1734 he persuaded *Maman* to let him take lessons under the abbé Blanchard, music master at the cathedral of Besançon. Rousseau was well received but unfortunately the abbé was about to leave for a new post in Paris. To crown his bad luck, Rousseau heard from his father, whom he had visited at Nyon, that the customs had seized his trunk at the frontier post of Les Rousses because of a Jansenist parody of Racine's *Mithridate* which he had imprudently left in one of his pockets. There was nothing for it but to return to Chambéry the poorer by an outfit worth 800 francs and, of course, the fees he would have received from the music pupils he had deserted. But these, one gathers from a letter to Mme de Warens, could easily be regained since Jean-Jacques, encouraged by Blanchard, now really felt for the first time that he was competent to teach music.[1] He did, in fact, on his return to Chambéry resume all his former activities. It was now that Rousseau met the comte de Conzié who had come back to reside on his estates at Les Charmettes, a lovely valley just outside Chambéry. Rousseau gave him music lessons but found in De Conzié an indifferent pupil who preferred to talk about the latest books: Voltaire's correspondence with the Prussian Crown Prince and his *Lettres philosophiques*. Of these talks with De Conzié, Rousseau writes: 'Le germe de littérature et de philosophie qui commençait à

[1] *C.G.* I, no. 5.

fermenter dans ma tête et qui n'attendait qu'un peu de culture et d'émulation pour se développer les trouvait en lui.'[1]

The trip to Besançon was not Rousseau's only absence from Chambéry. To escape from the distractions of fashionable society, he slipped off to Lyons and probably to Geneva and Nyon combining his own pleasure with errands for Mme de Warens, spending money which would have been squandered anyhow. Thus, in June 1735 Rousseau went to Lyons, perhaps, suggests Courtois, to visit Suzanne Serre, whom he had met as a little girl four years earlier at the convent des Chaseaux. Was she the cruel one to whom Jean-Jacques wrote that despairing, passionate love-letter on the draft of which he later inscribed the words: *jeunesse égarée*?[2] I think it quite possible, for Suzanne was only sixteen, a heartless age. That Rousseau was genuinely in love there is no doubt, though in certain passages one can detect the idiom of Prévost's unhappy chevalier des Grieux. It was probably during this visit that Rousseau, from the rue de Genti, wrote to another girl later identified as Mlle La Bussière confessing that he was the peeping Tom who had spied on her in the ladies' bathing-pool at Lyons, maliciously advertising his presence by a snatch of song. Both letters prefigure, by their style, that interfusion of sensibility and carnal desire which we shall rediscover in the effusions of Saint-Preux, the hero of *La Nouvelle Héloïse*. But the moral lecture which concludes the letter to Mlle La Bussière reminds one rather of his heroine, Julie d'Etange: 'Permettez-moi, cependant de vous donner un avis; n'allez plus au bain, Mademoiselle, ou prenez-y plus de précautions; à la fin, vous ne seriez plus tout à fait si excusable.'[3] I have no printable comment to make on these stupefying words.

At Chambéry, Rousseau made at least one friendship which was to endure the test of time and events. He was introduced at a party given by D'Entremont, to one of those rare individuals

---

[1] *Conf.* 210: 'The germs of literature and philosophy which were beginning to ferment in my brain and only needed a little culture and encouragement to develop fully, found these in him.'

[2] *C.G.* I, no. 12: 'mis-spent youth.'

[3] *C.G.* I, no. 13: 'Allow me, however, to give you a piece of advice. Don't go bathing again, Mademoiselle, or else take more precautions; in the long run, you would no longer be so excusable.'

who seem born to be happy and to radiate happiness. He was Jean-Vincent Capperonnier de Gauffecourt, a Parisian by birth and by trade a watchmaker who quickly rose, however, in the social scale. De la Closure, the French Resident at Geneva, took a fancy to Gauffecourt and granted him the monopoly of supplying salt to Le Valais, which earned him 20,000 francs a year. Though he was twenty years Rousseau's senior and was believed to have made, on one occasion, improper advances to Thérèse Levasseur, their affectionate relations were terminated only by Gauffecourt's death, at Lyons, in 1766. The latter's private printing-press at Montbrillant, just outside Geneva, went to Mme d'Epinay who used it to print two little books: *Mes moments heureux* (1758) and *Lettre à mon fils* (1759). And, ironically, it was under the pseudonym of Mme de Montbrillant that she wrote the romanced autobiography later, as we shall observe, doctored by Diderot and Grimm in order to vilify Rousseau and Duclos.[1] The other acquaintances of this Chambéry period derived mostly from Rousseau's ardour for music, which was cooled, however, by a temporary loss of prestige. At the public concerts organised by the comte de Bellegarde, by his sister, the comtesse de la Tour and his brother, the comte de Nangy, it was felt that Jean-Jacques, though he had composed a few trifling pieces, was not yet a competent musical director. He was, therefore, more than grateful when the young marquis de Senecterre, son of the French ambassador at Turin, publicly and generously praised his talents at the house of Mme de Menthon, for whom Rousseau had scored a song written by his new friend. Many years later, in Paris, Jean-Jacques felt impelled to remind him of the episode but delicately refrained, De Senecterre having meanwhile lost his eyesight.

Rousseau's newborn interest in literature, stimulated by his conversations with De Conzié, is reflected in various fragments discovered and published, in 1905, by that eminent scholar, the late Théophile Dufour.[2] Writing to his former benefactor,

---

[1] *Les pseudo-mémoires de Mme d'Epinay. Histoire de Madame de Montbrillant,* ed. G. Roth, 3 vols. (Paris: Gallimard, 1951).

[2] *Ann.* I and II. 'Pages inédites de Rousseau. Sur les Femmes; Sur l'éloquence; Sur Dieu; Essai sur les événements dont les femmes ont été la cause secrète etc.'

De Bonac, in December 1736, Rousseau mentions a programme of studies which he is following as regularly as his delicate health will permit. By a fortunate chance we can form some idea of their nature because Jean-Jacques, in July 1737, placed with a Genevan bookseller, Jacques Barillot, an order for the following titles: P. Bayle, *Dictionnaire historique*; le Père Lamy, *Eléments de mathématiques*; Mallez, *Géométrie pratique*; Newton, *Arithmetica*; Boileau, *Oeuvres complètes*; Prévost, *Clèveland*; Marivaux, *La Vie de Marianne*; Cicero, *Opera omnia*; Usserii, *Annales*.[1] Despite its high cost Rousseau was extremely anxious to acquire Bayle's *Dictionnaire*. His net, it will be seen, was cast widely, for he was no doubt eager to repair the deficiencies of his perfunctory schooling, especially in mathematics. Not, however, until 1739, and in circumstances we shall relate, did Rousseau embark on an intensive, methodical course of self-instruction. Indeed, the moment was not yet ripe. He was still in a rather 'flighty' mood, distracted by the endless stream of visitors who besieged Mme de Warens. Her pension had been continued by the new monarch, Charles Emmanuel III, but Jean-Jacques was still worried by her debts and by anxiety about his health. Moreover, in June 1737, whilst trying to make invisible ink, he nearly lost his eyesight. About this time, he made his will, being convinced, as he told De Bonac, that he had not long to live. He was probably now on the verge of the nervous breakdown which reached its climax two years later. In July 1737 Rousseau set out for Geneva to claim his mother's dowry, having attained his majority. He had hoped to combine business with recreation but found himself short of money, fretting at the law's delays and consumed with anxiety.[2] His lawyer advised him to remain incognito until the legacy was paid. This was no doubt prudent in the circumstances since Jean-Jacques was an apostate, though as it turned out, his legal status was not thereby affected. The claim was not opposed by Isaac Rousseau who had dipped into the capital. Finally, Rousseau got his half-share of 6,500 florins with the minimum of delay owing to the intervention of De la Closure who had been in love with his mother when she was Suzanne Bernard.

[1] Probably the Irish bishop and ecclesiastical historian, Usher.
[2] *C.G.* I, no. 15 (to Mme de Warens).

The late summer of 1737 was a critical period in Genevan history. For many years there had been protests from the reform party in the *Conseil Général* at the growing tendency of the two executive Councils to deprive the citizens of their sovereign powers and, in August, the Republic was on the verge of civil war. There were, in fact, armed clashes and a few deaths. One day during a call to arms Jean-Jacques saw the Barillots, father and son, leave the house, each to defend his post, liable at any moment to be at one another's throats. Appalled by this dreadful spectacle, Rousseau swore never to defend liberty in a civil war by force of arms, either personally or by lending his approval. He recorded these sentiments, it should be noted, in 1766, that is to say after the violent political quarrels which again convulsed Geneva in 1764 and which Rousseau was accused by his enemies of having deliberately fomented for purely selfish motives in his *Lettres de la montagne.* The experience of 1737, he admits, did not immediately turn him into an ardent patriot and as evidence of his indifference he relates a curious incident which probably occurred in 1734 during his return journey from Besançon to Chambéry. Early in that year, his uncle Bernard, the engineer, left for Charlestown, Virginia, not as Rousseau states to plan that city which was already built, but simply as one of a party of Swiss emigrants. He left with his wife several papers, including a memoir by the Genevan patriot Micheli Ducrest, severely criticising various weaknesses in the newly erected fortifications. Out of sheer vanity, to show that his relatives were 'somebodies' in Geneva, Rousseau displayed this pamphlet of which, he says, all the other copies had been destroyed, at a party given by one Coccelli, the Director of the Sardinian Customs. His host quietly annexed the document and undoubtedly passed it on to his superiors. Rousseau, who salves his conscience with the reflection that Sardinia was unlikely to attack his native city, nevertheless harshly condemns the silly vanity which prompted his irresponsible act. He does not tell us what was the comment of that professional agent Mme de Warens on such an amateur performance.

It was Proust who observed that the only real paradise is a paradise lost. For Rousseau, paradise was Les Charmettes where, in the summer of 1736 he experienced, in the company of *Maman*, a brief yet unforgettable moment of perfect happiness. Unfortunately, as he truly remarks, the one thing language is powerless to communicate is the quality of one's happiness:

> Encore si tout cela consistait en faits, en actions, en paroles, je pourrais le décrire et le rendre en quelque façon; mais comment dire ce qui n'était ni dit, ni fait, ni pensé même, mais goûté, mais senti, sans que je puisse énoncer d'autre objet de mon bonheur que ce sentiment même? Je me levais avec le soleil, et j'étais heureux, je voyais Maman, et j'étais heureux; je la quittais, et j'étais heureux; je parcourais les bois, les coteaux, j'errais dans les vallons, je lisais, j'étais oisif; je travaillais au jardin, je cueillais les fruits, j'aidais au ménage, et le bonheur me suivait partout: il n'était dans aucune chose assignable, il était tout en moi-même, il ne pouvait me quitter un seul instant.[1]

To some extent, certainly, Rousseau's new sense of inner harmony, of blissful indifference to the material aspect of existence was due to his improved state of health. He had just emerged from what was probably a prolonged bout of influenza with its classic symptoms: languor, melancholy, hysterical fits of weeping, feverish anxiety coupled with the premonition of imminent death. At Chambéry, brooding over Mme de Warens's financial situation and unable to sleep he used to visit her in the small hours, sitting on her bed and urging her to follow his advice until, finally reassured, he fell asleep. Jean-Jacques does not tell us what his benefactress thought of these nocturnal irruptions but, from her subsequent conduct, one can guess at the strain they imposed even upon her patience and kindness. Complacently, Rousseau tells us that he became entirely her child, more than if she had been his real mother. But the point is that Mme de Warens was not his mother and that their equivocal relationship which he describes as unique

---

[1] *Conf.* 222: 'Again, if all that were made up of facts, actions, words, I could describe and, in a way, communicate it; but how can one describe what was neither said, nor done nor even thought, but enjoyed, felt, without my being able to indicate any other source of my happiness than the feeling itself? I rose with the sun and I was happy; I saw *Maman* and I was happy; I left her and I was happy; I roamed the woods, the hills, I wandered in the valleys; I read, idled, worked in the garden; I picked the fruit, I helped in the house and everywhere happiness followed me; it resided in no definite thing, it was wholly within myself; it could not leave me for a single instant.'

among human beings was already approaching its inevitable term. She was essentially a woman of affairs and Jean-Jacques, however much he may have appealed to her protective maternal instinct, was a complete failure as a successor to Claude Anet. She had been obliged to give up the herbal garden in the suburbs and, though pestered by Jean-Jacques to move for good to the country, dared not offend her landlord, the comte de Saint-Laurent, Comptroller-General of Finances. Besides, her protégé had now given up his teaching because of ill-health. Finally, Mme de Warens compromised by renting, in the summer of 1736, a house in the valley of Les Charmettes. Then and not in 1738, as Jean-Jacques would have us believe, was enacted the memorable 'idylle des Charmettes' so lovingly re-created in the sixth book of the *Confessions*.

It has taken Rousseau's biographers years of patient research to solve the tricky chronological puzzle which he bequeathed to posterity. The initial source of confusion, as I see it, must be traced not to a faulty memory but to wounded *amour-propre*. Unable to face the brutal fact that as early as the summer of 1737 a rival called Winzenried had supplanted him in the affections of *Maman*, Jean-Jacques, in writing his memoirs, postdated this unpleasant event by a year. Perhaps, therefore, it may be advisable to set forth in their true sequence the incidents mis-leadingly recorded in the *Confessions*. In the summer of 1736 Jean-Jacques and Mme de Warens took up residence in a house she had rented in the valley of Les Charmettes and stayed there until the autumn. Early next spring, probably in April or May, they returned there, though in July Rousseau had to leave for Geneva on family business. As we know, it was not a pleasant visit and in addition to his other worries he was 'mortally anxious' at receiving no reply from Mme de Warens to his letters.[1] He returned to Les Charmettes in August or early September but left on the eleventh of this month for Montpellier to consult the famous Dr Fizes, convinced that he had heart disease. Proceeding by way of Grenoble, Valence and Monté-limar as 'Mr Dudding', an English Jacobite, he had a passionate but purely carnal *affaire* with a fellow-traveller, Mme de

[1] *C.G.* I, no. 15.

Larnage. They separated at Pont-Saint-Esprit on the understanding that Jean-Jacques, after his cure, would rejoin her at
Bourg-Saint-Andéol. Disgusted with Montpellier, consumed
with resentment and jealousy at the thought of Winzenried,
ignoring the advice of *Maman* to continue his treatment until
the following spring, Rousseau informed her of his intention to
leave Montpellier for home in December by way of Provence.
'C'est un air excellent; il y aura bonne compagnie, avec laquelle
j'ai déjà fait connaissance.'[1]

Having failed, however, to excite the jealousy of Mme de
Warens by this clumsy manœuvre, Rousseau left Montpellier in
January or in early February 1738, torn between the desire to
renew his affair with Mme de Larnage and jealous curiosity
about what was going on at Chambéry. Jealousy, sharpened by
the indifference of Mme de Warens, carried him back to her.
Yet, although his arrival had been announced, he met with a cool
reception. Winzenried was now solidly installed in his place.
Note how disingenuously this situation is reported in the *Confessions* in order to conceal the bitter truth that, before leaving
for Montpellier, Rousseau knew all about Winzenried and his
relations with Mme de Warens: 'Je le connaissais', he remarks
vaguely, 'pour l'avoir vu déjà dans la maison avant mon départ;
mais cette fois il y paraissait établi; il l'était.'[2] A painful interview ensued and Rousseau, indignantly refusing to share in a
ménage à trois, crept to his solitary room, immersing himself in
his studies, as an antidote to lacerated pride. The idyll of Les
Charmettes was over. Mme de Warens, by what Jean-Jacques
regarded as a wanton desecration of their unique love, had forfeited his trust and esteem. But nothing could destroy the
memories of his paradise lost. With every passing year they
were to acquire fresh lustre and vitality, residing always just
below the surface of his consciousness, ready at any moment,
when Rousseau called, to interpose a shimmering, radiant veil
between him and sordid actuality.

---

[1] *C.G.* I, no. 19 (to Mme de Warens, 23 Oct. 1737): 'The air is excellent and
there will be good company whose acquaintance I have already made.'

[2] *Conf.* 257–8: 'I knew him from having already seen him in the house before
my departure; but this time he seemed to be established there; he was.'

Yet the general impression projected by Rousseau's account in the *Confessions* of that unique experience is not one of unalloyed happiness. He relates, for instance, in minute detail, the symptoms of an extraordinary physical commotion which, we are told, instead of killing his body, only killed his passions: pounding arteries, buzzings and deep-toned whistlings in the ears followed by insomnia and digestive troubles. These, however, may have been caused by his 'water cure'. He absorbed four or five pints from a mountain stream every morning till Dr Salomon insisted on a more sensible régime. Haunted now by the spectre of imminent death, he had long earnest talks with *Maman* about religion. Her views on this subject, though they must have astonished her confessor, brought her much comfort. She could not bear the idea of a punishing God yet, whilst rejecting Hell, believed in Purgatory since, after all, the souls of the wicked must be accommodated somewhere. On the other hand, she stoutly asserted that she was a good Catholic, obediently accepting the doctrine of her Church. In these queer maxims Jean-Jacques found the reassurance which he so urgently needed as to the fate of his soul after death. And every morning, in an access of Pantheistic fervour, he used to offer up, on the hillside, a silent prayer to the Creator of Nature. Then, when *Maman* opened her shutters, he bounded to greet her, still abed, with a tender, filial embrace. Accustomed now to the idea of an early demise, Rousseau felt serenely happy and infected Mme de Warens with his love of country life. In fact, to judge from his excellent appetite, it would seem that Jean-Jacques had almost recovered from his malady. But soon the time came to return to Chambéry and with a sigh Jean-Jacques said farewell until the following spring to his tame pigeons and his bees. Yet, doubtful whether he would see another spring, he did not leave Les Charmettes without kissing the ground and the trees, quite unnecessarily as it transpired, for as soon as the snows had melted he and *Maman* returned in time to hear the early nightingales. Though still out of condition he made valiant attempts at gardening but found that the digging exhausted him. This time, however, Rousseau had brought a small library with him and, seized with an insatiable appetite for knowledge, began to devour books on history, theology, geometry, philosophy and astronomy.

It seems certain that Winzenried, who later called himself De Courtilles, was now at Les Charmettes. It is known, for instance, that in September 1737 he witnessed a deed by which Mme de Warens leased a small farm belonging to a widow called Révil. Meanwhile Rousseau was dallying with Mme de Larnage en route for Montpellier. His abrupt departure for that town, so soon after his return from Geneva was due, I think, largely to the presence of his hated rival at Les Charmettes. In a letter to *Maman* from Grenoble, moreover, there is a barbed phrase obviously levelled at the eupeptic Winzenried.[1] Rousseau's letters from Montpellier suggest that he had displeased Mme de Warens, and betray his despair: 'Ah! ma chère maman, n'êtes-vous plus ma chère maman?'[2] And his postscript makes it plain that she had issued her ultimatum. There was no question of getting rid of Winzenried and it was open to Jean-Jacques to accept the situation or make his own arrangements. Briefly, Winzenried was in, to stay. Rousseau in guarded terms wrote that he agreed to all her conditions save one to which he could not possibly consent: meaning presumably that he could not share her favours with Winzenried. His letter ends, however, with a really cryptic remark: 'Vous savez qu'il n'y a qu'un cas où j'accepterais la chose dans toute la joie de mon cœur. Mais ce cas est unique. Vous m'entendez.'[3] What the unique case was must remain a secret of the alcove.

For very good reasons, there is no allusion in the *Confessions* to the above correspondence which shows that Jean-Jacques had no scruples in deceiving *Maman* whilst at the same time accusing her of infidelity. That is why, for instance, he pretends that only on his return from Montpellier was he aware of the shattering change in their relations. Restored to its proper temporal and

[1] *C.G.* I, no. 17 (13 Sept. 1737). Describing the effects of Voltaire's *Alzire* on his own tender heart, Jean-Jacques refers darkly to the insensibility of others who seem born only 'to wallow in their squalid sentiments' ('pour ramper dans la bassesse de leurs sentiments').

[2] *C.G.* I, no. 21 (4 Dec. 1737): 'Ah! dear mamma, are you no longer my dear mamma?'

[3] *Ibid.*: 'You know there is only one case in which I would accept the thing with heartfelt joy. But that case is unique; you understand me.'

psychological context, here in greater detail is the story of Rousseau's escapade. On 14 September he set out for Montpellier and *en route* fell in with the wedding cortège of a Mme de Colombier, one of whose companions was a certain Mme de Larnage of Bourg-Saint-Andéol. She was not, Rousseau admits, a beauty though extremely amorous. She was, in fact, forty-four, and the mother of ten daughters, of whom Jean-Jacques mentions only one. The reason for the 'Mr Dudding' farce was apparently that he hoped to make a more favourable impression on the ladies as an English gentleman in exile than as a Genevan apostate. What follows confirms Boileau's dictum: 'Le vrai peut quelquefois n'être pas vraisemblable.' Questioned by an amiable old marquis called De Taulignan about the Jacobites, sweating with embarrassment lest someone discover his ignorance of English, Rousseau finally survived the ordeal. Intrigued by this bashful, attractive foreigner, undeterred by his ungallant taciturnity, Mme de Larnage undertook his seduction. Jean-Jacques, painfully aware of the sorry figure he cut in the presence of these ladies, gradually yielded to the blandishments of Mme de Larnage who listened sympathetically to a long recital of his symptoms. At Romans, they left the bridal party and Rousseau stopped sulking. Recalling the heroes of his favourite romances he began to respond to Mme de Larnage's advances in the idiom of Céladon under the amused eye of the marquis. Soon, in a *tête-à-tête*, the enterprising matron contrived to make her desires perfectly clear and Jean-Jacques dropped his Céladon nonsense and at last became himself: 'Jamais mes yeux, mes sens, mon cœur et ma bouche n'ont si bien parlé.'[1] The lady, he boasts, was well rewarded for her pains. For about five days, until their parting at Pont-Saint-Esprit, Rousseau enjoyed for the first time to the full the pleasures of sensual love. He leaves us in no doubt on that point: '. . .je me gorgeai, je m'enivrai des plus douces voluptés. Je les goûtai pures, vives, sans aucun mélange de peine: ce sont les premières et les seules que j'ai ainsi goûtées.'[2]

---

[1] *Conf.* 248: 'Never have my eyes, my senses, my heart and my lips spoken so well.'

[2] *Conf.* 250: 'I gorged myself, intoxicated myself with the sweetest pleasures. They were pure and lively, without the least admixture of pain: they are the first and only pleasures of the kind I have enjoyed.'

This is a significant admission for the illumination it sheds on Rousseau's subsequent relations with women and also because it made him acutely conscious, by contrast, of the degrading character of his sexual intimacy with Mme de Warens. Nevertheless, it was torture to picture her in the arms of Winzenried, an ignorant barber's assistant, a *coq de village*, fatuously bragging of his fashionable conquests, a noisy brute, proud of his muscular strength: in short a creature of infra-human intelligence totally devoid of sensibility.

One can understand, therefore, why his letters to Chambéry are laden with self-pity and resentment. They offer a very different picture of his life at Montpellier from that presented in the *Confessions* which is no doubt more truthful. As a boarder in the house of an Irish doctor, Fitzmorris, he consorted with medical students some of whom were also Irishmen. From them he acquired a few words of English which might come in handy if 'Mr Dudding' were to meet at Bourg-Saint-Andéol someone with a smattering of that language. He was not unhappy at Montpellier when he forgot Chambéry. Mme de Larnage had cured him of his hysterical bouts of crying and the doctors could find nothing wrong with his heart. They regarded him, says Rousseau petulantly, as a *malade imaginaire*. Probably they were right, for in the same breath Jean-Jacques complains of the meagre fare provided by Fitzmorris.

Haunted by visions of the opulent Mme de Larnage, whose face, one gathers, was the least of her charms, Rousseau set out for her village in late January or early February. The story he told Mme de Warens was that Dr Fizes had ordered a régime of asses' milk at Pont-Saint-Esprit[1] a place from which, incidentally, one could proceed either to Chambéry or to Bourg-Saint-Andéol. In two senses, therefore, it marked a turning of the ways: towards Mme de Larnage or Mme de Warens. As I have said, the impulse which drove Rousseau to the latter was jealous curiosity and not, as he asserts in the *Confessions*, the prompting of conscience, the lively feelings of remorse aroused by her letters. On the other hand, Rousseau admits that the fear of being unmasked at Bourg-Saint-Andéol also influenced his

[1] *C.G.* I, no. 19.

decision. Besides, Mme de Larnage had a daughter. What if Jean-Jacques were to fall in love with her, sowing hatred and jealousy in a peaceful household? As his imagination played upon this dramatic contingency Rousseau was seized with horror. His duty lay at the side of kind, generous *Maman*.

At Pont-Saint-Esprit, therefore, 'reason' triumphed, and, glowing with righteousness, Jean-Jacques set out for Chambéry. Yet, on second thoughts, he wondered whether his decision was due to pride or virtue. Certainly pride, he says, had its share. But what does he mean in this context by *orgueil* or pride? The following passage is illuminating:

> voilà la première obligation véritable que j'aie à l'étude. C'était elle qui m'avait appris à réfléchir, à comparer. Après les principes si purs que j'avais adoptés il y avait peu de temps, après les règles de sagesse et de vertu que je m'étais faites et que je m'étais senti si fier de suivre, la honte d'être si peu conséquent à moi-même, de démentir si tôt et si haut mes propres maximes, l'emporta sur la volonté.[1]

Now, it would be difficult to find in the *Confessions* a passage illustrating more clearly the limitations of Rousseau's introspection, which, if pursued, he always insisted, in *le silence des passions*, is an infallible guide to self-knowledge. But, as we can observe in this case as in so many others, his passions were rarely silent. It was not the laudable resolve to be true to his moral principles which triumphed over his erotic desires but, as the *Correspondance* reveals, his burning sense of humiliation and his jealous anxiety. One must, however, charitably assume that, whilst composing the sixth book of the *Confessions*, he had forgotten the letters of his Montpellier phase, of which, indeed, he had retained no copies.

What he never forgot was the scene that confronted him on his arrival at Chambéry. He had expected to find Mme de Warens on the doorstep: instead, she was discovered quietly talking to Winzenried. Jean-Jacques rushed to embrace her but

---

[1] *Conf.* 256: 'This was the first real advantage I derived from my studies; they had taught me to reflect and to compare. After the pure principles I had so recently adopted, after the rules of wisdom and virtue I had drawn up for myself and which I had felt such pride in following, the shame of being so little consistent with myself, of belying so soon and so flagrantly my own maxims, triumphed over my desire.'

was greeted with no enthusiasm. 'Ah! te voilà, petit,' she re-marked, casually, 'As-tu fait un bon voyage? Comment te portes-tu?' and in answer to his question, she admitted having received his note, whereupon, inwardly seething, he observed icily: 'J'aurais cru que non.'[1] In a private interview Rousseau's pent-up grief and rage erupted volcanically but *Maman*, who was no doubt accustomed to such explosions, remained quite unperturbed. People did not die of these things, she observed calmly, reminding Jean-Jacques, moreover, of his frequent absences and neglected duties as if, he remarks cattily, a frigid woman like her needed a permanent bedfellow. This comment, recorded nearly thirty years after these painful interviews, reveals the incurable nature of the wound inflicted by Mme de Warens. And, still unable to accept the harsh facts of the situation, he pictures Winzenried as her dupe: in order to obtain his services as her foreman, she gave him in return that to which men attached great importance and Mme de Warens none at all. But how does Jean-Jacques explain her growing coldness to himself? Simply that in refusing to continue their former relations he had been guilty of the one insult that women never forgive.

This shattering experience coincides with an important phase in Rousseau's intellectual life. During his previous sojourns in the valley of Les Charmettes he had indulged in much desultory reading: Descartes, Malebranche, Leibniz, Locke and, notably, *La Logique de Port-Royal* by the Jansenists Nicole and Arnauld. Picnics and rambles with *Maman*, long conversations about his spiritual problems with her Jesuit friends, Père Coppet and Père Hémet and of course, the anxieties provoked by his state of health: all these had made intensive reading impossible. But now, in early March 1738, alone at Les Charmettes in that house of poignant memories, Jean-Jacques shut himself up with his books or else, as he confesses, sighed and wept in the woods. He does not dwell on the events of these two years of virtual isolation. In March, Mme de Warens renewed her lease of the Révil farm and in July signed another for a house belonging to

---

[1] *Conf.* 236: 'Ah! there you are, little one. Did you have a good journey? How are you?'...'I should have thought not.'

a M. Noëray. Her affairs were now in a sorry state and from one of Rousseau's letters it appears that she was the subject of malicious gossip.[1] He still acted as her amanuensis and, in March 1739, obviously at her instigation, made two attempts to raise funds. The first was by a memoir to the Governor of Savoy asking for a pension on the grounds that he was afflicted with a disfiguring malady and had not long to live. It is doubtful whether this pathetic appeal was ever despatched, which was just as well, since inquiries might have revealed that the disfigurement, caused by a laboratory accident, was of ancient date and not permanent. In a second, persuasively worded memoir, Jean-Jacques tried, without success, to establish presumption of his brother's death and to inherit the remaining part of the maternal dowry.[2]

It was probably in the spring of 1738 that he composed *Le Verger de Madame la Baronne de Warens*. These verses, as the author correctly observes, have no literary merit but they tell us what were his occupations and sentiments during this troubled period. Having resolved, obviously, to heap coals of fire on the head of the 'sage WARENS, élève de Minerve', the exiled poet praises her virtue, wisdom and generosity. Nor does he neglect Winzenried, to whom, surely, applies the epithet 'cœur bas' in a passage associating him with other 'mercenary souls' who tried to dissuade Mme de Warens from financing Jean-Jacques. Their insensitive minds, he remarks bitterly, cannot appreciate the 'delicate pleasures' she derives from her liberalities. Ignoring their 'inhuman guffaws' Rousseau assures these wretches that he will never stoop to accept their help. Alone at Les Charmettes, 'raised above the vulgar herd', he devotes himself to the pursuit of knowledge. And, in proof, Rousseau gives a detailed catalogue of his favourite authors. We are invited to picture a student nurtured in the philosophy of Pascal, Leibniz, Newton, Malebranche, Locke; a mind capable of grasping the problems of physics and mathematics yet sensitive to the

---

[1] *C.G.* I, no. 23 (? late August 1738). Writing to his paternal aunt, Mme Fazy, about her daughter-in-law who had been justly deserted by her husband, Rousseau, in a passage afterwards crossed out, refers indignantly to the calumnies levelled at his 'benefactress and mother' by ignorant and sanctimonious people.

[2] *C.G.* I, no. 38.

aesthetic qualities of 'le tendre Racine' and of 'le touchant Voltaire'. The poem closes on an interesting note recalling the author's Plutarchian, pre-Warens outlook on life. Neither grief, loneliness, poverty, nor ill-health, he states, can daunt Jean-Jacques, for he is armed with the stoic pride, 'la stoïque fierté' of Epictetus and, above all, by the consciousness of his own moral integrity. But he does not stress this theme which will be the leitmotif of his Parisian symphony.

From an allusion in the *Verger*,[1] it seems that the hermit of Les Charmettes was still dependent on the generosity of Mme de Warens, which hitherto he had always taken for granted, looking on himself as her adopted son. But now, though Rousseau sneered at the noisy axe-swinging Winzenried, he was uneasily aware for the first time that this oaf, in the eyes of *Maman*, was a doer and not, like clinging, sickly *Petit*, a constant source of worry and expense. The latter, therefore, was obliged to alter his behaviour towards Winzenried. We read in the *Confessions* that, taking as his model the deceased Anet, he assumed the role of mentor and friend in order to please, he says, Mme de Warens. It was also, no doubt, a salve to his flayed *amour-propre*. But whereas Anet had found in Jean-Jacques a docile pupil, Winzenried, now De Courtilles, was the reverse. Garrulous, conceited, openly despising Rousseau's book-learning, he rudely laughed at the latter's earnest attempts to introduce him to the higher things of life. So, whilst Jean-Jacques radiated sweetness and light, Winzenried hefted his axe and pick, loaded waggons and bawled at the workmen to the great satisfaction of *Maman*. Yet, observes Jean-Jacques loftily, he was not altogether a bad fellow. True, Winzenried was often brutal to his mistress and slept with one of her servants, a tooth-less red-haired slut. On the other hand, this coarse individual, realising his abysmal ignorance, sometimes ruefully admitted he was a fool. How much of all this is true, how much due to jealous spite, it is impossible to say. But we do know that Winzenried served Mme de Warens for many years with great

---

[1] 'Que si jamais ce sort m'arrache à vos bienfaits...' ('If ever that fate wrests me from your benefactions...'). Rousseau goes on to say he would rather starve than accept help from another hand.

fidelity, that he held eventually a responsible post in the Government service and died at Chambéry in his fifty-sixth year.

Contrary to the impression given by Rousseau in his *Confessions*, this turbulent, unpleasant period lasted two years, from about February 1738 to April 1740. His leisure was not entirely spent in study for, as we have seen, he was a budding poet. In more serious vein was the article he sent to the *Mercure de France* on the question 'Si le monde que nous habitons est une sphère'. Apparently the editor did not much care whether the earth was spherical or oblong for the memoir was returned with thanks. Meanwhile, through a Grenoble friend, D'Eybens, the active Mme de Warens obtained for Jean-Jacques a post as tutor to the children of Jean-Bonnot de Mably, Prévôt-Général of the province called Le Lyonnais. This event, which had a tonic effect on Rousseau's self-esteem, revived his old tenderness for 'ma très chère maman', though an allusion to 'Monsieur de Courtilles' suggests no change in his attitude to Winzenried. His letters to Mably and D'Eybens reveal a diffident Jean-Jacques, reluctant to leave the solitude of Les Charmettes, unsure of his competence but eager to please his future employer whom he begs to treat him as a respectful son. To D'Eybens he writes that whilst the question of salary is important, what really matters is his social status. He would hope to receive the consideration due to a gentleman scurvily treated by fortune. Mably was a kindly indulgent man who discreetly ignored, for instance, the tutor's curious habit of pilfering his Arbois wine which he drank secretly in his room whilst nibbling a biscuit and devouring a novel. Jean-Jacques observes naïvely that he had never been tempted to filch anything at Mme de Warens's because nothing was locked up. Mably, who had entrusted him with the key of his wine-cellar, merely retained it, with no comment. Rousseau frankly admits that he was a complete failure as a tutor, lacking patience and, above all, method: '. . . Je ne savais employer auprès d'eux que trois instruments toujours inutiles et souvent pernicieux auprès des enfants: le sentiment, le raisonnement, la colère.'[1]

---

[1] *Conf.* 263: 'I could only think of three methods to employ with them. They are always useless and frequently pernicious with children: sentiment, argument, anger.'

Yet his experience was by no means wasted: it set Rousseau's mind on the track that led to *Emile*, the revolutionary treatise on education which he preferred, however, to describe as a treatise on the original goodness of man. But there is nothing about natural human goodness in the memoir Rousseau composed, in 1740, on the art of education and of which only a fragment has survived.[1] He advances, on the contrary, the 'astonishing paradox' that the only calm and modest people are those who live a great deal in society. And, since the object of all education is happiness, a boy's social training cannot begin too soon. It is an error, Jean-Jacques insists, to imagine that society is the theatre of the grand passions which nearly always originate in 'solitary melancholy hearts'. Polite society fosters 'the petty tastes' for music, painting, plays, light verse and pretty women. These, he infers, agreeably occupy the surface of our consciousness, thus enervating the passions. Therefore, the ideal tutor is a man of the world, familiar with modern literature and art. Unlike the dusty pedant steeped in the classics or the bigoted priest for whom all men are monsters from Hell, Jean-Jacques would teach his pupil that polite society consists of people subject no doubt to the usual human weaknesses, but fundamentally decent and honourable.

Yet the real subject of this memoir is Rousseau himself. Certain individuals had more than once represented him to Mably as a gloomy misanthropist and pedant, unaccustomed to polite society and therefore unfit for his post. Such is indeed, he admits, the impression that might be formed by a superficial observer for he is awkward and bashful in company. But it is unjust, he protests, to conclude that his nature is harsh and insensitive or that his lack of urbanity is due to a bad upbringing. His defects spring from an invincible tendency to melancholy. And, in a passage which is uncannily reminiscent of the abbé Prévost, he dwells on this fascinating theme:

Soit tempérament, soit habitude d'être malheureux, je porte en moi une source de tristesse dont je ne saurais démêler l'origine. J'ai presque toujours vécu dans la solitude, longtemps infirme et languis-

---

[1] *C.G.* I, pp. 367–79 (*Fragment du Mémoire présenté à M. de Sainte-Marie pour l'éducation de son fils*). Sainte-Marie was the name of Mably's elder son. Rousseau probably never submitted his memoir to Mably, though at the request of Mme Dupin he sent her a copy in April 1743. (*C.G.* I, no. 55.)

sant, considérant la fin de ma courte vie comme l'objet le plus voisin, un vif désir de sensibilité dans une âme qui n'a jamais été ouverte qu'à la douleur, portant continuellement dans mon sein, et mes propres peines et celles de tout ce qui m'était cher. Ce n'était là que trop de quoi fortifier ma tristesse naturelle.[1]

Truth or fiction? Probably a little of both. Jean-Jacques, brooding over the apostasy of *Maman* in his lonely room at Mably's, turns with a sigh to his Arbois and to his Prévost, the sufferings of whose hero, Clèveland, he once said affected him even more than his own, though that seems hardly credible.[2]

We must not picture Rousseau, however, as a neglected recluse. Whilst tutor at Mably's he made several good friends: Charles Bordes, the writer; the Intendant, Du Ruau; the *prévôt des marchands*, Perrichon; the surgeon, Parisot; Mably's brother, the famous philosopher, Etienne Bonnot, abbé de Condillac and the musician David. Besides, since Rousseau's name figures as witness at the baptism of Mably's daughter in April 1741, one may assume he was a favoured member of the household. Nevertheless, after a year of tutoring, he resigned his post, no longer able to resist the urge to revisit Chambéry and make one last appeal to Mme de Warens in the name of their former friendship. It was May and five years had passed since the brief idyll of Les Charmettes, which had never ceased to haunt his thoughts. But he was forced to accept the bitter reality that for *Maman* the past no longer existed.

Affreuse illusion des choses humaines! Elle me reçut toujours avec son excellent cœur qui ne pouvait mourir qu'avec elle; mais je venais rechercher le passé qui n'était plus et qui ne pouvait renaître. A peine eus-je resté une demi-heure avec elle que je sentis mon ancien bonheur mort pour toujours.[3]

---

[1] *C.G.* I, p. 377: 'Whether from temperament or from the habit of misfortune, I bear within me a source of sadness whose origin I cannot really discover. I have almost always lived in solitude, long infirm and listless, regarding the end of my short life as imminent; with a keen desire for sensibility, in a soul which has never been exposed to anything but grief, nursing continually in my bosom both my own misfortunes and those of all that are dear to me. That was more than sufficient to fortify my natural sadness.'   [2] *Conf.* 216.

[3] *Conf.* 266: 'Frightful illusion of human life! She received me with the same excellent heart which could only die with her; but I had come to seek a past which no longer existed and could never return. I had scarcely been with her half an hour when I felt that my former happiness was dead for ever.'

These are pregnant words, for if Rousseau from that moment resigned himself to the loss of Mme de Warens, he never renounced the dream of perfect felicity symbolised in the idyll they had shared and which had been so cruelly broken by her caprice. Now she and Winzenried made it impossible for him to inhabit the house of which he once had been the very soul, the child.[1] Mme de Warens's affairs were now in a desperate plight and it looked as if her pension might be distrained and stopped. Unable to remain in the place where once he had been everything and was now a stranger, Rousseau left, probably in July 1741, for Lyons where he stayed perhaps until December. But as he does not mention this sojourn in the *Confessions*, his biographers have had to wrestle with one more chronological problem. The omniscient Courtois surmises that Jean-Jacques was drawn to Lyons by his love for Mlle Serre and also by the artistic and literary attractions of that city. Possibly, too, he was already preoccupied with his marvellous plan for rescuing *Maman* from financial disaster: the *Projet concernant de nouveaux signes pour la musique*, a system of musical notation by numbers which was to revolutionise the teaching of music, bringing fame and wealth to its inventor. Now this necessitated a trip to Paris which Courtois thinks had to be postponed because of an illness that drove Rousseau back to Les Charmettes early in 1742.

Here, until July, he dabbled in literary composition and put the last touches to his *Projet*. From a little poem, *A Fanie*, in which he attributes his recovery to Mme de Warens, it seems that he had been dangerously ill.[2] On 19 April he sent to one Boudet, an Antonine monk who was writing a life of the late De Bernex, Bishop of Annecy, a memoir later published, with malicious intent, by Fréron in his *Année littéraire*. Referring to miraculous actions performed by the deceased prelate, one of which, presumably, was the conversion of Mme de Warens, Jean-Jacques testifies that once, when her house was threatened by a fire in an adjoining bakery, De Bernex began to pray in the garden, whereupon the wind suddenly veered round, driving away the flames. Even more interesting is his account of the

[1] *Conf.* 262, 267.   [2] *C.G.* I, no. 48 (14 March 1742).

conversion of Mme de Warens, depicted here as an extremely wealthy 'person of distinction' who was deeply moved by one of the bishop's sermons. After an interview with De Bernex, she espoused the true faith, sacrificing her great possessions and 'brilliant rank' to the dismay of her adoring tenants who threatened to set fire to Evian and abduct their châtelaine. Rousseau's version bears no resemblance to that of De Conzié and was obviously edited by *Maman*. Equally romantic is his story that, after the bishop's death she devoted herself entirely to meditation, completely detached henceforth from worldly affairs. In fact, the enterprising lady was now busily squabbling with a local lawyer, Renaud, who described her as a woman fond of disputes and chicanery.[1]

Rousseau was now about to pass out of Mme de Warens's life although, ironically enough, the chief object of his visit to Paris was to establish himself triumphantly as her saviour. The unpractical bookworm, jeered at by Winzenried, was now about to astonish the capital with his *Projet* and bring home the galleons. In July 1742 he went to Lyons and sold his library to raise funds for the Paris trip. All his old friends rallied to Jean-Jacques. The generous Perrichon paid his stage-coach fare and a brother of his former employer, the abbé de Mably, gave him letters of introduction, amongst others, to Fontenelle and the comte de Caylus, a well-known connoisseur of the arts. The kindly surgeon, Parisot, received from Jean-Jacques an *Epître* to which we shall return; it was finished on 10 July 1742. Was it now that Rousseau bade farewell to Suzanne Serre or during his previous visit in 1741? On learning that she was being courted by a young tradesman called Genève he virtuously abstained from declaring his love which, he thinks, was returned. But they were both poor; marriage was out of the question and Genève, whom he met occasionally, appeared to be a worthy man, likely to make a good husband. So Jean-Jacques, rather than disturb their innocent love affair, bravely departed, offering up prayers for their happiness which were not, alas! granted, for Suzanne died after two or three years of marriage. That, however, is a fiction, because Suzanne married Genève in 1745 and did not die

[1] *C.G.* I, nos. 50, 51 (written for Mme de Warens by Rousseau).

until ten years later. That she might have been really in love with her honest tradesman never, of course, entered Rousseau's mind.

Before following him to Paris, we might briefly discuss two poems which reflect his general outlook on society at this stage: the *Epître à M. Bordes* and the *Epître à M. Parisot*.[1] The first and shorter of these proclaims the independence of the poor but proud Republican who will not stoop to flatter the stupid, vile financiers noı yet to prostitute his pen by calumny or satire. At moments, he is tempted by the theme of virtuous happy indigence, of the good old days when men were content to live a simple, natural life. But the truth is that these days never existed save in the imagination of the poet, who is a liar by trade. Where poverty reigns, there is no goodness. Happy indigence is a myth invented by well-fed philosophers in their armchairs; the brutal fact is that the poor are often lazy and vicious:

J'honore le mérite aux rangs les plus abjects;
Mais je trouve à louer peu de pareils sujets.[2]

The poet will find a more profitable theme in the achievements of industry and commerce which multiply the amenities of life and strengthen the bonds of society. Here, Rousseau launches into a eulogy of Lyons, 'séjour charmant des enfants de Plutus',[3] rivalling London and Turin as a centre of the useful and decorative arts.

Even more subjective is the long *Epître à M. Parisot* where Jean-Jacques retraces the evolution of the 'vil enfant', 'l'orgueilleux avorton',[4] steeped in the austere, republican doctrine of his native Geneva but gradually converted by Mme de Warens to a saner, more tolerant outlook on life. Under her loving tuition, he realised the absurdity of his childish vision of a society based on complete equality; of that 'fierté burlesque'[5] which led him to declaim against the arrogant country gentry who imagined that their title-deeds, acquired by favouritism, dispensed them

---

[1] *C.G.* I, nos. 47 and 52.

[2] 'I honour merit in the lowest classes of society. But I can find few such individuals to praise.'

[3] 'Charming abode of the children of Plutus.'

[4] 'Base-born child'; 'bumptious little shrimp'.   [5] 'Ludicrous pride'.

from the obligation to live a virtuous life. Mme de Warens taught him to appreciate true nobility and to accept the fact that:

> Il ne serait pas bon dans la société
> Qu'il fût entre les rangs moins d'inégalité[1]

Under her kindly influence, he abjured for ever those 'savage maxims' which the Genevan child imbibes with his mother's milk. Thenceforth, he saw that one can love humanity and yet respect the privileges of birth and wealth. And if he smarted under the humiliations inflicted on him by the great, Jean-Jacques was consoled by the reflection that he could at least rival them in virtue. Besides, a more intimate acquaintance with polite society, a deeper appreciation of its amenities, have weaned him from the 'triste austérité' preached by his old masters, the Stoic philosophers, though he still shares their generous contempt for false moral values. Such, Rousseau tells Parisot, is the short yet faithful history of his errors.

Rightly, this *Epître* should have been inserted in the *Confessions*, of which it forms really an integral part and perhaps that would have happened if Jean-Jacques had been able, as he intended, to revise his memoirs. In Parisot, it is clear, Rousseau found a wise counsellor, 'un tendre ami, un Père' to whom in 1741 he unburdened his soul and whose advice he had sought on his plan to leave Mme de Warens, of which Parisot, by his silence, disapproved. Anxious to justify an action which his friend might attribute to ingratitude, Jean-Jacques pleads in his *Epître*:

> Pèse mes sentiments, mes raisons et mon choix,
> Et décide mon sort pour la dernière fois.[2]

He protests that he cannot remedy Mme de Warens's distress by sharing it: that would be, in effect, an unfilial and ungrateful act. Therefore, in resolving to leave Les Charmettes for Paris, he is impelled solely by a sense of duty, not by any desire for fame or the foolish illusion that he is an unrecognised genius. He makes no allusion, in the *Epître*, to his famous musical system on which, secretly, he built such high hopes. On the

---

[1] 'It would not be a good thing if there was less inequality of rank in society.'
[2] 'Weigh my sentiments, my reasons and my choice, And for the last time, decide my fate.'

contrary, he depicts himself as a *raté* whose failure is due not to an ill-spent youth but to that ingrained sincerity and diffidence which are incompatible with material advancement. Lacking the talent for hypocrisy and flattery, he will never attain a brilliant position in society. But, thanks to Parisot and his other Lyons friends he has at least abandoned his former narrow, rigid attitude to the social amenities. Only God, he realises, can be entirely self-sufficing and passionless. Remove man's passions and you remove the source of his happiness. Initiated by Parisot to the intellectual and artistic life of Lyons, he has learned to enjoy the innocent pleasures of good conversation and good cheer, the charms of elegant verses and of the fine arts. 'Rien ne doit être outré,' concludes Jean-Jacques, 'pas même la vertu,'[1] a Voltairian and startling maxim.

In August 1742 Rousseau arrived in the capital, putting up at the Hôtel de Saint-Quentin, rue des Cordiers, a street which used to open into the rue de Cluny, now called Victor Cousin. It was a wretched place but had housed several distinguished men: Gresset the playwright, Bordes, Mably and Condillac. Jean-Jacques's only visible assets were his *Projet*, a comedy, *Narcisse*, fifteen louis and his letters of introduction of which only three proved useful. These were addressed to De Boze, Secretary of the Académie des Inscriptions; the comte d'Ameysin, a Savoyard gentleman who later married Mlle de Menthon, one of Rousseau's pupils; and the Jesuit Père Castel, famous as the inventor of a *claveçin oculaire* or colour-keyboard. Rousseau lost no time in presenting his system to the Académie des Sciences, thanks to the intervention of De Boze and Réaumur. He read it to that body on 22 August, and was told to explain the details to a sub-committee with whose members he had several interviews. The verdict was that it was interesting but neither original nor useful. The Academy gave him, however, a flattering certificate. In January 1743 Rousseau published his work as a *Dissertation sur la musique moderne* and tried out the system on a young American, Mlle des Roulins, who made rapid progress. Nevertheless, it did not set the Seine on fire because, as Rameau pointed out to the inventor, his signs could not be read without

[1] 'Nothing must be exaggerated, not even virtue.'

a difficult mental operation. It was, remarks Jean-Jacques philosophically, another broken Hiéron fountain. Not quite, for it brought him into contact with Academicians and other men of letters such as Fontenelle and Marivaux, who was kind enough to praise and touch up his *Narcisse*. But the *Dissertation* earned him not a sou though the abbé Desfontaines and other journalists gave it a favourable press.

At this time Rousseau was greatly aided by Castel whom he dismisses rather ungratefully as 'mad, but a good fellow'. Let us note, therefore, Castel's first impressions of Rousseau.[1] He portrays a frank, naïve young man, 'a rather lofty philosopher', spurning the type of career which leads to honours and riches. His ambitions were centred on poetry and music: he had just, indeed, composed an opera. It was probably *La Découverte du nouveau monde* which, according to the *Confessions*, was thrown into the fire along with another in more tragic vein, his *Iphis et Anaxerète*, composed at Chambéry.[2] Castel was not encouraging. He disapproved of opera and said that Rousseau's verses had a strong provincial or rather Swiss flavour. He disliked also his music as over-elaborate, Italianate and obviously inspired by the school of Mondonville, Le Clerc and, especially, Rameau, whom the ungrateful Jean-Jacques later affected to despise.

Castel, whose advice to the eager neophyte was to 'try the women' introduced him to Mme de Bezenval, mother of the marquise de Broglie and to the brilliant salon of Mme Dupin, wife of a *fermier-général*. His first hostess, misled by Rousseau's humble appearance, insulted him by suggesting he should dine in the servants' hall, a blunder quietly rectified by her daughter. The little drama had a pleasant *dénouement* when Jean-Jacques, to make up for his lack of small talk, moved the ladies to tears by reading his *Epître à Parisot*. At Dupin's, he mingled with the *élite* of fashionable Paris, dukes, ambassadors, *chevaliers du Saint-Esprit*, savants and men of letters. Dazzled by the marmoreal beauty of his hostess who received him *en négligé*, the speechless Jean-Jacques ventured to declare his passion in a

---

[1] In *L'Homme moral opposé à l'homme physique ou Réfutation du Discours sur l'inégalité*, 1755.

[2] Fragments of both, however, have survived.

letter. Two days later, she personally returned it with a few curt words of reproof which, he says, 'froze my blood'. This was followed up by the suggestion, communicated by her stepson, Francueil, that he might discontinue his visits. He called less frequently and was later asked to take charge of Mme Dupin's son for a week, pending the arrival of a new tutor.

That Rousseau neither forgot nor forgave the humiliation produced by Mme Dupin's icy rebuff is evident from the *Confessions*. Referring to his brief experience as tutor to her son, a problem child, he observes grossly that he would not have continued for another week even if Mme Dupin had offered herself in payment. Here, one might not unjustly apply to Rousseau his favourite maxim that we may pardon others for the injuries they do us, but never for those we inflict on them. Incidentally, there is no allusion in the *Confessions* to the grovelling letter he wrote to this lady, beseeching her forgiveness,[1] or to the other in which he naïvely asks her husband to intercede on his behalf.[2] One gathers that Rousseau was already being considered for the post he later occupied as one of Dupin's secretaries, which explains, perhaps, why he was able to eke out his scanty store of louis. Otherwise, how did he contrive to pay for the *privilège*[3] of his *Dissertation*, his bi-weekly visits to the theatre, his chess sessions at the Café Maugis and the fees for the lecture-course which he and Francueil attended under the famous chemist, Rouelle? To be near Francueil, who shared his passion for music, Rousseau moved to the rue Verdelet, close to the Dupin residence in the rue de la Platrière. Shortly afterwards, he had an attack of pleurisy and whilst still running a high temperature, began to compose the songs and duets for his opera *Les Muses galantes*.

At the end of June 1743 something occurred which seemed to announce a happy revolution in Rousseau's material and moral existence. A friend of Mme de Bezenval, the abbé Alary, obtained for him the offer of a post as secretary to the newly

---

[1] *C.G.* I, no. 55 (9 April 1743).

[2] *C.G.* I, no. 56 (10 April 1743).

[3] The royal permission without which no book could be legally printed and published under the old régime. It was always reproduced on the last page.

appointed French ambassador at Venice. It was not, as Jean-Jacques always insisted, a permanent post as *secrétaire d'ambassade* for which, as a foreigner, he would not have been eligible. At first, on Francueil's advice, he declined the offer because the salary proposed by the ambassador, the comte de Montaigu, was only 1000 francs. Another person was appointed but Montaigu, according to Rousseau, quarrelled with him. Again approached, this time through Montaigu's brother, Rousseau accepted on learning that certain privileges were attached to the post. He left for Venice on 10 July 1743 and, airily dismissing the matter of his obligations to Montaigu, and consulting as usual only his personal convenience, he proceeded to Marseilles by way of Lyons and Avignon. In the *Confessions* he expresses regret at not having taken the Mont Cenis route so as to visit Mme de Warens. But owing to the war and for economy, he went down the Rhône. It is quite certain, however, that he did, in fact, branch off at Lyons for a week's sojourn at Chambéry, to the natural annoyance of his employer. 'M. de Montaigu,' complacently observes Jean-Jacques, 'ne pouvant se passer de moi, m'écrivait lettre sur lettre, pour presser mon voyage.'[1] An obligatory delay of twelve days in a lazaret at Genoa because of plague further prolonged his journey, to the exasperation of Montaigu. This was not a propitious beginning to a relationship which, for various reasons, rapidly deteriorated into a violent mutual antipathy.

Here, as with all of Rousseau's quarrels, it is extremely difficult to sort out the rights and wrongs of the situation. His case is fully and persuasively argued in the *Confessions* and in various letters.[2] The reverse of the medal is presented in one letter from the ambassador to Alary.[3] It is, however, most instructive. Montaigu could not, for instance, have invented the following striking tableau. Whilst he was in the throes of dictation, racking his brains for the appropriate word, Jean-Jacques used to pretend to read a book or else looked at his superior with an

---

[1] *Conf.* 285: 'M. de Montaigu, unable to do without me, sent me letter after letter to hasten my journey.'
[2] *C.G.* I, nos. 66, 84, 85, 87, 89, 90 (to Alary and Du Theil of the Department of Foreign Affairs).
[3] *C.G.* I, no. 87 A (incorrectly numbered as no. 87).

insufferable air of amused pity. Multiply such examples of studied insolence and it will be understood why the ambassador one day expressed his regret that he could not throw Rousseau out of the window like an insolent valet. But these scenes had their origin in a fundamental disparity of character, outlook and upbringing. Montaigu, a noble and an ex-officer of Guards, declined from the outset to treat his secretary as an equal, strongly resenting, as familiarities, Rousseau's friendly overtures. Now, the latter, forgetting that he was not a French subject, naïvely envisaged his new post as a stepping-stone to a brilliant career in the diplomatic service, a profession compatible with his talents and ambitions. Invested for the first time with authority, he formed an exalted opinion of his importance. Montaigu uses the term *folie* to describe his secretary's antics: his reiterated, peremptory demands for a private gondola; his refusal to dine with the ambassador's Italian major-domo whilst His Excellency entertained the duc de Modène; his pedantic insistence on the literal observance of the privileges and rights attached to the post of *secrétaire d'ambassade*, which he was not; his failure to appear at Montaigu's country house because only a public conveyance was available. Much of this silly snobbery can be traced to the influence of Mme de Warens who, as a *déclassée*, was extremely conscious of the regard due to 'Madame la Baronne de la Tour de Warens.' On the other hand, it is obvious that Jean-Jacques was a keen and efficient secretary who took his functions very seriously but regarded his employer as a half-wit. That was probably an exaggeration. Montaigu was no doubt lazy and incompetent, but not a complete zany. Accustomed to military discipline and, moreover, quick-tempered, he was no match for the logical Jean-Jacques in their frequent altercations. Chronically hard up, since his salary was always in arrears, he was often unable to pay his secretary who accuses him of annexing his perquisites. The threat of defenestration, it seems, arose from a violent dispute over Rousseau's claim for travelling expenses which, he asserts, the ambassador illegally reduced by overcharging him on the carriage of a parcel.

Summarily dismissed for insolence on 6 August 1744, Rousseau hurried to the French Consulate where, at a dinner party given by his friend, the Consul Le Blond, he poured out his grievances. The guests, who were all French, condemned Montaigu and generously offered their purses; for Rousseau, having refused to accept his employer's settlement, was reduced to a few louis. Montaigu, in a rage, asked the Venetian Senate to deport Rousseau who left, however, before the Inquisitors completed their investigation. On 22 August he set out for Paris by the postal route via Padua, Verona and Brescia, visiting the Borromean Islands before proceeding by the Simplon Pass to Geneva. *En route* he went through Nyon, without seeing his father but, recalled to a sense of duty by his friend Duvillard, a Genevan bookseller, he went back to Nyon. Here we take leave of Isaac Rousseau, who never saw his son again and died in 1747. Meanwhile, stopping only at Lyons to verify the exact weight of the parcel overcharged by the ambassador, Rousseau made for Paris, arriving in mid-October. For days he besieged the Department of Foreign Affairs with his complaints and wrote to the Minister appealing for justice. Finally, on receiving no reply, he dropped the whole affair. Montaigu, who had to dismiss Rousseau's successor for dishonesty in 1747, was himself relieved of his functions in 1749. On returning to Paris he settled his account with Jean-Jacques.

This encounter with officialdom, says Rousseau, planted in him the seeds of indignation against our stupid civil institutions which always subordinate the public weal to a false concept of order, and place the seal of authority on injustice and oppression. He explains, however, that in 1744 this incipient spirit of revolt was held in check by the reflection that the affair concerned only his private interest, and this can never inspire a pure love of justice.[1] He told Jonville, the French envoy at Genoa, that never again would he be the subordinate of anyone. Jonville was on friendly terms with Rousseau and thought of lending him his Paris apartment but was repelled by his irreligious views.[2] It is difficult to resist the conclusion that Jean-Jacques, largely owing

---

[1] *Conf.* 320.
[2] *Ann.* xvii, 219. P. Chaponnière, 'Quelques Notes d'un compilateur contemporain de Rousseau'. Jonville's confidant was the abbé Trublet who also collected impressions of Rousseau from Duclos, Marivaux and Mme Geoffrin.

to the defects of his early upbringing, was now quite unemploy-
able in any position demanding a sense of social obligation, a
spirit of co-operation and the willingness to adhere to a fixed
routine.

But Rousseau did not spend all his time in Venice squabbling
with Montaigu and the latter's major-domo, Dominico Vitale,
'a Mantuan bandit', 'a pimp', who turned the Embassy, he
asserts, into a haunt of rogues and profligates, abetted by a
fellow-pimp who kept a public brothel. It was really their baleful influence over Montaigu, we are told, which forced his
secretary to resign. On the other hand, Rousseau had many
good friends in Venice: Le Blond, Saint-Cyr, the Spaniards,
Carrio and Altuna, the Neapolitan Minister, Fiocchetti and two
or three cultured but anonymous Englishmen, who shared his
love of music. An assiduous opera-goer, Rousseau used to steal
away from the Embassy box to a secluded corner where nothing
might distract him from the music. Every Sunday, with Carrio,
he listened to the exquisite singing of the young girls trained in
the *scuole*, imagining them as creatures of angelic beauty until
one day Le Blond maliciously took him behind the scenes. Yet,
when they sang, Jean-Jacques utterly forgot their physical
defects and almost, he says charmingly, fell in love with these
ugly songsters. He devotes three pages of the *Confessions* to an
experience of a more banal character which, however, left an
indelible trace in his memory. This was his purely sensual infatuation for the professional courtesan, Zulietta, more ravish-
ingly beautiful and piquant than any houri of paradise. But his
flaming desire had an ignominious *dénouement*, evoking from
Zulietta the ironic advice to leave the ladies alone and study
mathematics though Rousseau attributed the fiasco to a peculiar
congenital blemish in her otherwise impeccable physical equip-
ment. A third rendezvous was arranged but Zulietta did not
appear, leaving Jean-Jacques with yet another memory of
frustration.

CHAPTER III

LA VIE PARISIENNE
1744–1756

Paris, malheureux qui t'habite! *Epître à M. de l'Etang*

Discours sur les sciences et les arts; Préface de 'Narcisse'; Discours sur l'inégalité with *La Dédicace à la République de Genève*

THE Venetian fiasco left Jean-Jacques with a rankling sense of injustice. Yet, from a letter written to Mme de Warens early in 1745, it does not seem to have shattered his morale. 'Alas! Mamma, I love you, I think of you, I complain about my lout of an ambassador. People commiserate with me, respect me but that is all the justice I get. Not that I do not hope some day to have my revenge by showing him not merely that I am the better man but that I am more esteemed than he is.'[1] In short, pride had emerged intact from his tussle with Montaigu. Compared with that, the collapse of his material ambitions was an affair of little moment. He was, meantime, busy with various schemes though none, he confessed, showed much promise.

Rousseau was now the guest of Manoel-Ignazio de Altuna, a Spanish gentleman with whom he had struck up a close friendship. Of no one else, save George Keith, Earl Marischal of Scotland, does Jean-Jacques write in such glowing terms. Apart from himself, he claimed, Altuna was the only really tolerant person he had ever known. They disagreed on almost every subject but neither would have wished the other to be different. The Spaniard who was ten years younger than Jean-Jacques, was one of those rare individuals who never interfere with the personal liberty of their friends. Though quick-tempered he

---

[1] *C.G.* I, no. 73 (25 Feb. 1745): 'Hélas! maman, je vous aime, je pense à vous, je me plains de mon cheval d'Ambassadeur, on me plaint, on m'estime et l'on ne me rend pas d'autre justice. Ce n'est pas que je n'espère pas un jour me venger en lui faisant voir, non seulement que je vaux mieux mais que je suis plus estimé que lui.'

never sulked or bore malice and used, indeed, to say that no man could offend him. Unlike Rousseau, and to the latter's huge amusement, Altuna lived according to a rigid time-table in which every hour of the day had its special and different occupation: meditation, talk, divine service, John Locke, telling his beads, music and painting. The two were inseparable and arranged to spend their days together on Altuna's estate at Ascoytia, but this, like Rousseau's other *châteaux d'Espagne*, never materialised. Altuna left Paris in March 1745 and married some years later. He died in 1762 when only 40.

That they corresponded at least until 1748 is evident from a letter written to Altuna in June of that year by Rousseau.[1] He was already suffering from the painful stricture which later became a chronic source of physical and mental distress and to which, in the opinion of Dr Elosu, we must attribute his subsequent attacks of persecution mania, caused by the toxic effects of uraemia.[2] It is clear from his letter to Altuna and from another written three months afterwards to Mme de Warens that Rousseau's courage was severely undermined by the sudden and unexpected onslaught of his malady. Convinced after only a fortnight's treatment that it was incurable, he adopted a fatalistic 'patience and resignation'. His affliction, Rousseau confided to Altuna though not to *Maman*, was probably an act of divine justice and chastisement from which he extracted consolation and hope: 'I have so greatly deserved castigation that I have no right to complain. And since He begins with Justice I hope He will end with mercy.'[3] These sentiments are in tune with the general theme of Rousseau's letter to Altuna who had been for some time gravely perturbed by his friend's attitude to religion and especially to the dogma of original sin. At least so I interpret Rousseau's allusion to a 'certain point' on which his sentiments, he reminds the Spaniard, are unshakable because they are based upon evidence and demonstration, the only foun-

---

[1] *C.G.* I, no. 100 (30 June 1748).

[2] *Bulletin de la Société française d'Histoire de la Médecine*, nos. 1 and 2, 1929. Dr Suzanne Elosu, *La maladie de Rousseau*.

[3] *Loc. cit.* 'J'ai tant mérité de châtiments, que je n'ai pas le droit de me plaindre de ceux-ci, et puisqu'il commence par la Justice, j'espère qu'il finira par la miséricorde.'

dation of any doctrine. Though faith, Jean-Jacques continues, has taught him many things that are above reason, it was reason primarily which obliged him to submit to faith. But he will not discuss such matters with Altuna who has the great advantage of being able to express his views openly. Even in this private letter to a trusted friend, Rousseau is very guarded about his religious beliefs though it appears certain that already, in 1748, whilst paying tribute to 'the divine and sublime principles of Christianity' he is defending his own system of morality which, he claims, is in no way inferior to Altuna's and certainly no less agreeable to God. He calls it his 'morale de principes' in order, clearly, to distinguish it from the Christian morality based on the dogma of original sin. Rousseau, it might seem, was already intuitively convinced of man's natural goodness. The statement that his sentiments are founded on 'evidence and demonstration', on the other hand, has a familiar Lockean ring. For John Locke, it will be recalled, defined reason as 'natural revelation' and revelation as 'natural reason enlarged by a new set of discoveries communicated by God immediately, which reason vouches the truth of by the testimony and proofs it gives that they come from God.'[1] Reminiscent of Locke, too, is Rousseau's preoccupation with morality and the good life which, he implies, will offset in the eyes of God the unorthodoxy of those sentiments deplored by Altuna as incompatible with Catholic doctrine. They will both share, affirms Jean-Jacques, the same eternal happiness in the bosom of their Creator.

We know relatively little about Rousseau's life from 1745 to 1750. This Balzacian period is condensed into some twenty pages of the *Confessions*, though the most illuminating reflection of his moral and material situation is caught in the letters he wrote to Mme de Warens during August 1748.[2]

I am wearing out my mind and my health in an effort to behave wisely in these difficult circumstances; to try, if possible, to get out of

[1] *Essay concerning the human understanding*, IV, 19.
[2] *C.G.* I, no. 101: 'J'use mon esprit et ma santé pour tâcher de me conduire avec sagesse dans ces circonstances difficiles, pour sortir, s'il est possible, de cet état d'opprobre et de misère; et je crois m'apercevoir chaque jour que c'est le hasard seul qui règle ma destinée et que la prudence la plus consommée n'y peut rien faire du tout.'

this state of poverty and ignominy; and every day it seems to me that chance alone rules my destiny and that the most consummate prudence is of absolutely no avail.

Now this was not entirely true: chance was not solely responsible for Rousseau's plight. After the departure of Altuna, he moved to the Hotel Saint-Quentin in the rue des Cordiers and there became intimate with Thérèse Levasseur who was to share his chequered existence, first as mistress, then as *gouvernante* or housekeeper and, after 1768, as Madame Rousseau. In the difficult circumstances to which he alludes this was scarcely an act of 'consummate prudence'. But Jean-Jacques, wearied by the 'perpetual distrust' of Mme de Warens, knowing that their former relations could never be resumed, felt an intense longing for feminine sympathy, or, as he puts it more simply, wanted someone to replace *Maman*.

Thérèse Levasseur, then 24, was the daughter of a former employee in the Mint at Orleans, a quiet and harmless man who lived in terror of his wife. Mme Levasseur had been in business and was, from all accounts, a crafty, smooth-tongued and rapacious woman. She quickly despised the feckless Jean-Jacques and, whilst privately milking his influential friends, did her utmost to poison his relations with Thérèse. Her first move was to summon to Paris a numerous brood of children and grandchildren. Of Thérèse we read in the *Confessions* that she was a simple creature who attracted Jean-Jacques by her lively but gentle looks; above all, by her timid, modest air. Although sometimes she astonished his aristocratic friends by her shrewd common sense, she often amused them vastly by her malapropisms, of which he composed a small dictionary. She never learned to tell the time and could not remember the days of the week. It is not easy to form an objective impression of her character as, in general, we see Thérèse only through the eyes of Jean-Jacques who pays warm tribute to her loyalty, devotion and unselfishness. Many of his female admirers, however, have portrayed her as a malevolent gossip and trouble-maker who exercised a baleful influence on Jean-Jacques by her irrational suspicions and dislikes. In the minority are those who think that a woman who could live for thirty-five years with a man of his temperament must needs have been a remarkable and admirable person. But we shall observe, in due course, that she had her less admirable traits.[1]

The liaison began with a misunderstanding. Rousseau was puzzled at the reluctance of Thérèse to satisfy his desires and suspected venereal disease. He was immensely relieved to learn the true cause. As a girl, she had been the victim of a 'cunning seducer'. It is significant that, from the outset, Rousseau had entertained no illusions on this score and would have been astonished, indeed, if the successor to *Maman* had been a virgin. That, he observes ironically, would have been a miracle in Paris. Though their intimacy dates probably from the spring of 1745, Jean-Jacques did not set up house with Thérèse until early in 1750, when he rented an apartment on the fourth floor of the Hôtel de Languedoc, in the rue de Grenelle-Saint-Honoré: the Levasseur family were installed two stairs higher up. Meanwhile, in 1745, Rousseau moved from the Hôtel Saint-Quentin to the rue Jean-Saint-Denis, near the Opéra. What he lived on it is hard to guess, since in addition to his Venetian debts he owed money to a compatriot, later affectionately referred to as 'Papa'. Roguin. To this kindly creditor he wrote in July, describing his terrible struggle with poverty and disgust with 'the society and commerce of men'. Rousseau's hopes were now centred on *Les Muses galantes*, an opera of which a fragment was played at Passy, in September, in the salon of that famous eighteenth-century Maecenas, La Popelinière. The whole work was later staged by the Intendant des Menus,[2] Bonneval, in the presence of the duc de Richelieu who asked the composer to change the first act. Rousseau, who had incurred the enmity of Mme de la Popelinière and her protégé Rameau, introduced a veiled allusion to his unhappy situation. Mme Dupin's stepson, Francueil, used his influence to get *Les Muses galantes* performed at the Opéra in 1748 but Rousseau, discouraged by the rehearsals, withdrew the

---

[1] Jean Senebier, in his *Histoire littéraire de Genève* (1786), III, 267, says she deserved Rousseau's gratitude but was unfit to be his confidante and guide. All his friends, he adds, complained of her bitterly as the cause of his worries and quarrels. Senebier did not know Rousseau, but he strikes one as an impartial historian.

[2] I.e. 'des menus plaisirs du roi'. These officials were responsible for the management of the royal theatres.

piece. Unjustly, in the *Confessions*, he asserts that Francueil and Mme Dupin were secretly pleased at his setback, neither being very anxious to see him acquire a reputation in society.

In October 1745 Jean-Jacques made his first contact with Voltaire, whose tragedy *La Princesse de Navarre* had been turned into an opera, *Les Fêtes de Ramire*, with music by Rameau. As both were otherwise engaged, Richelieu asked Jean-Jacques to recast the words and score of the *divertissements*. Elated by the prospect of collaboration with the great man, he wrote in suitable terms and received one of those charming letters reserved by Voltaire for dewy-eyed admirers. Perhaps, as Rousseau later surmised, he wanted to flatter a ducal protégé. In the event, the neophyte got neither money nor prestige for his pains. The implacable Mme de La Popelinière did her utmost to belittle his efforts in the eyes of Richelieu who staunchly defended Rousseau but was called away on military business. Rousseau was instructed to make fresh alterations which would have meant consultation with Rameau so that, in the end, the opera was produced with his original contributions unchanged. All the credit went to his rival as the latter's patroness had intended. Profoundly distressed, Jean-Jacques fell ill and was laid up for six weeks. Having tried in vain to interest the Opéra in his *Muses galantes* he offered a comedy, *Narcisse*, to the Théâtre Italien which accepted but did not stage it though the author received his *entrées* or free pass. Probably in February 1746 the Dupins, through Voltaire's close friend, Thiériot, approached Rousseau in regard to a secretaryship which he accepted in return for Francueil's promise to procure an audition for *Les Muses galantes*.

The post carried a salary of 900 francs. This, complains Rousseau somewhat unreasonably, was barely enough to meet his essential needs, especially as he was obliged to take a room near the Dupin residence in addition to the lodging he had rented for Thérèse in the rue Saint Jacques. But his duties were not onerous. With Francueil, he continued, for instance, to attend Rouelle's lectures on chemistry and, it would seem, even projected a text-book on the subject.[1] Dupin, a wealthy *fermier-*

---

[1] *Ann.* XII and XIII, *Les Institutions chymiques*.

général, had acquired the historic and superb Château de Chenonceaux in Touraine and here, far from the noise and dirt of Paris, his secretary enjoyed himself, in the autumn of 1747, composing music, verses and a comedy entitled *L'Engagement téméraire.*[1] As the Dupins kept an excellent table, Jean-Jacques became 'as fat as a monk'. Meanwhile, Thérèse was *enceinte* and in November a baby arrived which Rousseau in the circumstances found embarrassing. Therefore, despite the pleadings of Thérèse, but with the eager connivance of her mother, he arranged with a midwife to have the infant handed over to the *Enfants Trouvés* or Foundlings' Hospital. Thérèse bore him four other children who were all disposed of in the same way except that, unlike the first, there was no monogram by which they could be later identified.

Inevitably, this affair has aroused more controversy amongst Rousseau's biographers than any other disclosure in the *Confessions.* Of much greater moment, however, are the repercussions produced in Rousseau's own consciousness by the haunting memories of his 'fatal conduct'. What is now called the 'problem' of his children has given rise to various theories or, rather, conjectures. These derive either from an intuitive faith in Rousseau's moral integrity or from necessarily inadequate medical data. According to one school, it is doubtful whether he had five children: probably only four or three or one. The late Mrs Macdonald, not content with having, by her brilliant researches, justified Rousseau's indictment of Diderot, Grimm and Mme d'Epinay, maintained that he was gulled by the Levasseur women and never was a father. She alleged, moreover, that Mme Levasseur blackmailed him by threatening to inform his friends. An anonymous biographer thinks that Jean-Jacques knew he was a cuckold but accepted paternity to avoid a scandal. A view held by many doctors is that Rousseau was impotent. This is denied by Dr G. Variot, in an interesting article published in 1925 which recalls the discovery made by J. Lemaître of an entry in the registers of *La Maison de la Couche* recording the admittance of an infant called Joseph-Catherine

[1] In this tenuous comedy, Rousseau tries unsuccessfully to exploit a typical Marivaux situation. The hero simulates indifference in order to bring the lady to heel.

Rousseau on 19 November 1746. Dr Variot accepts, in fact, Rousseau's own statement that he had five children by Thérèse and abandoned them for the reasons given in the *Confessions*. Whether he actually was or not the father of these children is a puzzle that may never be solved. What concerns us is the moral problem which tormented Jean-Jacques till the end of his life. That he believed himself to be the father seems beyond doubt. It followed, therefore, that his 'fatal conduct' in handing all five over to the *Enfants Trouvés* would stamp him in the view of all right-thinking men as an unnatural father. On this head, Rousseau distinguishes between the motives which induced him to desert the first two and those which led him to dispose of the others. The latter, one should note, were born after he became famous as the author of the prize essay, *Le Discours sur les sciences et les arts*. Now, in 1746, Rousseau took his meals at a *table d'hôte* kept by a tailor's wife, Mme La Selle. It was frequented by a mixed crowd of *viveurs*, officers and business-men whose conversation was amusing but cynical, bearing largely on their amorous conquests, the husbands they had cuckolded and the by-blows they had sent to the *Enfants Trouvés*. In such an atmosphere of careless goodfellowship, says Jean-Jacques, it seemed the most natural thing in the world to follow the custom of the country and he did so with not the smallest scruple, persuading Thérèse that there was no other way of saving her honour. But, in 1750, his whole outlook on life had changed, witness, for example, the contrast between the tone of his *Epître à Parisot* (1742) and that of the *Epître à M. de l'Etang, vicaire de Marcoussis* (1749).[1] Here there is no trace of the docile and grateful pupil of Mme de Warens. Sobered and embittered by the experience of adversity and injustice, seething with class hatred, he launches into a violent diatribe against Parisian society. With obvious pleasure Rousseau lashes the favourites of fortune, the 'scum' called *grands seigneurs*; the boudoir-spaniels who become statesmen; the imbeciles known as *beaux esprits*; the mediocre scribblers hailed as geniuses by an ignorant public; the swashbuckling officers with their boring military 'shop'; the inane *petits-maîtres*; the vindictive prudes

[1] *C.G.* I, no. 105.

and the snobbish country nobles—in short, the fools, rogues and charlatans for whom honest men are objects of contempt in this abode of vice, injustice and arrogance. By a piquant coincidence, in 1748 Voltaire had expressed his own disgust with Paris in an *Epître à Mme Denis*. His poem, however, is conceived in a mood of philosophic disillusionment and bears no trace of class rancour.

When Thérèse gave birth in the spring of 1751 to her third child, a profound change had occurred in Rousseau's moral situation. As we shall note in discussing the *Discours sur les sciences*, the immediate stimulus to write this book came from a quasi-mystic experience which transformed him spiritually. Meanwhile, let us briefly review the events that preceded Rousseau's 'conversion'. Early in 1749 he was asked by Diderot to do the articles on music for the *Encyclopédie*, an enterprise destined to become the organ of advanced opinion in France. Here, as Jean-Jacques gleefully informed Mme de Warens, was an ideal opportunity for paying off old scores. 'I've got my enemies by the short hairs.'[1] In July Diderot was arrested and imprisoned in the *donjon* at Vincennes but released from close confinement in August and allowed to receive visitors. Rousseau, then suffering from his bladder complaint, was deeply shocked, and as soon as possible made frequent journeys on foot to Vincennes. There, amongst other friends of Diderot he made the acquaintance of a German called Grimm, employed as reader to the young prince of Saxe-Gotha. Very soon, owing to their common passion for music the two became inseparable comrades. Through this German, Rousseau was introduced to the Baron d'Holbach whose *salon* gradually became the rendezvous of several *philosophes* noted by the police for their subversive ideas on religion and philosophy. It is probable that Jean-Jacques, even at this period was, at heart, opposed to their ideals but remained for some time unconscious of any fundamental difference of outlook owing to his warm friendship and admiration for Diderot. Probably, however, D'Holbach scented in Rousseau, from the first, a potential rebel and a source of trouble to the 'party'.

[1] *C.G.* I, no. 102 (27 Jan. 1749): 'Je tiens au cu et aux chausses des gens qui m'ont fait du mal.'

In abjuring the religion of Geneva, Rousseau had automatically forfeited his status as citizen of that Republic. It is, therefore, interesting to note that he subscribes himself, in a flattering letter to Voltaire written in January 1750, as 'Citoyen de Genève'. And in November his prize essay was published anonymously as 'par un Citoyen de Genève'. Evidently Rousseau was anxious to reassume a style in accordance with his 'new principles'. So, when his third child arrived, he was no longer the gay commensal of Mme La Selle's *table d'hôte* but the author of a highly moral treatise the success of which, he confesses, rekindled his enthusiasm for truth, liberty and virtue. What would have happened to these smouldering embers had the laurels crowned another brow is a matter for speculation. As it is, heartened by the verdict of the Dijon Academy, Rousseau began to remodel his life according to the principles adumbrated in his first *Discours*. He recalled the teachings of early childhood, the love of virtue and heroism inculcated in him by his father, by Plutarch and Geneva. But he did not recall, apparently, the memories of *Cassandre* and the other old romances which used to temper the austerity of his boyish republicanism, his 'Roman pride'. Nowhere, perhaps, is the quality of his new mood expressed more transparently than in the second of Rousseau's *Dialogues* though it was written in old age.[1]

Beguiled by the absurd hope of procuring the final triumph of reason and truth over prejudice and lies and of making men wise by showing them where lay their true interest; excited by his vision of the future happiness of the human race and by the honour of contributing to it, he (Rousseau) discovered an idiom worthy of so great an enterprise.

Clearly, now, the fate of Rousseau's third child could no longer be a mere matter of routine. According to the *Confessions* this was a problem to be considered in the light of nature, justice, reason and of religion. What religion? Not, Rousseau

---

[1] *H.* IX, 214. *Rousseau Juge de Jean-Jacques, Dialogues*: 'Bercé du ridicule espoir de faire enfin triompher des préjugés et du mensonge la raison, la vérité et de rendre les hommes sages en leur montrant leur véritable intérêt, son cœur échauffé par l'idée du bonheur futur du genre humain et par l'honneur d'y contribuer, lui dictait un langage digne d'une si grande entreprise.'

implies, Catholicism or even Genevan Calvinism but 'that religion, pure, holy, eternal like its author, which men have polluted whilst claiming to purify it and which they have transformed by their formulas into a mere religion of words since it costs little to prescribe the impossible when one is not obliged to practise it.'[1]

This has a familiar ring and, indeed, is but the echo of sentiments already expressed by many writers, notably by Saint-Evremond in his *Discours sur les félicités promises aux religieux.* On the other hand, it must be remembered that the passage in question was written about 1769, that is to say, after Jean-Jacques had adopted his 'natural religion'. It is, therefore, quite possible that he viewed the past in the light of his actual religious sentiments. Otherwise, we must conclude that already in 1751 he was not an orthodox Christian.

In the end, the third infant went the way of its predecessors and for reasons which had, it seems, very little to do with the 'laws of nature, justice, reason and religion'. We find them in a letter written by Jean-Jacques to Mme de Francueil who had spoken to him about his conduct. It is the angry, truculent letter of a man who is guiltily conscious that his actions cannot be made to conform with his principles. He dwells, therefore, at length on the material obstacles that keep him from fulfilling his paternal obligations: his poverty and his 'mortal malady', the indifferent health of Thérèse, the impossibility of earning a living by his pen in a house full of squalling brats. The latter, moreover, handicapped by the stigma of illegitimacy, would never be able to find honest employment. And why are they illegitimate? 'Ask your unjust laws, Madame. It did not suit me to enter into an eternal contract and no one will ever prove to me that any duty obliges me to do so. What is certain is that I never did so and never shall.'[2] But why have children unless

---

[1] *Conf.* 349: '...cette religion, pure, sainte, éternelle comme son auteur que les hommes ont souillée en feignant de vouloir la purifier et dont ils n'ont plus fait, par leurs formules, qu'une religion de mots, vu qu'il en coûte peu de prescrire l'impossible quand on se dispense de le pratiquer.'

[2] *C.G.* I, no. 113 (20 April 1751): 'Demandez à vos injustes lois, Madame. Il ne me convenait pas de contracter un engagement éternel et jamais on ne me prouvera qu'aucun devoir m'y oblige. Ce qu'il y a de certain, c'est que je n'en ai rien fait et que je n'en veux rien faire.'

one can feed them? Because, argues Jean-Jacques, such was Nature's intention and, since she has provided food for all, the real culprits are the rich like Mme de Francueil and her kind who rob him of the bread meant for his children. To them he owes the means of subsistence and that, fortunately, is provided by the Foundlings' Hospital which is not the terrible institution pictured by Mme de Francueil. Governed by sound regulations, it furnishes the type of rustic upbringing Rousseau himself would have given his offspring. True, the children are not coddled, like little gentlemen. Adequately fed, they grow up to be sturdy peasants and labourers, leading a happy and innocent life, more fortunate than their father, he writes, having obviously forgotten why he, as an apprentice of sixteen, bolted from Geneva. Mme de Francueil, he concludes, is therefore unjust in reproaching him with a crime when, in fact, he has sacrificed the sweet pleasures of fatherhood in the interests of his children. He has rescued them from misery at his own cost. Here, but only as an afterthought, Rousseau invokes the authority of Plato who lays down in his *Republic* that the child should be brought up by the State, 'remaining unknown to its father'. The most decisive of all his reasons Jean-Jacques could not disclose to Mme de Francueil, since it concerned Mme Levasseur and her family.

Substantially, these are the arguments Jean-Jacques later reproduced in the *Confessions*. From the purely rational standpoint, we are told, they always seemed to him unassailable. But the heart, as Pascal said, has reasons which reason can never know. To this view Rousseau tacitly assents when he confesses that many a time, during these fifteen years, the poignant regrets of his heart had condemned him. But he passionately rejects the suggestion that his motives were ever bad, that he could ever have deliberately and cynically spurned the sweetest of all human obligations. The truth is that, at the time, his decision seemed wholly admirable, rational and legitimate. Although, out of regard for Thérèse, he did not openly boast of it, he told all who were aware of his liaison with her: Diderot, Grimm and, later, Mme D'Epinay and the duchesse de Luxembourg. But why then, in the *Confessions*, does he violently attack the 'false friends' who maliciously betrayed his 'secret', having just told us that he never made any mystery of his conduct because, in fact, he really saw no harm in it?

Rousseau warns us here that we were promised not a justification but a confession, yet it is painfully evident from the *Rêveries du promeneur solitaire* that, until the end of his life, he was tortured by the desire to justify his conduct and thus reintegrate himself in society. Now, it is almost impossible to comment on this wretched affair without appearing to assume the rôle of moral arbiter so that, perhaps, it might be salutary to recall Talleyrand's shrewd remark that in writing his *Confessions*, Jean-Jacques put us all in the confessional. The latter's final word on the matter is: 'It is my duty to be truthful; the reader's to be just. I shall never ask of him more than that.'[1] The trouble, however, is that Jean-Jacques presents the reader with two different sets of motives to explain the same action. When he confesses frankly why the first two children were sent to the *Enfants Trouvés* few of us, I imagine, can be sure that, in his place, we would have resisted the temptation to which he succumbed. But when he claims that, in disposing of the other three, he was actuated not by weakness but by lofty and rational motives it is difficult not to suspect 'principles' which impelled him to behave exactly as he had done originally when the question of scruples or obligations never entered his consciousness. It is true that in the *Confessions* we read that, intuitively, Rousseau knew from 'les regrets de mon cœur' that he had been wrong to follow his republican principles even if they were endorsed by Plato. Yet, in the *Rêveries* which was his last work, Jean-Jacques stoutly maintains that in abandoning his children he acted in their best interests since the only alternative was to have let them be brought up by Thérèse and her family who would have made 'monsters' of them. 'I would do it again', he asserts, 'with fewer doubts, if it had to be done.'[2] Rousseau's attitude is clear. In principle, it is a father's natural obligation to bring up his children, but in his case that was materially

---

[1] *Conf.* 351: 'C'est à moi d'être vrai, c'est au lecteur d'être juste. Je ne lui demanderai jamais rien de plus.'
[2] *Promenade* 9: 'Je le ferais encore, avec bien moins de doute, si la chose était à faire.'

impossible. It was, however, still his duty to see that they received a good upbringing. Therefore, although it involved a painful ordeal he turned a deaf ear to the voice of Nature and virtuously sacrificed his happiness and reputation for the good of his children. No one, he assures us, would have been a more tender father if only 'custom had aided Nature'. Here Rousseau is simply restating the conviction which lies at the root of his whole philosophy. The social order is wrong because it is based on a false notion of man's true nature. Otherwise the talents of a Jean-Jacques would have been adequately rewarded and he would have been able to share with Thérèse the delights and obligations of parenthood in lawful wedlock.

Yet we learn from the *Confessions* that for nearly seven years they enjoyed 'the most perfect domestic bliss compatible with human frailty'.[1] In the summer evenings, seated at the open window of their modest fourth-floor apartment with a trunk for a table, they used to enjoy a frugal supper of bread, wine, cherries and cheese, gazing down at the busy rue de Grenelle-Saint-Honoré. Or else, during their long walks in the suburbs, they would dine grandly for a few sous in some little rustic inn. Less innocent, however, were the pleasures indulged in by Jean-Jacques before his moral transformation in the company of Grimm and the chaplain to the Prince of Saxe-Gotha, Klupfell, who kept a mistress, a mere child, in the rue des Moineaux. Here occurred the sordid *partie carrée* recorded by Jean-Jacques in his autobiography, an incident he recalled with shame and remorse in composing for *La Nouvelle Héloïse* the scene where the hero, Saint-Preux, made drunk by a trick of his friends, spends the night in a house of ill fame. And just as Saint-Preux confessed to Julie so did Jean-Jacques to Thérèse, thus anticipating Grimm who regaled her next morning with an exaggerated version of the scabrous affair. One might have expected that Rousseau would have parted company then and there with Grimm, but not until 1757 did they become mortal enemies.

It is hard to form an objective impression of Friedrich Melchior Grimm who is portrayed in the *Confessions* as a

---

[1] *Conf.* 346: 'le plus parfait bonheur domestique que la faiblesse humaine puisse comporter.'

sinister hypocrite and dangerous conspirator. As we shall observe in discussing the notorious Montmorency quarrel, the German had strong personal reasons for detesting Rousseau and his peculiar views on the obligations of friendship. I doubt, however, whether this typical *Gelehrter* possessed the Machiavellian talents attributed to him by Jean-Jacques. So, at least, one may judge from his *Correspondance*, a review of the French literary scene which he used to despatch fortnightly to a limited *clientèle* of noble subscribers. Nothing in the style or tone of his own contributions suggests, for instance, that he was hand in glove with the *coterie holbachique*. Intimate with most of the *philosophes*, he damned them indiscriminately, not with faint praise but by the simple device of cancelling in one paragraph whatever he had noted to their credit in the preceding one. As a result, many of the judgments of this Bavarian Pococurante coincide with those of posterity. Yet none reveals the author as a man of subtle perceptions. Often, too, this disciple of Diderot imitates the most tiresome of the latter's mannerisms: his habit of ranting on the beauties of sensibility and friendship. Probably, as Rousseau suspected, Grimm was *un faux sensible* for, as a young man, he created a nine days' sensation in Paris by his queer conduct after having been rejected by the actress, Mlle Féel. He lapsed into a sort of coma, refusing all food whilst Rousseau and the abbé Raynal watched anxiously day and night at his bedside. One morning, Grimm got up, dressed and without a word of explanation or thanks, went about his business. This earned him a brief reputation amongst women as the model inconsolable lover. It was brief, says Jean-Jacques wickedly, because although Grimm used always to walk with a handkerchief held before his eyes whilst in sight of the windows, a suspicious observer noted that, once out of sight, the heartbroken lover quietly changed his white flag of desolation for a book.

It was in August 1747 that Rousseau first met Grimm and Klupfell at Fontenay-sous-Bois where he spent two days at the invitation of the Prince's tutor, Baron von Thun. On his return to Paris he began his visits to Diderot, now on parole with permission to receive friends at the château or in the park of

Vincennes. To relieve the tedium of an uninteresting walk he used to take a book and rest occasionally in the welcome shade of the adjoining forest. Thus, one hot October afternoon, he chanced to read in the current number of the *Mercure de France* the title announced by the recently founded Academy of Dijon of their 1750 prize-essay: *Le rétablissement des sciences et des arts a-t-il contribué à épurer ou à corrompre les mœurs?* Now, although from time immemorial writers had preached the virtues of happy ignorance and the futility of art and learning, the subject proposed by the Academy, we learn from Saint-Foix, created a general scandal.[1] Rousseau, in his *Confessions*, describes the volcanic upheaval produced in the depths of his consciousness by this provocative title. 'The instant I read it, I saw another universe and I became another man.'[2] All he was able to remember clearly was that on arriving at Vincennes he was in a state of agitation bordering on delirium which Diderot perceived. Having told him its cause, Jean-Jacques read out the 'Proseopopoea of Fabricius' which he had hastily scribbled under an oak-tree. Thereupon Diderot urged him to give free rein to his ideas and compete for the prize. Rousseau did so, choosing the second of the alternatives suggested by the Academy. Now Marmontel and Morellet, in their memoirs, assert that Rousseau's account of this incident is false; that he arrived at Vincennes intending to defend the cause of the arts and sciences but was advised by Diderot to adopt the more original approach. But if their charge is true, we must regard as a pure fabrication what Jean-Jacques wrote in 1762 to Malesherbes about the illumination which, in a quarter of an hour, altered his whole outlook on the universe; the sudden revelation that man is naturally good and, if men are wicked, the cause is to be found in the institutions of modern civilisation.[3] However, the accusations of Marmontel and Morellet rest upon a statement made by Diderot in a work composed at a time when he knew that Mme d'Epinay, Grimm and he were severely handled in the unpublished second part of

[1] *Oeuvres* (1778), IV, 220 and 397. *Essais historiques sur Paris*, written circa 1753.
[2] *Conf.* 344: 'A l'instant de cette lecture je vis un autre univers et je devins un autre homme.'
[3] *Seconde Lettre à Malesherbes* (12 Jan. 1762).

the *Confessions*. The statement, which occurs in the *Essai sur les règnes de Claude et de Néron* was designed to vilify Jean-Jacques and thus, as the author naïvely admits, to 'forestall the effects of a great calumny'. It forms part of a methodical attempt to present Rousseau as a liar and an ingrate, linking up with Diderot's *Tablettes* and with the bogus memoirs of Mme d'Epinay in the doctoring of which he played a leading part. Diderot's version of the scene at Vincennes is that, consulted by Jean-Jacques, he advised the latter to take the line which no one else would take, to which his friend remarked: 'Vous avez raison.' It is much more probable that Rousseau had already decided to take the line he did and that Diderot approved, not necessarily because he himself believed that the arts and sciences had corrupted modern civilisation, but because he loved a controversy. Now, at no time does Diderot deny that Rousseau arrived in a state of agitation and that is a decisive point. For why on earth should Jean-Jacques have been so excited if he had merely resolved to defend the banal and orthodox alternative?

This is not to say, however, that Rousseau, in 1749, on the road to Vincennes literally experienced the semi-mystic conversion which he related, thirteen years later, to Malesherbes:[1]

Oh! Sir, had I been able to write down the quarter of what I saw and felt under that tree, how clearly would I have shown up all the contradictions of the social system; how forcibly I would have exposed all the abuses of our institutions; with what simplicity I would have demonstrated that man is good naturally and that it is by their institutions alone that men become wicked.

This looks like a classic example of what Bergson calls the retroactive influence of the present on the past. When, in January 1762, Jean-Jacques attempted in all sincerity to re-create his emotional experience of October 1749 he superimposed on it, unconsciously, the image of his actual state of soul. For there is nothing at all in his *Discours sur les sciences et les arts* about

---

[1] *Loc. cit.* 'Oh, Monsieur, si j'avais jamais pu écrire le quart de ce que j'ai vu et senti sous cet arbre, avec quelle clarté j'aurais fait voir toutes les contradictions du système social, avec quelle force j'aurais exposé tous les abus de nos institutions; avec quelle simplicité j'aurais démontré que l'homme est naturellement bon et que c'est par ces institutions seules que les hommes deviennent méchants.'

human natural goodness. On the contrary, he remarks that men are perverse, that human nature was not fundamentally better when they lived in happy ignorance and simplicity, but at least, they could read each other's thoughts. Now, when Jean-Jacques wrote his letter to Malesherbes he had just completed *Emile*, the work in which his doctrine of natural goodness corrupted by modern civilisation is fully elaborated for the first time although he was now firmly convinced that his first *Discours* must have sprung immediately from this concept of human nature. It is, however, possible that his illusion began to crystallise earlier, in 1754, when Jean-Jacques drafted a second reply, never completed, to one of the most formidable opponents of his prize-essay.[1] Only a fragment of its preface survives, but it is not without interest, for here Rousseau defends his 'sad and great system', the fruit, he says, of a sincere examination of the nature, faculties and destiny of man. It is because most men have inopportunely abandoned this system that they have degenerated from their primitive goodness and become the victims of error and misery. However, Rousseau continues, he dared not fully reveal in the *Discours sur les sciences* the full scope of a 'true but distressing system of which the question treated in the *Discours* is only a corollary'. Note the reason advanced by Jean-Jacques to explain his restraint. The essay aroused a great scandal. What would have happened if he had then expounded his complete system with all its implications? His adversaries would have accused him of disturbing the public peace and it would have been easy to ridicule the work of an unknown writer, nay, to ruin him for 'the greater glory of philosophy'. He was obliged, therefore, to take precautions.

It was so as to be able to explain the whole (system) that I did not tell everything. Only successively and always for a few readers, have I developed my ideas.... Often I have been at great pains to enclose in a sentence, in a line, in an apparently chance word, the results of a long suite of reflections. Often the majority of my readers have found my *Discours* disjointed and almost entirely incoherent because they did not

---

[1] *Oeuvres et Correspondance inédites de J.-J. Rousseau publiées par M. G. Streckeisen-Moultou* (Paris, 1861), pp. 317–22. *Préface d'une seconde Lettre projetée à M. Bordes.*

perceive the trunk whose branches I showed them. But it was sufficient for those who are quick on the uptake and I never write for the others.[1]

Courtois, in his *Chronologie*, tentatively places the composition of this *Préface* in the summer of 1753, but Rousseau's use of the plural, 'mes *Discours*', indicates a later date. At the earliest, this fragment could not have been written before early spring of 1754 when the second *Discours* was completed. I doubt, therefore, whether Jean-Jacques, as an immediate result of his emotional experience on the road to Vincennes in 1749, acquired the sudden conviction that men had progressively degenerated from their primitive goodness and that it was his mission to announce from the housetops this painful and humiliating truth. On the other hand, the tone of the first *Discours* certainly betrays the influence of a recent psychological shock which produced a reorientation of his consciousness. What most probably occurred on the road to Vincennes is best understood if we reflect on that gradual change in Rousseau's outlook on society which has already been noted: his reversion to the sentiments, aspirations and ideals of the pre-Warens phase. What he desperately needed in 1749 was a sense of inner harmony, a release from his consciousness of the frustration and failure that had dogged all his attempts to win fame and fortune since the summer of 1742 when he set out to astonish Paris with his new and wonderful system of musical notation. At a critical moment in his psychological existence, Rousseau's attention was seized by the title of the Academy essay. In the words: '*Si le rétablissement des arts et des sciences a contribué à épurer ou à corrompre les mœurs*', he discerned a mysterious directive, so aptly did they conform to the new trend of his inner consciousness. None could answer that question better than Jean-Jacques who had failed ignominiously to make

---

[1] *Ibid.*: 'C'est pour pouvoir tout faire entendre que je n'ai pas voulu tout dire. Ce n'est que successivement et toujours pour peu de lecteurs que j'ai développé mes idées.... Souvent je me suis donné beaucoup de peine pour tâcher de renfermer dans une phrase, dans une ligne, dans un mot jeté comme au hasard le résultat d'une longue suite de réflexions. Souvent la plupart de mes lecteurs ont dû trouver mes discours mal liés et presque entièrement décousus faute d'apercevoir le tronc dont je leur montrais les rameaux. Mais c'en était assez pour ceux qui savent entendre et je n'ai jamais voulu parler aux autres.'

a name in the arts and sciences. And did not the Academy imply, by phrasing the question in such a challenging manner, that perhaps true merit has nothing to do with artistic or intellectual superiority? Thus, it seems to me, Jean-Jacques was led unerringly back to the plane from which, in childhood, he had envisaged life, weaving into his father's maxims and into Plutarch's *Lives*, the representations of a boy's vivid imagination. In a sudden flash of illumination his course was brightly revealed. For he knew well, from bitter experience, what the unrewarded pursuit of the arts and sciences can do to a man's soul. But it was not too late to recapture the innocence, the austere and virtuous ideals of youth. So, as his imagination played on the subject proposed by the Dijon Academy, Jean-Jacques universalised his personal experience. His own life history, undoubtedly, was that of all those who had foolishly abandoned the candour and simplicity of their golden age for the cult of the arts and sciences. Such was the 'truth' revealed to Rousseau on the road to Vincennes and from which he derived a profound feeling of liberation and inner harmony. May we not, in this sense, interpret the well known passage from the second *Lettre à Malesherbes*?

I chanced upon the Academy of Dijon question which gave rise to my first publication. If anything ever resembled a sudden inspiration, it is the emotion aroused in me by that reading; suddenly I felt my mind dazzled by a thousand flashes of enlightenment; swarms of vivid ideas presented themselves to me with a force and confusion which threw me into a state of indescribable turmoil. I felt overcome by a giddiness resembling intoxication. A violent palpitation oppressed me, causing my breast to heave. Unable to breathe whilst walking, I sank down under a tree in the avenue and there spent half an hour in such a state of agitation that, on getting up, I saw the whole front of my jacket wet with my tears although unconscious of having wept.[1]

---

[1] 'Je tombe sur la question de l'académie de Dijon, qui a donné lieu à mon premier écrit. Si jamais quelque chose a ressemblé à une inspiration subite, c'est le mouvement qui se fit en moi à cette lecture; tout à coup je me sens l'esprit ébloui de mille lumières, des foules d'idées vives s'y présentent à la fois avec une force et une confusion qui me jeta dans un trouble inexprimable; je sens ma tête prise par un étourdissement semblable à l'ivresse. Une violente palpitation m'oppresse, soulève ma poitrine; ne pouvant plus respirer en marchant, je me laisse tomber sous un des arbres de l'avenue, et j'y passe une demi-heure dans une telle agitation qu'en me relevant j'aperçus tout le devant de ma veste mouillé de mes larmes, sans avoir senti que j'en répandais.'

Viewed as a reflection of Rousseau's nostalgia for the innocent and happy climate of his boyhood, the first *Discours* is a significant document. Judged as a contribution to the history of ideas it is a shoddy piece of reasoning as the author later admitted.[1] But we must not forget that it is a thesis, with all the defects inherent in this method of grasping realities when it is applied to human, as distinct from purely scientific, problems. From the outset, wearing blinkers, Rousseau moves along that narrow strip in the field of history which is illuminated and predefined by his *a priori* concept. As he naïvely infers, it was not his business to reveal the forest surrounding his favourite tree. Now, in the eighteenth century it was usual to regard this procedure with indulgence and to make allowances for the author's enthusiasm. Thus, for example, the severe La Harpe comments on Jean-Baptiste Rousseau's much admired *Ode à M. le marquis de la Fare* the theme of which, oddly enough, is that of our Rousseau. It praises the carefree existence of the untutored Huron whose natural vigour has not been enervated by our modern 'luxe asiatique' or by those baleful arts which have increased our misery by multiplying our wants. La Harpe observes urbanely that if the ideas presented in this contrast between savage and civilised man are not always true from the rational standpoint, they are true enough for poetry which may, 'like eloquence, present them only under one aspect.'[2] And such, on the whole, was the attitude of those who read the passionate diatribes of Jean-Jacques. The *Discours*, as M. Gonzague de Reynold has shown, did, however, inspire sixty-eight articles defending the arts and sciences.[3]

The subjective character of the first *Discours* is almost immediately visible. All its ideas spring from an emotional state generated by Rousseau's bitter personal impressions of the cultured society in which he moved, not by virtue of his literary talents, but as secretary to Dupin. This is of capital importance. As his friend Duclos observes, in his excellent *Considérations sur les mœurs de ce siècle* (1750), the profession of letters did not exactly rank as an *état* or social category.[4] Yet literary distinc-

[1] *Conf.* 345.   [2] *Oeuvres choisies de J.-B. Rousseau* (Paris, 1808), p. 109, n. 2.
[3] *Revue de Fribourg*, July 1904.
[4] Ed. F. C. Green, Camb. Univ. Press, 1939, p. 136.

tion conferred upon a plebeian something resembling a social status, placing him on an equal footing with his superiors in fortune and lineage. ' Now, in 1749, Jean-Jacques had not achieved that position and, at 37, intensely conscious of his unrecognised genius, appeared destined to remain indefinitely in the rut of poverty and dependence. This complex and unhappy psychological state was aggravated by Rousseau's domestic cares and obligations. His pent-up emotions, as we have noted, reached their flash point on the road to Vincennes. The resultant explosion of sensibility produced a reorientation of his consciousness followed by the consoling illusion of a moral rejuvenation. *Integer vitae, scelerisque purus.* Transported by an act of self-hallucination to the exquisite climate of youthful innocence and of noble idealism, haunted by the vision of a golden past which, for him, was symbolised by the magic name of Sparta; yet still obsessed by rankling memories of Paris the modern Sybaris, a regenerated Jean-Jacques invested a *cliché* with the quality of a new and original emotion. Unfortunately, it is precisely his systematic hammering on the Sparta-Sybaris theme which vitiates the whole *Discours* for the critical and history-conscious reader of today.

A bare summary of Rousseau's thesis is enough to reveal its weakness. From his galling personal experience of the Parisian *beau monde* he concludes that the cult of the arts and sciences always generates moral corruption. Their adepts display a uniform urbanity which masks a *cortège* of vices: false bonhomie, suspicion, fear, hatred, treachery and insensibility. Gone are the sterling, rugged virtues of our rude forefathers. Their intense patriotism has been replaced by a selfish apathy masquerading as cosmopolitanism; their simple faith by a politely veiled blasphemy; their happy ignorance by a dangerous pyrrhonism. But this is not a recent phenomenon. History, Jean-Jacques asserts, shows that culture always rots the moral fibre of a nation and, by fostering inequality and the love of luxury, inevitably brings about its military and political decay. Operating with the regularity of a physical law, this recurring historical pattern is strikingly exemplified in the annals of ancient Egypt, Greece, Rome and Constantinople. All were doomed to spiritual and material destruction from the moment they abandoned the essential virtues of patriotism, equality, self-sacrifice, honesty and frugality in order to cultivate art, philosophy and science.

Everyone knows and quotes Rousseau's lapidary phrase: 'le besoin éleva les trônes; les sciences et les arts les ont affermis,'[1] and his striking metaphor of the iron chains wreathed with the garlands woven by the arts and sciences. Yet how much more significant is the preceding, more drably expressed, statement: 'L'esprit a ses besoins, ainsi que le corps. Ceux-ci font les fondements de la société, les autres en font l'agrément.'[2] Implicit in these apparently banal words is a concept which, if true, makes nonsense of what we call civilisation and progress. But, of course, we have here one of the numerous half-truths that compose the tissue of Rousseau's thesis. Obviously, the existence of the individual depends on the satisfaction of his biological needs and in this sense the latter form the basis of any society. But to assert that man's intellectual needs represent an in-essential element in society is to abolish what is specifically human in our species. We must not, however, take Jean-Jacques too seriously. In a moment, he will hold up as the model of a perfectly organised society that of Sparta, based not indeed on man's intellectual but on his spiritual or moral needs: innocence, self-denial, industry, mutual esteem, truthfulness, military courage, fanatical patriotism—almost godlike virtues. For Sparta, says Rousseau, was a republic of demi-gods rather than of men. There is a savage, exultant note in Rousseau's fanatical admiration for these untutored and warlike Spartans, Goths and Scythians whose toughness and endurance he contrasts with the softness of our modern troops who, for all their discipline, fall an easy prey to disease and the elements. There is a strange undercurrent of ferocity, also, in the prosopopoeia, sole sur-viving fragment of his mediumistic inspiration under the oak-tree at Vincennes. Jean-Jacques pictures the shade of the noble Fabricius contemplating the terrible spectacle of a Rome stripped of her antique simplicity and moral grandeur, lapped in

---

[1] *H.* 1, 3: 'necessity erected thrones; the arts and sciences consolidated them.'
[2] *Ibid.* 'The mind has its needs, like the body. The latter are the foundations of society, the former its ornamental trimmings.'

luxury, dominated by poets, painters, sculptors, philosophers and rhetoricians:

> What are these effeminate manners? What is the meaning of these statues, pictures and buildings?...The spoils of Carthage have become the booty of a flute-player! Up, Romans! Overthrow those amphitheatres; smash those marbles; burn those pictures; drive out those slaves who keep you in bondage and whose baleful arts are corrupting you...[1]

For the arts and sciences, read the Whore of Babylon, and we have the authentic idiom of the early, militant Genevan pastors nurtured in the Old Testament prophets. And, indeed, the main sources of the *Discours* are Rousseau's memories of the Bible, Plutarch, Montaigne and his father's stories of the good old days.[2]

So much for Rousseau's 'historical inductions' which derive from a systematically biased approach to history. The fallacy of his thesis and the inaccuracy of his so-called facts were quickly detected by his earliest critics. There is no evidence that the collapse of great nations was due to their love of the arts and sciences; that the latter necessarily generate a passion for luxury or, on the other hand, that illiterate peoples hold a monopoly of the human virtues. Even more puerile is Rousseau's attempt, in the second part of the *Discours*, to trace the origins of the various arts and sciences to the human vices: astronomy to superstition; rhetoric to ambition, hatred or flattery; geometry to avarice; physics to idle curiosity. Nowhere in his thesis does Jean-Jacques ever quite discard this banausic attitude to culture. Significantly, it never occurs to him that the masters in every branch of art and thought achieve greatness precisely because of a disinterested love of their craft; that man has always employed art, not for utilitarian ends or for love of fame but for the sheer love of beauty in form, colour and sound.

---

[1] *H.* 1, 9: 'Quelles sont ces mœurs efféminées? Que signifient ces statues, ces tableaux, ces édifices....Les dépouilles de Carthage sont la proie d'un joueur de flûte! Romains, hâtez-vous de renverser ces amphithéâtres; brisez ces marbres, brûlez ces tableaux, chassez ces esclaves qui vous subjuguent et dont les funestes arts vous corrompent...'

[2] For a complete examination of this question, see L. Delaruelle, 'Les Sources principales de J.-J. Rousseau dans le Premier Discours', *Revue d'Histoire litt. de la France.* vols. XIX, XX. One may also consult with profit the introduction (pp. 61–82) to G. R. Havens's edition of this *Discours* (Oxford Univ. Press, 1946).

Intoxicated by the vision of himself as a modern Cato, Jean-Jacques sternly calls upon the philosophers, artists and scientists to justify their civic *raison d'être*: 'Answer me, I say,' he declaims, 'you from whom we have received so much sublime knowledge; if you had never taught us any of these things, should we be less numerous, less well governed, less redoubtable, less flourishing or more perverse?'[1]

However, in the closing pages of his essay, Rousseau modifies his Boeotian attitude, recalling no doubt that he was a candidate for an Academy prize. The truly great and original savants, he generously allows, are the 'preceptors of the human race' and ought to be admitted by rulers to their councils. Nothing can be said, on the other hand, for the swarms of obscure hedge-scholars and scribblers inspired solely by an ignoble desire for publicity. Others there are, who constitute a definite menace to the State. They sap the foundations of religion, virtue and patriotism by their insidious paradoxes and subversive opinions the latest of which is the pernicious doctrine that luxury is an economic advantage to all classes. We have no lack of physicists, mathematicians, chemists, musicians, dramatists, painters and sculptors but France has no longer any citizens. Morality and virtue no longer count, says Rousseau bitterly, in an age when men are evaluated like herds of cattle and the only standards are commercial and financial. And so an individual of extraordinary talent who refuses to pander to the false values of his century, is doomed to oblivion and indigence. Still, one may draw consolation from the reflection that happiness depends, not on public opinion but on a man's inner consciousness of his own value. That is the only true science, the perennial philosophy. The intuitive conviction of one's individual moral worth, implies Jean-Jacques, is the one equalising factor in modern society. It is worth noting Rousseau's insistence on this question of social inequality which he obviously regards as the first and, by its consequences, the most pernicious effect of culture.

---

[1] *H.* 1, 11: 'Répondez-moi, dis-je, vous de qui nous avons reçu tant de sublimes connaissances; quand vous ne nous auriez jamais rien appris de ces choses, en serions-nous moins nombreux, moins bien gouvernés, moins redoutables, moins florissants ou plus pervers?'

The decay of morality, writes this aspirant for a competitive literary award, has its original source in the baleful inequality caused by the distinction accorded to superior talent in the arts and sciences. The public no longer asks if a man is upright but if he is talented; no one cares whether a book is useful provided it is attractively written. There are a thousand prizes for fine essays, none for good actions. But suddenly conscious of his delicate position, Jean-Jacques adroitly skates over the thin ice with the not v..y convincing remark that the merit of having founded the Dijon Academy competition is far superior to the laurels that will crown the successful candidate. The truth is that, as the essay drew to a close, its author began to realise uncomfortably to what extremes he had been carried by his initial enthusiasm and to reflect that some of his wilder utterances might one day come home to roost. Belatedly, therefore, he prescribes for ordinary folk, like himself, a Spartan abstinence from literary and scientific activity. In any case, he observes sententiously, why chase a reputation which, 'in the present state of things', will never make up for what it cost to acquire it? In short, the grapes are not only sour but poisonous.

On the whole, the eighteenth-century public refused to take the *Discours* seriously, treating it rather as an amusing paradox, a clever exercise in dialectic. Rousseau himself, more than twenty years later, viewed this work as an integral element of his 'system' or doctrine. At a critical moment, he suggests, in the formation of his ideas the Academy question 'removed the scales from his eyes' and produced order out of chaos by solving a problem which had long tormented him. Whilst admiring the intellectual progress of the modern age he was perturbed to observe that it seemed to be accompanied by a corresponding decay in moral values. The cult of progress, he felt, was incompatible with man's true nature and might ultimately destroy what is really human in our species. These views, if not explicitly expressed in the *Second Dialogue*, faithfully reflect its meaning. What the Academy question revealed to Rousseau was, briefly, the intuitive knowledge that the original goodness of human nature is still intact, though the minds of men are corrupted by the prejudices derived from their deplorable education and social milieu. The *Mercure* announcement, says Jean-Jacques, showed him the vision of another universe purged of all these evils, in which he then discerned the source of all human misery.[1] Here again, I would make generous allowances for the retroactive influence of the present on the past, especially after reading the following manuscript note which to the best of my knowledge is unpublished. Commenting on the statement that the destiny of literature in a State must decide that of its morals, Rousseau observes that the opposite view was 'sustained with much eloquence and wit in a *Discours* which won the Academy of Dijon award in 1750'. He continues:

May we be permitted to say that the judges who crowned this work ought perhaps not to have awarded the prize without having insisted on the author defending in a second *Discours* the thesis he had attacked in the first? Thus, as an Oracle once replied, the lance of Achilles *must cure the wound it had made*.[2]

In this connexion, it should also be noted that Jean-Jacques, in 1751, wrote an essay on the following question proposed by the Academy of Corsica: *Quelle est la vertu la plus nécessaire aux héros et quels sont les héros à qui cette vertu a manqué?* But on second thoughts, he did not compete for the prize and his *Discours*, which he coarsely described as 'un torche-cul', only appeared in print in 1769 when, to the author's intense annoyance, Fréron published it in his journal, *L'Année litteraire*. Rousseau's approach to the subject is quite objective and his style reveals no trace of the fire which glowed in the first *Discours*. And, far from regarding military valour as a sterling virtue, he doubts very much whether it should ever be counted as a virtue at all. Still more surprising when one recalls his eulogies of the ancient Romans, is the calm statement that temperance is not the characteristic virtue of the hero and that his former idol, Cato,

[1] *H.* ix, 213.
[2] Bib. de Neuchâtel, MS. 7842, fol. 1: 'soutenue avec beaucoup d'éloquence et d'esprit dans un Discours qui a remporté le prix de l'académie de Dijon en l'année 1750. Nous serait-il permis de dire que les Juges qui ont couronné cet ouvrage auraient peut-être dû n'adjuger le prix à l'auteur qu'en exigeant de lui qu'il défendît par un second Discours la thèse qu'il avait attaquée dans le pr [premier] ? C'est ainsi qu'un Oracle répondit autrefois que la Lance d'Achille *devait guérir la blessure qu'elle avait faite*.'

who loved wine and money, had ignoble vices but was yet greatly admired by his countrymen who were connoisseurs in glory. What of patriotism which figures in the first *Discours* as the finest of the antique virtues? The great men of the past, intoxicated by their ardent love of country, never hesitated to employ the most odious and unjust means in her service. Patriotism is one thing, justice is another. Cromwell, for all his crimes, was probably one of the greatest men who ever lived. Finally, as if to show with what virtuosity he could alter his principles in defence of a new thesis, Rousseau congratulates the Corsicans on their choice of a liberator, that warrior-philosopher, Paoli, whose first act on casting aside the sword was to establish in his country the arts and sciences: 'Oh, spectacle worthy of heroic times! I see the Muses in all their splendour, march proudly in your battalions.'[1] We need not wonder why Jean-Jacques, now fully committed to the awkward task of justifying his first *Discours*, prudently decided to pigeon-hole his Corsican essay.

I will deal rather summarily with the half-dozen serious *Réfutations* provoked by the *Discours sur les sciences et les arts* and with the author's ingenious but futile efforts to escape from the web spun by his own eloquence. Gautier, a professor of history from Nancy, opposed real facts to Rousseau's 'inductions historiques', proving for example that the military decay of Athens was due to political corruption and not to artistic or intellectual progress. In a second *Réfutation* he ruthlessly exposed his adversary's technique which was to dodge fundamental objections by enlarging on bagatelles. Jean-Jacques, in replying to Stanislas, the exiled king of Poland, adopted a more respectful and conciliatory tone, protesting disingenuously that he had never denied the utility of the arts and sciences. His sole object was to discover why the sciences, so pure at their source, had engendered so much impiety, so many heresies, errors and false systems. It was because science was never made for the average man whose passionate nature inevitably leads him to abuse knowledge. The alliance of science and virtue is to be

---

[1] 'O spectacle digne des temps héroïques! Je vois les Muses dans tout leur éclat, marcher d'un pas assuré parmi vos bataillons.'

found only in a few 'privileged souls'. To the king's blunt argument *ad hominem* Jean-Jacques replies with a metaphor which really begs the question. If someone threatened his life and he was lucky enough to seize the malefactor's weapon, is he forbidden to use it against his enemy? Indeed, the Fathers of the Church employed profane knowledge to attack the pagan philosophers. Alarmed lest he be suspected of including Catholic sacred literature in his general proscription, Rousseau adduces in support of his thesis the religious polemics of the Reformation. And with typical eighteenth-century insensibility to the beauty of Gothic architecture, Church ritual and music, he asks ineptly what profit religion has derived from the arts. The Evangelists, he maintains naïvely, communicated their gospel in language which owes nothing to art. And in an outburst of pious wrath, 'plus royaliste que le roi', he summons the ministers of God to cast aside their prideful learning, to prostrate themselves at the feet of the Master, communicating thus by their example His divine message. One important criticism, however, had still to be answered. It concerned the theme of 'happy ignorance' which is identified in the *Discours* with probity and described as the state in which man had been placed by 'the eternal wisdom'. Rousseau explains that he is using the word 'ignorance' in the special sense of 'ignorance raisonnable', not to be confused with the ignorance born of wickedness. 'Reasonable ignorance' leads the individual to adjust his intellectual curiosity to his intellectual capacity, so acquiring an indifference to everything not immediately conducive to virtuous behaviour. This happy or reasonable ignorance, he adds, is the distinctive quality of the pure and contented soul which draws its felicity solely from the contemplation of its own innocence. It does not, therefore, need to seek the false empty happiness deriving from what the public thinks of one's intellectual or artistic talents. Yet, despite all these lofty sentiments, his appetite now whetted by the success of his prize essay, Jean-Jacques secretly resolved to win fresh laurels. But that is not the reason he gives for throwing up a lucrative post which Francueil had obtained for him in the *Finances*, in order to earn a living by copying music. Apart from literary ambition he seems to have been actuated by two motives.

Office routine bored him and when Francueil, during a brief absence, left Jean-Jacques in sole charge, the thought of being responsible for 30,000 francs drove him almost crazy with worry. But the real cause of his apparently quixotic behaviour was a fresh and painful attack which he suffered in November 1751 of his bladder complaint now diagnosed by the specialists as incurable. Rousseau, in the *Confessions*, attributes it pathetically to an inflammation of the kidneys brought on by his journeys to see Diderot at Vincennes. This was pure illusion, as is proved by a letter of 26 August 1748 to Mme de Warens minutely describing his 'colique nephrétique' and other symptoms.[1] Convinced, as he always was at every new attack, that he had not long to live, Jean-Jacques decided to reform his mode of life and, as far as possible, bring it into line with the lofty principles of his *Discours*, a plan which in no way conflicted with his literary ambitions. He had only to exploit his reputation as an original and persuasive lay-writer on moral questions in order to establish himself as *arbiter morum* in a country which, for half a century, had witnessed a steady reaction against intellectualism. The case for sentiment against geometric reason had been pleaded by dramatists and poets, by *libertins* such as De la Fare and Chaulieu, in the *comédies larmoyantes* of La Chaussée and Destouches and more eloquently by the widely read marquise de Lambert whose celebrated salon was a temple dedicated to the worship of friendship, sensibility, platonic love and virtue. There were schools established, she complained, for the cult of intellect; why not have schools devoted to the cult of the heart?[2] Jean-Jacques was to be the answer to her prayer and he was frequently inspired, I think, by this wise and subtle lady.

Jean-Jacques soon became, as Castel remarks, 'l'homme du jour'.[3] Francueil told everyone he had gone crazy, unable to understand how any sane man could refuse a lucrative post in the inland revenue. Fashionable society was inclined to share this view when Jean-Jacques embarked on his 'sumptuary reform'. Discarding his gold lace, sword, white stockings and watch, he

---

[1] *C.G.* I, no. 101.   [2] *Oeuvres* (1748), p. 116.
[3] *Supplément à la Collection des oeuvres de Rousseau* (Geneva, 1782), v, 126.

wore a plain round wig to go with his sober attire. Thérèse's ne'er-do-well brother accelerated Rousseau's sartorial transformation by stealing his ample stock of expensive shirts. Always timid in company, acutely concious of his *gaucherie*, he affected a boorish disregard of the social proprieties and silenced his interlocutors by his caustic retorts. Naturally, the *beau monde*, enchanted with his bearishness, importuned him with invitations, visits and presents. In more intimate company, however, Bruin was a very docile and gentle creature, more than ever attached to Grimm and Mme d'Epinay whose friendship was to alter the pattern of his existence, with deplorable results. She married in 1745 her cousin, Denis-Joseph La Live d'Epinay, a *fermier-général* who owned the château of La Chevrette at Montmorency. Here, in the summer of 1749, on the occasion of a marriage, they performed Rousseau's *Engagement téméraire*, a mediocre comedy in verse. In passing, let us note that Mme d'Epinay had at least two lovers: Francueil, by whom she had a son in 1753 and Grimm whom Rousseau introduced to her in September 1750. In 1753 Grimm and Rousseau became involved in the famous *Querelle des Bouffons*. An Italian operatic troupe arrived in Paris and was ordered to play at the Opéra. The public, entranced with the foreign music, refused to wait for the French works that followed. Ever since his Venetian sojourn, Jean-Jacques had been an enthusiastic admirer of Italian music and, in the violent polemic over the merits of the two schools, intervened with a *Lettre sur la musique française*, published at the end of 1753. In January, Grimm had joined the fray with a brochure, *Le petit prophète de Boehmischbrode*, which missed fire. Not so the *Lettre* which, according to its author, caused such an explosion that the public forgot the other great quarrel, then at its height, between Church and Parlement. Rousseau's brutally expressed opinions gave deep offence since he claimed that, if French music had neither harmony nor tempo, it was because the French language itself was not musical. French singing, he added, was a continuous yelping, painful to foreign ears. His *Lettre* evoked at least fifteen vigorous refutations and the author was described by one reviewer, Fréron, as 'un furieux, un frénétique, un pédagogue bilieux, un Dracon...

un Missionnaire suisse'.[1] The last epithet is significant, for le
Père Castel also considered it shocking on the part of a foreigner
to abuse the hospitality so generously extended to him by 'an
amiable and gracious nation'. Since Rousseau was attacking not
French morals but French taste, he stirred up a wasp's nest,
though we need not swallow without a grain of salt his statements that the orchestra of the Opéra had conspired to murder
him or that he narrowly escaped deportation, if not the Bastille.
After all, the Italians had many allies amongst French lovers of
music, known collectively as *le coin de la Reine* because, at the
Opéra, they sat under the Queen's box whilst the patriots composed *le coin du Roi*. In 1754 Rousseau published a clumsily
facetious *Lettre d'un symphoniste* accusing the Opéra musicians of
having cunningly sabotaged their rivals' performances. This was
because the management had unjustly withdrawn from him the
free pass always granted to composers whose works were
accepted for performance and given to Rousseau for his operetta,
Le Devin du Village, first presented at the Opéra in March 1753,
though it had scored a dazzling triumph six months earlier at
Fontainebleau in the presence of Louis XV and a brilliant
assembly of courtiers. Now, this event must be situated in its
original ambience if we are to understand Rousseau's complex
psychological state. His staunch friend Duclos, who had got
Le Devin accepted by the Opéra, was against a court performance. However, authority had the last word. So the 'ancient
Roman' was whisked out to the rehearsal in a royal coach,
accompanied by Grimm, the abbé Raynal and the leading lady,
Mlle Féel, all of which, Rousseau confesses, imposed a severe
strain on his austere republicanism. On the great day, after much
heart-searching, he decided to appear before royalty with un-
combed wig and stubbly beard in a box facing that of the king
and Mme de Pompadour. Incidentally, considering the poor
lighting of the average eighteenth-century theatre, Rousseau
seems to have worried unnecessarily. On the other hand, surrounded as he was by ladies, the frequent exits necessitated by his
infirmity must have been most embarrassing. Yet Jean-Jacques

---

[1] *Lettres sur quelques écrits de ce temps* (1753): 'a frantic madman, a bilious pedant,
a Draco...a Swiss missionary.'

saw nothing but kindliness in the politely curious glances which he intercepted. And as the play unfolded, in an atmosphere of mounting excitement and admiration, he entered the gates of paradise.

In the scene between the two good little people, this effect reached its climax. There is never any clapping in the presence of the King, so everything could be heard; the play and the author gained thereby. I heard around me the whispering of women who seemed to me beautiful as angels, saying to each other in undertones: 'Charming! delightful! Every single note speaks to the heart!' The pleasure of inspiring emotion in so many lovable people moved me to tears which I could not restrain during the first duet, observing that I was not the only one to weep.... Yet I am sure that, at this moment, I was much more affected by sensual voluptuousness than by an author's vanity.[1]

That evening, Rousseau was commanded to appear at the Château on the following day to be presented to Louis XV. According to his informant, the king intended to announce the grant of a pension. But after a sleepless night, Jean-Jacques decided to plead ill-health and return to Paris, thus causing much surprise and adverse comment. Next evening, on setting out to visit Mme d'Epinay, he was waylaid by Diderot who approved his refusal to be presented, yet strongly urged him to accept the pension as a matter of duty to the Levasseurs. A lengthy dispute ensued which, says Jean-Jacques, prefigured many others of a similar nature where Diderot invariably laid down the law, throwing him on the defensive. Rousseau believed he was defending his principles, for he could not accept a pension and continue to preach the virtues of independence and disinterestedness. Besides, he adds dryly, it was one thing to be awarded a pension but quite another to obtain its regular payment. His reasons for shirking the royal interview are more convincing.

---

[1] *Conf.* 371: 'A la scène des deux petites bonnes gens, cet effet fut à son comble. On ne claque point devant le Roi; cela fit qu'on entendit tout; la pièce et l'auteur y gagnèrent. J'entendais autour de moi un chuchotement de femmes qui me semblaient belles comme des anges, et qui s'entre-disaient à demi-voix: Cela est charmant, cela est ravissant; il n'y a pas un son qui ne parle au cœur! Le plaisir de donner de l'émotion à tant d'aimables personnes m'émut moi-même jusqu'aux larmes et je ne pus les contenir au premier duo, en remarquant que je n'étais pas seul à pleurer.... Je suis pourtant sûr qu'en ce moment la volupté des sens y entrait beaucoup plus que la vanité d'auteur.'

Here Rousseau was influenced not by principles but by timidity and *amour-propre* reinforced by a vivid imagination. What if his wretched bladder chose the crucial moment to play its devilish tricks? And how, with his accursed shyness, could he be sure of finding *le mot juste*, the lapidary phrase which would combine 'some great and useful truth' with the homage due to a monarch? More likely, in his agitation, he would blurt out some idiotic remark. Rousseau shuddered at the mere thought. As it was, *Le Devin du Village* netted him more than any of his other works except *Emile*, though that cost twenty years of meditation and took three to write. He conceived his operetta at Passy whilst on a visit to a distant relative, Mussard, and virtually completed it in six weeks. In that rustic suburb, Rousseau spent many happy days in congenial society. Mussard was a practical philosopher but with a strange bee in his bonnet. Mad on conchology, he saw the whole globe as a vast shell composed of shell-dust. Though tortured by a cancer of the stomach which eventually starved him to death, Mussard was the soul of gaiety and fortitude. A profound admirer of Italian music, it was he who encouraged Rousseau to compose *Le Devin*. At Passy, too, the latter met the famous abbé Prévost, a simple, lovable man with no trace of the sombre melancholy that darkened the lives of his novel heroes. To Passy also came Boulanger, whose *Antiquité dévoilée*, published after his death by D'Holbach, caused a sensation with its theory that religion originated in primitive man's fear of Nature's cataclysms. Another visitor was Mlle Denis, the niece and, as their recently discovered correspondence has revealed, the mistress of Voltaire. Jean-Jacques had many talks at Passy with an old friend and political exile Lenieps, who was very intimate with an even more celebrated Genevan patriot, Micheli Ducrest. We shall have occasion, later, to consider the possible implications of this filiation.

Is it true, as Rousseau alleges in the *Confessions*,[1] that *Le Devin* was the original cause of his eventual rupture with Grimm, Diderot and the D'Holbach clique, who might have forgiven him for writing successful books but were secretly jealous of his triumph as a composer? He complains that, on entering

[1] *Conf.* 452.

D'Holbach's salon, the company used to break up into little whispering groups, studiously ignoring him, though Mme D'Holbach was always charming. Her husband, when he deigned to look at Jean-Jacques, was deliberately malicious and, on one occasion, grossly insulted him. That much is probably true for, as Rousseau elsewhere reveals, other guests were frequently revolted by the baron's Teutonic sense of humour. However, we have it from Palissot de Montenoy that, at this time, Rousseau was regarded as being hand in glove with the *philosophes* by the general public who detested their dangerous ideas and jeered at their emphatic, pontifical style. 'The Philosopher of Geneva is one of their associates and everyone knows that these *philosophic* potentates form an offensive and defensive league.'[1]

I suspect, however, that the activities of Jean-Jacques were beginning to excite, inside the D'Holbach coterie, not envy but speculation. These professors of materialism dismissed Rousseau's first *Discours* as an amusing paradox and it is doubtful whether they discerned anything in the behaviour of Jean-Jacques, the Cato of the *salons*, to indicate that he was no longer in sympathy with the general aims of the *Encyclopédie*. D'Holbach, indeed, seems to have treated him as an egregious *poseur*. But Rousseau's so-called *Dernière Réponse* to his old friend, Charles Bordes, and especially the *Préface* to his comedy *Narcisse*, must have excited unfavourable comment at the headquarters of the 'parti philosophique'. Bordes, whose first criticisms were embodied in a lecture delivered at the Académie de Lyon in June 1751, was easily Rousseau's most formidable adversary, for he concentrated his attack on the substructure of the *Discours*, forcing its author to take evasive action.[2] Ignoring, as far as possible, objections concerning specific questions of historical fact, Jean-Jacques made a selection of the criticisms levelled at his thesis not only by Bordes but by all his opponents, hoping in this way to end a distasteful controversy.

The interest of the *Dernière Réponse* lies in its general tone

---

[1] Bibl. de l'Arsénal, MSS. 2759, fol. 64, 77: 'Le Philosophe de Genève est un de leurs associés et personne n'ignore qu'il y a entre ces puissances *philosophiques* une ligue offensive et défensive.'

[2] *Discours sur les avantages des sciences et des arts* (pub. in *Le Mercure*, 1 Dec. 1751).

rather than in Rousseau's arguments. From the outset, in order
to conceal his embarrassment, he assumes the manner of an
expert patiently replying to the amateurs whose objections, he
coolly remarks, display none of 'those luminous truths which
impress no less by their evidence than by their novelty'.[1]

Bordes had pictured man in the savage state as ignorant, lawless
and barbarous. But history, Jean-Jacques proclaims, favours the
'contrary supposition'. It was not until someone invented those
terrible expressions, *mine* and *thine*, that man lost his original
virtues. But even supposing that man is naturally wicked, it is
obvious that intellectual progress could only have made him
worse. And so by this very hypothesis alone, Rousseau continues,
his adversaries ruin their own case. On the other hand, they
cannot maintain that if man is naturally good, culture would have
been good for him since, from the moment man evinced a desire to
perfect his intellect, his primitive goodness began to deteriorate.
This pitiful dialectic is not the only symptom of Rousseau's
embarrassment which is betrayed by an increasing note of
irritation. Thus, as if angrily conscious that Bordes had sapped
the historical foundations of his thesis, he suddenly produces
with a flourish his trump card. What would his adversaries not
give, he exclaims, to be able to say that Sparta had never existed?
Sparta is the thorn in their flesh: Sparta, the one State in Greece
where virtue was purest and lasted longest precisely because it
had no philosophers. Bordes had got under Rousseau's skin at
another point. In rebutting the latter's statement that ignorance
is always associated with virtue, he remarked dryly that, on the
other hand, no traveller had ever returned from darkest Africa to
tell the tale. That, Jean-Jacques lamely retorted, was no proof
that the Africans were vicious, adding the following gratuitous
remark: 'If I were chief of one of those tribes in Nigritia,
I declare that I would erect on the frontier of the country a
gallows from which I would hang, out of hand, any European
who dared to enter it and the first citizen who tried to get out.'[2]

---

[1] 'Ces vérités lumineuses qui ne frappent pas moins par leur évidence que par
leur nouveauté.'

[2] 'Si j'étais chef de quelqu'un de ces peuples de la Nigritie, je déclare que je
ferais élever sur la frontière du pays une potence où je ferais pendre sans rémission le
premier Européen qui oserait y pénétrer, et le premier citoyen qui tenterait d'en sortir.'

We need not of course take too seriously an outburst due to Rousseau's pent-up annoyance. Yet it reveals an aspect of his personality on which we shall have occasion to comment later in discussing that final chapter of *Du Contrat social* entitled *De la religion civile*.

The *Dernière Réponse* did not silence Bordes. Meanwhile, early in 1753, Rousseau published the *Préface de 'Narcisse'* which is really an indictment of intellectualism as reflected in the eighteenth-century doctrine of scientific progress. Wisely discarding the historical approach, Jean-Jacques reaffirms his conviction that the cult of science is incompatible with man's true nature. The savants, he remarks, no longer enjoy his esteem for he has seen through their *vaine pompe scientifique*. The new philosophy he condemns as antisocial because it weakens the links which really attach man to society: benevolence and mutual esteem. 'What I complain of is that the sciences, the arts and all the other objects of human intercourse knit the bonds of society closer by means of self-interest.'[1] And applying to the *philosophes* the phrase coined by La Bruyère to scarify the financiers, Rousseau concludes. 'Family, country become for him words devoid of meaning; he is neither a parent, a citizen nor a man; he is a philosopher.'[2] One can picture the impression produced by these sentiments on D'Holbach, D'Alembert, Raynal and other *habitués* of the baron's salon, all of whom constantly stressed the obligations of the individual to society, to humanity, to the family and to the State.

To some extent, the *Préface* modifies the extremism of the first *Discours*. Rousseau denies ever having said or thought that science is worthless and evil by its nature; that cultured peoples are necessarily corrupt, and ignorant communities always virtuous, or that all schools and universities should be closed. In other respects, however, the *Préface* is more Boeotian than the *Discours*. Everything, we are told, that facilitates communication between nations leads to the interchange, not of

---

[1] 'Je me plains de ce que les sciences, les arts et tous les autres objets de commerce resserrent les liens de la société par l'intérêt personnel.'
[2] 'La famille, la patrie deviennent pour lui des mots vides de sens; il n'est ni parent, ni citoyen ni homme; il est philosophe.'

virtues but of vices. It is perhaps difficult for the twentieth-century reader, accustomed to 'iron curtains', to appreciate the effect which this maxim must have produced in the minds of the *philosophes* who were nearly all professed 'citizens of the world'.

More interesting is the footnote where Jean-Jacques, attacking 'the half-baked philosophers' who proclaim that men are everywhere the same because they are universally governed by self-love and self-interest, advances a really constructive idea. In considering the psychology of primitive peoples, suggests Rousseau, we must not confuse words with things. Owing to the enormous difference between the milieu of civilised and that of uncivilised man, it is quite wrong to identify the self-interest of the savage with that of a modern European. In primitive communities, men were linked only by a common love of their society and by a mutual interest in their self-defence; they were not divided by any question of self-interest in our sense of the term; their sole ambition was to earn the esteem of their fellows. Everyone, obviously, will not endorse these views, but the implications of his initial remarks are true and valuable. It is essential, if we are to understand the psychology of primitive peoples, to remember that the radical difference between civilised and uncivilised men derives solely from the differences in the social *milieux* into which they are born.

Having no intention of giving up his writing and musical composition, Rousseau now explains the apparent contradiction between his principles and practice. Precisely because the French are irremediably corrupted by the arts and sciences, these must be cultivated intensely lest the vices they have engendered degenerate into crimes. After all, it is better to live with polite rogues than with ferocious ruffians. Rousseau's one desire, now, was to retire from this polemic without loss of face. But the obstinate Bordes launched a second devastating essay[1] which effectively silenced Jean-Jacques and, I think, made him realise the unconstructive and illiberal character of his *Discours*. Bordes, whilst not disputing the military valour of the Ancients, their

[1] *Réplique de M. Bordes à la Réponse de M. Rousseau, ou Second Discours sur les avantages des sciences et des arts* (Aug. 1753). It should be noted that although Rousseau had entitled his answer to Bordes' first discourse, *Dernière Réponse* he had never published another previously.

poverty, frugality and patriotism, pointed out that these cease to be virtues when subordinated to the lust for domination. His cruellest thrusts are directed at Rousseau's beloved Spartans whose vices are ruthlessly exposed: their tolerance of adultery and sexual inversion; their unspeakable inhumanity towards their Helots and prisoners of war and infants of delicate constitution; their base flattery of the Asian satraps; their cowardice and cruelty in the Peloponnesian wars; their economy based on slave labour. In short, Bordes exploded Rousseau's theory that the happiest phase in the history of every nation is that of its greatest ignorance. If a golden age ever existed, asked Bordes, why and how did men abandon it? This is one of the criticisms which deeply influenced Rousseau's thought when, a few months later, he began to compose his *Discours sur l'inégalité*. Another was the comment of Bordes on the problem of man's original nature. He himself agrees that men are not naturally wicked yet finds it hard to accept the theory of natural human goodness: 'But when I see, in three quarters of the universe, ignorance united with the vices, if the latter are not in man's nature what gave birth to them?'[1] It was to answer this question that Rousseau wrote his *Emile*. Anticipating the Academy of Dijon, Bordes goes on to discuss the origins of political and civil inequality and remarks: 'If we seek the origins of that vaunted system of equality imputed to the Ancients, we shall find that it rested upon a false principle which supposes all men equal in the natural order.'[2]

In November 1753, the *Mercure* published the subject proposed by the Dijon Academy for its 1754 literary competition: *Quelle est l'origine de l'inégalité parmi les hommes et si elle est autorisée par la loi naturelle?* Jean-Jacques, once again a candidate, went on a week's holiday with Thérèse and their landlady to Saint-Germain. During his solitary walks in the adjacent forest, he brooded on two questions, both inextricably linked up

---

[1] 'Mais quand je vois dans les trois quarts de l'univers l'ignorance et les vices réunis, si ces vices ne sont pas dans la nature de l'homme, qu'est-ce donc qui leur a donné naissance?'

[2] 'Si nous recherchons l'origine de ce système d'égalité tant vanté chez les anciens, nous trouverons qu'il portait sur un faux principe qui suppose tous les hommes égaux dans l'ordre de la nature.'

with the problem of human happiness. What is the original configuration of man's nature? Is social inequality artificial or, as Bordes maintained, a necessary extension of natural inequality?

Tout le reste du jour, enfoncé dans la forêt, j'y cherchais, j'y trouvais l'image des premiers temps, dont je traçais fièrement l'histoire; je faisais main basse sur les petits mensonges des hommes; j'osais dévoiler à nu leur nature, suivre le progrès du temps et des choses qui l'ont défigurée, et comparant l'homme de l'homme avec l'homme naturel, leur montrer dans son perfectionnement prétendu la véritable source de ses misères. Mon âme, exaltée par ces contemplations sublimes, s'élevait auprès de la Divinité, et voyant de là mes semblables suivre, dans l'aveugle route de leurs préjugés, celle de leurs erreurs, de leurs malheurs, de leurs crimes, je leur criais d'une faible voix qu'ils ne pouvaient entendre: 'Insensés qui vous plaignez sans cesse de la nature, apprenez que tous vos maux viennent de vous.'[1]

Rousseau's opponents, no doubt, had seriously undermined the historical basis of his first *Discours*, but nothing could shake his intuitive belief in his mission. It was perfectly clear and simple, like the truth he had now to announce to the world. Modern civilisation is corrupt because it rests upon a totally false notion of human nature. Men are unhappy because they have created a social organisation where crime knits closer ties than virtue. Man, as he emerges from the hands of Nature is good, in the sense which Rousseau will explain in his second *Discours*. He will also reconstruct the chain of events that led to our present deplorable situation. Some of these were, no doubt, accidental: others were due to human blindness. Such is the tragedy stylised in Rousseau's metaphor of the statue of Glaucus, recovered from the ocean but so disfigured by corrosion

---

[1] *Conf.* 381: 'All the rest of the day, I buried myself in the forest. There I sought and found the image of those primitive times of which I proudly sketched the history. I made short work of the petty lies of men; I dared to strip their nature to the buff, to follow the progress of time and of the things that have disfigured it; and, comparing man as men have made him with natural man, I boldly revealed, in his so-called perfectibility the true source of his misery. My soul, exalted by these sublime contemplations, ascended to the Godhead and from there, seeing my fellow creatures following, along the blind path of their prejudices, that of their errors, their misfortunes and their crimes, I cried aloud to them with a feeble voice they could not hear: "Madmen, who complain unceasingly of Nature, learn that all your ills come from yourselves."'

as to resemble now a wild beast rather than a god.[1] Turn, however, to the pages of the *Discours* where we shall gaze on another
image: that of man as originally fashioned by Nature.

How does Rousseau propose to embark on what one might
call his *Recherche de l'homme perdu*? Simply by brushing aside all
the facts, since they have no bearing whatsoever on the question.
He means, of course, historical facts which, indeed, are irrelevant to a prehistoric problem. As for the awkward matter of
Genesis, the less said the better. After all, there is nothing
irreligious in speculating on what the human race might have
been if God had not, immediately after the Creation, withdrawn
it from the state of nature and willed that men should be un-
equal. At this point, Rousseau makes an observation in which
lurks a brilliant and suggestive idea:

it is no light enterprise to disentangle what is original from what is
artificial in the actual nature of man and to know well a state which no
longer exists, which perhaps never existed, will probably never exist,
about which, however, we must acquire accurate notions in order to
judge properly of our present state.[2]

Rousseau outlines a method of approach to his problem
which, although he himself employed it wrongly, has since
revealed its potentialities, thanks to the genius of Bergson. In
seeking a clear idea of man's original psychological sub-
structure, Jean-Jacques quickly realised that no help was to be
obtained either from history or from what we call sociological
science, then at the embryonic stage. He noted, moreover, that
the so-called primitive peoples whose habits were exciting the
curiosity of missionaries and explorers, had a considerable social
history behind them. Besides, the accounts furnished by these
amateurs struck him as unreliable. He foresaw, indeed, the
emergence of a new science, experimental psychology, but
doubted whether it would ever yield decisive results. So far, all
that the savants had achieved was to complicate the problem

---

[1] *V.* i, 135, *Préface.*

[2] *V.* i, 136: 'ce n'est pas une légère entreprise de démêler ce qu'il y a d'originaire
et d'artificiel dans la nature actuelle de l'homme, et de bien connaître un état qui
n'existe plus, qui n'a peut-être point existé, qui probablement n'existera jamais, et
dont il est pourtant nécessaire d'avoir des notions justes, pour bien juger de notre
état présent.'

by a fundamental error of method, by transposing 'to the state of nature, ideas which they got from society: they talked about savage man and depicted civilised man.'[1] Then Rousseau suddenly saw the light. We need not look for primitive man in history or in some remote corner of the globe. He resides within each of us, though buried under a mass of civilised accretions which may, however, be penetrated by an effort of introspection; by 'stripping' civilised man 'of all the supernatural gifts he may have received and of all the artificial faculties he can only have acquired by long progress: by considering him, in a word, as he must have emerged from the hands of Nature'.[2] We have here the key to the second *Discours*. Unfortunately, however, Rousseau was temperamentally incapable of employing the introspective method in the disinterested search for truth. No doubt he frequently asserts that introspection must always be pursued 'dans le silence des passions', a word which was used in his day to embrace all the affective states. But Rousseau's passions were rarely silent. In fact, his whole doctrine of natural human goodness was the involuntary projection, on a universal scale, of Rousseau's own moral and spiritual dilemma. He had committed wicked deeds. But since he was a natural man and Nature is good, how could Jean-Jacques be wicked? Belief in the original goodness of human nature was for him, therefore, a vital spiritual need.

It cost Rousseau no great effort of introspection to retrace the history of our species back to the state of nature. He had only to transfer to primitive man his own new reactions to the external world. In the pure state of nature, the human soul bore the imprint of a 'celestial and majestic simplicity'.[3] The individual always acted from certain and invariable principles. In addition to physical inequality deriving from differences in age, health and bodily strength, men in the pure state of nature had dif-

---

[1] *V*. I, 141: 'à l'état de nature des idées qu'ils avaient prises dans la société: ils parlaient de l'homme sauvage, et ils peignaient l'homme civil.'

[2] *V*. I, 143: 'En dépouillant (cet être ainsi constitué) de tous les dons surnaturels qu'il a pu recevoir, et de toutes les facultés artificielles qu'il n'a pu acquérir que par de longs progrès; en le considérant, en un mot, tel qu'il a dû sortir des mains de la nature.'

[3] *V*. I, 135, *Préface*: 'cette céleste et majestueuse simplicité.'

ferent 'qualities of mind and soul'. There was no such thing, however, as moral and political inequality which derives not from Nature but from a kind of man-made convention. How did this type of inequality supersede the other? How was Nature subjected to Law?

Primitive man's needs were simple: food, sex, sleep, which were all easily satisfied. He led, therefore, a uniform, solitary existence amongst the animals, all of whose instincts he acquired by imitation. And, since Nature deals with sickly infants in Spartan fashion by killing them off, primitive man was never ill. Rousseau contrasts her admirable method with that of civilised society where the State, by making parenthood a burden, slaughters the children promiscuously before they are born. In a passage which is always mutilated when quoted, Rousseau observes that if Nature intended us to be healthy, he would venture to say that reflection must be an unnatural state and that 'l'homme qui médite est un animal dépravé'.[1] Isolated from its context, this phrase sounds more shocking than it is. In all fairness to Rousseau, he simply meant that primitive man, viewed physically, shared the immunity from sickness enjoyed by the lower, unreflecting animals but must have become a 'depraved' or imperfect animal when he began to meditate. He does not suggest that reflection is necessarily a form of human depravity, though later he will have much to say on this head.

Rousseau asserts that because early man had annexed all the instincts of the animals, he had less difficulty in satisfying his hunger, ignoring the fact that *homo faber* had the specifically human power to manufacture tools and hunting weapons. But it does not suit his book to dwell upon this matter. He stresses, on the other hand, the distinction between man's free-will and the automatism of animal instinct for a reason that will shortly be evident. Man's consciousness of his faculty of choice, he says, constitutes *par excellence* the spirituality of his nature. Another quality which distinguishes him from the animal is his perfecti-bility, that faculty which, in favourable circumstances, succes-sively develops all the others. Yet Rousseau is tempted to regard it as the source of all human misfortunes and to applaud

[1] *V.* I, 146: 'the man who meditates is a degenerate animal.'

those savages who deliberately compress the skulls of their infants, thus preserving to some extent their 'imbecility and original happiness', an odd remark from one who consistently deprecates any interference with Nature's plan. It accords perfectly, however, with his conviction that when man began to exploit his intelligence, he entered upon a career which was to carry him farther and farther from his true nature, 'from that original condition in which he would have spent quiet and innocent days'.[1] An anonymous critic, the brilliant young Genevan scientist, Charles Bonnet, writing under the pseudonym of Philopolis, sensibly objected that since perfectibility is a natural human attribute, modern civilised society is natural. Not so, retorted Jean-Jacques, because, although the initial development of perfectibility depended on circumstances some of which were fortuitous and inevitable, others could have been avoided by the exercise of man's free-will. All scientific progress, Rousseau implies, is the work of a few savants whose inventions usually contain a hidden threat to man's happiness and security. This view is illustrated by a little parable. Imagine, he says to Bonnet, that a scientist has discovered a means of accelerating the oncoming of old age and urges its adoption on a gullible public which angrily dismisses the warnings of someone, like Jean-Jacques, who dares to question the authority of science in the name of common sense and humanity. Is not this, he suggests, the pitiful history of universal man who forfeited the golden age, the youth of his species, in a foolish effort to attain immediately the wisdom, serenity and security naïvely associated with old age?[2] It is perhaps significant that this 'misoneism' or resistance to innovation which is so typical of Rousseau, is a well-known characteristic of primitive societies.

In addition, then, to sensation and perception, early man had free-will and intellectual perfectibility which, thinks Rousseau, must have been very slow to develop. Our primitive ancestor, he claims, had no knowledge or fear of death. But surely a rudimentary intelligence, sharpened by the instinct of self-preservation coupled with the sight and smell of corpses must have

---

[1] *V.* 1, 150: 'de cette condition originaire dans laquelle il coulerait des jours tranquilles et innocents.'   [2] *V.* 1, 222, *Lettre à M. Philopolis.*

taught man that death awaited him too. One must also question the statement that primitive man abandoned himself to the 'sheer sentiment of his immediate existence' with no thought of the future. For although lack of foresight is common in uncivilised peoples, early man must have experienced a sentiment of anticipation in the chase. But Jean-Jacques is influenced by his pet obsession. To think of the future is a beginning of reflection, a step in the direction of intellectual perfectibility. He prefers to visualise primitive man basking in the enjoyment of his sensations, deterred by his 'mortal hatred of continuous labour' from any activity requiring the exercise of intelligence. So aeons must have elapsed before he discovered the use of fire or the art of cultivating the soil. Jean-Jacques now encounters the problem of language. Rejecting the obvious hypothesis that man's unique faculty of speech conceals a virtual instinct, and that language is a natural product of family life, he racks his ingenuity to prove that in the state of nature there could have been no family life at all. All sexual contacts were fortuitous and ephemeral: the family never assembled in the same dwelling since there were no houses, huts or property of any sort. Males and females lived the same solitary life and the child, as soon as it could fend for itself, abandoned the mother. This concept need hardly surprise us. The family, after all, is a society in miniature, an organisation implying an ensemble of laws and obligations, in short, everything which natural man, according to Rousseau, detested and must have resisted as long as possible. Language, therefore, must have originated in *le cri de la nature*, the sounds uttered by the primitive infant to communicate its urgent needs. Variations of this cry extended his vocabulary but Rousseau is stupefied at the miraculous transition from a language of proper nouns to one of ideas. He cannot, in fact, conceive why early men should have needed language at all since Nature 'did so little to prepare their sociability'.[1]

Primitive man had no morality: the ideas of good and evil belong to a more advanced stage of human intelligence. Yet Hobbes is wrong in supposing that he was *homo homini lupus*. Why confuse with the natural human instinct of self-preserva-

_____
[1] *V*. i, 158: 'combien elle (la Nature) a peu préparé leur sociabilité.'

tion the multitude of subsequently acquired passions which derive from society and necessitated the invention of laws? The pure state of nature, Rousseau thinks, was the most conducive to peace, a view supported not so long ago by several archaeologists, though it seems generally agreed that primitive man's instruments were probably used indiscriminately for war or peace. Hobbes's great error, however, was to have overlooked an innate disposition which, though discernible in certain animals, is specifically human. It is pity, man's innate feeling of commiseration for his suffering fellow men. Nowhere in the *Discours* is Rousseau's style more urgent than in the pages devoted to this theme which will recur so often in his writings and always with momentous effect. It is notable that in the second *Discours*, in order to define *la pitié*, man's innate and irresistible sympathy for his suffering fellow creatures, he uses the term *sentiment* and not *instinct*, as if to underline its peculiarly spiritual quality. Yet, at the same time, he insists that it operates automatically, preceding reflection. It is the germ of all the social virtues: generosity, clemency, humanity, charity. But, unhappily, this sentiment, which in primitive man was 'obscure yet intense', deteriorated with his first social contacts so that, today, the last vestiges of his original humanity have been almost obliterated by scientific progress. That is why, in order to know what natural pity must have been in the state of pure nature, we must observe the reactions of the uneducated *canaille*. In street quarrels, asserts Jean-Jacques, it is always the women of the *Halles* who rush to separate the combatants and prevent bloodshed, a fallacy certainly not entertained by the more observant Marivaux and brutally shattered by the *tricoteuses* of the Terror.[1] Rousseau's theory of natural, spontaneous, unreflecting pity is based on the following error. He confuses physiological sympathy which might be described as a contagion of gestures and actions and is indeed natural, with psychological sympathy which belongs to a more advanced intellectual stage. No doubt the former contains the germ of the latter but the natural effect produced by the sight of suffering seems to be one of horror, inspiring a desire for instant flight as Rousseau ought to have

[1] Marivaux, *Sur la Populace de Paris.*

known from his own conduct when the organist Le Maistre fell writhing in an epileptic fit at Lyons. Then, in fact, Jean-Jacques followed instinctively the direction of his primitive nature. I need not elaborate the point but it corroborates what has been said about his misuse of the introspective method.

This section of the *Discours* reveals the author's purpose which is to prove that modern society is corrupt because the civilised individual has almost lost that primordial pity which formerly 'took the place of laws, morals and virtue'.[1] Primitive man did not, of course, know the Christian maxim: 'Do unto others as you would be done by.' But his natural pity inspired in him another maxim, much less perfect though more practical: 'Do what is good for yourself but with the least possible harm to others.' For Rousseau, the moral beauty of this precept resides in the fact that it presupposes no education or reflection. So far, then, we cannot apply the epithet *moral* to savage man who is also ignorant of vanity, esteem, contempt, property. He does not know what we call love but only sexual desire, which excludes jealousy or modesty. The introduction of the modern concept of love was a disaster for the human race. It is a product of civilisation fostered by woman for her own ends. Based on aesthetic notions foreign to savage man, it played no part in his life. Any female suited his purpose and we must not infer from the courtship behaviour of birds and animals that early man followed their example.

How, why and at what moment did man abandon the state of pure nature ? 'The species was already old, and man still remained a child.'[2] Certainly he possessed, as we have seen, faculties which could eventually make him capable of a social life. But these existed only in a virtual state and developed only under the extreme pressure of certain physical events which threatened the extinction of the human race, 'a fortuitous concourse of several external causes which might never have arisen'.[3] Briefly, the origins of society were accidental. In describing the

---

[1] *V.* I, 162: 'tient lieu de lois de mœurs et de vertu.'

[2] *V.* I, 166: 'l'espèce était déjà vieille, et l'homme restait toujours enfant.'

[3] *V.* I, 168: 'concours fortuit de plusieurs causes étrangères, qui pouvaient ne jamais naître.'

contingencies which produced the civilised state and, by accelerating intellectual progress, corrupted human natural goodness, Rousseau admits he is reduced to conjectures. But there will be nothing conjectural, he affirms, in his inductions from these hypotheses. Nevertheless, it is hard to discover on what he bases his account of the 'various hazards' which, it is alleged, perfected human reason and thus, by rendering man sociable, caused the human race to deteriorate. Modern scholarship has exploded the old belief in the accidental or contractual origins of society and favours the view that social life was, to quote Bergson, 'comprised in the structural plan of the human species as in that of the bee'. Rousseau always held, on the contrary, that primitive man had a natural repugnance for organised social life, fearing instinctively that whilst it offered certain advantages, like security, it would perhaps destroy for ever his individual liberty and independence. This is in keeping with the peculiar character of Rousseau's 'introspection'. It blinded him to what Bergson calls the dimorphism of our primitive nature which makes us alternately pacific or combative, sometimes eager to command, at others just as eager to obey. Jean-Jacques whilst violently refuting the Hobbesian fallacy that humanity is naturally, even biologically, divided into leaders and slaves, pictures just as wrongly a humanity consisting entirely of individuals whose natural repugnance for any sort of discipline bowed only to the yoke of harsh necessity. Nor could he have ever grasped the meaning of Bergson's profound remark that the obligation which links one individual to others, far from being incompatible with liberty, implies liberty.

The individual primitive man, because of climatic changes and growth of population was forced, in order to feed himself, into an association with other hunters. But such obligatory contacts were not durable. After countless centuries man, who had apparently not observed the building habits of birds and animals, began to construct rude dwellings, the first step towards luxury. Unwilling to admit the existence of *homo faber*, Rousseau assumes that Nature supplied man with some sort of hard, edged, stone axes. Then, ceasing to be nomadic, men adopted a family existence involving a rough notion of property which doubtless gave rise to quarrels. These were exacerbated by sexual preferences which, in turn, led to the arts of song and dance, 'the true offspring of love and leisure'. Superiority in these engendered jealousy, inequality, vanity, contempt, envy, humiliation. It does not occur to Jean-Jacques who did not watch his children grow up, that primitive man might have danced or sung for the sheer fun of it, with no sexual pre-occupation. Thus, chiefly as a result of violent climatic accidents, floods or earthquakes, men had to adopt a more gregarious life though the individual was not subject to any kind of law. Each was the judge and avenger of his private insults. Man's natural pity had already undergone some alteration yet, Rousseau maintains, 'this period of the development of the human faculties, representing a happy mean between the indolence of the primitive state and the petulant activity of our amour-propre, must have been the happiest and most durable epoch'.[1] It was the youth of our species, in which our distant ancestors could and should have lingered indefinitely for the happiness of mankind.

Man is now launched on the road leading to scientific progress, a fatal process which began the moment the individual was no longer self-sufficing. Then he lost his independence, happiness and equality. Someone conceived the baleful notion of enclosing a piece of land, saying: *Ceci est à moi.* That anonymous criminal was the true founder of civilised society. What horrors would have been spared to the human race, says Rousseau, if somebody had uprooted the stakes, crying to his neighbours: 'Don't listen to this impostor; you are lost if you forget that the fruits of the earth belong to all and that the earth belongs to no one!'[2] With property, labour became a necessity: agriculture and metal-working hastened the enslavement of the individual. 'It is iron and wheat that civilised men and ruined the human race.'[3] Agriculture brought in its train the division

---

[1] *V.* I, 175: 'ce période du développement des facultés humaines tenant un juste milieu entre l'indolence de l'état primitif et la pétulante activité de notre amour-propre, dut être l'époque la plus heureuse et la plus durable.'

[2] *V.* I, 169: 'Gardez-vous d'écouter cet imposteur; vous êtes perdus si vous oubliez que les fruits sont à tous et que la terre n'est à personne.'

[3] *V.* I, 176: 'Ce sont le fer et le blé qui ont civilisé les hommes et perdu le genre humain.'

of the land, property rights and laws. Skill in the crafts fostered inequality and war. That man, endowed by Nature with constructive intelligence might have found pleasure in craftsmanship is inconceivable to the ex-apprentice of the engraver Ducommun. The proliferation of inequality spawned new vices: cunning, hypocrisy, tyranny, servitude, brigandage until some rich man, worried about his possessions, evolved the most cunning plot ever conceived by the human mind. Cleverly exploiting the simplicity of the masses, he lured them into a pact of mutual defence which, in fact, robbed them of their natural liberty, established for all time the laws of property and of inequality, transforming an adroit usurpation into an irrevocable right. Yet how could these simple men have rejected such a wise and fair arrangement by which, it seemed, they merely sacrificed part of their liberty to preserve the rest? This one might call the false social contract. Rousseau will tell us later about the true one by which alone can the natural rights of man be preserved.

Incapable of dispassionate introspection, Rousseau formed an unreal impression of primitive human nature and an equally unreal notion of how political society and its laws originated. He thinks it unreasonable to suppose, for example, that 'men threw themselves straightway into the arms of an absolute master, unconditionally and irrevocably'.[1] Yet, to a modern sociologist, nothing is more probable if we consider the psychology of uncivilised man. Informed opinion, today, supports the view that man was naturally intended for very small societies whose dominant traits are patriotism, hatred of the foreigner, cohesion, hierarchy, the absolute authority of the chief, in short, discipline and belligerence. Sovereignty did not originate in paternal authority, says Rousseau. 'By the law of nature, the father is master of the child only so long as his help is necessary to the latter.'[2] Less debatable is his statement that paternal authority in the conjugal family emanates from the civil power,

---

[1] V. i, 184: 'les peuples se sont d'abord jetés entre les bras d'un maître absolu sans conditions et sans retour.'

[2] V. i, 185: 'Par la loi de la nature, le père n'est le maître de l'enfant qu'aussi longtemps que son secours lui est nécessaire.'

which was true in Rousseau's time. Where he goes badly astray is in supposing that primitive man was unconscious of family obligations or relationships. It is now known, on the contrary, that the totemic clan was, in fact, a domestic society, a family whose members, though not linked by consanguinity, were welded together by an ideal religious or mystic relationship. Later, however, as the clan became smaller, its authority and rights were concentrated in the father of the family. But the most serious defect of Rousseau's *Discours* springs from his failure to discuss the vital function of religion in the formation of primitive society.

The composition of his second *Discours* imposed a great emotional strain on Jean-Jacques. Deleyre, who had seen him at work, told the *Convention Nationale* in 1793: 'I have seen Rousseau...plunged in the deepest sadness turn aside for a moment to his spinet, strum a few pathetic airs, anoint the instrument with his tears then leave it, his soul relieved of its dejection.'[1] For some time, Geneva had been much in Rousseau's thoughts and on the first of June 1754 he set out for his native city accompanied by Thérèse and his old friend, Gauffecourt. In this nostalgic mood, he felt impelled to dedicate his essay to the Republic of Geneva. In May he sent the *Discours* to the Dijon Academy but did not finish the *Dédicace* until 12 June, probably at Chambéry. This work marks a critical stage in Rousseau's spiritual life as well as in the evolution of his political thought. The *Dédicace*, as the *Correspondance* reveals, sprang direct from Rousseau's urgent need to complete his moral rehabilitation; to purge the 'crimes' alluded to in the letter to his father. To begin with, he wanted to recover his status of Genevan citizen and that, of course, involved a return to the Genevan communion. Besides, since no one is really a prophet until he has been acclaimed as such by his townsmen, Jean-Jacques earnestly desired the esteem and applause of all Genevans. From beginning to end, therefore, the *Dédicace* is

---

[1] *Convention Nationale, Recueil de Discours*, Bibl. Nat. 8 L^{38}$_e$: 'J'ai vu Rousseau... plongé dans la plus profonde tristesse se détourner un moment vers son épinette, y préluder ou tâtonner quelques airs pathétiques, couvrir son instrument de larmes et le quitter, soulagé de l'abattement de son âme.'

fraught with a missionary zeal. For Rousseau was exalted by the belief, very privately communicated to the Genevan pastor and professor Perdriau, that he had been called to 'a sublime vocation' which was to labour for the public weal by fearlessly proclaiming the truth to his fellow men.[1] Perdriau, clearly, felt that in view of the unrest lately excited in Geneva by the *Représentants* or political reformers, the *Magnifique Conseil* might frown upon a dedicatory epistle addressed direct to 'La République de Genève' instead of through the *Procureur Général* whose office was the usual channel. But he dared not even hint that such a document emanating from one whose apostasy had, technically, deprived him of his civic rights, might create an unfortunate impression. Brushing aside Perdriau's tactful objections, Rousseau said that, having just devoted long and mature reflection to 'questions of government', he was not to be deterred by petty details of administrative procedure, a most illuminating remark. And, indeed, in the *Dédicace*, he surveys the Genevan political scene from the lofty plane of an arbiter or mediator, writing with the assurance of an expert in *matières de gouvernement*. The *Dédicace* is essentially a 'message', an exhortation addressed to the sovereign people of Geneva and their elected magistrates. Only in the light of this psychological fact can one seize its spirit and purpose. However, this work can be more usefully discussed in the chapter on Rousseau's political writings. At the moment we are concerned with his Genevan holiday, which lasted four months.

The journey had been marred by an unpleasant incident. Thérèse complained, privately, that Gauffecourt had made improper overtures to her in the coach. Such conduct, in a gouty and impotent sexagenarian, Rousseau observes in the *Confessions*, made him revise his views on the nature of friendship, especially since Thérèse, he remarks naïvely, had lost her good looks. Whether, at the time, he really believed her accusations seems questionable, for the *Correspondance* shows that he and Gauffecourt, until the latter's death in 1766, remained close friends. They parted at Lyons since Rousseau was bound for Savoy. At Chambéry he stood face to face with the woman to whom so often

[1] *C.G.* II, no. 196 (28 Sept. 1754).

he had sworn, on that very spot, that theirs was a union which only death could terminate. But in real life, as Jean-Jacques now realised, the inexorable, corrosive effects of habit and absence can destroy love more swiftly than death. Whatever sweet and poignant memories had accompanied him to Chambéry were instantly dissipated by the spectacle of Mme de Warens at fifty-four: 'Je la revis....Dans quel état, mon Dieu! quel avilissement! Que lui restait-il de sa vertu première? Etait-ce la même madame de Warens, jadis si brillante, à qui le curé de Pontverre m'avait adressé? Que mon cœur fut navré!'[1] She refused the urgent entreaties of Rousseau and Thérèse to share their life. They met again, for the last time, in August, near Geneva. His last impression of her, like the first, was of a *grande dame*, for she pressed on Thérèse a ring, the only pitiful relic of her former affluence. Thérèse gently returned it, kissing the generous hand from which it came.

Rousseau's farewell to the Church of Rome, on the other hand, cost him not a solitary pang since he had long ago rejected as unintelligible her dogmas and ritual. That much, he observes, should be placed to the credit of his Encyclopaedic friends though they never managed to shake his faith in the essential teachings of Christ. As Rousseau frankly admits, his chief motive for returning to the Genevan communion was to be reinstated as a *citoyen de Genève*. The situation was rather delicate because some of the ministers thought it improper that Thérèse should sleep in the same room as Jean-Jacques. The latter, apprised of these murmurs by his friend J.-F. De Luc, pointed out that, owing to his painful urethral complaint, it was physically impossible for him to justify the suspicions of the pastors. The inventive Thérèse, besides, produced a version of her relations with Jean-Jacques which satisfied De Luc.[2] The Consistory spared the prodigal the ordeal of a public appearance by

[1] *Conf.* 383: 'I saw her again....My God, in what a state! What degradation! What remained now of her former virtue? Was this the same Mme de Warens, once so brilliant, to whom the curé de Pontverre had sent me? How it tore my heart!'

[2] *C.G.* II, note to no. 172 (July 1754). When Rousseau, she said, was dangerously ill at Dupin's, he was nursed by her mother. One day, Thérèse, stumbling into a street-fight got a kick in the belly and, at Rousseau's request, was nursed in her mother's home. Out of gratitude, she swore to serve him to the grave.

appointing a small committee to receive his profession of faith. The ceremony took place on 29 July 1754 and was followed immediately by Rousseau's admission as a citizen. A few days previously, however, he had attended a meeting of the sovereign *Conseil Général* specially convened to swear in one of the Syndics, Pierre Mussard. It was this high official who waived the arrears of Rousseau's civic dues, only one of the many kindnesses showered on him by Genevans of all social classes.

In Geneva, he informed Mme Dupin, political liberty was solidly established. The machinery of government ran smoothly because the enlightened citizens, though firmly maintaining their rights, sensibly respected those of others.[1] Clearly this visit had a tonic effect on Rousseau's morale. It was a new and delicious sensation to bask in the esteem of his own people and to hear that his friends wanted him to come home for good. Their kindly solicitations, indeed, threw him into a state of 'violent perplexity' which continued for some months. On this matter, our only authentic source of information is the *Correspondance*. The *Confessions* give a quite inaccurate account of the reasons which actually prevented Rousseau from settling in Geneva. In these memoirs, he blames the importunities of Mme d'Epinay and the fact that Voltaire, in February 1755, had taken up residence just outside his native city. The *Correspondance* tells a very different story. There were insuperable objections, he informed Lenieps and Mme Dupin, which made it impossible to fall in with the kind offers of his Genevan friends: his sentimental ties with Paris; the promises he had made to Mme Levasseur and the difficulty of earning a living as a copyist in Geneva. But the theme of his letters to Mme d'Epinay and the Genevan pastors is independence. Mme d'Epinay had generously offered, rent free, a little cottage on her estate at Montmorency called *L'Ermitage*. Indignantly, Rousseau accused her of trying to make him her valet.[2] Her impulsive gesture, indeed, almost tilted the scales in favour of Geneva. On the other hand, as he told Jallabert, professor of philosophy at the Genevan Academy, whilst never doubting that his friends would relieve him of his

[1] *C.G.* II, no. 173 (20 July 1754).
[2] *C.G.* II, no. 276 (16 or 17 March 1755).

material anxieties, that was precisely what he feared.[1] As for Voltaire, we find Rousseau, in a letter of January 1755, allaying the misgivings expressed by the pastor Jacob Vernes regarding the distinguished fugitive and his possible influence on Genevan morals. 'I have never so strongly desired that he should justify my prejudices in his favour as now when he is in my native land.'[2]

Jacob Vernes was one of the many friends Rousseau met during his sojourn in Geneva. Then a young minister of 26, he later made a name as a man of letters. Until the publication of *Emile*, of which he disapproved, Vernes was a great admirer of Rousseau. Jean-François De Luc, a prominent member of the *Grand Conseil* afterwards led the *représentants*, or popular party, in their fight for sovereignty. It was in the company of De Luc, his two sons and Thérèse that Jean-Jacques in September 1754 enjoyed a week's boating holiday on Lake Geneva and there gathered impressions which were later woven into his novel, *La Nouvelle Héloïse*. At his own request, Jean-Jacques was introduced by Lenieps to Jacob Vernet, an able theologian and professor of belles lettres. But their relations were always rather formal despite Rousseau's obvious wish to make them more intimate. Paul Moultou, who was inducted as a pastor during this visit, made a very favourable impression on Rousseau. To him, eventually, was entrusted the manuscript final version of the *Confessions*. In Geneva, too, Jean-Jacques met his future publisher, Marc-Michel Rey of Amsterdam. Thus began a long association chequered with scoldings, complaints, ironic criticisms, apologies and effusions of friendship.

Returning to Paris via Dijon on 10 October, Rousseau sent to Rey the manuscript of his second *Discours*: it appeared in August 1755. A copy had been presented, however, in June to the *Grand Conseil* which replied courteously through the First Syndic, J.-L. Chouet expressing its satisfaction at the sentiments of patriotic zeal and virtue contained in the *Dédicace*. Chouet's predecessor, Dupan, wrote in like terms, yet remarked that the

---

[1] *C.G.* II, no. 262 (20 Nov. 1754).

[2] *C.G.* II, no. 206: 'Jamais je ne désirai si fortement qu'il justifiât mes préjugés en sa faveur qu'aujourd'hui que le voilà dans ma Patrie.'

Genevans were depicted not as they were but as they ought to be. De Luc and Jallabert were also most complimentary. Why then, in the *Confessions*, did Rousseau complain that no one was grateful for the 'cordial zeal' that pervades this work and of the cold reception generally accorded to the *Dédicace*? The key to this enigma is to be found in the letter to Perdriau which I mentioned. It seems clear that Jean-Jacques, obsessed by his 'sublime vocation', confidently hoped that his *Dédicace* would produce a moral revolution in Geneva, infecting all classes with the author's own enthusiasm for civic virtue. Instead, it merely evoked 'a few compliments'.[1] *Hinc illae lachrymae.* The *Discours* also fell flat, disappointing the author's hope of a controversy similar to that excited by its predecessor.[2] It elicited, however, a sparkling letter from Voltaire thanking Jean-Jacques for his 'new book against the human race' which, he said, made him want to crawl again on all fours, though that was rather difficult after having become accustomed, during sixty years, to the upright posture.[3] Amiably concurring with Rousseau's views on the 'horrors of society', Voltaire blandly refused, however, to blame them on intellectual progress. He closed on a paternal note, cordially inviting Jean-Jacques to share his simple rustic life at Les Délices. Rousseau's answer completely belies the statement in the *Confessions* that in 1755 he knew Voltaire would debauch the morals of Geneva and had hinted as much in his letter.[4] On the contrary, he hails the great man's arrival as a red-letter day in the annals of the Republic. On the old theme of literature and morals, he courteously defends the modified views expressed in his *Préface de Narcisse*. In this friendly duel with buttoned foils, the honours are even. But it is evident that these two men will always be separated by a fundamentally different concept of human progress. Each will continue to regard the other as an enemy of the human race.

[1] *Conf.* 387.
[2] *Vide* C.G. ii, no. 239 to Jacob Vernes, and no. 248 to the marquise de Créqui, 6 June and 8 Sept. 1755.
[3] *C.G.* ii, no. 243 (30 Aug. 1755): 'votre nouveau livre contre le genre humain.'
[4] *C.G.* ii, no. 244 (10 Sept. 1755).

CHAPTER IV

MONTMORENCY
1756–1761

Je n'ai commencé de vivre que le
9 avril, 1756. ROUSSEAU

Genesis of *La Nouvelle Héloïse*; *Lettre sur la providence*; *Lettres
à Malesherbes*; *Essai sur l'origine des langues*; *La Reine fantasque*;
Lettres à Sara.

HAVING decided to leave Paris for ever, Rousseau drew up
a list of the books he proposed to complete or write in the
solitude of Montmorency: *Les Institutions politiques*,[1] already
five years on the stocks; selections from the works of the abbé
de Saint-Pierre; *La Morale sensitive, ou le matérialisme du sage*;
a treatise on education and, for wet days, his *Dictionnaire de
Musique*. Nothing in their titles suggests that Rousseau's 'intoxication for virtue' had abated; that he had abandoned the
'sublime vocation' mysteriously revealed to him on the road to
Vincennes. Yet, out of this list, the only work to be completed
at Montmorency was the educational treatise, *Emile* (it was
begun in May 1759 after Jean-Jacques had vacated the *Ermitage*). On the other hand, two books not included in his programme were composed at Montmorency: *La Nouvelle Héloïse*
and *La Lettre à d'Alembert sur les spectacles*. Both of these,
Rousseau suggests, mark a radical change in his emotional life:
'Jusqu'alors l'indignation de la vertu m'avait tenu lieu d'Apollon;
la tendresse et la douceur d'âme m'en tinrent lieu cette fois.'[2]

---

[1] *Les Institutions politiques* was abandoned by Rousseau in 1759 as too vast an
enterprise. However, before destroying his notes, he extracted from them the
material for his *Du Contrat social* which was probably begun about 1751 and was
completed in 1761. The Saint-Pierre anthology was also virtually jettisoned except
for two *Extraits* accompanied by *Jugements*. These we shall discuss in Chapter VII.
Unfortunately, *La Morale sensitive* never materialised, for Rousseau gave it up in
1759. The *Dictionnaire de Musique* was not published until 1767.

[2] *Conf.* 487: 'Up till then, virtuous indignation had been my Apollo; it was now
supplanted by love and gentleness of soul.'

Condensed in these words is the psychological 'revolution' analysed by Jean-Jacques when, about 1770, he composed the ninth book of his *Confessions*, disclosing the genesis of *La Nouvelle Héloïse*. But this 'revolution' or reorientation of Rousseau's consciousness had already been transparently reflected in the first two parts of his novel (1757); in *La Lettre à d'Alembert* (February 1758) and in the four *Lettres à Malesherbes*. Here one must cling firmly to chronology so as to avoid a fertile source of error, for it is too easy to forget that Rousseau, whilst composing the second half of his *Confessions*, frequently viewed his past through the distorting medium of his immediate, troubled state of soul. One can, therefore, in some respects supplement the *Confessions* from the *Lettres à Malesherbes* and, in others, rectify them. Indeed, many factors must be taken into account if we are to form an accurate impression of the moral dilemma that faced Rousseau when, shortly after his arrival at the *Ermitage*, he gradually realised that he was actually conceiving a novel. It is, for instance, remarkable that, in 1769, looking back upon the astonishing reception accorded in 1761 to *La Nouvelle Héloïse*, he made this comment: 'It is dead, however, and I know the reason; but it will come to life again.'[1] Yet his novel had already run through a score of editions or reprints.[2] The truth is that Jean-Jacques, even after its dazzling success, never quite shook off his original guilty feeling that *La Nouvelle Héloïse* symbolised a betrayal of his principles. As the *Confessions* reveal, he feared lest his 'second revolution', the volcanic upheaval in the obscure depths of his consciousness that resulted in *La Nouvelle Héloïse*, might be interpreted as a deviation from the austere moral values which for some years had been associated with his name. After all, was this really the kind of book the public had a right to expect from the *citoyen de Genève*? In February 1761 he confessed to Mme de Luxembourg that its publication had cast him into a state of moral anxiety which none of his other works had aroused.[3] In April he wrote to

[1] *Conf.* 538: 'il est mort, je le sais, et j'en sais la cause; mais il ressuscitera.'

[2] M. Sénelier, in his *Bibliographie générale des œuvres de J.-J. Rousseau*, lists twenty-seven, many of which, however, must have been unknown to Rousseau.

[3] *C.G.* no. 1020 (16 Feb. 1761).

Moultou that the novel must not be included in his collected works.[1] And, significantly, there is no mention whatever of *La Nouvelle Héloïse* in his letters to Malesherbes. Moreover, he never subsequently claimed it as one of his principal works. This *trouble moral* is reflected in everything that Jean-Jacques tells us about the genesis of *La Nouvelle Héloïse* and also, as will be seen, in the tonality of the novel.

With these facts in mind, we may now attempt to re-create that period of Rousseau's material and psychological history which coincides with the genesis and growth of *La Nouvelle Héloïse*. In the France of 1756, no sensible man of letters ever dreamed of forsaking Paris indefinitely to pursue his craft in rustic solitude especially if, like Jean-Jacques, he had established himself in public opinion as an authority on the duties and virtues of the good citizen. Rousseau's decision to settle down at the *Ermitage* caused, therefore, much astonishment and some amusement. It was difficult, indeed, to reconcile this deliberate choice of a hermetical existence with his much-advertised vocation. How could one be useful to society in the solitude of Montmorency? It was, primarily, to answer such criticisms that Jean-Jacques in 1762 composed the four *Lettres à Malesherbes*, though his *apologia* is not their chief attraction for the modern reader. Briefly, Rousseau's case is that he can best serve humanity by avoiding that 'ordinary commerce with people' which he finds so distasteful. Yet nothing charms him more than the companionship of friends provided they respect his independence and do not try to make him happy in their way. That is one reason why he left Paris. Another, which of course could not be disclosed to Malesherbes was his resolve, at all costs, to get Thérèse away from her dreadful family circle. But there were other very strong if less tangible reasons one of which, probably, was his unexpected meeting, just before leaving Paris, with Venture de Villeneuve now sadly different from his former idol, the brilliant virtuoso of Chambéry. Of that infatuation nothing remained, for they parted as strangers. Yet, at the sight of Venture, a host of long-buried memories leapt into Rousseau's consciousness: memories

[1] *C.G.* no. 1079 (29 April 1761).

of that summer's day at Thônes; of his charming pupils; of Les Charmettes:

> ...tous ces ravissants délires d'un jeune cœur que j'avais sentis alors dans toute leur force, et dont je croyais le temps passé pour jamais; toutes ces tendres réminiscences me firent verser des larmes sur ma jeunesse écoulée, et sur ses transports désormais perdus pour moi. Ah! combien j'en aurais versées sur leur retour tardif et funeste, si j'avais prévu les maux qu'il m'allait coûter![1]

Strangely enough, Rousseau seems to have overlooked the importance of this incident when exploring, in a later Book of the *Confessions*, the psychological origins of *La Nouvelle Héloïse* and portraying his intolerable sense of isolation, frustration and self-pity. Yet it is almost certain that this, in fact, had been his state of soul before leaving Paris and the compelling force that drove him to the *Ermitage*, hoping there to find that perfect innocence and happiness which, but for Winzenried, might have rounded off a lifetime shared with Mme de Warens. In that dream, born long ago one afternoon in the lovely Annecy countryside whilst *Maman* was at Vespers, Jean-Jacques visualised a felicity pure of sex, arising wholly from the companionship of a sympathetic woman in beautiful natural surroundings. 'This singular need', he tells us, 'was such that the closest physical union had not been able to satisfy; I should have required two souls in the same body; failing that, I was always conscious of a void.'[2] Mme de Warens had proved a broken reed and her successor, the ignorant Thérèse, soon got bored with solitary rambles in the forest. Dominated by her mother, she furtively entertained her relatives at the *Ermitage* whilst Jean-Jacques was at La Chevrette visiting Mme d'Epinay. Moreover, it now leaked out that Mme Levasseur, in Paris, had gone behind Rousseau's back to Mme Dupin and Mme d'Epinay with

---

[1] *Conf.* 391: '...all the mad delights of a youthful heart I had then experienced in their full force, the time for which I thought was past for ever; all those tender reminiscences made me weep for my vanished youth and its joys, henceforth lost for me. Ah! what tears I would have shed over their belated and fateful return had I foreseen the sorrows it was to cost me!'

[2] *Conf.* 406: 'Ce singulier besoin était tel que la plus étroite union des corps ne pouvait encore y suffire; il m'aurait fallu deux âmes dans le même corps; sans cela je sentais toujours du vide.'

whining stories of hard luck. His informant was the garrulous Thérèse.

It is especially in solitude [he remarks] that one appreciates the advantage of living with someone who has a mind....So it came to pass that, half cheated in my expectations, leading a life after my own inclinations in a spot of my own choosing, with a person dear to me, I began, nevertheless, to feel almost isolated.[1]

Jean-Jacques really offers us two versions of his psychological revolution. I will deal first with that presented in the *Confessions* though the other, contained in the *Lettres à Malesherbes*, is closer by seven years to the situation described by Rousseau. Invaded by a sense of acute frustration, he turned his thoughts away from the fretful present, seeking in the memories of youth a happier spiritual climate. Something, clearly, had gone badly askew in the design of his sentimental life. Though endowed by Nature with extraordinary sensibility, he had never known the intoxicating pleasures which his soul had always craved. Now, on the brink of old age, tormented by an incurable malady, what could he look back upon? True there had been moments of intense happiness but none had been the prelude to a great and durable friendship or a splendid, immortal passion. Was this dynamic force pent up within his soul doomed to stagnation? Outside Rousseau's windows, June had returned. In the cool glades of the forest, lulled by the song of birds, the heavy scent of leaf and blossom, the caress of summer zephyrs, his sombre anxieties retreated before the advancing cohort of bright, enchanting memories. In this very season, in just such a countryside, at Thônes, a younger and nimbler Jean-Jacques had dallied with Mlle Graffenried and Mlle Galley. He remembered other pretty women whose love might, perhaps, have been his for the asking.

I saw myself surrounded by a seraglio of houris, by my old acquaintances, my ardent desire for whom was no new sensation. My blood began to surge and seethe, my head swam, despite my greying

[1] *Conf.* 413: 'C'est surtout dans la solitude qu'on sent l'avantage de vivre avec quelqu'un qui sait penser....Voilà comment, à demi trompé dans mon attente, menant une vie de mon goût, dans un séjour de mon choix, avec une personne qui m'était chère, je parvins pourtant à me sentir presque isolé.'

temples. And the grave citizen of Geneva, the austere Jean-Jacques, close on forty-five, suddenly became again a love-sick shepherd swain.[1]

Jean-Jacques harboured no illusions in regard to his sex-appeal and had no wish to figure in the role of elderly Adonis. Instead, he deliberately surrendered himself to the caprice of memory and imagination, seeking in a universe of his own fabulation the emotions denied him by a scurvy destiny. He peopled his ideal world with creatures of ineffable beauty and virtue, enjoying in their society hours and days of perfect bliss. These communions took place in secluded forest nooks whither Jean-Jacques sped every morning, scowling at any luckless visitor who threatened to stand between him and paradise. But reality is not lightly thwarted. A stinging attack of his old bladder complaint jerked him down from the Empyrean, 'like a kite on a string'. Preoccupied with his remedies and domestic worries, he forgot his 'angéliques amours'. And, indeed, houris assort ill with catheters.

Cooped up indoors, he read Voltaire's *Poème sur le désastre de Lisbonne*, a savage and disillusioned commentary on Leibnizian optimism. With the horrors of the Lisbon earthquake fresh in his mind, taking as his theme *Tout est bien dans le meilleur des mondes possibles*, Voltaire examined, one by one, the comfortable reasons adduced by Leibniz to explain the enigma of human suffering in a universe created by a God of justice and pity. He sent a copy through Duclos in July 1756 to Rousseau who felt at the moment that he was an authority on human suffering. He replied in August with his *Lettre sur la providence* which was handed to Voltaire by his physician, the famous Genevan, Dr Tronchin.[2] It is evident that Jean-Jacques looked on the poem as the petulant outburst of a spoilt darling of fortune whom it was his duty to reason with, very gently and discreetly.

---

[1] *Conf.* 418: 'Je me vis entouré d'un sérail de houris, de mes anciennes connaissances pour qui le goût le plus vif n'était pas un sentiment nouveau. Mon sang s'allume et pétille, la tête me tourne, malgré mes cheveux grisonnants, et voilà le grave citoyen de Genève, voilà l'austère Jean-Jacques, à près de quarante-cinq ans, redevenu tout à coup le berger extravagant.'

[2] It was first published, without Rousseau's permission, by Formey in his *Nouvelle Bibliothèque germanique*, 1759.

He approaches the problem of moral and physical evil in a calm and rational spirit. Except for death, most of our bodily ills are due to our artificial needs: the mortality at Lisbon would have been negligible had the inhabitants led a natural, rustic existence scattered over the land. Besides, he interposes slyly, had not Voltaire shown in *Zadig* that a sudden, violent death may be a blessing in disguise? But Rousseau's chief argument is drawn from Leibniz. Individual evil certainly exists, yet it is childish to induce therefrom the notion of a universal evil. No one really believes that, otherwise the human race would long ago have committed suicide. We all feel, on the contrary, that life is sweet and know intuitively that Providence has designed a cosmic system in which every material entity is situated in the best possible relation to the whole, and every intelligent, sentient being in the best possible relation to himself. One must view the problem in its true perspective, remembering that the earthly life of the individual is but a moment in the infinite duration of his spiritual existence. It is this certainty of survival, implies Rousseau, which explains his own optimism. Voltaire's real answer to *La Lettre sur la providence* was the novel, *Candide* (1759). Meanwhile, to the intense relief of Jean-Jacques, 'le grand homme' betrayed no sign of annoyance. Instead, he wrote urbanely regretting that illness prevented him from continuing the discussion. But no one, he concluded, admired Rousseau's books more than he: no one was disposed to love him more tenderly. Jean-Jacques, who had expected a brickbat, was delighted with this bouquet. A man who could take his letter in such a spirit, he told Tronchin, deserved the title of philosopher.[1]

These distractions, he remarks, ought to have cured him of his 'fantastic amours', but a malicious fate ruled otherwise. With convalescence, his lonely walks and reveries were resumed. Mindful, however, of his recent crash, Rousseau decided there should be no more high-altitude flights. But he was still obsessed with the vision of a little society composed of human beings 'as celestial in their virtues as in their beauty; of trusty, tender, loyal friends such as I have never seen in this world

[1] *C.G.* III, no. 336 (25 Jan. 1757).

below'.[1] In the event, one gathers, Rousseau came to terms with his too exuberant imagination which now presented a little group consisting of a youth and two charming girls, one dark, the other fair, called Claire and Julie. They were cousins and devoted friends, the former vivacious yet prudent; the latter gentle and weak 'but so touchingly weak that virtue seemed to gain by it'.[2] To Julie he gave a lover, Saint-Preux, to whom Claire was a tender friend and even something more. Yet not the faintest wisp of jealousy or rivalry clouded the friendship of the cousins.

'Smitten by my two charming models, I identified myself as far as possible with the lover and friend; but I made him young and amiable, investing him, moreover, with the virtues and defects of which I was conscious in myself.'[3] For these exquisite creatures, Rousseau finally chose, as a worthy setting, the birthplace of *Maman*, Vevey. As they gradually became more clearly defined in his imagination and associated with certain situations, he began to describe, in a few disjointed letters, their attitudes, emotions and reactions. At this stage, the three characters were still, it would appear, in search of a novelist. For, although these scattered letters were to constitute the first two parts of *La Nouvelle Héloïse*, the author had not yet conceived a definite plan for a novel. How the plan evolved will be discussed in another context. During the winter of 1756–57, 'in a state of the most erotic ecstasy',[4] Rousseau completed the first two parts and, for lack of a better audience, read them to Thérèse and her mother in the evenings.

We may now usefully consider the earlier version of Rousseau's 'inner transformation'. It is embodied in the four *Lettres à Malesherbes* and is, necessarily, more concise than the second account. That does not, however, explain why Jean-Jacques is

---

[1] *Conf.* 419: 'aussi célestes par leurs vertus que par leurs beautés, d'amis sûrs, tendres, fidèles, tels que je n'en trouvai jamais ici-bas.'

[2] *Conf.* 421–2: 'mais d'une si touchante faiblesse, que la vertu semblait y gagner.'

[3] *Conf.* 422: 'Epris de mes deux charmants modèles, je m'identifiais avec l'amant et l'ami le plus qu'il m'était possible; mais je le fis aimable et jeune, lui donnant au surplus les vertus et les défauts que je me sentais.'

[4] *Conf.* 539: 'dans les plus brûlantes ecstases.' In the Paris MS. 'les plus érotiques extases'.

almost completely silent about his 'erotic ecstasies' and his novel. Here, indeed, the only tangible link between the two versions is the following passage:

My imagination did not leave deserted for long a landscape thus adorned. I soon peopled it with creatures after my own heart and, sweeping aside public opinion, prejudices, all the factitious emotions, I transported to the sanctuaries of Nature men fit to inhabit them. Of these I formed a charming society, of which I did not feel unworthy. I created for myself a golden age according to my fancy and, filling those beautiful days with all the scenes of my life of which I retained sweet memories and with all those my heart could still desire, I shed melting tears over the true pleasures of humanity, pleasures so delightful, so pure and now so remote from man.[1]

There is no allusion here, it will be noted, to the prelude of this charmingly innocent vision of Rousseau's ideal society: the erotic phantasies evoked by memories of the houris he had known or desired in youth. On the contrary, he asks Malesherbes:

What times, Sir, would you think I now recall most often and most willingly in my dreams? Not the pleasures of my youth: those were too rare, interfused with too much bitterness and they are already too remote. It is the pleasures of my retreat, of my solitary rambles, those fleeting yet delightful days I spent with myself alone, with my good and simple housekeeper, my beloved dog, my old cat, with the birds of the countryside and the woodland deer, with all Nature and her inconceivable Author.[2]

---

[1] *IIIe Lettre*: 'Mon imagination ne laissait pas longtemps déserte la terre ainsi parée. Je la peuplais bientôt d'êtres selon mon cœur, et chassant bien loin l'opinion, les préjugés, toutes les passions factices, je transportais, dans les asyles de la nature, des hommes dignes de les habiter. Je m'en formais une société charmante dont je ne me sentais pas indigne, je me faisais un siècle d'or à ma fantaisie, et remplissant ces beaux jours de toutes les scènes de ma vie qui m'avaient laissé de doux souvenirs, et de toutes celles que mon cœur pouvait désirer encore, je m'attendrissais jusqu'aux larmes sur les vrais plaisirs de l'humanité, plaisirs si délicieux, si purs, et qui sont désormais si loin des hommes.'

[2] *Ibid.* 'Quels temps croiriez-vous, Monsieur, que je me rappelle le plus souvent et le plus volontiers dans mes rêves? Ce ne sont point les plaisirs de ma jeunesse; ils furent trop rares, trop mêlés d'amertume, et sont déjà trop loin de moi. Ce sont ceux de ma retraite, ce sont mes promenades solitaires, ce sont ces jours si rapides, mais délicieux, que je passais tout entiers avec moi seul, avec ma bonne et simple gouvernante, avec mon chien bien aimé, ma vieille chatte, avec les oiseaux de la campagne et les biches de la forêt, avec la nature entière et son inconcevable auteur.'

Lingering on this Arcadian theme, Rousseau communicated, in a new and exquisite idiom, the original emotions aroused by the familiar objects of his rustic environment. Such an attitude, by its very novelty, at first disconcerted his eighteenth-century readers, even the sympathetic Mirabeau who called it 'gaping at crows'.[1] The author of *L'Ami des hommes*, though he lived in the country farming his estates, simply could not understand how any intelligent man could waste his time, like Rousseau, day-dreaming in the fields and woods, staring at 'l'or des genêts et la pourpre des bruyères' for nothing but the sheer love of the thing.[2] And such, no doubt, was the reaction of Malesherbes to Rousseau's charming, perhaps too selective, account of his 'délire rustique'. In a passage which has no counterpart in the *Confessions*, Jean-Jacques seems to me indebted to Fénelon for an idiom which he employs, however, to express sentiments not to be found in the latter's *De l'Existence de Dieu*.[3] The following lines suggest, rather, the Pantheistic *élan* of a soul whose supreme happiness resides in a total voluptuous sense of fusion with the Eternal All:

...I felt stifled in the universe, I should have liked to launch into the Infinite. Had I unveiled all the mysteries of Nature, my situation would have been, I think, less delightful than the intoxicating ecstasy to which my spirit abandoned itself utterly and which, in the excitement of my raptures, made me cry out sometimes: 'O great Being! O great Being!' unable to say or think anything more.[4]

Except, then, by implication the *Lettres à Malesherbes* do not reflect the moral dilemma we have mentioned. On this point, the *Confessions* are more explicit. Perturbed, at first, to find himself, at Montmorency, no longer apparently consumed by that 'burning enthusiasm' for truth, liberty and virtue which, as reflected in the austerity of his conversation, attire and deport-

[1] *C.G.* xvi, no. 3237 (27 Oct. 1766): 'bayer aux corneilles.'
[2] 'The gold of the broom and the purple of the heather.'
[3] *Oeuvres philosophiques* (ed. 1731), i, 178.
[4] *Loc. cit.*: '...j'étouffais dans l'univers, j'aurais voulu m'élancer dans l'infini. Je crois que si j'eusse dévoilé tous les mystères de la nature, je me serais senti dans une situation moins délicieuse que cette étourdissante extase à laquelle mon esprit se livrait sans retenue, et qui, dans l'agitation de mes transports, me faisait crier quelquefois: "O grand Etre! O grand Etre!" sans pouvoir dire, ni penser rien de plus.'

ment, had impressed the Parisian world of fashion and culture, Rousseau anxiously searched his heart for the cause of this astonishing transformation. The explanation was beautifully simple. If there ever was a period when Rousseau's conduct stood in direct opposition to his true nature, we shall find it, he asserts, in the Parisian phase of his life.[1] Why then could he not attain, in the serene and lovely setting of Montmorency so conducive to solitary reverie, that permanent state of inner harmony described in the fourth letter to Malesherbes as 'the spiritual pride of a man who feels he is well adjusted'?[2] For he admits frankly in the *Confessions* that the 'revolution' had been too sudden and violent though certainly its original effect was to change his harsh, virtuous indignation into pity for the misery and wickedness of men. Yet this swift reorientation of his consciousness, he implies, proved fatal to his happiness which, it is clear from the fourth letter to Malesherbes, was just another name for Rousseau's self-esteem.

If the revolution had only restored me to myself and stopped there, everything would have been all right, but unfortunately it went further and carried me rapidly to the other extreme. From that moment, my quivering soul lost its centre of gravity and, as the result of ever-recurring oscillations, has never regained its equilibrium.[3]

Rousseau's pendulum metaphor stylises the train of devastating emotional shocks which made of his sojourn at the *Ermitage*, 'the terrible and fatal epoch of a destiny unparalleled in human experience'.[4] However, before we survey the events of that period, let us very briefly consider the projected treatise, *La Morale sensitive ou le matérialisme du sage*, jettisoned in 1759. If I have correctly understood Rousseau's short and sketchy account of his scheme, it was to evolve a psychological control of what he calls, no doubt after Aristotle, our *âme sensitive* or

---

[1] *Conf.* 409.

[2] 'La fierté d'âme d'un homme qui se sent bien ordonné.'

[3] *Conf.* 409: 'Si la révolution n'eût fait que me rendre à moi-même et s'arrêter là, tout était bien, mais malheureusement elle alla plus loin, et m'emporta rapidement à l'autre extrême. Dès lors mon âme en branle n'a plus fait que passer par la ligne de repos, et ses oscillations toujours renouvelées ne lui ont jamais permis d'y rester.'

[4] *Ibid.*: 'époque terrible et fatale d'un sort qui n'a point d'exemple chez les mortels.'

économie animale. Though hostile to the materialists, he was certainly influenced by the associationist determinism of his century which held that our conscious states are produced by the sensations deriving from our material environment. 'Climates, seasons, sounds, colours, darkness, light, the elements, food, noise, silence, movement, repose, all act upon our organism and on our soul.'[1] Empirically, chiefly by introspection, Rousseau tried to discover why, at various periods in their career, men are often 'dissimilar to themselves and seem to be transformed into quite different beings'. The cause, he implies, must be traced to the presence in our *âme sensitive* (in the self or soul which receives purely physical sensations), of sense impressions which subtly and continuously influence what Aristotle called our *nous*, our intellectual soul. But although he discovered the cause of the malady, Rousseau unfortunately does not precisely explain how he proposed to cure it. He merely suggests vaguely that since we are aware of the psychological facts, we ought to be able in some way 'to control, at their origins, the feelings by which we allow ourselves to be dominated'.[2]

In April 1757 Rousseau showed the first two parts of *La Nouvelle Héloïse* to Diderot and to Mme d'Epinay. Now, a letter from his friend Deleyre reveals an interesting fact. Referring to the 'two lovers', he asks Jean-Jacques what has become of *Les amours de Claire et de Marcellin* who, unlike Saint-Preux and Julie, are obviously peasants.[3] A fragment, indeed, has survived of this essay in the popular, rustic genre of fiction. Marcellin, betrothed against his will by a grasping father, falls in love with Claire whose chief asset is her irresistible sensibility. To postpone the marriage, the hero swallows a whole bottle of his invalid mother's medicine, with alarming results. Meanwhile, Claire has inherited a small legacy and uses it to buy off Marcellin's fiancée. Presumably, the sordid and brutal father will relent in time. Rousseau's mawkish style does nothing to

---

[1] *Conf.* 401: 'Les climats, les saisons, les sons, les couleurs, l'obscurité, la lumière, les éléments, les aliments, le bruit, le silence, le mouvement, le repos, tout agit sur notre machine, et sur notre âme.'

[2] *Ibid.*: 'pour gouverner dans leur origine les sentiments dont nous nous laissons dominer.'

[3] *C.G.* II, no. 318 (23 Sept. 1756).

relieve the dullness of these few pages of what would have been an insipid production. Another rustic fragment, *Le petit Savoyard ou la Vie de Claude Noyer*, dates probably from the same period. Its style is more alert and the heroine, also named Claire, resembles her famous namesake. She is, however, more frolicsome and we are obliged to leave her at an exciting moment, stoutly defending her virtue against the advances of an enterprising young marquis.[1]

Until the early spring of 1757, nothing occurred to cloud Rousseau's happiness as the pattern of Julie's destiny emerged from the busy play of imagination on his youthful reminiscences. 'Oh! how you will despise me', he wrote to Tronchin in February, 'when you know the sort of work I'm engaged upon and what is worse, pleasurably!'[2] To the artist for whom nothing matters but the work of art, winter in the country, he realised, can be a valuable ally. True, in January, the obligations of friendship had summoned him twice to Paris where Gauffecourt was seriously ill. There he had been able to talk about his novel to Diderot and to hear about the latter's new play, *Le Fils naturel*. He heard also that Dr Tronchin might find a home for Mme Levasseur, thus leaving him free to settle down permanently in Geneva, a plan they had discussed secretly at La Chevrette the previous year. His scheme was to be divulged to no one, not even Mme d'Epinay. Pleased and excited by this news, Tronchin at once used his influence to obtain for Jean-Jacques a post as sub-librarian at Geneva which was regretfully declined, however, in February. Though greatly tempted, Rousseau felt that he did not possess the necessary qualifications. Besides, his chronic malady would prevent him from carrying out his duties regularly.

Early in March a violent altercation with Diderot interrupted for a month Rousseau's intercourse with his enchanting lovers.[3] He himself, after the reconciliation, dismissed it as a storm in a tea-cup but that is not the impression one gathers from the

---

[1] Both fragments were published in 1861 by M. G. Streckeisen-Moultou in his *Oeuvres et Correspondance inédites de J.-J. Rousseau.*

[2] *C.G.* III, no. 340: 'O que vous me mépriserez quand vous saurez de quelle sorte d'ouvrage je m'occupe et, qui pis est, avec plaisir!'

[3] *C.G.* III, no. 347, p. 28.

Correspondance which reveals, incidentally, that Diderot possessed a talent for malicious innuendo sharply contrasting with
the legendary portrait of 'le bon Denis', the outspoken, impetuous but loyal and affectionate friend. To grasp the adequate,
as opposed to the immediate cause of this quarrel we must
replace it in its proper context. The D'Holbach coterie strongly
disapproved of Rousseau's decision to remain permanently in the
country, an action which the public might interpret to the
detriment of the 'party'. Genuinely incapable of conceiving any
rational motive that could induce a man to spend the winter at
Montmorency, cut off from his friends, the latter charitably
assumed that Jean-Jacques was becoming a selfish, unhappy
misanthropist. Even Diderot, who knew that Rousseau was
blissfully occupied with his novel, felt that solitude and isolation
had altered his character. Jean-Jacques, who was well aware of
all this, happened to pick up the newly published *Le Fils naturel*
and lighted upon a phrase which he at once interpreted as a
veiled and cruel allusion to his own situation: 'the good man is
in society and only the wicked man is alone.'[1] Wounded to the
quick, he complained to Diderot in a touching letter of which no
copy survives.[2] We have, on the other hand, Diderot's reply
which produced an explosion of grief and indignation and drew
Mme d'Epinay into the quarrel though she had never met 'le
bon Denis' who had no desire to meet her. Here, in brief, is the
substance of the letters concerning this sorry affair.[3] Granting
that Rousseau's suspicions were baseless and even offensive, so
were Diderot's sly and provocative innuendoes. The callous and
selfish Jean-Jacques, he hinted, was preventing a bed-ridden old
lady of eighty (Mme Levasseur was sixty-nine and in rude
health) from returning to her family in Paris. He called himself
a citizen, yet lived the life of a recluse, neglecting his duties to
the poor whom he had formerly assisted in Paris. Diderot's

[1] Act IV, 3: 'l'homme de bien est dans la société et [qu'] il n' y a que le méchant
qui soit seul.'   [2] *Conf.* 447.
[3] *C.G.* III, nos. 342-52, 355-8, 361 *bis*, 362. We may regard as false nos. 354,
356, 360. Reprinted from Mme d'Epinay's pseudo-memoirs, these letters are
known now to have been 'doctored' by her at the instigation of Diderot and Grimm
in order to vilify Rousseau and thus to discredit his references to them in the
Confessions. For a fuller account of this conspiracy, see p. 355.

subsequent effusions are couched in the same vein of truculence, self-pity and crocodile tearfulness. Furious at this unpardonable interference in his private life, Rousseau threw discretion to the winds. In his letter to Mme d'Epinay, asking for her sympathy and counsel, he accused Grimm, who was her lover, of having corrupted Diderot. In revenge, Mme d'Epinay came down solidly on the side of the *philosophe* and in a tortuous letter oozing suppressed malice and cheap sentiment, tried to persuade the bewildered Rousseau that he was the sole offender. Meanwhile Diderot, who cared not a straw for Mme Levasseur, wrote saying that he was 'terrified' at her situation whilst she, having been informed of this letter by Jean-Jacques broke into piteous lamentations and upbraidings. He wrote to Mme d'Epinay admitting that his remarks about Grimm were unjust but flatly refusing to apologise to Diderot who remained aggressive and unrepentant. Finally, Mme d'Epinay solved the Levasseur problem by offering to find her a home and the quarrel subsided. But it had rubbed the bloom off Rousseau's friendship for the three persons involved. From one of Diderot's letters to his mistress Sophie Volland[1] it is clear that he too was subsequently enlightened as to the true character of Mme d'Epinay.

But for Rousseau's eagerness to resume his novel, I doubt whether his reconciliation with Diderot would have been so quickly effected. It took place at the *Ermitage* on 3 April, when both agreed to let bygones be bygones. Spring, Rousseau confesses, had redoubled his 'erotic transports'. In this mood, he composed the third part of *La Nouvelle Héloïse* where Saint-Preux leaves Julie and sets sail with Anson for distant lands. For the fourth part, which was to have been the last, he wrote several letters exteriorising his rapturous emotions. Now, dramatically, fiction met and coalesced with reality. Just when Rousseau's dreams had achieved almost perfect materialisation in the image of Julie d'Etange, a real woman, Sophie, comtesse d'Houdetot, swept on to the brilliantly lit theatre of his consciousness. True, she had already visited the *Ermitage* at the end of January 1756, on a rainy day when her carriage was bemired, wet and demanding shelter, wearing her coachman's

[1] 18 July 1762.

enormous boots and shouting with laughter. But then, as Stendhal would have said, the moment of crystallisation had not arrived, no doubt because Rousseau was having trouble with his bladder. Now, probably in May 1757, Mme d'Houdetot re-appeared at the cottage, piquantly attired in masculine riding-kit bearing greetings from her lover, the philosopher-poet, Saint-Lambert, who was absent on military service. This time it was the *coup de foudre*

Elle vint; je la vis; j'étais ivre d'amour sans objet; cette ivresse fascina mes yeux, cet objet se fixa sur elle; je vis ma Julie en madame d'Houdetot, et bientôt je ne vis plus que madame d'Houdetot, mais revêtue de toutes les perfections dont je venais d'orner l'idole de mon cœur.[1]

Rousseau's one and only grand passion, therefore, had its genesis in a fiction. He had first met Mme d'Houdetot in 1748, just before her marriage. She was then Mlle de Bellegarde, sister to M. d'Epinay the son of De La Live de Bellegarde and thus, sister-in-law to Mme d'Epinay. Sophie or 'Mimi' d'Houdetot was 27 when Jean-Jacques fell in love with her. According to the remarkably objective portrait in the *Confessions*, she was not a conventional beauty. Her complexion was marred by the effects of smallpox and her short-sighted eyes were slightly round. But she had masses of beautiful curly hair which, he says, came down to her knees. What enchanted Jean-Jacques was the caressing sweetness of her expression and her graceful vivacity. Utterly frank, often absurdly indiscreet, Sophie radiated the infectious gaiety of an overgrown schoolgirl. She was quite incapable of disguising her feelings or thoughts. Diderot, who got to know her after the unhappy affair with Rousseau, amply confirms the latter's impressions and, in connexion with a certain *Hymne aux tétons*, praises her talent for graceful, excessively voluptuous verse. She was, it seems, a tireless chatterbox with 'a hundred thousand enthusiasms of every shape and colour', leaping from one topic to another, exasperating her husband who cared

---

[1] *Conf.* 431-2: 'She came; I saw her; I was intoxicated with love without an object. This intoxication cast a spell over my vision. This object became centred in her. I saw my Julie in Mme d'Houdetot, and soon I saw only Mme d'Houdetot but clad in all the perfections with which I had just adorned the idol of my heart.'

only for horses and cards.[1] Of the latter, Rousseau says that he was a brave soldier but a gambler and a shuffler with few amiable qualities. Mme d'Houdetot's lover, Saint-Lambert, was on the contrary a man of great intelligence, virtue and talent.

She had rented for the summer months a country-house at Eaubonne, barely three miles from the *Ermitage* and it was there or in the neighbouring woods that Sophie and Jean-Jacques walked and conversed, mostly about the absent Saint-Lambert of whom she spoke in the language of passionate love. Bewitched by her charming voice, Rousseau completely lost his heart and head. Finally, after a severe tussle with his conscience, he revealed his secret to Mme d'Houdetot who treated him with a tender and understanding pity which merely inflamed Rousseau's ardour. Painfully sensible of the difference in their ages he suspected at first that she and Saint-Lambert were amusing themselves at the expense of a superannuated beau. Reassured on this score, his passion knew no bounds: 'We were both intoxicated with love; she for her lover, I for her. We mingled our sighs and our delightful tears.'[2]

One summer evening, under a blossoming acacia in Sophie's moonlit garden, they re-enacted the famous *scène du bosquet* where Saint-Preux receives from Julie the kiss which transfigures their existence. That night, Jean-Jacques modestly records: 'Je fus sublime.' Once, if only for a brief moment, he had been admitted into the sanctuary reserved for Saint-Preux. More experienced than Julie, however, Mme d'Houdetot knew how to handle the situation.

Enfin, dans un transport involontaire, elle s'écria: 'Non, jamais homme ne fut si aimable, et jamais amant n'aima comme vous! Mais votre ami Saint-Lambert nous écoute, et mon cœur ne saurait aimer deux fois!' Je me tus en soupirant; je l'embrassai: quel embrassement! Mais ce fut tout.[3]

---

[1] *Lettres à Sophie Volland* (30 Sept. 1760 and 14 July 1762). 'Cent mille enthousiasmes de toutes les couleurs.'

[2] *Conf.* 435: 'Nous étions ivres d'amour, l'un et l'autre, elle pour son amant, moi pour elle; nos soupirs, nos délicieuses larmes se confondaient.'

[3] *Conf.* 436: 'At last, in an involuntary transport, she exclaimed: "Never, no, never was a man so lovable, never did a lover love like you! But your friend Saint-Lambert is listening to us and my heart cannot love twice!" I sighed and fell silent; I kissed her: what a kiss! But that was all.'

And so, Rousseau adds with pathetic fatuity, Mme d'Houdetot emerged from the grove and from the arms of her friend, in the middle of the night, 'as pure in body and in heart as when she entered'.[1] Jean-Jacques asks us to weigh these circumstances and we may as well take him at his word.

From the *Correspondance* one can almost re-create the highly charged emotional climate in which Rousseau, the ardent lover, composed the last two or perhaps even three parts of *La Nouvelle Héloïse*. As in the novel so also in reality, passionate love brings sorrow, humiliation and disillusionment. Yet from its smouldering embers there arises the pure and steady flame of a much greater love and a more durable happiness. In a letter to Mme d'Houdetot it is described by Jean-Jacques as 'the sovereign good' which derives from 'sublime virtue and holy friendship'.[2] Whether, in fact, he ever achieved it seems very doubtful because in all his relations with Sophie he was always unconsciously influenced by the image of a Julie who had, before marriage, given herself to Saint-Preux. To a great extent, this explains the persistent illusion that, but for his extraordinary respect for the sacred obligations of friendship, Mme d'Houdetot might have betrayed Saint-Lambert. 'Je puis mourir de mes fureurs mais je ne vous rendrai jamais vile.'[3] But the dramatic alternative existed only in Rousseau's fevered imagination. For Sophie, the one thing that counted on earth was Saint-Lambert's love. Rousseau was merely a sympathetic friend to whom she could safely open her heart though, no doubt, she valued the friendship and esteem of an elderly man who had acquired by his writings and by his conduct a reputation for virtue and integrity. Somewhat naïvely, knowing his stern views on adulterous liaisons, both she and Saint-Lambert were profoundly comforted by a phrase in one of his letters to the effect that, henceforth, he would regard Sophie's fidelity as one of her virtues.

Jean-Jacques, rejuvenated by the 'flamme invisible' of a passion such as he had never experienced even in the flower of youth,

---

[1] *Conf.* 436: 'aussi pure de corps et de cœur, qu'elle y était entrée.'

[2] *C.G.* III, no. 417 (31 Oct. 1757): 'la vertu sublime et la sainte amitié sont le souverain bien des humains.'

[3] *C.G.* III, no. 374: 'I may die of my furious passion but I will never make you vile.'

made no secret of his infatuation which was soon the talk of La Chevrette and of the D'Holbach clique. A memorable page of the *Confessions* illuminates the violent, almost pathological effects produced by the image of Mme d'Houdetot on Rousseau as he reeled and stumbled on his way from the *Ermitage* to Eaubonne, in a frenzy of erotic desire, with pounding heart, the blood whistling through his middle-aged arteries. Obviously, this could not last and, one day, he arrived to find Mme d'Houdetot in tears, greatly agitated by an ill-humoured letter from Saint-Lambert. Someone had told him of Rousseau's 'insensate love' and, whilst casting no doubts on Sophie's innocence, he implied that she was not blameless. Either their relations must cease or Jean-Jacques must behave simply as a dear friend. Who were the vile informers? Rousseau's suspicions lighted at once on Mme d'Epinay and on Grimm who held a secretarial post at Army Headquarters in Westphalia, not far from Saint-Lambert. Ignoring Mme d'Houdetot's urgent advice to do nothing, Jean-Jacques despatched a cryptic, menacing note to Mme d'Epinay who had just written artlessly complaining of his neglect. He still awaited definite proof. But meanwhile, let her be certain that whoever the slanderers were, outraged innocence would find in him an implacable avenger. In rapid succession five letters passed to and fro on that fateful autumn day.[1] The fertile Thérèse, on being questioned, came out with the startling news that Mme d'Epinay had repeatedly attempted to intercept the correspondence between Jean-Jacques and Mme d'Houdetot. She had even searched his study and, by playing on the jealousy of Thérèse, tried to persuade her to collect scraps of torn-up letters. Mme d'Epinay, when bluntly accused of blackening the reputation of a guiltless woman and of plotting to ruin the happiness of two lovers, faltered between evasion and indignant denial. It is significant, perhaps, that instead of demanding an immediate retractation of Rousseau's charges, she held the door wide open to a reconciliation. He might come, she wrote, whenever he chose, with the assurance of being received better than his suspicions deserved. In the circumstances, it is a remarkably

---

[1] The *Correspondance générale* gives the date, 29 June. H. Guillemin, however, suggests 31 August, which seems more probable (*Ann.* xv, 157).

mild letter capable of various interpretations except that which postulates her complete innocence. On the other hand, it would be a sheer waste of time to examine the statements of Thérèse. The point is, however, that Rousseau believed them all, including a titbit of scandalous gossip from the servants at La Chevrette who said that as the result of her amours with Grimm, their mistress would be leaving shortly for Geneva on a professional visit to Dr Tronchin. This explains Rousseau's mysterious remark that even if Mme d'Epinay were to become his enemy, her secrets would always be respected. To revert to the famous 'day of the five letters', I do not think that Mme d'Epinay, although she was certainly the original source of the information divulged by Grimm to Saint-Lambert, ever for a moment felt guilty of the crimes imputed to her by Rousseau. In the eyes of the D'Holbach coterie he was a figure of fun, an elderly Adonis infatuated with a flighty young woman who was certainly neither pure nor innocent. That is why, some years later, when Mme d'Epinay was induced to 'doctor' her *Mémoires* in order to vilify Jean-Jacques retrospectively, she never troubled to alter the letters in which Grimm maliciously asks for the latest news about the 'mysterious' rendezvous in the forest and the 'mysterious' visits to Eaubonne. This was legitimate gossip which Mme d'Epinay passed on without the slightest misgivings,[1] seeing in it no connexion with Rousseau's charge that she had been guilty of an infamous plot to wreck her sister-in-law's liaison with Saint-Lambert by informing the latter that his friend was a treacherous seducer. Jean-Jacques, it is very important to note, was most reluctant to believe Mme d'Epinay capable of harbouring such a 'base thought' though he knew she had a loose tongue. 'But I tax you only with having said it,' he wrote, 'not with having believed it.'[2] The real culprit, in his mind, was the malevolent Grimm who had corrupted his mistress as he had corrupted the 'good and too easy-going Diderot'.[3] Not until later did Rousseau acquire the conviction

---

[1] *Mémoires de Mme d'Epinay* (1818), II, 258, 270.

[2] *C.G.* III, no. 378: 'Mais c'est seulement de l'avoir dit et non de l'avoir cru que je vous taxe.'

[3] *C.G.* III, no. 397 (5 Sept. 1757): 'le bon et trop facile Diderot.'

that Mme d'Epinay was no mere tattler but a jealous and cunning enemy who had sworn to separate him from Mme d'Houdetot.[1] The position was very different on the evening of 31 August when he arrived at La Chevrette. Unable to quote Mme d'Houdetot or Thérèse, he was at a loss to justify his violent indictments. But that proved quite unnecessary. His benefactress threw her arms around his neck and the whole affair evaporated in a mist of sensibility. Yet, though the sun had not gone down on his wrath, Jean-Jacques felt unhappily that the miserable business had imperceptibly altered his relations with Mme d'Houdetot whose friendship was now tinged with prudence and indeed, perhaps, with a certain evasiveness. Alarmed, in fact, by her lover's recent attitude, Sophie now privately resolved that Jean-Jacques must never again be allowed to overstep the frontier dividing friendship from passionate love. Entangled, however, in the complex web of emotions which Rousseau had spun round their friendship, she could not extricate herself without lacerating his incredibly sensitive *amour-propre*. Her secret fear, shared to a lesser degree by Saint-Lambert, was that Jean-Jacques in another of his Sir Galahad displays, might irretrievably ruin her liaison.

In July 1757, that is to say before, and not as the *Confessions* imply after, the stirring events of 31 August, Rousseau had met Saint-Lambert at Diderot's house in Paris, at the rue Royale as the guest of D'Holbach and a few days later at Montmorency. Sophie's lover, according to Jean-Jacques, rebuked him in blunt though friendly terms for what he regarded as an involuntary weakness and certainly not as a betrayal of friendship. Secretly gratified to find himself treated as a rival by a much younger and more attractive man, Rousseau meekly accepted the reprimand. But docility under reproof was foreign to his temperament. At first, Saint-Lambert's jealousy caressed Rousseau's vanity but this agreeable sensation vanished when he observed the growing aloofness of Mme d'Houdetot. A few days after the episode of the five letters, he wrote to Saint-Lambert complaining of her changed attitude and demanding an explanation. It was Saint-Lambert, after all, who had originally sent her to the *Ermitage*;

[1] *C.G.* iii, no. 430 (to Mme d'Houdetot): 'Elle jura de nous désunir....'

all her sentiments were governed by her lover's wishes. He alone, therefore, was responsible for Rousseau's present humiliation '...a man whom one wants to get rid of could not be treated differently than I am by her; at least so far as I can surmise, for I have never yet been cast off by anybody.'[1] Saint-Lambert did not immediately reply since he was paralysed in one arm and on one side. Jean-Jacques did not know this. He was still smarting from his last memory of Saint-Lambert snoring in a chair at the *Ermitage* during a reading of *La Lettre sur la providence*, an indignity which, at that time, had to be swallowed without protest.

Rousseau had been seriously ill during the whole of August. Now, in early September, he was plunged in black melancholy, sick of everything and everybody. 'My body is racked with every conceivable pain', he wrote to Mme d'Houdetot, 'and I bear within my soul the anguish of death.'[2] But he was able, on 15 September, to attend the fêtes in honour of her birthday and the dedication of the chapel at La Chevrette at which was sung a motet set to his own music. The arrival of Grimm, however, destroyed Rousseau's pleasure. The German, whose overbearing manner often enraged even Diderot, behaved on this occasion like a perfect boor, studiously ignoring Jean-Jacques to the distress of Mme d'Epinay. Rousseau departed, swearing never again to set foot in La Chevrette when Grimm was there. The latter, realising that he had gone too far, got his mistress to write to Jean-Jacques proposing a reconciliation which took place a week later. The kiss of peace, however, was a most perfunctory affair. The whole scene, observes Rousseau, was rather like the interview granted to a schoolboy by a master who has let him off a caning.[3]

Neglected by Mme d'Houdetot and also, it seemed, by her lover, Rousseau brooded over his sorrows. Winter was at hand and he did not expect to see another spring. No one, he

---

[1] *C.G.* III, no. 397 (4 Sept. 1757): '...un homme dont on veut se défaire n'est pas autrement traité que je suis d'elle; du moins autant que j'en puis juger car je n'ai encore été congédié de personne.'

[2] *C.G.* III. no. 394 ([7 Sept.] 1757): 'Je porte dans le corps toutes les douleurs qu'on peut sentir et dans l'âme les angoisses de la mort.'

[3] *Conf.* 464.

reflected, would ever understand the true meaning of friendship. 'I demand as much as I give,' he wrote to Sophie, 'and finding no one who returns it I withdraw within myself, pained to discover no responsive heart.'[1]

She arrived, however, at La Chevrette for M. d'Epinay's birthday celebrations and Jean-Jacques, as he watched her dancing, thought that once or twice her eyes sought him out. His smouldering passion leapt into flame and, returning to the *Ermitage*, he composed a love-letter more beautiful than any written by Saint-Preux to Julie. Every phrase is the lyrical transcript of a vital emotion. Rousseau never sent it to Mme d'Houdetot. He wrote it for his own consolation, for the bitter-sweet pleasure of recording the most exquisite moments of his sentimental existence. Here is a typical passage:

Souvenirs amers et délicieux! laisserez-vous jamais mes sens et mon cœur en paix? et toutefois les plaisirs que vous me rappelez ne sont point ceux qu'il regrette le plus. Ah! non, Sophie, il en fut pour moi de plus doux encore et dont ceux-là tirent leur plus grand prix, parce qu'ils en étaient le gage. Il fut, il fut un temps où mon amitié t'était chère et où tu savais me le témoigner. Ne m'eusses-tu rien dit, ne m'eusses-tu fait aucune caresse, un sentiment plus touchant et plus sûr m'avertissait que j'étais bien avec toi. Mon cœur te cherchait et le tien ne me repoussait pas. L'expression du plus tendre amour qui fut jamais n'avait rien de rebutant pour toi. On eût dit à ton empressement à me voir que je te manquais quand tu ne m'avais pas vu: tes yeux ne fuyaient pas les miens, et leurs regards n'étaient pas ceux de la froideur; tu cherchais mon bras à la promenade, tu n'étais pas si soigneuse à me dérober l'aspect de tes charmes, et quand ma bouche osait presser la tienne, quelquefois au moins je la sentais résister. Tu ne m'aimais pas, Sophie, mais tu te laissais aimer, et j'étais heureux.[2]

---

[1] *C.G.* III, no. 399 (1 Oct. 1757): 'J'exige autant que je donne, et ne trouvant personne qui me le rende, je rentre dans moi-même avec la douleur de ne point trouver de cœur qui me réponde.'

[2] *C.G.* III, no. 380 (Oct.? 1757): 'Bitter and delightful memories! Will you ever leave my senses and my heart in peace? And yet the pleasures you bring back to mind are not those it most regrets. Ah! no, Sophie, I had some that were sweeter still and from which the former derive their greatest value as being their pledge. There was, there was a time when my friendship was dear to you and when you could reveal it to me. Had you said nothing, had you given me no caress, yet should I have known, instructed by a feeling more touching and more sure, that all was well between us. My heart sought you and yours did not repulse me. You did not then recoil from the expression of the tenderest love that ever was. One would

Though their relations were to continue for some months, that letter is the swan-song of Rousseau's one and only true love.

At this critical moment, the egregious Diderot once again crashed into his friend's private life. In October Mme d'Epinay was preparing to leave for Geneva to consult Dr Tronchin, a visit already planned in early February. This fact disposes of the libellous story circulated by Thérèse yet accepted by Jean-Jacques to whom Diderot now wrote in the following vein: 'Je suis fait pour vous aimer et pour vous donner du chagrin. J'apprends que Mme d'Epinay va à Genève et je n'entends pas que vous l'accompagniez. Mon ami, content de Mme d'Epinay, il faut partir avec elle: mécontent, il faut partir plus vite.'[1] In the same insufferable style, Diderot proceeds to marshal and to refute one by one, the objections which Rousseau might adduce to justify a refusal, brushing aside, for instance, as quite irrelevant the trifling matter of his friend's bladder trouble. Diderot, in such a case, would seize his trusty staff and follow the postchaise on foot. However, he concludes sternly, Rousseau will no doubt obey the dictates of his conscience.

Trembling with rage, Jean-Jacques replied briefly and pungently that since Diderot obviously did not know what he was talking about, it was sheer humbug on his part to pose as a moral arbiter. He implied, moreover, that the good Denis was being used as a catspaw by certain unscrupulous individuals, meaning, of course, Grimm and Mme d'Epinay in whose presence Jean-Jacques read out Diderot's letter and his own reply observing how Grimm quailed before his flashing, accusatory gaze. Shortly afterwards, the latter received from Rousseau a long letter stating why it was materially impossible for him to accompany Mme d'Epinay. In his anger, Jean-Jaques was guilty of several

---

have said from your eagerness to see me that you missed me when you had not seen me: your eyes did not evade mine nor was there any coldness in their looks. When we went walking you took my arm, you were not so careful to hide from me the sight of your charms and when I dared to press my lips on yours, sometimes at least I felt them respond. You did not love me, Sophie, but you let yourself be loved and I was happy.'

[1] *C.G.* III, no. 404 (18 Oct. 1757): 'I am fated to love you and to cause you grief. I learn that Mme d'Epinay is going to Geneva, but I do not hear that you are accompanying her. My friend, if you are pleased with Mme d'Epinay, you must leave with her; if displeased, you must do so even more quickly.'

unpardonable remarks. These he bitterly regretted later, dismissing them very feebly as 'puerile outbursts'.[1] They represented, in fact, a concise balance-sheet of his sentimental transactions with Mme d'Epinay, revealing a dead loss to himself in time, money, liberty and peace of mind. She had prevented him by solicitations and intrigues from settling in Geneva; kept him for two years a slave to her tyrannical whims. And why, he asked maliciously, was Grimm not included in the Genevan equipage? Diderot's opinion, Rousseau implied, could be ignored. If he did accompany Mme d'Epinay, the *philosophe* would probably accuse him of deserting Thérèse to follow the wife of a rich *fermier-général*. He concluded by asking Grimm to pronounce judgment on his action.[2]

Meanwhile, Jean-Jacques received Saint-Lambert's long-expected reply which was as balm to his lacerated pride.[3] Sophie's lover frankly confessed he had been misled by false impressions. He alone was to blame for the behaviour of Mme d'Houdetot, caused by his silly jealousy. He had never thought Rousseau capable of treachery yet, knowing the austerity of his principles, was stupidly alarmed by his intimacy with Mme d'Houdetot. Eager to make amends, Saint-Lambert hoped that some day they might all three live happily together at Eaubonne. Rousseau, charmed by this prospect, gave the lovers his paternal blessing, almost in the very words of his hero's English friend, Lord Edouard Bomston: 'Oui, mes enfants, soyez à jamais unis; il n'est plus d'âme comme les vôtres, et vous méritez de vous aimer jusqu'au tombeau.'[4]

At last Grimm broke his enigmatic silence. There was nothing in his letter to warn Rousseau of what lay in store for him.[5] Mme d'Epinay had postponed her departure but Grimm advised Jean-Jacques to offer his company which, in view of his domestic and other commitments, she would no doubt decline. Altogether, a *nichtssagend* letter. Now it is clear from Rousseau's correspondence with Mme d'Houdetot that he was vaguely apprehensive.

[1] *C.G.* iii, no. 406 (19 Oct. 1757): 'puériles emportements.'
[2] *C.G.* iii, no. 406 (19 Oct. 1757).   [3] *C.G.* iii, no. 407 (11 Oct. 1757).
[4] *C.G.* iii, no. 413 (28 Oct. 1757): 'Yes, my children, be for ever united; there are no longer souls like yours and you deserve to love each other to the grave.'
[5] *C.G.* iii, no. 414 (approx. 28 Oct. 1757).

His petulant and unjust indictment of Mme d'Epinay weighed heavily on his conscience. If Grimm, normally so discreet, were to betray his confidence, Rousseau foresaw a rupture and, in a sense, it would come as a relief provided Mme d'Houdetot and Saint-Lambert remained his friends. Suddenly, on 1 November, Grimm's hatred of Rousseau erupted in a curt announcement that he could no longer have relations with a man whose 'horrible system' filled him with indignation. As the note has disappeared we can judge of its tenour only from the profound impression it left on Jean-Jacques who had anticipated, at the worst, another *brouillerie* or tiff. But this was a complete breach, threatening the ruin of his reputation. Shown to anyone unfamiliar with the history of his relations with Mme d'Epinay, the impetuous letter to Grimm must infallibly corroborate the latter's picture of an unprincipled ingrate. For how could Rousseau explain that it was not the letter of a wicked man bereft of all sense of gratitude, but of one who held absolute proof of Mme d'Epinay's hypocrisy and treachery? On 2 November, 'jour de deuil et d'affliction', he displayed his naked bleeding soul in a letter to Mme d'Houdetot, urgently beseeching her to pronounce words of consolation and reassurance. 'Ah! if I am wicked, how vile is the whole human race!'[1] Wild with anxiety because she did not immediately reply, he wrote again, on the following day: 'Your barbarity is inconceivable; it is not like you. This silence is a refinement of cruelty which has no parallel.... And you, also, Sophie believe that I am a wicked man!'[2] Her answer brought only partial relief to his tortured soul, for what he wanted was her unequivocal approval of his conduct and that she could not honestly give. Instead, she wrote sensibly that the only sure source of consolation lay in his own conscience. Only he knew whether he had anything to reproach himself with in regard to Mme d'Epinay. She begged him at all costs to see and consult Diderot who wrote to Jean-Jacques about the middle of November. The opening words

[1] *C.G.* III, no. 424 (2 Nov. 1757): 'Ah! si je suis un méchant que tout le genre humain est vil!'

[2] *C.G.* III, no. 452 (3 Nov. 1757) (date as amended by M. Guillemin): 'votre batbarie est inconcevable; elle n'est pas de vous. Ce silence est un raffinement de cruauté qui n'a rien d'égal.... Et vous aussi, Sophie, vous me croyez un méchant!'

betray Diderot's incurable penchant for cheap melodrama: 'Il est certain qu'il ne vous reste d'ami que moi; mais il est certain que je vous reste.' Thereafter, however, he writes like a man of sense and a kind friend. His previous letter ought never to have been read out to Mme d'Epinay since it contained remarks that were bound to offend her. Rousseau, he thought, would be ill advised to leave the *Ermitage* at once: it would look bad.

Am I not your friend? [he concludes] Have I not the right to tell you everything that comes into my head? Have I not the right to be mistaken? Is it not my duty to tell you what I think it is proper to do? Goodbye, my friend. I loved you long ago and I love you still.[1]

Rousseau, many years later, unjustly described this as the letter of a false friend, but he did not think so at the time.

We may now briefly observe the liquidation of Rousseau's friendship with Mme d'Epinay who left for Geneva on 30 October. On the eve of her departure, Jean-Jacques called at La Chevrette and swore that a whole lifetime would not be long enough in which to make amends for his insults to her. Yet on the same day he wrote from the *Ermitage* attributing his 'ill-humour' to her lack of frankness. Instead of trying to bring pressure on him by using Diderot and Mme d'Houdetot as intermediaries, which gave him an impression of 'tyranny and intrigue', she had only to appeal to their old friendship and Jean-Jacques would have accompanied her to Geneva. Not included, however, in the copy he made of this letter was an interesting paragraph in which Rousseau portrays the conflict between his affection for Mme d'Epinay and the suspicions aroused by her recent conduct. It ends on a curiously ambiguous note: 'I hasten to declare to you that my most ardent wish is to be able to honour you all my life and continue to entertain for you a friendship equal to the gratitude I owe you.'[2]

[1] *C.G.* III, no. 434: 'Ne suis-je pas votre ami? N'ai-je pas le droit de vous dire tout ce qui me vient en pensée? N'ai-je pas celui de me tromper? Vous communiquer ce que je croirai qu'il est honnête de faire, n'est-ce pas mon devoir? Adieu, mon ami. Je vous ai aimé il y a longtemps; je vous aime toujours.'
[2] *C.G.* III, no. 415: 'je me hâte de vous déclarer que le plus ardent de mes vœux est de pouvoir vous honorer toute ma vie et continuer à nourrir pour vous autant d'amitié que je vous dois de reconnaissance.'

Replying from Geneva a fortnight later, Mme d'Epinay reminded Jean-Jacques of their farewell conversation at La Chevrette. His conduct, she wrote, frightened her for his sake: it was unnatural to spend one's life suspecting and insulting one's friends.[1] Rousseau's answer made a reconciliation impossible. Their friendship, he announced, was extinguished, but he would never forget her past kindness. Though he wanted to leave the *Ermitage* and ought to, his friends advised him to wait for the spring.[2] On 7 or 8 December he got her reply. She was astonished to learn that, in the circumstances, his friends should have told him to remain. Personally, she never consulted her own as to her duties.[3] Stung into action, Rousseau vacated the *Ermitage* on 15 December and moved to *Mont-Louis*, a dilapidated house belonging to a M. Mathas, *procureur-fiscal* to the prince de Conti. Despite the pleadings of Thérèse, old Mme Levasseur was bundled off to Paris. Now that the affair was over, Jean-Jacques heaved a great sigh of relief. 'At last', he wrote to Sophie, 'I am free; I can resume the frank and independent character which Nature gave me.'[4] Better still, as this letter reveals, he had silenced the murmurs of an uneasy conscience by a dialectical *tour de force*. Mme d'Epinay, he explains to Sophie, has confirmed all his previous suspicions of her character by dismissing him brutally from the *Ermitage*; justifying therefore, Rousseau implies, his letter about her to Grimm. He can now magnanimously forget her deceitful conduct and ignore the censure of her friends. Indeed, he had been too magnanimous perhaps in concealing for so long his just indignation. Still, that was an honourable fault. At this point, the master-theme of Rousseau's letter emerges: his desperate anxiety to regain ascendancy over Mme d'Houdetot; to wring from her, at any cost, a positive statement that Saint-Lambert and she were on his side against her sister-in-law. A reference in Sophie's last letter to a difference in their principles had deeply mortified Rousseau and even more her remark that he

---

[1] *C.G.* III, no. 439 (12 Nov. 1757).   [2] *C.G.* III, no. 440 (23 Nov. 1757).
[3] *C.G.* III, no. 449 (1 Dec. 1757).
[4] *C.G.* III, no. 451 (17 Dec. 1757): 'Enfin je suis libre; je puis reprendre caractère de franchise et d'indépendance que m'a donné la nature.'

could rely upon her friendship so long as he continued to deserve her esteem.[1] Irritated by her non-committal attitude, he accused her of having been 'corrupted' by Grimm and summoned her, if she intended a rupture, to come out into the open. With the clairvoyance of the jealous, rejected lover, Jean-Jacques quickly perceived Sophie's dilemma. Although genuinely sorry for him, she was quietly determined to end a relationship which might, at any moment, bring disaster to her love owing to the unpredictable character of Rousseau. Of this he was only too conscious and his passion for Mme d'Houdetot was revived by the intolerable and desolating thought of losing her for ever. She represented, he confessed involuntarily, his last remaining link with the society of *honnêtes gens*, of those decent, cultured gentlefolk whose opinion he respected even when they deserted him.[2] And Mme d'Houdetot knew perfectly well that, to avoid a rupture, Jean-Jacques would not hesitate to adopt a cat and mouse technique by exploiting her secret apprehensions. Such, in fact, is the psychological design revealed in their correspondence from December 1757 to May 1758. Goaded by the announcement that in future her letters would be shorter and less frequent, he peremptorily demanded a clear assurance from Sophie and Saint-Lambert that they were still his friends,[3] a request which she dismissed as childish and unnecessary.[4] Infuriated by the epithet *puérile*, Rousseau sharply condemned the 'shifty and equivocal style' of her letters so typical of her class and so different from his own *puérile*, rustic frankness.

Since, therefore, instead of feeling honoured by my friendship, you are ashamed of it, I withdraw it....I declare to you that, from this instant, I shall look upon you only as Madame la Comtesse and on him [Saint-Lambert] with all his genius, only as M. le Marquis.[5]

With barely concealed eagerness Mme d'Houdetot accepted the rupture of a liaison which, she said, was becoming too 'stormy' and to which she could not contribute as much as Jean-

---

[1] *C.G.* III, no. 448 (14 Dec. 1757).   [2] *C.G.* III, no. 451, p. 237.
[3] *C.G.* III, no. 454 (26 Dec. 1757).   [4] *C.G.* III, no. 455 (30 Dec. 1757).
[5] *C.G.* III, no. 459 (5 Jan. 1758): 'Puis donc qu'au lieu de vous honorer de mon amitié, vous en avez honte; je la retire....Je vous déclare que, dès cet instant, je ne vois plus en vous que Madame la Comtesse, ni en lui avec tout son génie, que M. le Marquis.'

Jacques.[1] And, to make doubly sure, she repeated these sentiments in a letter despatched two days later,[2] assuring Rousseau
that she would continue to esteem his virtues but hinting that,
in view of her husband's expected return, it was perhaps just as
well that their correspondence should end now. Jean-Jacques,
however, had merely been playing his game of cat and mouse.
Admitting that his letter was unpardonably rude, he observed
slyly that she was, of course, only too glad to find a pretext for
the rupture she had long desired. Then, unsheathing his claws
he asked if it had ever occurred to her that if Jean-Jacques had
been less zealous in defending her reputation, he might still be
the friend of Mme d'Epinay.[3] Apologising for her *vivacité*, the
disconsolate Sophie agreed to resume their old footing but
stipulated that Rousseau must get rid of that *humeur solitaire*
which made him regard all social commerce as a source of evil
or a kind of slavery. He must also stop insulting and suspecting
his friends. Her sudden capitulation delighted Rousseau but
did not really surprise him for he knew that M. d'Houdetot was
now back. It amused him, however, to play with his victim:

> Oh! Sophie, is this so charming change of front quite natural? Is it
> really sincere? Don't I owe it partly to circumstances? Having to
> warn me against writing to you again, were you not afraid that anger
> might prevent me from listening to you and make me go on writing
> indiscreetly despite your orders?[4]

Her suggestion that M. d'Houdetot might disapprove of their
correspondence aroused Rousseau's suspicions. Why should he
object? Had the voice of calumny reached his ears? Had he
forbidden his wife to see Jean-Jacques? If so, surely there was
only one honourable course. Though Sophie alone now linked him
with the 'douceurs de la Société', their relations must cease.

Realising, perhaps, the stupidity and cruelty of these feline
tactics, Jean-Jacques hit upon a more sensible and dignified way

---

[1] *C.G.* III, no. 460 (7 Jan. 1758).   [2] *C.G.* III, no. 461 (9 Jan. 1758).
[3] *C.G.* III, no. 462 (10 Jan. 1758).
[4] *C.G.* III, no. 465 (15 Jan. 1758), p. 266: 'O Sophie, ce retour si charmant est-il
bien naturel? Est-il bien sincère? N'en dois-je rien aux circonstances? Ayant à
m'avertir de ne plus vous écrire, n'avez-vous point craint que la colère ne m'em-
pêchât de vous écouter, et ne me fît continuer indiscrètement d'écrire malgré vos
ordres?'

of repairing his tattered self-esteem and of regaining his ascendancy over Mme d'Houdetot. He now began to write a series of letters designed for her moral guidance and edification. These *Lettres morales* as they are called we shall examine in the next chapter along with *La Nouvelle Héloïse* and the *Lettre à d'Alembert sur les spectacles*. For all three works illuminate, from different angles, the psychological crisis unfolded in the *Correspondance* to which we may now return.

In February 1758, tormented by a severe recurrence of his malady and by the malicious gossip fomented in Paris by the D'Holbach coterie, Rousseau longed for the return of spring. Mme d'Houdetot's letters arrived less frequently though they were full of anxious inquiries about his health. Convinced, indeed, that his end was near, Jean-Jacques wrote pathetically to Diderot early in March, begging him to think of the comrade he had known for sixteen years and then ask himself whether such a man could be guilty of villainy.[1] Meanwhile, his candid friend Deleyre expressed his indignation at the terrible things he heard about Jean-Jacques in Paris.[2]

With the fine weather, Rousseau's health quickly improved. Once again the familiar storm signals are hoisted in his letters to Mme d'Houdetot. In the last month, he complained, her expressions of friendship had become more circumspect, more reserved, more conditional. If she persisted in that affected, equivocal style, her letters would remain unanswered. But this time Rousseau's cat and mouse technique did not work. After a silence of six weeks, Mme d'Houdetot informed him that their relations must cease immediately. His unfortunate passion for her was the subject of public gossip which had reached the ears of Saint-Lambert.

J'ai à me plaindre de votre indiscrétion et de celle de vos amis. Je vous aurais gardé toute ma vie le secret de votre malheureuse passion pour moi, et je la cachais à ce que j'aime pour ne pas lui donner de l'éloignement pour vous: vous en avez parlé à des gens qui l'ont rendue publique, et qui ont fait voir contre moi des vraisemblances qui pouvaient nuire à ma réputation. Ces bruits sont parvenus depuis quelque temps à mon amant, qui a été affligé que je lui eusse fait

---

[1] *C.G.* III, no. 479 (2 Mar. 1758).   [2] *C.G.* III, no. 475 (22 Feb. 1758).

mystère d'une passion que je n'ai jamais flattée et que je lui taisais dans l'espérance que vous deviendriez raisonnable et que vous pourriez être notre ami. J'ai vu en lui un changement qui a pensé me coûter la vie.[1]

Her lover's first reaction had been to suspect Rousseau's virtue, but he was now disposed merely to pity him. So far as they were concerned, the incident was forgotten. But she owed it to herself to break off all communication with Jean-Jacques of whose character they would always think highly. Mme d'Houdetot, in conclusion, begged him to remain calm and warned him especially not to enter the lists in defence of her innocence.

We do not know how Rousseau answered her shattering letter. In the *Confessions* he records simply that it plunged him into 'a fresh affliction, the most poignant I had so far experienced'.[2] He quickly selected Diderot as the false friend who had betrayed his confidence. Determined to break with him publicly, yet without compromising Mme d'Houdetot, he adopted a method which struck him as admirable. His *Lettre à d'Alembert* was in the press. On 21 June, before returning the first corrected sheets, he appended to the *Préface*, by way of footnote, a savage quotation from Ecclesiasticus, in Latin.[3] As Rousseau had intended, no one in the world of letters failed to recognise that the object of this terrible indictment was Diderot. Whether the latter was, in fact, guilty of betraying Rousseau is a matter that has aroused some controversy. It may be, as M. Guillemin has suggested, that Diderot's three conflicting versions of the affair point to an uneasy conscience.[4] On the other hand, by 1758,

---

[1] *C.G.* III, no. 494 (6 May 1758): 'I have a complaint to make about your indiscretion and that of your friends. I would have kept all my life the secret of your unhappy passion for me and I concealed it from the one I love so as not to estrange him from you: you have talked about it to people who have made it public and who have circulated plausible stories which could harm my reputation. For some time my lover has been hearing these rumours and he was distressed at my making a mystery of a passion I have never encouraged and which I kept from him in the hope that you would become reasonable and might be our friend. I noticed a change in him which nearly cost me my life.'

[2] *Conf.* 488: 'une affliction nouvelle, la plus sensible que j'eusse encore éprouvée.'

[3] XXII, 26–7. The English version is: 'Though thou drewest a sword at thy friend, yet despair not, for there may be a returning to favour. If thou hast opened thy mouth against thy friend, fear not: for there may be a reconciliation. Except for upbraiding, or pride, or disclosing of secrets, or a treacherous wound; for these things every friend will depart.'   [4] *Ann.* XXIX, ch. 2.

Rousseau's passion for Mme d'Houdetot was an open secret amongst his friends. Deleyre knew of it and Jean-Jacques himself admits that he was the talk of La Chevrette. I see no reason to doubt Diderot's story of what happened. He had advised Rousseau to make a clean breast of the affair to Saint-Lambert and, under the impression that the latter was fully informed of the situation, alluded to it without any malicious intention in the course of a conversation. In this he was guilty merely of an indiscretion. It is doubtful, moreover, whether Saint-Lambert looked on Jean-Jacques as a serious rival, for he paid him a brief visit at the *Ermitage* in May and in a letter of 23 June 1758 assured him that neither he nor Sophie would ever desert him. But next day, having read the terrible indictment of Diderot in his presentation copy of the *Lettre à d'Alembert*, he returned the book with an indignant note: 'cette atrocité me révolte... Monsieur, nous différons trop de principes pour nous convenir jamais. Oubliez mon existence!'[1] Rousseau, beyond remarking that he was astonished and grieved, made no attempt to justify his footnote. Saint-Lambert's letter, he thought, deserved no reply. Yet, at the end of the month, he accepted an invitation from M. d'Epinay to lunch at La Chevrette with Mme d'Houdetot, her husband and Saint-Lambert. This awkward meeting was robbed of embarrassment by the exquisite tact of D'Epinay and his guests. And, though Rousseau's conversation with Sophie and her lover was confined to banalities, they did not part as enemies. Indeed, two years later, when manuscript copies of *La Nouvelle Héloïse* were circulating among the chosen few, they asked Jean-Jacques for permission to show theirs to the King of Poland.

Rousseau's quarrel with Diderot was purely personal. It may be, however, that in smiting him with the Bible he was animated by the same motive which impelled him to write *La Lettre à D'Alembert* and to modify the eroticism of *La Nouvelle Héloïse* by composing two extra parts, namely five and six. In surrendering to the urgent call of his sensual nature, Rousseau had descended from that exalted moral plane which it was now imperative to

---

[1] *C.G.* IV, no. 552: 'this atrocity revolts me...Sir, we differ too much in our principles for us ever to suit each other. Forget my existence.'

regain if he was to attain inner harmony. In this light one must interpret his remarks on the success of *La Lettre à d'Alembert*: 'It taught the public to distrust the insinuations of the D'Holbach coterie.... People saw that I had returned to my element.'[1] His book, indeed, focused public attention on the *Encyclopédie* at an awkward moment and, incidentally, blasted Voltaire's cherished hopes of staging his tragedies in Geneva.

Had Rousseau wanted, at this stage, to dissociate himself publicly from the *philosophes*, the appearance of *De l'Esprit*[2] in July 1758 offered him an excellent opportunity. But his *Notes en réfutation de l'ouvrage de Helvétius intitulé 'De l'Esprit'*, composed at the end of the year, were not given to the public because the scandal aroused by that materialistic work had placed its author in a dangerous position. Even in 1766, when Rousseau sold his library to Louis Dutens, including the copy of *De l'Esprit* with his marginal notes, he stipulated that they must not be printed until after his death.[3] The importance of these *Notes* rests upon the rejection by Jean-Jacques of the materialistic theory implied in Helvétius's statement that the only two human faculties are physical sensibility and memory, which he defines as a continued but enfeebled sensation. Rousseau denies that this theory has any basis in experience and remarks: 'But I know very well that to feel the object present and the object absent are two operations the difference between which certainly deserves examination.'[4] It is fascinating to watch him groping towards the light which Bergson eventually shed on this problem in 1908 when he exploded the materialistic view that present perception is a strong state and revived recollection a feeble state; that perception passes into recollection by a process or diminution. Bergson confirmed the validity of Rousseau's intuition that the remembrance of a perception (sensation) is radically different from the perception itself. Rousseau also objected, rightly, that Helvétius was merely playing with words

---

[1] *Conf.* 493: 'Il apprit au public de se défier des insinuations de la coterie holbachique.... On vit que j'étais rentré dans mon élément.'

[2] By Claude-Adrien Helvétius.

[3] L. Dutens, *Oeuvres mêlées* (London, 1797).

[4] *H.* xii, 299: 'Mais je sais bien que sentir l'objet présent et sentir l'objet absent, sont deux opérations dont la différence mérite bien d'être examinée.'

when he identified sensation with judgment. 'To apperceive objects', retorted Jean-Jacques, 'is to feel: to apperceive relationships is to judge.'[1] In *Emile* he will elaborate this argument. As Louis Dutens notes, the 'luminous distinction' made by Rousseau between judgment and sensation riddled the materialistic doctrine that everything in the human mind derives from physical sensibility.

Rousseau's attack on the stage, *La Lettre à d'Alembert sur les spectacles*, fulfilled its author's main object which was to assure himself and his compatriots that he was still, at heart, the *Citoyen de Genève*. To his immense pride he learned that the book had won the approval of his idol, the venerable savant, Abauzit. Among other pastors it gained him new admirers like Moultou, Roustan, Vernes and Jacob Vernet. Whilst basking in their adulation Rousseau learned in February 1759 that his *Devin du village* was to be performed at the Opéra which, some five years earlier, had withdrawn his *entrées* or free pass. Aroused by such a cynical disregard of his rights, Jean-Jacques sent a memoir to the Director, Saint-Florentin, demanding the return of his operetta. His request was ignored, but through the good offices of Duclos he received an honorarium of 4000 francs and the restoration of his *entrées* which Rousseau no longer wanted. As he wrote sardonically to Leniens, why go to the Opéra since there was an excellent chorus of screech-owls in the forest outside his door at Montmorency?

Rousseau now began to frequent the exalted persons whose names will figure prominently in the *Correspondance* during the next few years: Malesherbes, son of the Grand Chancelier, and Director of the *Librairie* or Censorship; the maréchal and maréchale de Luxembourg who resided for a few weeks every year at their magnificent country seat near Montmorency; the comtesse de Boufflers, mistress of the great prince de Conti to whose kindness and wise counsel he was to owe so much in the dark days to come. Though the Luxembourgs had already made courteous overtures, it was not until Easter of 1759, after a visit by the maréchal to *Mont-Louis*, that Jean-Jacques responded to

[1] *Ibid.* 300: 'Apercevoir les objets, c'est sentir; apercevoir les rapports, c'est juger.'

the latter's offer of friendship. In an admirably phrased letter he explained with great tact and dignity why, as a social inferior, he felt reluctant to embark upon a relationship which might eventually prove a source of embarrassment to both. However, the exquisite simplicity and warmth of Luxembourg's reply quite disarmed Rousseau who gratefully accepted his offer of an apartment in the Petit Château until *Mont-Louis*, which was in a sorry state, could be made habitable. Rousseau's new abode was a charming house situated in the grounds of the great Château, between the orangery and a small lake. 'In this profound and delightful solitude, in the midst of woods and water, to the accompaniment of the songs of birds of every species, amongst the perfumes of orange blossom',[1] he composed the fifth book of his new work, *Emile*. The Luxembourgs were again in residence and Rousseau, captivated by their unaffected kindness, visited them twice a day. To amuse Mme de Luxembourg who knew that *La Nouvelle Héloïse* was in the press, he offered to read his novel to her. The maréchal came to these readings which took place every morning in her bedroom. Infatuated with Julie, she sang the author's praises to all her guests. Yet Jean-Jacques, knowing the fickleness of great ladies, was always secretly afraid of offending the maréchale. But in this he was unjust to Mme de Luxembourg whose friendship for him was no less sincere than that of her husband. What Rousseau with all his penetration failed to realise was that, from their point of view, genius was something to be prized far above rank and wealth when it is allied with sincerity and natural dignity. Rousseau's error lay in confusing Mme de Luxembourg with professional *salonnières* like Mme Dupin for whom men of letters were attractions, invited merely to entertain their bored and fashionable guests. The Luxembourgs, on the other hand, thought it perfectly natural that Jean-Jacques should prefer to call in the absence of their illustrious friends whose conversation, they felt, could not possibly interest him. He was jealous of his privileged situation as is evident from his scathing allusions in the *Confes-*

---

[1] *Conf.* 513: 'C'est dans cette profonde et délicieuse solitude qu'au milieu des bois et des eaux, aux concerts des oiseaux de toute espèce, au parfum de la fleur d'orange....'

sions to that dogsbody, Coindet, who arranged for the illustra-
tions to Mme de Luxembourg's copy of *La Nouvelle Héloïse* and
thus contrived to get himself invited to dinner. Fanatically
devoted to Jean-Jacques, by whom he was used as an unpaid
factotum, the hapless Coindet never succeeded in winning the
master's confidence and was given his *congé* in 1768.

In July 1760 Rousseau entertained the maréchale with readings
from *Emile* which were not very successful. However, convinced that he was a child in the hands of his publishers, she
begged him to let her negotiate the publication and sale of this
work. Rousseau, fearing that it would be 'mutilated' by a
French publisher because of the censorship, insisted on its being
printed in Holland. Greatly to his surprise, Malesherbes, when
approached by Mme de Luxembourg, wrote to Jean-Jacques
warmly praising the section entitled *La Profession de foi du
vicaire savoyard*. Presumably this was one of the letters returned,
at the writer's request, after the condemnation of *Emile*, since no
trace of it exists. At the end of August, whilst stipulating that
the book should be printed in Holland, Rousseau signed an
agreement negotiated by Mme de Luxembourg with Duchesne
of Paris though the French edition carried the imprimatur of
Néaulme, an Amsterdam publisher who subsequently issued an
edition of his own from sheets supplied by Duchesne.[1] Thus,
Rousseau, who wanted to deal with his usual publisher, Rey,
allowed himself to be overruled by the maréchale. He received
6000 francs from Duchesne whose associate, Guérin, was one of
his neighbours at Montmorency.[2] The edition proceeded very
slowly and Rousseau confided to Malesherbes his suspicions that
Guérin, in collusion with the Jesuits, was trying to sabotage his
book.[3] But two days later, in an agony of remorse, he exonerated
Guérin. It is important to note that for some months Rousseau
had been suffering intense pain, though Frère Côme, after a long
and trying examination, had relieved him of the fear that his
malady was the stone. This no doubt accounts to some extent

[1] *C.G.* no. 1204 (Rousseau to Moultou, 12 Dec. 1761).
[2] *C.G.* no. 1121 (approx. 29 Aug. 1761). Draft agreement returned to Duchesne
with corrections by Malesherbes.
[3] *C.G.* no. 1178 (18 Oct. 1761).

for his anxieties concerning *Emile*. At the end of November 1761 a fragment of a broken catheter lodged in his urethra, followed almost immediately by a recurrence of his suspicions regarding the Jesuits and *Emile*. To reassure him, Malesherbes did violence to his professional conscience though Jean-Jacques never mentions the fact. Officially, he was not supposed to know that *Emile* was being printed in France.[1] Yet he personally investigated the whole situation and during a visit to Montmorency was able to calm Rousseau's fears. The latter had the grace to acknowledge his kindness in the *Confessions*. But he never thanked Mme de Luxembourg who saw Duchesne, convinced herself of his good faith and obtained from him an offer to return, if necessary, the manuscript from which he was printing. The delays, it transpired, had been caused by Rousseau's frequent corrections. One significant point emerges from this interview: Duchesne said he was eager to get the edition completed whilst Malesherbes remained in office.[2]

Du Contrat social, published by Rey, came out in April 1762; the Duchesne edition of *Emile*, about the middle of May. We shall presently observe the upheaval which they produced in Rousseau's material and psychological existence. At the moment, he was not unhappy despite his physical sufferings. It will be recalled that, by the spring of 1759, Jean-Jacques had recovered his self-esteem, grievously shaken by the rupture with Mme d'Epinay and the defection of Mme d'Houdetot. So, with a clear conscience, he could once again proclaim himself as 'le défenseur de la vérité', 'l'ami de la vérité',[3] 'l'ami du genre humain'.[4] He began, too, at this time to employ in his correspondence the proud device: *vitam impendere vero*.[5] Now confident of his moral integrity, Rousseau was in no mood, therefore, to accept meekly the unctuous homilies of Dr Tronchin on

[1] *C.G.* no. 1210. Malesherbes wrote to Rousseau on 16 Dec. 1761 that, owing to the latter's cruel state of anxiety, he had been obliged to take more cognisance of this edition than he should have liked, since he had to speak to Duchesne about it.

[2] *C.G.* no. 1209 (Mme de Luxembourg to Rousseau, 15 Dec. 1761).

[3] *C.G.* iv, no. 620 (to Lenieps, 5 April 1759).

[4] *C.G.* iv, no. 615 (to Tronchin, 28 April 1759).

[5] Juvenal *Satires*, iv, 91. The quotation occurs frequently as an epigraph to Rousseau's letters and also on the title page of the *Lettres de la montagne*.

the theme, *mens sana in corpore sano*. Hypocrisy and malevolence positively trickle from the doctor's clumsy pen. Misanthropy, caused by ill-health, he wrote to Jean-Jacques, had lost him Diderot and his other friends. Why not come to Geneva, he urged, and share the sweetness and innocence of Tronchin's mode of life? Thoroughly aroused by this gratuitous intrusion on his private affairs, Jean-Jacques retorted sharply that he had detached himself from certain friends but had never lost one, adding that if Tronchin's notion of friendship was typical of Geneva he preferred to live with foreigners. Common sense, evidently, was not one of Dr Tronchin's attributes since a moment's reflection would have told him that, as the physician and intimate of Voltaire he was bound to be suspect to Rousseau whose hatred and contempt of the *baladin* or mountebank of Ferney is forcibly expressed in a letter to Moultou written in January 1760. Not, however, until June did he find an opportunity of communicating these sentiments to Voltaire himself. Formey had printed the famous *Lettre sur la providence* and, as Jean-Jacques felt bound to explain, without his authorisation. So far, the style of Rousseau's letter is neutral and courteous. Suddenly, however, his suppressed emotions of hatred, self-pity and indignation explode in a veritable *cri du cœur*:

Je ne vous aime point, monsieur, vous m'avez fait les maux qui pouvaient m'être les plus sensibles, à moi votre disciple et votre enthousiaste. Vous avez perdu Genève pour le prix de l'asile que vous y avez reçu. Vous avez aliéné de moi mes concitoyens pour le prix des applaudissements que je vous ai prodigués parmi eux: c'est vous qui me rendez le séjour de mon pays insupportable; c'est vous qui me ferez mourir en terre étrangère, privé de toutes les consolations des mourants et jeté, pour tout honneur dans une voirie; tandis que tous les honneurs qu'un homme peut attendre vous accompagnent dans mon pays. Je vous hais enfin puisque vous l'avez voulu; mais je vous hais en homme encore plus digne de vous aimer, si vous l'aviez voulu. De tous les sentiments dont mon cœur était pénétré pour vous, il n'y reste que l'admiration qu'on ne peut refuser à votre beau génie et l'amour de vos écrits.[1]

[1] *C.G.* v, no. 811 (17 June 1760): 'I do not like you, Sir. The injuries you have inflicted on me, your disciple and enthusiastic admirer, are those to which I am peculiarly sensitive. You have ruined Geneva in return for the sanctuary accorded to you there. You have alienated from me my fellow citizens in return for the

Voltaire made no reply, but he wrote to his friend Thiériot: 'I have received a long letter from Jean-Jacques Rousseau. He has gone completely mad. It is a pity.'[1] Rousseau, in the *Confessions*, airily dismisses this strange incident as a petty literary squabble.[2] It was very much more because from that moment he was marked down by Voltaire as a rogue and a renegade. As the latter wrote to D'Alembert on 19 March 1760:

> This arch-maniac who might have been something if he had allowed you to guide him, has broken off on his own. He writes against the theatre after having composed a bad comedy; he writes against France which feeds him; he picks up a few rotten staves from Diogenes's tub and gets inside them to bark; he deserts his friends; he writes me the most impertinent letter ever scrawled by a fanatic.[3]

But Rousseau was not yet openly an *anti-philosophe* and when he received from Duchesne in May 1760 a copy of *Les Philosophes*, a satirical comedy by Palissot de Montenoy, he refused to accept a work in which his former friend Diderot was vilified and ridiculed. Moreover, when the abbé Morellet was imprisoned for insulting, in his *Vision de Charles Palissot*, the princesse de Robecq, daughter of the maréchal de Luxembourg, Rousseau successfully exerted his influence on behalf of the Encyclopaedist whose letter of thanks, he complains, did not appear to come straight from the heart. His surmise was correct since Morellet, in his *Mémoires*,[4] does not even mention Rous-

---

applause I lavished on you in their midst. It is you who make residence in my country intolerable. It is you who will cause me to die in a foreign land, deprived of all the consolations of the dying, with no other reward than to be cast upon a muck-heap whilst all the honours a man can expect surround you in my country. In short, I hate you since you have so wished; but I hate you as one still more worthy of loving had you so desired. Of all the feelings which I cherished for you there remains only the admiration which no one can deny to your fine genius, and my love of your writings.

[1] 'J'ai reçu une grande lettre de Jean-Jacques Rousseau, il est devenu tout à fait fou, c'est dommage.'

[2] *Conf.* 533.

[3] 'Cet archifou, qui aurait pu être quelque chose, s'il s'était laissé conduire par vous, s'avise de faire bande à part; il écrit contre les spectacles, après avoir fait une mauvaise comédie; il écrit contre la France qui le nourrit; il trouve quatre ou cinq douves pourries du tonneau de Diogène, il se met dedans pour aboyer; il abandonne ses amis; il m'écrit la plus impertinente lettre que jamais fanatique ait griffonnée.'

[4] Ed. Paris, 1823.

seau's intervention. The latter, on 5 February 1761, categorically announced to Mme de Créqui his rupture with the *philosophes*:

...je me suis absolument détaché du parti des philosophes. Je n'aime point qu'on prêche l'impiété: voilà déjà de ce côté-là un crime qu'on ne me pardonnera pas. D'un autre côté, je blâme l'intolérance, et je veux qu'on laisse en paix les incrédules; or le parti dévot n'est pas plus endurant que l'autre. Jugez en quelles mains me voilà tombé.[1]

These are prophetic words, for they describe exactly the position in which Rousseau was to find himself after the publication of *Emile*. Meanwhile, the only cloud on his horizon was the anxiety caused by his malady. In truth, his present situation was unique. Caressed by the Luxembourgs, honoured by two visits at *Mont-Louis* from the prince de Conti, overwhelmed by the astonishing success of his novel, Jean-Jacques revelled in glory and adulation. Yet, cannily, he resolved to have no truck with the god of chance. His one desire now was to give up writing and, by amassing a capital of 10,000 francs, to buy an annuity which would allow him to retire with Thérèse to some quiet retreat in Touraine. He might, indeed, have achieved financial security by accepting Margency's offer of a demi-sinecure on *Le Journal des Savants*. The honorarium was 800 francs and the work trifling: two extracts a month from a list of books furnished by the editor. But that very fact made Rousseau decline: 'My indifference for the thing would have frozen my pen and deadened my mind. They imagined I could write to order, like all other men of letters whereas I could never write except from passion.'[2] At the end of May 1761 he told Moultou that he had finished with the 'tumultuous business of authorship.'

---

[1] *C.G.* v, no. 987: '...I have detached myself absolutely from the party of the *philosophes*. I don't like people who preach irreligion and there you have already one crime they will not pardon me for. On the other hand, I condemn intolerance and I want unbelievers to be left in peace. Now, the devout party is not any more long-suffering than the other. So you can see into what kind of hands I've fallen.'

[2] *Conf.* 505: 'Mon indifférence pour la chose eût glacé ma plume et abruti mon esprit. On s'imaginait que je pouvais écrire par métier, comme tous les autres gens de lettres, au lieu que je ne sus jamais écrire que par passion.' Nevertheless, between 1746 and 1749, Rousseau ventured into journalism with *Le Persifleur*, in association with Diderot. They were to have written alternate numbers. Only the first appeared. It contains a self-portrait of Jean-Jacques, in the humorous style of *The Spectator*.

and, tormented by the fear of imminent death, begged his friend in that event to come to Paris and select from his papers the material for a complete edition of his writings. With *Emile* in mind, Rousseau warned the Genevan pastor that he would come across certain views on religion that might shock him.[1] In June he told Mme de Luxembourg about his children and asked her to trace the eldest through the records of the Foundlings' Hospital. Despite the most exhaustive inquiries, however, she had to inform Jean-Jacques in August that her search had been fruitless.

Though Frère Côme, or to give him his real name, Jean Baseilhac, had dispelled Rousseau's fears of the stone, the accident with the catheter in November 1761 seems to have aggravated his malady. For, in January 1762, he wrote to Moultou: '...day and night, I am not free from pain a single moment and it is driving me absolutely crazy.'[2] Moultou, who had just finished reading a private copy of *La Profession de foi*, was less distressed about his friend's health than about what would happen after the publication of *Emile*. In France, he foresaw, it would be savagely attacked both by the orthodox Catholics and by the *philosophes*. 'What an outcry and clamour your are going to excite in Geneva! How difficult it will be for your friends to defend you!'[3] But Rousseau, whose urethral canal was healing, laughed at these croakings, observing that his position in regard to the authorities could not be more regular. Of course, if trouble did arise, he could not decently implicate Malesherbes and the Luxembourgs. But the humane and hospitable French would never persecute a poor invalid preaching virtue and concord.[4] To Néaulme who was worried about the attitude of the Dutch government, he replied in the same optimistic vein. His book consolidated what was socially useful without destroying the rest. In April, a little more impressed by Moultou's persistence, he admitted that perhaps the un-

---

[1] *C.G.* vi, no. 1079 (29 May 1761).

[2] *C.G.* vii, no. 1255 (18 Jan. 1762): 'je ne suis ni jour et nuit, un seul instant sans souffrir ce qui m'aliène tout à fait la tête.'

[3] *C.G.* vii, no. 1268: 'Quels cris, quelles clameurs vous allez exciter à Genève. Que vos amis auront de la peine à vous défendre!'

[4] *C.G.* vii, no. 1280 (16 Feb. 1762).

believers and the *dévots* might try to incite the authorities against
him but such threats had never deterred Jean-Jacques from doing
what he thought right.[1]

The first hint of trouble, however, came from *Du Contrat
social*. Rey, on the advice of a Dutch magistrate, urged Rousseau
to remove his name from the title-page since the work embodied
principles which might ruin him in France. But Rousseau, who
knew that in May the importation of the *Contrat* had been
prohibited by Malesherbes, rejected Rey's advice. After all,
Holland was a Republic and his treatise was purely abstract and
speculative. That *Emile* might also cause trouble seems not to
have occurred to Rousseau for he wrote, at the end of May, to
the Chief of Police, Sartine, denouncing a pirated Lyons edition
of the book which was about to be hawked in Paris, under the
rose.[2] A few days later Malesherbes informed the police that he
had given Duchesne orders to stop the sale of *Emile*, acting no
doubt under pressure from a very high level. The machinery of
French law, once started, functioned with alarming rapidity.
Emile was denounced on 7 June to the Sorbonne. The same afternoon, Martin, the *curé* of Deuil, wrote to the maréchal de
Luxembourg that the Parlement intended to deal severely with
Rousseau who now informed Moultou that the only man in
France who believed in God was to be the victim of the defenders
of Christianity. Refusing, however, to be panicked by his
friends, he bravely decided to live up to his motto: *vitam impendere vero*. Next day, a warrant was issued for his arrest.
Mme de Luxembourg wrote urgently entreating Jean-Jacques,
who had gone off on a picnic with two Oratorians, to come at
once to the Château, bringing his papers. Her steward, La Roche,
would fetch him that night and explain her reasons. Rousseau
spent the evening as usual, reading a chapter of the Bible.
Either he did not receive her note or his memory is at fault
because, according to the *Confessions*,[3] the appearance of La
Roche at 2 a.m. on 9 June was a complete shock. A hurried discussion took place at the Château where a letter had arrived from
Conti warning them that Rousseau would be *décrété* or arrested by

[1] *C.G.* vii, no. 1341 (25 April 1762).
[2] *C.G.* vii, no. 1377 (28 May 1762).   [3] *Conf.* 571.

warrant that day. He spent the morning arranging his papers, some of which were set aside for his memoirs: the rest were handed for safe-keeping to the maréchal. In the afternoon, Jean-Jacques said goodbye to the tearful Thérèse, the Luxembourgs, the duchesse de Mirepoix and the comtesse de Boufflers who suggested England as a sanctuary. He set out at four in the afternoon in a cabriolet and passed, near Montmorency, the police-officers sent to arrest him. Rapidly crossing Paris, he stopped at the Château de Villeroi to obtain from the duke, who was Governor of Lyons, a safe-conduct to that town. At this point we must leave the fugitive for a time, bound not for Lyons but for Yverdun, there to seek refuge with 'Papa' (Daniel) Roguin, an old and dear friend. In Paris, *Emile* was being ceremoniously burnt at the foot of the great staircase of the Palais de Justice. That was on the eleventh of June: eight days later, Geneva followed the example of Paris, adding *Du Contrat social* to *Emile*. These and other major products of Rousseau's rustic meditations we shall discuss in the next two chapters. First, however, we may briefly consider four minor writings that belong roughly to the same period.

The *Essai sur l'origine des langues*, as Masson has shown,[1] was composed originally as a long Note to the *Second Discours* but, in 1761, it was enlarged, by the addition of various remarks on harmony and melody, into an independent essay. In 1763 it was divided into chapters with a view to publication; it was not printed, however, until 1781.

Speech, Rousseau thinks, cannot have originated in man's physical needs but in his passions, especially the passion of love. This idea may have been suggested to him by Condillac's *Essai sur l'origine des connaissances humaines* (1746). On the other hand, it fits into Rousseau's general picture of primitive times when man led a roving, independent existence and, having few contacts with his fellows, required only a sign language. Speech, therefore, belongs to the later early social phase described in the *Second Discours* and, Rousseau implies, must have resulted from a kind of social convention. Since language was originally

---

[1] *Ann.* IX, 48–9 (1913). See also XXIV, 95–119 (1935) for an interesting parallel by E. Claparède between Rousseau's theories and those of Jespersen.

designed to express emotions, it must have resembled song and was probably figurative. Its vocabulary was rich in synonyms but grammatically irregular. The first elements of speech were not words but phrases: or rather, the word had the sense of a whole proposition. When language came to be written, it became more intellectual and, therefore, deteriorated, having lost its original emotional quality. Spoken language is the only true language. How much Rousseau was indebted for these ideas to Condillac and other writers is a moot point. In the *Essai*, however, they are expressed with his customary eloquence and persuasive charm.

La Reine fantasque, published in 1758, is a fairy-tale no better and no worse than scores of others written in the eighteenth century. The style is agreeable but, even so, cannot relieve the essential banality of Rousseau's theme: the squabbles between the Queen, Fantasque, and her husband over the sex of the expected infant; the traditional malice of the fairy, Discrète, and the *dénouement* which presents the royal couple with twins, a Prince Raison and a Princess Caprice.

The four *Lettres à Sara* were composed, possibly in the spring of 1761, in order to prove, says Rousseau, that a man of fifty can write at least four passionate love-letters to a girl of twenty without forfeiting the good opinion of decent people. In fact, Rousseau retains our esteem and wins our sympathy, since the *Lettres à Sara* are merely a pretext for relating once again the pathetic story of his fruitless passion for Mme d'Houdetot.

As Jean-Jacques tells us, the piece entitled *De l'Imitation théâtrale* is simply a paraphrase of certain passages from Plato's *Republic* dealing with the relationship between reality and art. Rousseau wrote these pages originally for his *Lettre à d'Alembert sur les spectacles*, but found them unsuitable for that purpose. They were published as an opuscule in January 1764.

CHAPTER V

INDIAN SUMMER

Il n'y aura jamais qu'une Julie au monde. *La Nouvelle Héloïse.*

La Nouvelle Héloïse; Lettres morales; Lettre à d'Alembert sur les spectacles.

THE original title of Rousseau's novel was *Lettres de deux amants, habitants d'une petite ville au pied des Alpes.* Why, in the second edition it was altered to *Julie ou La Nouvelle Héloïse* is a matter for conjecture. As I have shown elsewhere, the Eloisa of history and Rousseau's Julie represent two very different concepts of sensibility.[1] Abelard's unhappy nun was a passionate, sensual woman tormented by the fear of Hell and eternal damnation. The theme of *La Nouvelle Héloïse* is quite different. It is reflected in the device appended to the frontispiece: *Aidé de la Sagesse, on se sauve de l'Amour dans les bras de la Raison.*[2] The choice of the ambiguous *sagesse* which applies equally to profane or divine wisdom is certainly not fortuitous. What probably induced Rousseau to change his first title was the current vogue for Colardeau's adaptation of Pope's *Eloisa,* called *La Lettre amoureuse d'Héloïse à Abailard*[3] in which the erotic aspect of the medieval Letters is brazenly exploited. In this art, the French poet rivals Jean-Jacques himself who was no doubt aware that the public which applauded Colardeau would be attracted even more strongly by the piquant sensuality of Saint-Preux's letters to Julie d'Etange.[4] That did not prevent him, in the instructive, dialogued *Préface* to the second edition from advertising his novel as a work of moral utility and, therefore, as an innovation in French fiction.

---

[1] *Modern Language Review,* XXXII, no. 4 (October 1937), 'Medieval and modern Sensibility'.

[2] 'With the help of Wisdom, one escapes from Love into the arms of Reason.'

[3] 1758.

[4] *Le Temple de Vénus* (Londres, 1777) includes a selection of these letters. The title of this anthology aptly describes its contents.

The average French novel, Rousseau observes, portrays ordinary people involved in a network of extraordinary situations and events. *La Nouvelle Héloïse*, on the contrary, reveals a little society of *âmes d'élite*, or 'dedicated souls', variously distinguished by their rare spiritual qualities: intense sensibility, the innate love of moral beauty, an exceptional sense of personal dignity, a unique concept of friendship and its sacred obligations. They live in a private spiritual world of their own. Originally celestial creatures born of Rousseau's day-dreams, they still retain, even when transposed to that inferior plane in which a novelist must place his characters, something of their primitive other-worldliness. As we are frequently reminded, they are 'hors de la règle commune' and may not therefore be judged by ordinary ethical standards. Thus, whilst an ordinary girl who loses her virginity out of wedlock cannot expect to be reintegrated in society, a *belle âme* like Julie d'Etange who has erred only through excess of natural pity will achieve complete social and spiritual rehabilitation. Moreover, in the role of wife, mother and chatelaine, she will serve as a model to women technically more chaste yet inferior in all other respects. As Julie herself complacently remarks, although quite a few ordinary lovers have managed to conquer a grand passion, she and Saint-Preux have purified and transfigured theirs into a beautiful, tender friendship.[1]

In an avowed attempt to bring his characters nearer to earth, Jean-Jacques situates them in a homely milieu, a country-house near Vevey, because, as he explains, people whose lives are passed in rustic solitude have different ways of seeing and feeling from urban dwellers. Always surrounded by the same objects, they have unusually intense sentiments and emotions. However, readers accustomed to the energetic, picturesque idiom of the traditional novel may, he warns us, find their modes of expression too natural, undramatic and often diffuse. When heart speaks direct to heart, one must not expect elegantly turned phrases. Genuine passion, Rousseau suggests, is communicated in transparent words, in a lyrical, disorderly style which exercises an irresistible appeal. Some of the hero's letters are, indeed, as

[1] *N.H.* vi (vi^e Partie), Lettre 6.

Rousseau says, *hymnes*: in these, love borrows the ardent language of religious devotion. *La Nouvelle Héloïse*, he continues, is unique for another reason. Its interest derives solely from the reactions to commonplace events of three people who follow invariably the contours of their natures which are unspoilt by commerce with urban sophistication.

Let us briefly review the 'natural and simple events' which form the texture of Rousseau's novel. The hero, Saint-Preux, is a youth of 20. Though a *roturier* or commoner, he is the son of a gallant officer killed in his country's service. For a year Saint-Preux has been acting as unpaid tutor to Julie d'Etange and her adoring cousin, Claire. Both are 18 and the daughters of country noblemen. Julie's father is with his regiment but is about to retire from the army. Her mother, a confirmed invalid, is a somewhat colourless woman, dominated by her irascible husband. The novel opens, like a classic tragedy, on a crisis. Saint-Preux confesses to Julie that for months he has been hopelessly in love with her. He is startled and delighted by the transformation produced in Julie by his declaration, for she loses her carefree gaiety and becomes sombre, pale and distraught. This does not, however, surprise Claire who reminds her cousin that their former governess, a Frenchwoman called La Chaillot, had always foreseen that once Julie's sensibility was aroused, she would be lost. Claire's reminder is distasteful to Julie who had always disliked La Chaillot and prides herself on her strength of mind. Precisely, however, because Julie is so rational she eventually falls, where a girl less sure of herself would have confided in her mother and escaped undamaged. As Claire points out, her cousin refuses to forgo the honour of a single-handed contest: 'you want to avoid the possibility of a lapse but not the honour of struggling.'[1] It will be observed that the cousins are not exactly rustic *ingénues*.

Meanwhile, Saint-Preux offers to go away but is told to remain. Driven almost frantic by Julie's apparent indifference, he darkly hints at suicide. Then Julie confesses her love but, terrified at her weakness, throws herself on the chivalry of

---

[1] *N.H.* i, 7: 'tu veux t'ôter le pouvoir de succomber mais non pas l'honneur de combattre.'

Saint-Preux. Claire, apprised of Julie's new and disturbing emotions is profoundly anxious, knowing her cousin's serious, passionate nature. With her it will be all or nothing. For a time, the lovers drift along in the happy illusion that they have found in their Platonic relationship the secret of perennial felicity. Naturally, however, the ardent Saint-Preux quickly tires of his impossible role and, with a sigh of relief, agrees to entrust their common destiny to Julie. The latter, rashly sure of her virtue, plays with fire. To reward her faithful Galahad, she arranges a rendezvous in a certain *bosquet* where, in Claire's presence the lover receives his first embrace. This 'fatal, mortal kiss' transforms the *fin amant* of courtly romance into the exigent lover of actuality. In language charged with sensual, lyrical passion, Saint-Preux swears that he will expire either at Julie's feet or in her arms.

Her father's return and his disparaging remarks about the low-born tutor bring Julie face to face with reality. Prudently, she orders her lover to pay a long overdue visit to his native place. At this point it becomes clear that she will always be the stronger vessel. She insists, for example, on paying for Saint-Preux's travelling expenses, scornfully exposing the fallacy of his scruples about taking money from a woman. Her poet-lover, alone in the mountains of Le Valais, dreams voluptuously of married bliss in a rustic sanctuary. Nature, to be perfect, requires only the eternal presence of Julie who realises now that her father will never consent to a *mésalliance*. The passion of both lovers is intensified by separation and a growing sense of hopelessness saps Julie's courage. At this critical moment, she receives a despairing letter from Saint-Preux. Winter is approaching and the desolation of his soul seems to be reflected in the bleakness of Meillerie. From his rocky eyrie he looks down on Vevey and pictures Julie the dutiful daughter, loved and cared for by her family whilst he, the homeless orphan, languishes, by her cruel decree, outside the gates of paradise. In a furious, heart-rending appeal, he implores Julie to desert her parents and follow him. Otherwise, he will hurl himself from the beetling crags. He learns from Claire that she is dangerously ill, calling out for him in her delirium. On her recovery, Julie hears that her father proposes to 'sell' her to the baron de Wolmar, an old regimental comrade who had once saved his life. Now, seeing herself trapped in a moral impasse, she gives herself to her lover. 'Il fallait donner la mort à l'auteur de mes jours, à mon amant ou à moi-même. Sans savoir ce que je faisais, je choisis ma propre infortune.'[1] Tortured by remorse, still more by the loss of her self-esteem, Julie has full need of Claire's consoling letters: Julie, her cousin insists, is really much more chaste than she herself who could not have struggled so long. And Saint-Preux tries to lull her conscience with the romantic doctrine that they are married in the sight of God. She is his mystic bride, his 'cold and mysterious sweetheart'.[2] But Julie, unlike the original Eloisa, is incapable of glorying in her surrender. They are now, she tells Saint-Preux, just ordinary lovers since they have stooped to enjoy a pleasure within the reach of the basest mortals.

For various interesting reasons, Rousseau departs here from the medieval story. There is no public exposure of Julie's lapse and its consequences though she toys with the idea of begetting a child and of extorting parental consent to her marriage under threat of a public declaration. A new character is now introduced, an English peer called Lord Edouard Bomston whom her lover, out of jealousy, challenges to a duel. It is averted when Julie writes to Bomston, confessing her relations with Saint-Preux and threatening to commit suicide if he is killed. The magnanimous Englishman not only apologises to the younger man in the presence of witnesses, but offers to settle the young couple on one of his estates. 'Vos deux âmes', he says, 'sont si extraordinaires qu'on n'en peut juger par les règles communes.'[3] Bomston imprudently approaches the baron, offering to settle a third of his fortune on Saint-Preux. Julie's father, in a towering rage, strikes his daughter who has a miscarriage which is luckily concealed from her parents.

Now the unmanly despair of Saint-Preux is sharply contrasted

---

[1] *N.H.* I, 29: 'I had to destroy the author of my being, my lover or myself. Without knowing what I was doing, I chose my own misfortune.'

[2] 'Froide et mystérieuse amante.'

[3] *N.H.* I, 60: 'Your two souls are so extraordinary that they cannot be judged by the ordinary rules.'

with the energy and resource of his mistress who orders him off to Paris. Suddenly, Mme d'Etange discovers Julie's guilty correspondence and falls dangerously ill. Saint-Preux is persuaded by Claire to write, promising to cease all relations with her daughter. Mme d'Etange then realises the unique quality of their love, 'hors de la règle commune', and dies regretting the cruel fate that makes their marriage impossible. Tortured by remorse, Julie accuses Saint-Preux of having made her a wicked daughter and he is haunted by the idea that perhaps the death of Mme d'Etange lies at his door. Claire reassures him on this point: Julie's mother died of a long-standing malady aggravated by her husband's brutality. Inconsolable, Julie demands and obtains her lover's permission to dispose of her hand according to her father's wishes. Stricken with smallpox, she thinks, in her delirium, that Saint-Preux is at her bedside and takes this as a dreadful omen until assured by Claire that it was no hallucination. Saint-Preux, finally convinced that Julie's life and honour are at stake, leaves with Bomston for Paris in an agony of grief. He is prevented from committing suicide only by his friend's irresistible logic and eloquence. Julie's farewell letter discloses her tragic moral dilemma. At every stage, it seems, the hand of Providence is visible. God, to crown His mercies, grants her divine grace because, just before the marriage ceremony, she undergoes a spiritual transformation. She thinks of Saint-Preux now only as the lover of her soul and will respect the sanctity of her vows to Wolmar.

Six years elapse during which Saint-Preux has sailed on distant seas with Anson's expedition. Claire is now a widow with one small daughter: Julie de Wolmar is the happy mother of two boys. But her conscience troubles her. Though no longer in love with Saint-Preux who is probably dead, ought she not to confess their former relations to her husband? She does so on learning that the wanderer has returned safe and sound. But Wolmar, as Claire had guessed, had known of the affair before his marriage and indeed possesses the fatal letters. Convinced that Saint-Preux is now only in love with a memory, with the non-existent Julie d'Etange, he decides privately to employ the young man as tutor to his children, envisaging a happy *ménage à trois*: ex-lover, wife and husband. Saint-Preux is therefore invited to their country-house, *Clarens*, but warned to search his heart before accepting the invitation which is endorsed by Julie. Wolmar, we learn, is an honest atheist and, it would seem, a psychologist of the associationist school. Having observed, presumably, that the simplest psychic states occur as accessories to well-defined physical phenomena, he concludes that Saint-Preux, once he has perceived the changes wrought in Julie by time, will realise that the love he preserves for his mistress, Julie d'Etange, no longer applies to Mme de Wolmar, the wife and mother. 'I wipe out one picture by another,' says Wolmar, 'and cover the past with the present.'[1] That is why Saint-Preux is invited to *Clarens* and thrown into the daily society of Julie who also benefits from her husband's experiment. Finally, in order to prove to them that they are cured of their former love, Wolmar goes away for a week, leaving them alone. His very logical theory is almost wrecked, however, by a contingency he could not possibly have foreseen. During an outing on Lake Geneva, a storm drives Saint-Preux and Julie to seek refuge at Meillerie where, ten years previously, he had suffered the agonies of frustrated passion. Though summer has now transformed the natural scene, he writes to Bomston: 'I realised how powerfully the presence of objects can reanimate the violent emotions by which one was agitated near them.'[2] But Julie's virtue withstands his supreme, passionate appeal. They row back to *Clarens* in the moonlight. In a final convulsion of rage and despair, Saint-Preux is tempted to hurl himself and Julie into the lake. But his frenzy subsides in a torrent of passionate weeping and, to all appearances Wolmar's psychological experiment has been successful.

Yet, when Julie discovers that Claire is in love with Saint-Preux, her behaviour is governed by a subconscious resolve to prevent a marriage which she undertakes, however, to negotiate. In this she succeeds by employing a technique which, in anyone

[1] *N.H.* IV, 14: 'J'efface un tableau par un autre et couvre le passé du présent.'
[2] *N.H.* IV, 17: 'J'éprouvai combien la présence des objets peut ranimer puissamment les sentiments violents dont on fut agité près d'eux.'

less perfect, could only be described as refined bitchery. By marshalling certain objections and unpleasant criticisms which she imputes to those 'sordid souls' whom Claire must of course ignore, Julie effectively nips the projected union in the bud, eliciting at the same time from Saint-Preux the vow that nothing will ever efface from his heart the memory of their 'first and unique love'. Now ripe for apotheosis, Mme de Wolmar trumpets her swan-song: 'Je suis trop heureuse; le bonheur m'ennuie. Malheur à qui n'a plus rien à désirer!'[1] Her soul now yearns for a greater, more durable felicity.

In saving her child from drowning, Julie contracts pneumonia and on her deathbed reveals, if possible, added virtues. Thanks to the special grace of God, she is snatched from this world at the moment of supreme perfection. For, as her posthumous letter to Saint-Preux discloses, she has never ceased to love him. But, fortunately, Julie only became conscious of this situation when it could no longer be a danger to her virtue. During her married life she had always thought and lived blamelessly. 'La vertu me reste sans tâche et l'amour m'est resté sans remords.'[2] But her insatiable egotism must have hostages in the world she has left. So Mme de Wolmar bequeaths Claire to Saint-Preux but with the reminder that the memory of Julie will always be interposed between their two souls. Ironically, this symbolic marriage is frustrated by Claire who warns Saint-Preux that any man who, having been loved by a Julie, should dare to contemplate marriage with another, is a coward and a cad. One wonders with a certain malice whether the ghost of Mme de Wolmar really applauded her cousin's gesture. After all, it must be rather tiresome to be outdone in sensibility even by one's best friend and adoring understudy. Wolmar, it need scarcely be mentioned, experiences a change of heart, and the three *âmes d'élite*, to be joined shortly by Lord Edouard, dedicate their lives to the cult of Julie de Wolmar.

This was not the ending originally designed for *La Nouvelle Héloïse*, an extremely important fact disclosed in a letter from

---

[1] *N.H.* vi, 8: 'I am too happy; I am sated with happiness. Woe betide anyone who has nothing left to desire!'

[2] *N.H.* vi, 12: 'My virtue remains unspotted and my love without remorse.'

Deleyre to Rousseau dated 23 November 1756, in which he asks:

> Have you got to the end of your novel yet? Are your people drowned? You are very wise to adopt this course because, as you have depicted them, this earth is not worthy to possess them; and when one has no great rewards to give to virtue, one must overwhelm it with misfortunes in order to render it interesting and to make people flee from virtue whilst adoring it. For, after all, who will have the courage to follow it through all the perils with which you surround it?[1]

Now, that is the *dénouement* implicit in the last chapter of Part IV which describes the momentous boating excursion on Lake Geneva. Here, presumably, Julie and Saint-Preux were to have perished during the storm or perhaps as a result of the hero's mad impulse. When and how did Rousseau abandon this ending? We know that, as late as February 1758, he intended to publish his novel in four parts only, but had composed a fifth solely for Mme d'Houdetot and never to be printed.[2] Yet, in September of the same year, he announced to his publisher Rey that *La Nouvelle Héloïse* was completely finished and consisted of six parts.[3] But in November 1760 we find Rousseau anxiously consulting Duclos as to whether or not he should suppress the fifth and sixth parts. The latter replied that this would be a great mistake and suggested, moreover, an additional part containing the *Histoire des aventures de Lord Edouard Bomston*.[4] The novel was, however, already in print.

What conclusions are we to draw from these facts? M. Mornet, who appears not to have known of Deleyre's letter, advances the following theory about the composition of *La Nouvelle Héloïse*. By the end of 1756, he thinks, Rousseau had composed 'a simple love story about a seduction and a departure':[5] the idea of Julie's marriage and of the *ménage à trois* at Clarens only occurred to

---

[1] *C.G.* II, no. 318: 'Etes-vous encore à la fin du Roman? Vos gens sont-ils noyés? Vous faites fort bien de prendre ce parti, car la terre n'est pas digne de les posséder tels que vous les avez dépeints; et quand on n'a pas de grandes récompenses à donner à la vertu, il faut l'accabler de malheurs pour la rendre intéressante et la faire fuir en l'adorant. Car enfin qui aura le courage de la suivre à travers les périls dont vous l'environnez?'

[2] *C.G.* III, no. 471 (to Mme d'Houdetot, 13 Feb. 1758).   [3] *C.G.* IV, no. 539.

[4] *C.G.* V, nos. 924, 931, 932.

[5] In t. I, pt. II, ch. 1, of his classic edition of *La Nouvelle Héloïse* (Hachette, 1925): 'un simple roman d'amour, l'histoire d'une séduction et d'un départ.'

Rousseau after he saw Julie in Mme d'Houdetot. We must therefore ignore, according to M. Mornet, what Rousseau narrates in the *Confessions* about his original plan for *La Nouvelle Héloïse*. In short, his theory is that until May 1757, when Jean-Jacques fell in love with Mme d'Houdetot, he had not conceived the idea of writing a novel about a young girl who allows herself to be seduced yet, as a married woman, finds the strength to conquer her love and recovers her virtue. For various reasons, I find it impossible to accept this view. Admittedly, Rousseau's memory often deceived him in regard to dates but it is incredible that he should have completely forgotten the original theme of his novel. Again, from Deleyre's letter, it is reasonable to suppose that his original *dénouement*, the drowning of the two lovers, was connected with the boating excursion which closes Part IV. Further, his avowed intention in February 1758 to publish his novel in four parts shows that at that date, although he had composed a fifth for Sophie's private edification, he had not yet written the sixth in which Julie alone dies, not from drowning but as a result of having saved her child from drowning. Finally, why must we disbelieve Rousseau's statement in the *Confessions* that he had always intended his love story to be a work of moral utility? In the circumstances, nothing seems more natural.

With all deference to the authority of my eminent colleague and friend, M. Mornet,[1] I suggest that it is possible to interpret the available facts without impugning the validity of the *Confessions*. It is evident from Rousseau's youthful love letters and, above all, from the tone of the first two parts of *La Nouvelle Héloïse*, that it was not Mme d'Houdetot who first taught him, as M. Mornet claims, the meaning and the authentic idiom of passionate love. On the contrary, she was merely the screen upon which Jean-Jacques projected his actual state of soul at the beginning of 1757. We must not forget that there had been previous opportunities for him to fall in love with Sophie; but for that to happen, she had to pass at a critical moment into the field of a consciousness magnetised by passion. Thereafter, the

---

[1] These pages were written before the recent death of this great scholar, who possessed a unique knowledge of eighteenth-century French literature and ideas.

pattern of Rousseau's relations with Mme d'Houdetot and Saint-Lambert gradually influenced the tone and design of his novel. His daily conversations with Sophie made him realise that he had not fully developed the character of Julie de Wolmar. After all, his 'youthful reminiscences' had never included a serious passionate affair with a married woman,[1] complicated by the sacred obligations of friendship towards her husband, for so he regarded Saint-Lambert. From that moment it became clear to Rousseau that his original *dénouement* was unconvincing. He abandoned it, therefore, and gave to the last chapter of Part IV its present form. That this change had already been made by the end of January 1758 is implicit in a letter from Deleyre to Rousseau:

> Cependant le Citoyen, sans demander ce qu'on dit ou qu'on pense de lui, voit tous les jours le petit étang qui ramène ses pensées aux bords du fameux lac, ou la pauvre Julie faillit se jeter; je m'en souviens bien. Etait-ce elle pourtant ou son amant?[2]

As we have noted, Rousseau still intended, in February 1758, to close his novel with Part IV, Julie and Saint-Preux having, by a supreme effort of will, sacrificed their love to virtue and reason. But it will be recalled that in May his dream of a Platonic *ménage à trois* was shattered when Mme d'Houdetot wrote that their relations must cease. That, as we know, was a cruel wound to his pride. He discovered, however, a marvellous specific. It was, of course, alien to the 'natural order' of things that a Saint-Lambert should be preferred to a Jean-Jacques or a Wolmar to a Saint-Preux. He conceived, therefore, a *dénouement* which, at the twelfth hour, restores the natural order without detracting from the moral perfection of Julie de Wolmar. On her deathbed, she discovers her illusion. Deep in her heart, she had always been faithful to the lover intended for her by Nature. So much for the rational theories of the too confident Wolmar who, like Saint-Lambert, had rashly thrown his wife, so to speak, into the arms of his rival. It is, therefore, pleasant to be able to record that Mme d'Houdetot remained the faithful mistress of

---

[1] One cannot so describe his *passade* with Mme de Larnage.

[2] *C.G.* III, no. 469 (25 Jan. 1758): 'The Citizen, however, without wondering what people say or think about him, sees every day the little pond which carries his thoughts to the famous lake into which Julie nearly threw herself. I remember it well. Was it she, however, or her lover?' (It was, of course, Saint-Preux.)

Saint-Lambert until 1803 when, at the age of 87, he died in her arms.

Rousseau lacked the kind of creative imagination which enables the born novelist or playwright to dissociate his personal experience from the fictitious life of his characters. So, whilst *La Nouvelle Héloïse*, if judged purely as a novel, seldom achieves the illusion of reality, it displays, perhaps more completely than any other of his works, the soul of Jean-Jacques Rousseau. In his twenties, passionately in love with a girl pledged to another man, he wrote despairingly:

> Mais, Hélas en me plaignant de mes tourments, je m'en prépare de nouveaux; je ne puis penser à mon amour sans que mon cœur et mon imagination s'échauffe et quelque résolution que je fasse de vous obéir en commençant mes lettres, je me sens ensuite emporté au delà de ce que vous exigez de moi; auriez-vous la dureté de m'en punir?[1]

Prefigured in these words is the sentimental history of Saint-Preux and the Jean-Jacques with whom Mme d'Houdetot had to part because their liaison was becoming 'trop orageuse'. In *La Nouvelle Héloïse*, fact and fiction, remembered experience and its extension in Rousseau's imagination are hopelessly interfused. Take, for example, that incident in the cherry-orchard at Thônes which inspired the scene in the *bosquet* where Julie bestows on Saint-Preux the innocent but fatal kiss that leads to disaster:

> mais que devins-je un moment après que je sentis...la main me tremble...un doux frémissement...la bouche de rose...la bouche de Julie...se poser, se presser sur la mienne et mon corps serré dans tes bras! Non, le feu du ciel n'est pas plus vif ni plus prompt que celui qui vint à l'instant m'embraser.[2]

Now turn to the letter written but never sent to Mme d'Houdetot by Jean-Jacques after the scene enacted under the acacia tree at

[1] *C.G.* I, no. 12 (à Mlle * * *, 1735 or 1741): 'But alas! in bewailing my torments, I pave the way for others. I cannot think of my love without my heart and my imagination catching fire and whatever resolve I make to obey you on beginning my letters, I feel myself then being swept on beyond what you demand of me; would you be so harsh as to punish me for it?'

[2] *N.H.* I, 14: 'But what became of me a moment afterwards when I felt...my hand trembles...a sweet shuddering...your rosy lips...Julie's lips...pressing on mine and my body clasped tightly in your arms! No. The fire of Heaven is not more intense or more swift than the fire which at that moment consumed me.'

Eaubonne: 'Quoi! mes lèvres brûlantes ne déposeront plus sur ton cœur mon âme avec mes baisers! Quoi! je n'éprouverai plus ce frémissement céleste, ce feu rapide et dévorant qui, plus prompt que l'éclair... moment! moment inexprimable!'[1] Finally, re-read, in the *Correspondance* for 1735 the following typical passage from the love-letter already quoted: 'Dieux! si j'avais pu parvenir à cette charmante possession, j'en serais mort assurément! et comment trouver assez de ressources dans l'âme pour résister à ce torrent de plaisirs!'[2]

In the presence of these texts, I cannot endorse M. Mornet's view that Rousseau's infatuation for Mme d'Houdetot transformed what had been up till then merely 'an idyllic dream', 'a tender, graceful and mendacious romance' into 'the novel of passion'.[3] On the contrary, these extracts confirm what Rousseau has to say on this subject in the *Confessions*:

Everybody was persuaded that it was impossible to express so vividly feelings one had not personally experienced or depict thus the transports of love unless they came straight from one's heart. In that they were right and it is certain that I composed this novel in the throes of the most burning ecstasies. But they were wrong in thinking that it had needed real objects to produce them; they were far from understanding to what an extent I am capable of being inflamed by purely imaginary beings. But for a few reminiscences of my youth and Mme d'Houdetot, the loves I felt and described would have had only sylphs as their object. I wished neither to confirm nor refute an error which was to my advantage.[4]

[1] *C.G.* III, no. 380 (approx. 15 Oct. 1757): 'What! shall my burning lips no longer place my soul on your heart with my kisses! What! Am I never again to experience that celestial shuddering, that rapid, devouring flame which, swifter than lightning....Oh! inexpressible moment!'

[2] *C.G.* I, no. 12: 'Ye Gods! If I had managed to attain that charming possession, I should assuredly have died of it! And how could I find sufficient resources in my soul to resist that torrent of pleasures!'

[3] *Rousseau, l'Homme et l'Oeuvre* (Boivin), p. 70: 'un rêve d'idylle...un roman tendre, gracieux et menteur...le roman de la passion.'

[4] *Conf.* 539: 'Tout le monde était persuadé qu'on ne pouvait exprimer si vivement des sentiments qu'on n'aurait point éprouvés ni peindre ainsi les transports de l'amour, que d'après son propre cœur. En cela l'on avait raison, et il est certain que j'écrivis ce roman dans les plus brûlantes extases; mais on se trompait en pensant qu'il avait fallu des objets réels pour les produire; on était loin de concevoir à quel point je puis m'enflammer pour des êtres imaginaires. Sans quelques réminiscences de jeunesse et Mme d'Houdetot, les amours que j'ai sentis et décrits n'auraient été qu'avec des sylphides. Je ne voulus ni confirmer ni détruire une erreur qui m'était avantageuse.'

Now, as we have noted, this tallies exactly with Rousseau's earlier account in the *Confessions*, of the role played by Mme d'Houdetot in the evolution of his novel. She did not, as M. Mornet claims, 'reveal' to Jean-Jacques the meaning of passionate love. He merely transferred to her the flaming passion already inspired in him by his heroine. Nor was the renunciation theme the work of Mme d'Houdetot though it is tempting, in retrospect, to ascribe it to Rousseau's illusory picture of their relationship. In fact, the renunciation motif is implicit in the first part of *La Nouvelle Héloïse* where Julie learns of her father's intention to marry her to Wolmar. As we have observed, however, the novel most probably owes its final *dénouement* to the author's relations with Mme d'Houdetot and Saint-Lambert. But where the influence of Sophie is even more strikingly reflected is in the progressive spiritualisation of the heroine who begins to reveal, after the fourth part, a remarkable likeness to Rousseau's idealised portrait of Mme d'Houdetot in the *Lettres morales* which he composed in the winter months of 1757–8. It so happens that the following passage occurs in the novel but it would fit equally well into the context of the *Lettres morales*. Saint-Preux writes from *Clarens* to Bomston:

> Il n'y aura jamais qu'une Julie au monde. La Providence a veillé sur elle et rien de ce qui la regarde n'est un effet du hasard. Le Ciel semble l'avoir donnée à la terre pour y montrer à la fois l'excellence dont une âme humaine est susceptible et le bonheur dont elle peut jouir dans l'obscurité de la vie privée sans le secours des vertus éclatantes qui peuvent l'élever au-dessus d'elle-même ni de la gloire qui peut les honorer.[1]

In these last two parts, Rousseau is situated once more on the moral plane which he abandoned, in the spring of 1756, to compose those passionate love-letters which display his amazing flair for the image or epithet that intensifies the carnality of Saint-Preux's sensations. Not a trace now remains of that

---

[1] *N.H.* v, 2: 'There will never be more than one Julie in the world. Providence watched over her and nothing that concerns her is a result of chance. Heaven seems to have given her to our earth so as to demonstrate the excellence of which a human soul is capable and also the happiness it can enjoy in the obscurity of private life without the help, either of the dazzling virtues which may lift it above itself or of the fame by which they may be honoured.'

'erotic frenzy'. Instead, Rousseau glorifies the love that has been purified by suffering; the sweetness of a friendship which is most eloquently communicated in its silences; the happiness that resides in the daily fulfilment of humble, domestic tasks; the charity that finds an outlet in practical acts of kindness; the serene faith in God that robs death of its sting.

In this process of glorifying Julie de Wolmar, the author greatly enlarged the original design of his novel which was to show merely how Julie the married woman recovered the virtue she had lost by her pre-marital lapse. She is now not only virtuous, but a unique model whom few women will have the courage to emulate but whom they will involuntarily admire.[1] How, one might ask, was such a transformation effected without a reversal of the traditional moral values? Rousseau implies that there is no question of a transformation. What happens in the church where the heroine stands at the altar is an act of renovation by which she is restored to her real self, her primitive innocence. Deeply impressed by the prevailing atmosphere of holiness, by the dim light and the hush that falls upon the congregation, she seems to hear the voice of God in her pastor's exhortations. With a shudder of awe, Julie feels that the 'all-seeing eye' is scrutinising her soul. These sensations are followed by a sudden 'inner revolution', a reorientation of her emotions. Under the influence of this 'unseen Power', the disorder in her soul is stilled, its passions re-established 'according to the law of duty and nature'.[2] Her heart, Rousseau suggests, is now in harmony with her will, her whole being engaged in the vows she now pronounces. Julie sees the marriage bond as a new state which will purify her soul and restore it to its original essence. She feels, as it were, reborn, 'freshly emerged from the hands of Nature'. And to test the quality of her conversion, she asks for an hour of solitude and self-contemplation. Deliberately, she thinks of Saint-Preux and, to her ineffable joy, finds that although her love for him persists, it has changed its nature. She can dwell on his image with a quiet conscience, with emotions

---

[1] *N. H.* v, 2: 'que peu de femmes voudront imiter, mais qu'elles aimeront en dépit d'elles.'

[2] *N.H.* iii, 18: 'selon la loi du devoir et de la nature.'

drained of sensual desire, shame or humiliation. From this new plane Julie views with horror the road she might have followed, realising the fallacy of that 'inner feeling' which all lovers think they experience. For, having once lapsed from innocence, what guarantee was there that she would have remained eternally faithful to Saint-Preux? A single lapse can initiate the habit of vice. But the hand of God mercifully intervened, saving her from that fatal second step, preserving her reputation, on the brink of the abyss. As to how this act of renovation occurred, Julie is not quite clear. She desired it intensely and God did the rest. A soul once corrupted, she is inclined to believe, is doomed to permanent corruption without a sudden inner revolution such as she experienced. It is granted, Julie implies, only to certain privileged souls, a doctrine repudiated by her lover as incompatible with divine justice. Since her letter initiates a dialogue with Saint-Preux which is pursued in the sixth part, it might be convenient, at this point, to consider their views on various questions connected with the religious life. However, this section of *La Nouvelle Héloïse* is clearly only a prelude to *La Profession de foi du vicaire savoyard* which represents the *summa* of Rousseau's religious thought. The dialogue between Julie and Saint-Preux is deliberately inconclusive and the author himself does not take sides. It becomes clear, however, that he rejects the dogma of original sin. It is also significant that Julie and her lover leave Christ and the Redemption out of their discussion which centres on the nature of God, free-will, the function of prayer and divine grace. Only once does the author allow Julie to utter the word *péché* and then only in a traditional formula, when she declares to the pastor that she is bringing to God 'ma vie entière pleine de péchés et de fautes mais exempte des remords de l'impie et des crimes du méchant'.[1] Even so, it might be objected, the admission contained in the first part of her statement is virtually cancelled in the second; for what is a consciousness of sin which excludes that of wickedness? But in Rousseau's lexicon the word *méchant* implies a deliberate intention to harm others. And Julie is not really conscious of having

---

[1] *N.H.* vi, 11: 'My whole life full of sins and faults, but exempt from the remorse of impiety and of the crimes of the wicked.'

sinned: she does not really think of her moral lapse as *un péché* and normally refers to it as *une faute* or *une erreur*.

How are we to interpret the divine act which, according to Julie, lifted the veil of error and restored her to herself despite herself?[1] Were she a Jansenist, one might compare it to the victorious delectation of grace which surmounts the delectation of that concupiscence whose chief property, says Saint Augustine, is to attach us to the search of an elusive good incapable of bringing us anything but misery. Yet, although the notion of predestination is implicit in Julie's concept of divine grace, can one describe it as the 'prevenient, operating and co-operating' grace of Saint Augustine? No doubt it predisposes her will to seek conformity with the divine Will, thus enabling it to co-operate in the work of salvation. On the other hand, the Augustinian doctrine is incompatible with the usual concept of free-will, of a will free to determine itself, and on this point Julie eventually finds herself in conflict with Saint-Preux. Meanwhile, whilst admitting that God gave us liberty, she describes Him as the Being 'qui soutient ou détruit quand il lui plaît par nos propres forces la liberté qu'il nous donne.'[2] Possibly the key to her cryptic statement is to be found in Rousseau's favourite theologian, Fénelon, who says that whilst the idea of Man deprived of liberty and abandoned by God is contrary to the divine order and goodness, it is not contrary to His order to suppose that God leaves to Man, succoured by grace, the choice of making himself happy by virtue or miserable by sin so that if Man is deprived of the celestial reward, it is because he rejects it whilst it is, so to speak, within his grasp. Man, as the work of God, cannot have the perfection of his Architect. Probably, like Fénelon, Julie believes that God suffers a flaw in his creatures so as to have the glory of repairing it by mercy.[3] Her greatest source of consolation lies in the thought that God knows our human limitations.

Saint-Preux, who has also read Fénelon, violently rejects Julie's suggestion that divine grace is accorded to special, chosen

---

[1] *N.H.* iii, 18: 'qui lève à mes yeux le voile de l'erreur et me rend à moi-même malgré moi-même.'

[2] 'Who sustains or destroys when it pleases Him, by our own strength, the freedom He gives us.'

[3] *Sur le culte de Dieu*, ch. 3.

individuals, a doctrine which is an insult, he thinks, to divine justice. If it is in the Bible, he would rather believe the Bible to be wrong than accept it. The Supreme Being, in creating Man, endowed him with all the faculties necessary to carry out His will: reason, to know the Good; conscience, to love it and liberty, to choose it. Divine grace consists in these gifts. Here, Saint-Preux merely summarises the views of Fénelon who says that life is continual grace. Saint-Preux implies that Julie had no need of an 'inner revolution', of an infusion of supernatural grace; she had only to follow the deepest instincts of her own nature in order to be impeccable. That is, of course, sheer Pelagianism. What alarms Saint-Preux is the suspicion that Mme de Wolmar is drifting into Quietism about which we shall have more to say in the next chapter.

Rousseau, in portraying the special quality of the heroine's piety seems to follow a path traced out by Fénelon. For Julie, the love of God, is a necessary extension of her excessive sensibility. Her love, being infinite, requires an infinite object. On the other hand, since the heart attaches itself only through the intermediary of the senses and the imagination, she despairs of ever gaining contact with the divine Essence. As Rousseau observes in a footnote obviously inspired by Fénelon, one must 'fatigue' the soul in order to lift it up to the sublime idea of God.[1] Here Fénelon's precept is a constant fidelity to prayer: the mind, by constant exercise, will acquire facility.[2] Less ambitious, Julie prefers to diminish the divine majesty by interposing tangible objects between it and her mind. Unable to contemplate God in His Essence, she loves Him in His works though always painfully conscious that such an interested form of gratitude is a poor substitute for pure love. Still, her rough and ready cult brings God within her purview and saves her, probably, from the extremes of mysticism. At any rate, Rousseau interjects, Julie does not, like Saint Theresa, confuse profane and divine love: '. . . if the God of the universe eludes her feeble vision, she sees everywhere the common Father of men.'[3]

---

[1] N.H. v, 5.   [2] Discours sur la prière.
[3] N.H. v: 'Si le Dieu de l'univers échappe à ses faibles yeux, elle voit partout le père commun des hommes.'

In her final phase, Julie experiences a new and strange emotion which she calls 'le dégoût du bien-être', the ennui that comes from a happiness so complete as to leave nothing more in life to be desired. 'Le pays des chimères est en ce monde le seul digne d'être habité et tel est le néant des choses que, hors l'Etre existant par lui-même, il n'y a rien de beau que ce qui n'est pas.'[1] Mme de Wolmar has everything she could desire. Could any woman, she asks, have more sensibility or love her father, children, friends and neighbours more dearly? Or be better loved by them? Lead a life more to her taste; be freer to choose another mode of life; enjoy better health; have more resources against ennui; more ties linking her with society? And yet, she sighs; '. . .j'y vis inquiète; mon cœur ignore ce qui lui manque; il désire sans savoir quoi.'[2] In an attempt to escape from this hopeless state, her avid soul seeks refreshment in the contemplation of God, the source of all being and feeling, in the vision of an existence that has nothing to do with the passions of the body. These pseudo-mystic *élans* have a tonic effect on Julie's spirit which loses its languor and aridity and becomes infused with new energy. I use the expression 'pseudo-mystic' because it is clear from the letter which Julie asks Saint-Preux to read after her death, that she had never ceased to love him. Hers is not, therefore, a truly mystic soul which has eliminated from its substance all that is earthy and impure so as to become God's instrument. Viewed in retrospect, in the light of Julie's admission: 'One day more, perhaps, and I might have been guilty,'[3] her pious ecstasy, as she admits, is simply 'un état agréable' or as Wolmar puts it more crudely, 'an opiate for the soul'.

Unique in her life, Julie is unique in her last hours which furnish Rousseau with the excuse for a veritable orgy of sensibility. He alludes casually to certain doctrinal matters on which the heroine and her minister do not see eye to eye. However,

---

[1] *N.H.* vi, 8: 'The land of phantasy is in this world the only one worth living in and such is the nothingness of things that, outside the Being existing in Himself, nothing is beautiful save what is not.'

[2] *Ibid.*: '. . .I live anxiously; my heart knows not what it lacks; it knows not what it desires.'

[3] *N.H.* vi, 12: 'Un jour de plus, peut-être, et j'étais coupable.'

the latter exclaims admiringly: 'Madame...I thought I was instructing you, but it is you who are teaching me. I have nothing more to say to you. You have the true faith, that which inspires the love of God.'[1] What is the true faith? According to the dying Julie, she is still a member of the Genevan communion. Yet, significantly, she does not once, in her profession of faith, mention the name of Christ. She has, in fact, no need of a Mediator: her salvation is entirely a matter between God and herself. She dispenses also with Revelation, witness her remark that she has never pretended to believe anything in Holy Writ which her reason could not accept. Julie modestly allows, however, that she may have been wrong. But what really matters to God is the purity of her intentions. And He is too kind and just to expect a degree of enlightenment surpassing that which He has bestowed on her. In short, if God had intended us to believe what is rationally absurd we should have been endowed with a special faculty for that purpose. Yet, whilst rejecting the beliefs of the spiritualists, Julie does not find it absurd to suppose that the soul, liberated from the body, hovers round those who were dear to it on earth, in order to know what they are thinking and feeling. For this immediate communication, she says, resembles that by which God reads our thoughts and by which, reciprocally, we shall read His when we meet Him face to face in the after life.

Essentially, Julie's creed rests on the belief that God's kindness and clemency is always greater than our guiltiness provided we have always sincerely loved Him and tried, according to our lights, to seek that which conforms to His glory and truth. Therefore, she prepares to meet her Creator without fear, serenely confident that she will enjoy eternal happiness because she has always striven to live so as never to require to think about dying. Her death, exclaims her pastor, is as beautiful as her life. Having lived for charity, she dies a martyr to maternal love. Mme de Wolmar, in her last hours, cordially endorses his strictures on Catholicism, that venal religion which, for material gain, exploits the terrors of the dying, selling paradise to the

[1] *N.H.* VI, 11: 'Madame...je croyais vous instruire, et c'est vous qui m'instruisez. Je n'ai plus rien à vous dire. Vous avez la véritable foi, celle qui fait aimer Dieu.'

rich and thus transporting to the very gates of the other world the inequality that reigns on earth. The dying Julie, on the contrary, radiates joy and sweetness in a bedchamber gay with flowers, its windows opened to admit the summer breezes, surrounded by her adoring subjects. In a succession of pathetic tableaux, we observe Julie, the incarnation of sensibility; Julie, the perfect friend gently preparing Claire for the end; Julie, the ideal wife in converse with Wolmar. Finally, in the melodramatic episode of the mysterious stranger, we have Julie the peacemaker who reunites Fanchon, the maid, with her long-lost, ne'er-do-well husband, Claude Anet. The real Claude Anet, it will be remembered, had established a moral ascendancy over Mme de Warens and her young protégé. Now, in symbolic fashion, Rousseau dishonours the shade of his former mentor, thus dispelling an intolerable memory. But how are we to explain the macabre and idiotic scene of the bogus resurrection due to the hallucinations of the baron's venerable retainer? Possibly, in depicting the mass credulity of Julie's servants, Rousseau intended to show how miracles originate. More probably, to judge from the author's footnote, this ghoulish incident merely serves as a prelude to Claire's theatrical gesture when she covers Julie's face with the golden veil spangled with pearls, threatening with her curse the hand that shall remove it or the eye that shall dare to gaze upon the disfigured features of her dead friend. Claire, explains the author, is subconsciously impelled to re-enact thus a terrible dream in which Saint-Preux had seen Julie, on her deathbed, similarly veiled. An event is not predicted, he remarks, because it will happen: it happens because it was predicted. But the true explanation of this and subsequent excursions into cheap melodrama is that Rousseau did not possess the talent that enables the born novelist to depart from the pattern traced by his own life and to create situations which, although imaginary, yet bear the stamp of reality. That is painfully evident in the surviving fragments of his other essays in fiction. When Jean-Jacques diverges from the channel grooved out by his personal experience, his imagination is apt to plunge into sheer hallucination. Note for instance the scene where, in order to portray Claire's grief after Julie's death, he makes her roll on the floor, twisting her hands and biting the legs of the chairs! Equally inane is the experiment devised by Wolmar 'to soften the harshness of despair by more gentle sentiments'.[1] He dresses up Claire's little daughter, Henriette, in the dead woman's clothes and installs her at the dinner-table where the child proceeds to imitate Julie's gestures, tone and speech. Not unnaturally, the effect of this masquerade is to drive Claire into hysterics and to leave the reader with the impression that he has stepped out of *Clarens* into Bedlam.

'Je suis en femme une espèce de monstre.'[2] It is Claire who makes the remark though it would have come more appropriately from her cousin. Physically, as the author frequently reminds us, Julie is lavishly feminine. Psychologically, she is a kind of monster, combining the sentimentality of a village Gretchen, the sexual wisdom of a midwife, the austerity of a Cato, the pedantry of a blue-stocking, the virtuousness of an elderly prude and, on occasion, the analytic powers of a delicate psychologist. The only quality Julie lacks is simplicity, a defect shared by Claire, Wolmar and Bomston. Of Rousseau's characters, a friendly eighteenth-century critic shrewdly observed: 'We are too much aware that it is the same man who makes them talk.'[3] The author, conscious of their family likeness, tried to explain it away in his *Seconde Préface*. One notes, he says, in a society of intimate friends not only a confusion of styles, but of ways of thinking, feeling and speaking. The fact is, however, that Jean-Jacques cannot permit his characters to lead their imaginary lives unmolested. Besides, it is evident from the letters of Claire and Julie that he knew little about the psychology of young girls. The cousins, though presented as intelligent but unsophisticated country maidens, display the precocious wisdom of 'enfants terribles', and this cannot be justly attributed to the influence of their late governess, La Chaillot, to whom both refer in tones of indulgent contempt. From beginning to end, the love affair between Julie and Saint-Preux is governed by a code

---

[1] *N.H.* vi, 11: 'amollir la dureté du désespoir par un sentiment plus doux.'
[2] *N.H.* i, 64: 'For a woman, I am a kind of monster.'
[3] L.-M. Chaudon, *Bibliothèque d'un homme de goût* (1772), ii, 255: '...l'on sent trop que c'est le même homme qui les fait parler.'

summarised in *La Lettre à d'Alembert* which embodies the following articles. Feminine modesty, *la pudeur*, is not a social invention designed to safeguard the institution called the family, as
the *philosophes* stupidly assert. It is a natural sentiment whose
function is to perpetuate the species. Wise Nature sees beyond
the mere act of procreation which, but for *la pudeur*, would result
in a purely animal union. Having destined woman for a retired
existence as wife and mother, Nature gave her modesty and
timidity, qualities essential to a happy domestic society. Love
springs from mutual and equal desires in man and woman, but
Nature has carefully established 'the order of attack and defence'.
Love is woman's kingdom where, necessarily, she lays down the
law because, according to the natural order, it is her privilege to
resist. And unless he is a satyr, a lover will respect her *pudeur*
and even when she reciprocates his desires will refrain from
satisfying them until he has the consent of her will as well as of
her heart. The whole art of love consists in extracting this tacit
consent.[1]

All the leading characters bear the imprint of Rousseau's
personality. Lord Edouard Bomston, who has always been a
puzzle to interpreters of *La Nouvelle Héloïse*, derives probably
from the *Clèveland* of l'abbé Prévost, a novel much admired by
Jean-Jacques. Prévost's hero is the prototype of the 'stage'
English gentleman we meet in eighteenth-century literature.
Honourable, eminently just and reasonable, he stands above the
ordinary prejudices. Slow to yield to passion, he plumbs untold
depths of misery when, like Bomston, he falls in love. He is, in
short, the ideal friend for a Saint-Preux whose rare qualities
Bomston instinctively discerns because there is a 'certain unison
of souls which is instantaneously perceptible'.[2] Immediately,
too, Bomston perceives the uniqueness of Julie's character and
situation and plays an important part in her destiny. But why
does Rousseau, who disliked the English, make Bomston an
English peer? Because, in the first place, he has a little homily
to deliver on caste prejudice which could not be attributed to a

---

[1] *Lettre à M. d'Alembert sur les spectacles*. Ed. M. Fuchs (Geneva, Droz, 1949),
pp. 111–120. All references are to this edition.
[2] *N.H.* I, 45: '...un certain unisson d'âmes qui s'aperçoit au premier instant.'

French nobleman. Pronounced by the English aristocrat in his interview with Julie's father, it acquires weight and conviction. Bomston also helps to illuminate an aspect of Saint-Preux's character unsuspected by Julie. For he who had been obliged to reason with the passionate, impetuous youth is saved by his friend's loyalty and common sense from a dishonourable marriage with the courtesan, Lauretta. Converted by the irresistible eloquence of Saint-Preux, she retires to a convent.

Eighteenth-century admirers of the novel were repelled by Wolmar: the cad who, although fully informed of Julie's relations with Saint-Preux, virtually forced her to marry him and later cruelly exposed her to temptation. As one critic remarked: 'the principles of such conduct are impenetrable to my feeble intellect.'[1] Perhaps Wolmar's *raison d'être* would have been more intelligible if Rousseau, as he so long intended, had closed his novel with Part four. We should not then have been left with a Julie who, but for her opportune death, might at any moment have again been guiltily in love with Saint-Preux, a *dénouement* which soothed the author's bruised *amour-propre* though it befogs the moral issue. To understand Wolmar's unorthodox attitude towards his wife's former lover, one must realise that he is an extraordinary person. A Cossack of princely rank, he has devoted his life to the objective study of human nature in even the humblest classes of society. Devoid of sensibility, he is governed by two passions only: a passion for moral order and for scientific observation. But he derives an aesthetic pleasure from watching the symmetrical, mechanical interplay of Chance and human actions. His conclusion is that the basic element of human psychology is love of self which is originally non-moral but becomes moral or immoral according to the various modifying influences exercised by the individual's social and material environment. In saving the life of Julie's father, however, Wolmar saw that man may perform completely disinterested actions. But it is Julie who is responsible for the first real emotion he had ever experienced. And, on learning her history, Wolmar experienced also his first temptation. He could have surrendered

---

[1] *Lettre de M. * * * à M. D * * * sur 'La Nouvelle Héloïse'* (Geneva, 1762): 'les principes d'une pareille conduite sont impénétrables à mes faibles lumières.'

her to Saint-Preux, but love was too strong. Now he realises that

> only souls of fire can fight and win: all the great efforts, all the sublime actions are their work: cold reason has never achieved anything illustrious, and you can only triumph over the passions by setting one against another. When the passion for virtue gets the upper hand, it reigns supreme and keeps everything in equilibrium.[1]

Moreover, when chance brings the lovers' correspondence into his hands, Wolmar becomes convinced of two things: Julie has recovered her original virtue and, if anyone can make her happy, it is he and not Saint-Preux. No longer young, faced with the problem of his children's education which, as an atheist, he hesitates to undertake, Wolmar decides to entrust it to Saint-Preux. Of Julie's virtue her husband is certain though she must be cured of her foolish self-distrust. Saint-Preux, in turn, must be made to realise that he is in love with a Julie who exists solely in an imagination haunted by memories of dead emotions and the inanimate objects connected with them. But it is a fallacy to assume from the apparently eternal character of external nature that human nature is static. As Rousseau notes, everything in human nature is in a continual state of flux. Therefore, Wolmar takes his wife and ex-lover to the fatal *bosquet* and makes them kiss again, remarking merrily: 'Julie, ne craignez plus cet asyle, il vient d'être profané',[2] and Julie afterwards confides to her cousin: 'I learned that my heart had changed more than I had hitherto dared to believe.'[3] Finally, Saint-Preux sees Julie not as he had liked to imagine her, but as she now is, the wife of Wolmar and mother of his two children. But the Meillerie episode was, as he says, *la crise* because it was associated, directly for Saint-Preux, indirectly through his letters, for Julie, with the most violent phase of their broken romance. She could read,

---

[1] *N.H.* IV, 12: 'il n'y a que les âmes de feu qui sachent combattre et vaincre; tous les grands efforts, toutes les actions sublimes, sont leur ouvrage: la froide raison n'a jamais fait rien d'illustre, et l'on ne triomphe des passions qu'en les opposant l'une à l'autre. Quand celle de la vertu vient à s'élever, elle domine seule et tient tout en équilibre.'

[2] *Ibid.*: 'Julie, fear this sanctuary no longer, it has just been profaned.'

[3] *Ibid.*: 'Je connus que mon cœur était plus changé que jusque là je n'avais osé le croire.'

moreover, carved on the surrounding rocks, the inscriptions reminding her of her lover's agony. Now, if Rousseau had closed the novel on this episode, the validity of Wolmar's system would have been completely vindicated. As Saint-Preux writes to Bomston: 'Voilà, mon ami, le détail du jour de ma vie où sans exception j'ai senti les émotions les plus vives. J'espère qu'elles seront la crise qui me rendra tout à fait à moi-même.'[1]

La Nouvelle Héloïse produced no sudden revolution in the eighteenth-century attitude to external nature. For over half a century, in real life and in the arts, there had been many signs of a new aesthetic sensibility to the spectacle of rustic nature. Yet, in the main, these were rather vague and elementary sentiments, akin to sensations. Rousseau, especially in his later writings, created a profound and original emotion in regard to nature. But the feeling for natural beauty evinced in *La Nouvelle Héloïse* is, on the whole, a by-product of the hero's sexual emotions. Stendhal was thinking of Saint-Preux when he wrote, in *De l'Amour*: 'A lover sees the woman he loves in the sky-line of all the landscapes he perceives and, when he travels a hundred leagues to catch a glimpse of her, every tree, every rock speaks to him of her in a different way and teaches him something new.'[2] Such is precisely the 'feeling for nature' expressed in one of Saint-Preux's letters to Julie:

Je trouve la campagne plus riante, la verdure plus fraîche et plus vive, l'air plus pur, le ciel plus serein; le chant des oiseaux semble avoir plus de tendresse et de volupté; le murmure des eaux inspire une langueur plus amoureuse; la vigne en fleurs exhale au loin de plus doux parfums; un charme secret embellit tous les objets ou fascine mes sens; on dirait que la terre se pare pour former à ton heureux amant un lit nuptial digne de la beauté qu'il adore et du feu qui le consume.[3]

[1] *N.H.* IV, 17: 'Such, my friend, is the detailed account of the day in which I experienced, without exception, the most intense emotions of my life. I hope they will be the crisis which will restore me completely to myself.'
[2] Ch. lix: 'Un amant voit la femme qu'il aime dans la ligne d'horizon de tous les paysages qu'il rencontre, et faisant cent lieues pour aller l'entrevoir un instant, chaque arbre, chaque rocher lui parle d'elle d'une manière différente et lui en apprend quelque chose de nouveau.'
[3] *N.H.* I, 38: 'I find the countryside more smiling, the verdure cooler and more intense, the air more pure, the sky more serene; the song of the birds seems more tender and voluptuous; the murmur of the waters inspires a more amorous languor; the vines in bloom exhale sweeter perfumes; a secret charm beautifies every object

Whilst it is true that the ultimate effect of *La Nouvelle Héloïse* was to transform the eighteenth-century horror of mountains into aesthetic enjoyment, I cannot agree with Bergson that we derive this emotion today not so much from the mountains themselves as from Rousseau's descriptions of them.[1] One has only to turn to the novel itself to realise that what Saint-Preux felt about mountains is something very different from the emotions they subsequently aroused in the Romantics—for example, in Byron:

> I live not in myself, but I become
> Portion of that around me; and to me
> High mountains are a feeling.

On the sole occasion when Saint-Preux contemplates mountain scenery otherwise than through the tinted screen of his passionate love for Julie, his dominant emotions are of astonishment mingled with intellectual curiosity. His perceptions are those of a scientist or of an aquafortist for whom the chromatic splendour of the Alps is non-existent. At second-hand, after Petrarch, he notes the black pine-trees, the oaks and beeches, the foaming torrents and beetling crags. But what really interests Rousseau is the bizarre juxtaposition of contrasts: the differences in vegetation due to the various exposures; the theatrical effects produced by the play of light and shadow and by the vertical perspectives; the sense of disorientation created by the spectacle of strange birds and plants but, above all, the tonic effect on the morale due to the inalterable purity of the mountain air. Physicians, he thinks, ought to exploit its therapeutic properties. What delights Saint-Preux even more during his rambles in Le Valais is his 'commerce with the inhabitants'. And the really eloquent pages of his letter are those which express his enthusiasm for the antique simplicity and primitive goodness of the Valaisans and his dreams of perfect married bliss, with Julie, amongst these kindly, happy mountain folk.[2]

We discover, however, emotions of a more interesting and

or fascinates my senses; the earth, as it were, adorns herself so as to present to your happy lover a nuptial couch worthy of the beauty he adores and of the flame that consumes him.'

[1] *Les deux sources de la morale et de la religion* (ed. Alcan), p. 37.

[2] *N.H.* I, 23.

original quality in the letter written by Saint-Preux to Julie from his wild and lonely eyrie amidst the rocks of Meillerie:

O Julie! que c'est un fatal présent du ciel qu'une âme sensible! Celui qui l'a reçu doit s'attendre à n'avoir que peine et douleur sur la terre. Vil jouet de l'air et des saisons, le soleil ou les brouillards, l'air couvert ou serein, régleront sa destinée, et il sera content ou triste au gré des vents.[1]

Unconsciously, in these words, Rousseau illuminates the gulf that separates him, in spirit, from the Pascalian outlook on the external world: '*Lustravit lampade terras.* Le temps et mon humeur ont peu de liaison; j'ai mes brouillards et mon beau temps au dedans de moi; le bien et le mal de mes affaires même, y fait peu.'[2] We must not, however, leap to the conclusion that Saint-Preux is a precocious Romantic for he has no Romantic illusions about Nature. Perhaps, he writes, Meillerie contributes to his melancholy because it is sad and horrible. But inanimate Nature has no mysterious power to shape his inner life: only Julie can determine the quality and colour of his deepest emotions. Nature, he says, is insensible and dead until animated by their love. In short, the feeling for natural beauty reflected in *La Nouvelle Héloïse* is genuine and finds expression in a new and original idiom. It lacks, however, that sense of more intimate communion with Nature which we shall find in *Les Dialogues* and in *Les Rêveries du Promeneur solitaire.* As yet, it cannot be said that Jean-Jacques perceives with the disinterested eye of the artist whose vision of external nature reveals beauties which, but for him, the ordinary spectator would never have suspected. The idyllic *Clarens* scenes, on the other hand, show him in his true element, lingering happily on the theme adumbrated in the tenth Note to the *Second Discours* and restated in the *Seconde*

---

[1] *N.H.* I, 26: 'Oh Julie! What a fatal gift of Heaven is a feeling heart! He who has received it must expect nothing but pain and grief on earth. Base plaything of the air and of the seasons, his destiny will be governed by the sun or the fogs, by clouds or fair weather and he will be happy or sad according to the caprice of the winds.'

[2] Pensée 107: '*Lustravit lampade terras.* The weather and my humour have little in common; I have my fine and foggy days within me; my fortunes, even my misfortunes, have little to do with the matter.'

Préface of his novel. In these charming pictures of country life we behold Rousseau's vision of society as it must have been long ago before men turned from their natural sentiments to chase the mirage of a universe made perfect by scientific reason: Julie's *jardin à l'anglaise* with its hidden, chuckling streams, leafy thickets, wildflowers and meandering paths; the harvesting of the grapes in vineyards blue with the haze of a September morning; the simple pleasures of a rustic fête enjoyed alike by contented peasants and their *bon seigneur*; the atmosphere of tranquil happiness that clings like woodland scent to every nook and cranny of *Clarens*.

The impact of *La Nouvelle Héloïse* on public opinion was sensational and immediate and, as we have noted, it remained a 'best-seller' until the Revolution. For a detailed account of the reception accorded by the press and general public to Rousseau's novel one must, however, consult the fine Introduction to M. Mornet's now classic edition. The reviewers were largely hostile, either because they were *philosophes* or else men of letters genuinely repelled by the author's 'immoral' sentiments and unorthodox style. From 'the mute but irrefutable evidence' of the numerous editions, the eulogies of friends, but above all, from 'the letters Rousseau received in hundreds, which he kept and which are deposited in the Library of Neuchâtel', M. Mornet concludes that the carping objections of the critics were drowned in the torrential enthusiasm of the general public. The latter found in *La Nouvelle Héloïse*, he says, not only 'the delights of sentiment' but 'the delights of virtue'; besides the 'intoxication of passion', they discovered also 'the enthusiasm for duty', the 'divine flame, the principle of all heroism'.[1] And such, beyond question, are the impressions one gleans from some of the letters, for the most part still unpublished, written by Rousseau's French and Swiss correspondents about *La Nouvelle Héloïse*. However, after having read through this collection, I am not at all convinced that it provides sufficient material on which to base a valid appreciation of the reactions produced in the general public

---

[1] *Rousseau* (Boivin), pp. 90–1: 'les délices du sentiment'...'les délices de la vertu'...'les ivresses de la passion'...'l'enthousiasme du devoir'...'la flamme divine, le principe de tout héroisme'.

by Rousseau's novel. For, although the manuscript letters addressed to him fill twenty-one large tomes, those which specifically refer to *La Nouvelle Héloïse* number, not 'hundreds', but only about forty. Of the latter about fifteen, which are mostly from the author's friends, have been published in the *Correspondance générale* and are warmly eulogistic. The contents of the others are analysed below.[1] Whilst the numerous editions of *La Nouvelle Héloïse* testify to its popularity, we should be unwise to conclude, as a matter of course, that the majority of readers were chiefly attracted by the moral lessons contained in Rousseau's novel. It is significant that the editor of *Le Temple de Vénus*, some fifteen years after their first publication, thought it worth while to accord a place of honour in his erotic anthology to the most ardent letters of Saint-Preux and Julie. And one wonders how many of Rousseau's readers, like the ladies of Nantes mentioned by De Bruc, lost interest after Letter 55 of the first Part and were frankly bored by the details of domestic life at *Clarens*. The critic of our *Monthly Review*,[2] in his preliminary notice of *La Nouvelle Héloïse*, wrote archly: 'There are, indeed, some *warm ideas* in several of the love-letters; but they are not indecently expressed. However, there are Readers who will not be greatly displeased by these Circumstances.' It would be misleading, therefore, to ignore this aspect of Rousseau's novel and thus overestimate its moral influence though no doubt it was for many readers, as one admirer ingenuously remarked, 'the only book with morality in it that one can read without getting

---

[1] *Collection de lettres adressées à Rousseau.* Bibl. de Neuchâtel, Ancien fonds 7902. They include nine anonymous letters of which four (t. VII, ff. 95–7; IX, 'Philandre'; XII, ff. 125–6; XII, ff. 133–8) are sharply hostile: the remaining five are, on the whole, favourable. Uncritical enthusiasts are: Loiseau de Mauléon (III, ff. 129–30); Séguier de Saint-Brisson (V, ff. 129–30); D'Augier, a naval officer (VI, f. 11); Du Verger (VI, ff. 85–6); François, a former cavalry cornet (VI, ff. 87–8); Gallot, the nineteen-year-old son of a merchant (VI, ff. 95–6); De Guigneville (VI, ff. 101–3); Jullien, a student (VI, ff. 127–8); Lecointe, a cavalry captain (VI, (ff. 131–2); Mégy de Saint-Maurin, a young man in love (VII, f. 22); Rousseau, a teacher of mathematics at Nantes (VII, ff. 55–6); De la Sarraz (IX, ff. 31–2). The following temper admiration with criticism: Cahague (I, ff. 56–62); De Rochefort (VII, ff. 129–30); De la Roche (X, ff. 112–30). The letters of De la Chapelle (II, ff. 60–7) and De la Neuville (VI, ff. 129–30) seem to me the inventions of practical jokers. De Bruc of Paimbeuf (VI, ff. 54–5) said that the ladies of the Nantes district regarded the death of Julie as that of an outcast from the Church.

[2] T. XXIII, 492 (1760).

bored'.[1] On the other hand, as M. Mornet reminds us, *La Nouvelle Héloïse* did not breed any Romantics of the René or Lélia persuasion. Those who sympathised with the lovers, he observes, 'only really loved them in the sublime practice of their renunciation, in their chaste, well-doing, pious life at Wolmar's country-house'.[2] Indeed, it is questionable whether the eighteenth-century reader fully grasped the implications of *La Nouvelle Héloïse.* It has not, I think, been remarked that it is the first serious French novel of manners where no character represents the traditional attitude to moral, religious or social questions. We can dismiss, in this connexion, the ridiculous Baron d'Etange and Julie's infatuated pastor. Saint-Preux, Julie, Claire, Bomston and Wolmar compose a small, select community, the nucleus of Rousseau's new social order and he presents to us only their actions, sentiments, ideas, opinions and values, careful always never to expose them to the criticism of outsiders. We gather, however, that the Wolmars do not live in isolation and receive many visitors at *Clarens.* Yet not once do we hear the faintest whisper of public opinion. That this unreal situation was accepted without comment by Rousseau's public is a tribute to the hypnotic quality of his style and the transparent sincerity of his faith in the heroine's power to enslave all who come under the influence of her irresistible, natural goodness.

But for us, today, *La Nouvelle Héloïse* no longer holds its original appeal. Judged solely on its intrinsic merits, it cannot, as a novel, stand comparison with the authentic masterpieces of fiction. The characters express their sentiments and passions in an idiom which too often strikes us as false or absurd, like their theatrical gestures and attitudes. Nevertheless, just as often, one lights upon pages that transform our exasperation into sheer delight. Then, surrendering to the spell of Rousseau's pellucid language we recapture, if only for a moment, that vision which evoked such a complete response from his eighteenth-century disciples. Still, when all is said, we can no longer really see *La*

---

[1] Bibl. Neuchâtel, Ancien fonds 7902, vii, ff. 102–3: '...votre livre est le seul livre où il y ait de la morale que l'on puisse lire sans ennui.'

[2] *Op. cit.* p. 91: 'Ils ne les ont vraiment aimés que dans l'exercice sublime de leur renoncement, dans la vie chaste, bienfaisante, pieuse du château de Wolmar.'

Nouvelle Héloïse through their eyes, admiring it purely as a product of the novelist's art. Rousseau made such an approach impossible when, in the *Confessions*, he revealed the tissue of intimate personal experiences which forms its true substance and now constitutes its chief attraction. For the twentieth-century reader, who is familiar not only with the *Confessions* but with the *Correspondance*, this book holds the peculiar fascination, not of a great novel, but of a veiled autobiography whose disclosures are all the more illuminating because they are involuntary. The force that has ensured the survival of *La Nouvelle Héloïse* is, therefore, extrinsic to the art of the novel since it derives mainly from the continuously felt presence of the author. Unlike the genuine classics of fiction, *La Nouvelle Héloïse* is not a self-sufficing organism, endowed by the novelist with such independent vitality that, even if it had remained anonymous, we should still rank it as a masterpiece. *La Nouvelle Héloïse* is the first example in French literature of that hybrid which Flaubert was to condemn in his well-known gibe at those novelists who neglect to sever the umbilical cord linking the artist with his creation.

★   ★   ★   ★   ★

With pathetic naïveté, in these words addressed to Mme d'Houdetot, her rejected lover discloses the object of *Les Lettres morales*: 'May my zeal help to raise you so far above me that, in you, *amour-propre* may compensate me for my humiliations and, in some sort, console me for not having been able to attain you.'[1] As we have noted, Sophie had repelled his passionate advances but Jean-Jacques was determined to retain his moral ascendancy over her by assuming the function of spiritual director. Almost immediately, he persuaded himself that his *libido dominandi*, born of jealousy, was an irresistible moral obligation, nay, a divine command: 'I feel within myself the invincible compulsion of genius. I believe myself to have been sent by Heaven to perfect its most noble work. Yes, Sophie, the occupation of my closing years will honourably redeem my

---

[1] *C.G.* III, p. 346: 'Puisse mon zèle aider à vous élever si fort au-dessus de moi, que l'amour-propre me dédommage en vous de mes humiliations, et me console en quelque sorte de n'avoir pu vous atteindre!'

sterile youth.'[1] In expounding his views on what constitutes the good life, Rousseau will make, at the same time, his 'profession of faith'. Later, but only with the consent of Mme d'Houdetot, these letters will be published: 'je vous charge de ma gloire, O Sophie!'[2] Implicit in this first letter as in all the *Lettres morales*, is Rousseau's anxiety to still the murmurs of a conscience perturbed by the memory of his conduct towards Mme d'Epinay and of the injury which his reputation had suffered from the publicity given to that affair by the *coterie holbachique*.

Therefore, in the second *Lettre* the theme of which is happiness, he launches a violent attack on the rationalists. We live in the climate and in the century of philosophy and reason. Yet, with all the facilities for intellectual progress at our disposal, are we wiser or better? Do we really know what are the essential duties, the moral obligations of our species? For all our material progress we are less happy than our ancestors. In a formidable onslaught on the empirical methods of his former colleagues, Rousseau exposes the fundamental weakness of their system. Materialists, fascinated by the mechanical order governing the physical universe, they foolishly imagine, he suggests, that human nature obeys the same laws. As a result, they generalise on one 'little fact' only to find their theories contradicted by a multitude of exceptions. They cannot grasp the truth that, as science is based on sense experience, which is unreliable, it can never lead to a true knowledge of human nature. What of Cartesian philosophy? Even Descartes, starting off from his 'unique and incontestable' principle *cogito ergo sum*, believed he was moving towards truth and found only lies. For Newton has proved that the essence of matter is not extension; Locke has shown that the essence of the soul is not thought. But already their systems, in turn, are beginning to collapse. Newton did not even suspect the marvels of electricity 'which appears to be the most active principle of Nature'[3] and Locke's sensationalism cannot define spirit because our senses were given to

---

[1] *C.G.* III, p. 347: '...j'éprouve en moi l'invincible impulsion du génie. Je me crois envoyé du Ciel pour perfectionner son plus digne ouvrage; oui Sophie, les occupations de mes derniers jours honoreront ma stérile jeunesse.'

[2] *C.G.* III, p. 349: 'I place my fame in your charge, O Sophie!'

[3] *C.G.* III, p. 357, Lettre 3: 'qui paraît être le principe le plus actif de la nature.'

us for our self-preservation and not to instruct us. And so, Rousseau implies, the philosophers juggle with words, with concepts that have no basis in real experience: substance, soul, body, eternity, movement, liberty, contingency. Having rejected as useless both the *a priori* and the *a posteriori* approaches to knowledge, he concludes that we are back where Descartes began: *Je pense, donc je suis*. However, inspired by Plato, he dallies with the following theory, purely conjectural and perhaps improbable, yet hard to refute. Might there not be a hierarchy of minds of different degrees of perfection, to each of which Nature has given a body organised according to its faculties, ascending from the oyster to man and from man to the most sublime species? Perhaps what essentially distinguishes man from the animal is not the fact that the latter has no more faculties than its body has sensations but that the human soul, whose faculties are compressed and restricted by its bodily envelope, is constantly striving to break through the sense-barrier in an effort to attain the celestial and intellectual regions. Perhaps, indeed, that is what genius partially achieves.[1]

The first lesson of wisdom, therefore, is humility. Yet, though man, viewed as a reasoning creature is puny, he is great by his innate love of justice and goodness. This 'sentiment intérieur' is his real title to nobility. And in words vibrant with sincerity, Jean-Jacques tells of the volcanic upheaval produced sometimes in the depths of his being by the spectacle of moral beauty:

If this sacred flame could endure, if this noble frenzy animated our whole life, what heroic actions could daunt our courage, what vices would dare to approach us, what victories should we not win over ourselves and what could there be so great as to be unattainable by our own efforts!...this holy enthusiasm is the energy of our faculties shaking off their earthly bonds and which perhaps it only depends on ourselves to maintain constantly in that state of freedom. However that may be, at least we feel within us a voice that forbids us to despise ourselves. Reason crawls, but the soul rises aloft. If we are small intellectually, we are great by our feelings...[2]

---

[1] *C.G.* III, p. 359.
[2] *C.G.* III, pp. 860–1, Lettre 4: 'Ah si ce feu sacré pouvait durer, si ce noble délire animait notre vie entière quelles actions héroïques effrayeraient notre courage,

In a brief survey of his chequered moral existence, Rousseau wonders why he was sometimes happy in misfortune and yet anxious in times of prosperity. He felt within him some hidden force that counterbalanced his destiny. It derived, Jean-Jacques discovered, from a secret judgement 'which I pronounced, unthinkingly, on the actions of my life and on the objects of my desires'.[1] Frequently, he tells Sophie, the verdict of his private conscience was at variance with that of public opinion. Nevertheless, it is this 'principle' which governs his present actions and enables him to form an accurate valuation of his past conduct. Here we have one of the most illuminating pages of the *Lettres morales*. Written early in 1758, that is to say nearly ten years before the *Confessions*, it concerns Rousseau's second 'moral revolution' which we described as a reorientation of his consciousness. Originally, it will be remembered, in abandoning himself to a purely retrospective attitude of mind and spirit, Jean-Jacques felt guilty of a kind of self-betrayal. Now, on the contrary, he states explicitly that only by living wholly in the past can he achieve that inner peace and harmony which results from a clear vision of one's moral life.

After having exhausted all the good and evil that a sentient being can experience, I am gradually losing sight and expectation of a future which no longer holds for me any charm; my desires are fading along with my hope; my existence resides now only in my memory; I live now only in my past life and I cease to care about its duration since my heart has nothing new to feel. In this state, it is natural that I should like to turn my eyes towards the past, from which henceforth I derive my whole being; then it is that my errors are corrected, that good and evil make themselves felt within me, unalloyed and with no prejudices.[2]

quels vices oseraient approcher de nous, quelles victoires ne remporterions-nous point sur nous-mêmes et qu'y aurait-il de grand que nous ne pussions obtenir de nos efforts!...ce saint enthousiasme est l'énergie de nos facultés qui se dégagent de leurs terrestres liens, et qu'il ne tiendrait qu'à nous peut-être de maintenir sans cesse dans cet état de liberté. Quoi qu'il en soit, nous sentons au moins en nous-mêmes une voix qui nous défend de nous mépriser; la raison rampe, mais l'âme est élevée, si nous sommes petits par nos lumières, nous sommes grands par nos sentiments...'

[1] *C.G.* III, 361: '...que je portais sans y penser sur les actions de ma vie et sur les objets de mes désirs.'

[2] *C.G.* III, 362, Lettre 4: 'Après avoir épuisé tout ce que peut éprouver de bien et de mal un être sensible, je perds peu à peu à la vue et l'attente d'un avenir qui n'a

The substance of the fifth *Lettre morale* was later embodied in *Emile* and will be discussed in the next chapter. In the sixth and last of the *Lettres* Rousseau stylises, in the following metaphor, that atrophy of the Conscience which is so typical of modern, civilised man. 'I picture a little insect spinning out of its substance a great web, by which alone its sensibility is apparent though one would think it dead in its hole. Human vanity is the spider's web which man stretches out over all that surrounds him.'[1] How then will Sophie learn to know and follow the dictates of her moral conscience? To begin with, she must rediscover, says Jean-Jacques, her *moi humain*, the fundamental self whose precious substance we draw upon and well nigh exhaust in order to create the social self we display to the world. By following the régime which he himself adopted with salutary results, she will finally obtain a clear vision of her 'human self'.

The first step is to separate it absolutely from its spurious facsimile the social self which consists, Rousseau implies, of our acquired, not of our natural sentiments. These must now be reassembled and concentrated within their natural boundaries, for they compose our real being. That is what Jean-Jacques means by the expression: *rentrer en soi-même.* To 'get back within herself', Sophie must acquire the habit of solitude, not the solitude of the cloister nor even of her room. Rousseau means that she must learn how to withdraw in spirit from the crowd; how to know her fundamental or individual self and prevent it from being obliterated by the constant demands made upon it by her social milieu. She need not become a hermit, though at first it might be wise to retire for a short time to the country where the beauties of Nature are conducive to self-contemplation and reverie and will help to revive 'le sentiment intérieur' which has

plus de quoi me flatter; mes désirs s'éteignent avec l'espérance; mon existence n'est plus que dans ma mémoire; je ne vis plus que de ma vie passée et sa durée cesse de m'être chère depuis que mon cœur n'a rien à sentir de nouveau. Dans cet état, il est naturel que j'aime à tourner les yeux sur le passé, duquel je tiens désormais tout mon être; c'est alors que mes erreurs se corrigent et que le bien et le mal se font sentir à moi sans mélange et sans préjugés.'

[1] *C.G.* III, 369: '...je crois voir un petit insecte former de sa substance une grande toile par laquelle seule il paraît sensible, tandis qu'on le croirait mort dans son trou. La vanité de l'homme est la toile d'araignée qu'il tend sur tout ce qui l'environne.'

become atrophied by her artificial mode of life. An expert practical psychologist, Jean-Jacques omits no practical details. For her solitary country walks, Sophie must choose a time when she is not preoccupied with lively emotions of pain or pleasure. There is no need, at first, to indulge in profound meditations: '... I ask you only to maintain your soul in a state of languor and calm which will allow it to turn inwards upon itself.'[1] By this, Rousseau is careful to add, he does not mean 'un affaissement total' or total collapse, that is to say, of her will. Indeed, Sophie can now gently revive her benumbed 'sentiment intérieur' by a kind of spiritual massage. She can flood her consciousness with memories of her good actions. She can think, for example, of Jean-Jacques whose heart she directed towards virtue. And, in the country, she must live like a countrywoman: no reading, simple meals, early to bed and early to rise. In an admirable page, Rousseau explains to Mme d'Houdetot the meaning of true charity which is so hard to practise if it is to be a virtue. For virtue, at first sight, is always ugly and frightening and Sophie will find that the poor are dirty, brutal, untruthful and selfish. But what of her own vices? What would they look like if they were not camouflaged by good breeding? It is not enough merely to distribute alms through her servants: Sophie must think of herself as the sister of these unfortunates. Humanity will soon triumph over her repugnance. Then she will never feel bored or lonely because the secret voice of Conscience will say to her heart: 'Thou art not alone: good deeds have a witness.'[2] Such, Rousseau assures Mme d'Houdetot, is the régime which he himself followed in search of his *moi humain*.

The doctrine of living roughly sketched out in these *Lettres* will be presented more elaborately in *Emile*. But we can see already why Jean-Jacques was bound to clash, on the one hand with the Christian Churches and on the other with the *philosophes*, their enemies. Implicit in the *Lettres morales* is the Humanist rejection of the dogma of original sin and the Humanist conviction that man can achieve his salvation by his

---

[1] *C.G.* III, 371: '...je demande seulement que vous puissiez maintenir votre âme dans un état de langueur et de calme qui la laisse replier sur elle-même.'

[2] *C.G.* III, 374: 'tu n'es pas seule, les bonnes actions ont un témoin.'

own natural resources, without divine assistance. At the same time, Jean-Jacques contemptuously dismisses rational philosophy as a guide to self-knowledge or to genuine human progress. These *Lettres* which Mme d'Houdetot almost certainly never read, remained unpublished until 1861.

Meanwhile, in February of 1758, Rousseau was busy with his *Lettre à d'Alembert sur les spectacles*, which he completed in three weeks. Its thesis possesses little actuality for the twentieth-century reader who no longer views dramatists as 'public poisoners' or believes that 'to tell the actor not to be immoral is like telling a man not to fall ill'.[1] On the other hand, from the standpoint of the social and literary historian, *La Lettre à d'Alembert* constitutes a valuable document. It was always Rousseau's favourite. No one, he proudly told Dusaulx in his old age, could ever rob him of the glory of having produced this 'virile' work which, he adds, was composed in the most lucid moments of his existence and practically wrote itself.[2] Even more interesting is the revelation that it saved his life at a moment when, but for this distraction, Rousseau would have died of grief and despair.[3]

Though *La Lettre sur les spectacles*, but for an article on Geneva contributed by D'Alembert to the *Encyclopédie*, might never have been written, it links up with an old controversy which did not, however, become really violent, as M. Fuchs has shown, until the close of the seventeenth century.[4] With the history of that quarrel we are not immediately concerned, except where it directly touches upon Jean-Jacques and his native city. In Geneva, M. Fuchs observes, the polemic had passed from the theological to the political plane, reviving long-standing class antagonisms. In 1737, for example, plays had been performed by the Gherardi troupe from Lyons on the

[1] *Lettre à d'Alembert sur les spectacles* (ed. M. Fuchs (Genève, 1948); all references are to this edition), p. 123: 'Défendre au comédien d'être vicieux, c'est défendre à l'homme d'être malade.'

[2] Dusaulx, *De mes rapports avec Jean-Jacques Rousseau*, 1798.

[3] *C.G.* IV, no. 546 (to Deleyre, October 1758): 'parce qu'il m'a sauvé la vie et qu'il me servit de distraction dans des moments de douleur, où, sans lui, je serais mort de désespoir.'

[4] Ed. cit. Introduction.

occasion of the *Médiations* or constitutional reforms imposed on the Genevans by France and the other guarantory Powers. These performances were applauded by the governing classes but not by their disgruntled political opponents who could see no reason for rejoicing. The actors indiscreetly boasted of the support they had received from the French envoy, whereupon many Genevan citizens openly identified the members of the Government with the defenders of the stage, accusing them of francophile, Papist and anti-republican sympathies. Consequently, after Gherardi's departure, there was a general tightening of the old regulations.

In February 1755 Voltaire took up residence at *Les Délices*, just outside Geneva, and persuaded the famous actor Lekain, then in Lyons, to come and play on his private stage to an audience which included several Genevan patricians. The Consistory, however, intervened and these performances were discontinued at the request of the *Grand Conseil*. Voltaire, who probably did not fully grasp the situation, resolved that Geneva should have a theatre. In 1756, D'Alembert arrived in Geneva to gather material for an article on that city which was to appear in Tome VII of the *Encyclopédie*. During his visit he was entertained by Voltaire who had moved to Vaudois territory and now ran his theatre with impunity, first at Monriond, later at Monrepos.

The article *Genève*, which appeared in 1757, was undoubtedly influenced by D'Alembert's conversations with his host at Monrepos. It consists of two distinct parts. The first is a glowing eulogy of the Genevan Republic, its democratic constitution and enlightened citizens. Yet, strange to say, they will not tolerate a theatre within their walls. This is not, the author insinuates, because the Genevans object to plays in themselves, but rather because they are afraid lest the immoral habits of the players might contaminate the youth of Geneva. The objection, D'Alembert agrees, is a very serious one, though surely the danger could be prevented by stringent regulations. Nowhere, it should be noted, does he advocate a permanent theatre.

It was, however, the second part of the article which got D'Alembert into hot water. A typical *philosophe*, blissfully ignorant of the role played by religious sentiment in the life of Geneva, he praised the broadmindedness of the Genevan clergy and referred admiringly to the 'perfect Socinianism' of certain pastors he had met. On 10 February 1758 *La Vénérable Compagnie des Pasteurs et Professeurs de l'Académie de Genève* swung into action with a Declaration which was both a protest and a profession of faith. They denied indignantly that any of their members held Socinian views and, in an oblique attack on the *Encyclopédistes*, vigorously condemned their 'licentious and sophistical philosophy'.[1] The *Vénérable Compagnie* completely ignored the suggestion that Geneva should have a theatre.

It is probable that Rousseau knew nothing of the article before its publication in November 1757. On the other hand, he did not inform D'Alembert of his *Lettre sur les spectacles* until the end of June 1758 when it was already in the press. Nor did he mention the new book when urged, in February, by Jacob Vernes to reply to D'Alembert's *Genève*: only Mme d'Houdetot was let into the secret. Rousseau and D'Alembert, though they did not write to each other, were then on good terms. Why, therefore, was the article *Genève* not entrusted to Jean-Jacques, a citizen of Geneva who had lived long enough abroad to treat the subject objectively?

We have already mentioned the terrible indictment of Diderot inserted in the final draft of the *Préface* where Rousseau, after a few banal compliments to D'Alembert, explains why he feels impelled, as a good Genevan, to attack his article: 'Justice and truth, those are the first duties of man. Humanity and fatherland, those are the primary objects of his affection.'[2] Rousseau, clearly, has no intention of becoming involved in a doctrinal controversy. But this does not prevent him from sitting in moral judgment on D'Alembert whose allusions to Socinianism, he politely implies, are worse than indiscreet, being tantamount to a betrayal of confidence. Thereupon, after a little homily on religious toleration, Rousseau develops his two main objections to the establishment of a theatre in Geneva. Drama, by its very

---

[1] 'Cette philosophie licencieuse et sophistique.'
[2] *Op. cit.* ed. cit. p. 3: 'Justice et vérité, voilà les premiers devoirs de l'homme. Humanité, patrie, voilà ses premières affections.'

nature and purpose must inevitably exercise an immoral influence: the same is true of the actors and actresses whose profession is incompatible with good morals. Assuming now that Geneva has adopted D'Alembert's suggestion, Rousseau vividly pictures the deplorable social and economic situation which would result from such an innovation. Finally, he proposes alternative modes of entertainment more suitable to a democratic nation.

Harsher even than Bossuet whom he quotes approvingly, Jean-Jacques has not a single good word to say for the theatre. The spectator, interested in purely fictitious creatures and events, selfishly forgets his domestic and social obligations. The dramatist offers a false picture of the human passions since he panders to the vanity and prejudices of the audience. The virtues he portrays we already know and admire, and the virtuous sentiments excited in the playgoer are sterile and ephemeral. For reasons intimately connected with his state of soul when he composed this work, Rousseau violently attacks the theatre of Molière whom he brands as a public enemy, citing as proof his own peculiar interpretation of *L'Avare*, *Le Bourgeois Gentilhomme* and *Georges Dandin*. His *bête noire*, however, is *Le Misanthrope*, ineptly described as the most typical product of Molière's dramatic 'system'. Alceste, he argues, is indubitably an upright and sincere man and no one can deny that he is presented as a ridiculous character. Ergo, Molière deliberately ridicules virtue on his stage. It is scarcely necessary to refute this absurd accusation. What Molière finds amusing in Alceste is, of course, not his virtue but his rigidity of outlook, his unsociability or lack of common sense. But Jean-Jacques saw in Alceste an *alter ego*, the virtuous, outspoken man deceived, abandoned and vilified by false friends. He admits as much in the *Confessions*: 'Unconsciously, I described my actual situation; I depicted Grimm, Mme d'Epinay, Mme d'Houdetot, Saint-Lambert, myself.'[1] Rousseau's savage little portrait of Alceste's reasonable friend, Philinte, was obviously intended to annoy the *coterie holbachique* and the passionate digression on feminine

---

[1] *Conf.* 487: 'Sans m'en apercevoir, j'y décrivis ma situation actuelle; j'y peignis Grimm, madame d'Epinay, madame d'Houdetot, Saint-Lambert, moi-même.'

pudeur which we have already noted was certainly inspired by Sophie d'Houdetot.

At last, ending where he should have begun, Rousseau deals with D'Alembert's proposal. The practical obstacles, he points out, are insuperable. Geneva with only 24,000 inhabitants could not maintain a playhouse without a State subsidy or a tax on the rich. But the real objections are of a moral nature. Such an innovation would upset the existing social and moral order by accentuating class distinctions and by introducing a taste for luxury and frivolity. Quite irrelevantly, Rousseau imagines the revolution which the proximity of a theatre would cause in a little community, that of the happy, frugal Montagnons situated near Neuchâtel. In Geneva itself, one effect would be the disappearance of the clubs separately frequented by men and women, of which Jean-Jacques paints a glowing but inaccurate picture. Such at least was the opinion of his friends, Perdriau and Lenieps who told him, frankly, that he was tilting at windmills. Every Genevan knew that the notion of a permanent theatre was fantastic: even the most ardent supporters of D'Alembert thought only in terms of performances limited to a few months in the year. But Rousseau, who had extended his condemnation of the French theatre to include the French aristocracy and cultured *bourgeoisie*, glorifies the Genevan *cercles* at the expense of the Parisian salons, contrasting the virile, frank, hard-drinking Genevans with the effeminate French *petits-maîtres*. The Genevan women, too, are held up as models of the Republican virtues and Rousseau describes admiringly the active role played by these vigilant matrons in the service of morality. It was thus, he remarks approvingly, that in the halcyon days of Rome the citizens used to watch and accuse each other publicly, out of zeal for justice.

That they cannot have a theatre is no reason, however, why the laborious Genevans should not have entertainments. But these must conform to the *mœurs* of a Republic and here Rousseau's model is the Sparta of his Plutarchian memories, a Sparta unknown to history. The Genevans already have their military reviews, shooting-matches and boat-races; Rousseau would extend the range of these manly entertainments so as to preserve the Republican virtues and train robust soldiers and workmen. For the winter he suggests public balls where, however, everything shall take place under the paternal eye of a *seigneur-commis* or commissary appointed by the State. At the end of the ballroom will be an enclosure reserved for the older citizens of both sexes. To these, before and after each dance, the young Genevans must make a profound obeisance. Less original, since there had been *rosières* in France since the sixth century, is his suggestion that the most virtuous girl should be crowned annually as queen of the ball and receive, on her marriage, an official decoration. Rousseau attaches great importance to these dances since they provide an ideal occasion for arranging suitable marriages. But he will not permit married women to 'profane conjugal dignity' by taking the floor. The best comment, perhaps, on all this came from Mlle Perdriau who remarked that if Jean-Jacques came back to Geneva he would find that the young people had no need of such organised rendezvous which could only result in loveless marriages,[1] an objection unlikely to impress Jean-Jacques who never believed that love was an indispensable condition of a happy marriage.

[1] *C.G.* iv, no. 574 (Perdriau to Rousseau, 15 Nov. 1758).

CHAPTER VI

'LA BONNE EDUCATION'

On trouve parmi nous beaucoup d'instruction et peu d'education.
Duclos, *Considérations sur les mœurs de ce siècle* (1750)

Emile, ou de l' Education

In 1760 Rousseau began to write two books, *Emile* and *Du Contrat social*, which have left their imprint on modern society. The first embodies his ideas on education and also a profession of his religious faith. The second establishes certain principles without which, according to Rousseau, it is impossible to safeguard the natural rights of the individual citizen and, at the same time, the integrity of the political community known as the State. This work may be most conveniently discussed in a later chapter although, in fact, it was published two or three weeks before the educational treatise, on 23 May 1762. Such had not, however, been Rousseau's intention. Indeed, he tells us that the political ideas contained in the last book of *Emile* represent a summary and a preview of those he intended to elaborate in the *Contrat social*. The latter, he reminds us, is an extract from a much larger work, *Les Institutions politiques*, which Rousseau had to abandon as 'beyond his powers'. It is worth noting, incidentally, that he himself, unlike many of his critics, does not appear to have discerned any essential contradiction between the concept of human nature on which the *Contrat* is based and that expounded in *Emile*. But this question need not, for the moment, detain us.

Emile is not Rousseau's first essay on education. In 1740 he composed the fragment entitled *Projet pour l'Education de M. de Sainte-Marie* which, as we have already suggested, contains nothing that could be said to prefigure *Emile*. On the other hand, nearly all the ideas crystallised in this great work are to be found in *La Nouvelle Héloïse* though in a fluid, unclarified state. The system employed by Rousseau in educating his imaginary pupil, Emile, substantially resembles Julie's although

GR

her children are still infants and, moreover, are blessed with unusual parents. Emile, on the other hand, is educated solely by his tutor in what might be termed a scientifically conditioned *milieu*. Besides, we know that the imaginary tutor, who is Rousseau, has been supervising Emile's upbringing since the latter's birth and will directly control the boy's education from the age of six to manhood. By this fiction, Emile enjoys virtually no other society but that of his tutor who is able to follow 'the progress of infancy and the course natural to the human heart' in applying his system. Above all, he can exclude the social influences which infallibly contaminate the child's original and natural goodness. Jean-Jacques chooses a boy from a wealthy family: the poor require no other education than that imposed upon them by their economic condition. Emile's parents are also persons of rank. He will thus be rescued from that class-prejudice which, in the eighteenth century, was inseparable from nobility. The boy, like Jean-Jacques, is motherless and, though his father is alive, is virtually an orphan since he will obey no one but his tutor. It would be absurd, of course, as Rousseau always said, to try to reduplicate this ideal setting. It is mere device intended to facilitate the demonstration of his principles. But these, like the fictitious incidents which illustrate them, are essentially practical. All, moreover, stem from the author's firm belief in the original goodness of human nature.

We can, as Bergson used to say, give any meaning we like to words but only if we define that meaning. Now, though Rousseau would cordially endorse this maxim, he often found it hard to observe, being hampered by the relative poverty of the vocabulary at his disposal. So one gathers, at least, from his statement that, in writing a long treatise, it is impossible to give always the same meaning to the same words. Here, probably, we have the true explanation of certain apparent inconsistencies that crop up in *Emile*. Like all pioneers, Jean-Jacques was often embarrassed when obliged to express his new thoughts in language which represents a crystallisation of old ideas and systems. He did not always pause to define the special meaning attaching, in a particular context, to certain important expressions. Rousseau mentions, for example, *raisonnement*, to which one might add others such as *le naturel, caractère, tempérament, bien né, mal né*. The last two, because of their implications, are peculiarly interesting. Thus, when in *La Nouvelle Héloïse* the heroine exclaims: 'Heureux les enfants bien nés!' she obviously means not gently born children but children not innately wicked, for she goes on to express the hope that no wicked children have emerged from her womb.[1] Now, in opening *Emile*, Rousseau explicitly states that everything, as it comes from the hands of Nature is good, but later in the same work he seems to contradict himself. We read, for instance, that a child who is not *mal né* and has retained his original innocence until twenty is the most lovable and generous of men.[2] And in another passage he observes that there are gentle, quiet characters which can be led a long way, without danger, in their primitive innocence. But there are also violent natures whose 'ferocity' develops at an early stage and whose education must be accelerated. Otherwise, we should have to chain up such individuals.[3] The apparent contradiction disappears, however, if we turn to *La Nouvelle Héloïse* where the Wolmars, in opposition to Saint-Preux, maintain that in addition to 'la constitution commune à l'espèce', that is, to the basic psychological traits which he shares with his species, the individual is born with a special temperament that determines his character and genius. Saint-Preux, on the contrary, holds that such differences are not the work of Nature but of environment. Here Julie intervenes with the remark that the infant, almost at birth, begins to leave the state of Nature and to show the effect of these environmental influences.[4] Rousseau, apparently, endorses Julie's opinion, thus avoiding an awkward dilemma. For the truth is that his theory of *la bonté naturelle* clashes with experience which shows that, at a very tender age, some children are little devils and others little angels. Whether he found Julie's solution conclusive is another matter though the implication of *Emile* is that no dilemma exists. We may accept with confidence Rousseau's guarantee that every new-born child carries the imprint of Nature's goodness. Is it possible to preserve the original beauty

---

[1] *N.H.* v, 3: 'Ma première espérance est que des méchants ne seront pas sortis de mon sein.'   [2] *E.G.* 259.   [3] *E.G.* 88.   [4] *N.H.* v, 3.

of this intaglio which seems to be so quickly effaced by the friction of social life? We have Rousseau's answer in *Emile*. A natural education can, to a large extent, preserve intact the pristine goodness, innocence and happiness of the individual from infancy through childhood and puberty to manhood. By a 'natural education' Rousseau means an education which interferes as little as possible with the free, natural development, both physical and psychological, of the child. Ideally, as in the case of Emile, the child should be continually protected from the demands of the social group which, by conflicting with his innate and essentially good passion for self-conservation, prematurely corrupt his natural sociability and lead him to regard parent, teacher and later, society, as a threat to his liberty and happiness. Jean-Jacques, by inviting us to observe his secluded human guinea-pig, throws into relief the fate of the average child, the victim of an educational system based on wrong principles and on a false concept of human nature.

This unnatural education begins, as Rousseau vividly demonstrates, in the cradle. The primitive dispositions of the individual lead him to seek pleasure and avoid pain. The infant, therefore, naturally loves the mother or nurse who satisfies his physical needs. But properly, there should be no wet-nurse. Nature entrusted this first and most important phase of the child's education to the mother and in moving accents Jean-Jacques pleads with her to discharge this sacred obligation, for her own sake as much as for that of humanity. 'Where there is no mother, there is no child.'[1] If the former neglects her duties so will the latter. 'The child must love his mother before knowing that he ought to.'[2] On the fashionable mothers with indulgent doctors who put their babies out to nurse Jean-Jacques has no mercy. Whilst they are gaily amusing themselves their wretched infant, swaddled and ligatured, is hanging from a nail on the wall. Meantime, sublimely indifferent to the chokings and screams of the purple-faced, crucified baby, the peasant foster-mother goes quietly about her household duties. Rousseau then lays down his precepts for the proper care of infants: mother's

[1] *E.G.* 19: 'Point de mère, point d'enfant.'
[2] *E.G.* 19: 'L'enfant doit aimer sa mère avant de savoir qu'il le doit.'

milk, loose and scanty clothing, country air, absolute freedom of movement at the risk of a few bumps and bruises, cold baths summer and winter, deliberately irregular times for food and sleep. For the only habit a child should be allowed to form is that of forming no habits. Our natural education begins at birth and from that moment the infant's five senses must be given free play. He must be accustomed, moreover, at an early stage to darkness and to seeing and touching unusual objects fearlessly.

The cries of the average infant evoke pettings and scoldings. Not content with gratifying his natural needs the mother, who constantly transfers her adult emotions to the child, foolishly indulges his fancies. Thus at an early phase, Society, as incarnated in the parent or nurse, interferes with and deforms Nature. Quite unnecessarily, the infant has acquired two vices which come, not from Nature but from human ignorance of human nature: the ideas of servitude and domination. The rest of the story is painfully familiar. To undo our own errors, we try to correct what we call the baby's 'natural naughtiness' by absurd appeals to his reason or to his vanity. Worse still, we employ fear, emulation, jealousy in order to make the child a good and useful member of society. And so, Rousseau suggests, the honest stuff of Nature is transformed into shoddy. Do not let us misinterpret his attitude to the problem of the individual and his relationship to society. Necessarily, he insists, all education must 'denature' man: otherwise society would cease to exist. Anyone naïve enough to believe he can preserve his natural sentiments completely intact and still live happily in society is marked down for obliteration by the mass. Education is a necessity and always involves a transformation of that self which the individual regards as a unit, into a fraction of the larger collective self we call Society. Yet this partial surrender of one's personal liberty need not entail unhappiness provided one is gradually accustomed to it by a natural process of education. But we must not, Rousseau implies, adopt the errors of the priest or the materialist. We must not assume like the former that human nature is originally wicked or, like the latter, that there is no such thing as human nature; that nature is just habit and that the individual is only what his environment makes of him. The first book ends with the author's remarks on teaching children to speak. We must not listen attentively to their infantile babble for this might encourage in them a spirit of domination. Do not be in too great a hurry to make the infant talk: he will talk plenty when he wants something. Finally, it is useless to correct the syntax of a very young child. One should introduce him to very few words but see to it that they are clearly enunciated. The vocabulary must never exceed the child's understanding.

The iconoclastic character of Rousseau's treatise emerges in the second book which deals with the education of his pupil from five to twelve. Here is the author's general directive: 'Do exactly the opposite of what is usually done and you will have hit on the right plan.' This is the phase of Emile's *éducation négative*. As every critic has observed, it is happily impossible to suspend the moral and intellectual life of a child from infancy to the age of twelve. Rousseau himself admits that this could not happen if Emile lived in society instead of in the sole company of himself and a handful of servants trained as actors in the little scenes invented for the pupil's benefit. What should interest us are the principles underlying Rousseau's *negative education*. His first principle is that education is made for the child and not contrariwise. Now, the child is not a miniature adult. Childhood has ways of seeing, feeling and thinking peculiar to itself so that nothing could be more absurd than to try to substitute ours in their place. The object of Rousseau's *negative education* is to protect Emile by a kind of *cordon sanitaire* from anything which will impede the natural growth and trend of his body and mind. In the first place, he must on no account be ordered to do this or that. Nature has already inculcated in him the knowledge of his weakness in relation to the external world of things and of grown-ups. The boy good-temperedly accepts this yoke because it is 'fashioned by the nature of things and not by the caprices of men'. Here, for Rousseau, is a vital point. Emile's tutor's *No* must be inexorable, a 'wall of bronze' imitating the harsh necessity of Nature's laws. So long as the child detects no personal intention to curtail his individual freedom, he will feel free. Thus Rousseau's system, illustrated also in the *Contrat*, might be described as education imitating the mechanism of physical nature. Primitive man willingly obeyed the physical laws because they are impersonal and necessary. Similarly, in the State based on Rousseau's social contract, the citizen will feel free because 'in him who governs he sees, not the man but the organ of the law', serene and impassive like a rock. Emile, therefore, will obey because he feels he must, never because he feels that obedience is a duty.

As a young child's first knowledge comes from the sense-impressions evoked by things, words mean nothing to him at the early pre-rational stage because words are merely symbols of things. Locke is, therefore, hopelessly wrong in telling us to reason with children. Amusingly, Jean-Jacques reproduces the typical dialogue resulting from such attempts at moral instruction. What happens, then, when Emile in a fit of anger, breaks his windows? He is put to bed in a cold room, at the risk of catching cold. Finally the broken panes are replaced, only to be smashed a second time. With no sign of anger, the tutor coldly points out that the windows are his and to make sure they will not be broken again, locks the boy up in a hut with no windows. Emile screams and rages, then sobs and moans. A servant passes and when appealed to for help merely remarks that he too has windows to protect. Finally, Emile offers to break no more windows if released. 'An excellent idea,' observes the tutor, 'why did you not think of it sooner?' By such artificial scenes, often involving elaborate preparations, Jean-Jacques illustrates his principles. Naïve often to the point of exciting ridicule these examples sometimes shake our faith in the validity of the author's maxims. Take, for instance, the miniature drama enacted with the connivance of the gardener who digs up the bean plants lovingly tended by Emile because he himself had previously sown the plot with melon seeds. Thus, we are told, the boy acquires the clear and simple notion that the origin of property is the time and labour expended by the first owner. But is it so clear and simple? A child, as Jean-Jacques truly remarks, usually reads the mind of his master better than the latter can read the heart of his pupil. Will not Emile perceive that the real culprit from first to last is the tutor who encouraged him to plant his beans in that particular plot? No matter. This second book is full of sound ideas which have since borne fruit, though it is now agreed that Rousseau's *éducation négative* must not be prolonged beyond the kindergarten stage.

It is virtually certain that Jean-Jacques, in formulating his system, was deeply influenced by memories of his own unsystematic upbringing. Therefore, in postulating no book-learning for Emile until twelve, he tacitly condemns the misguided paternal affection and pride which were responsible for his own precocious introduction to literature. 'Reading is the scourge of childhood.' Emile's only book is that of Nature. His head is not crammed with a smattering of history, geography, or of languages. All that is dead matter and merely prevents the child from exercising his own perceptive faculty. The great thing at this stage, says Jean-Jacques, is to waste time in order to gain time. Emile, he thinks, will learn to read and write before he is ten precisely because no one presses him to learn. Here Rousseau invents another little plot designed to appeal to the boy's self-interest and curiosity. Emile sometimes receives very short and plainly written invitations to exciting parties or picnics. But he cannot read them and, oddly enough, can never find anyone to do so for him till it is too late. The *dénouement* can be guessed. Rousseau does not tell us exactly how Emile learns to read and write and, indeed, apologises for boring the reader with 'such trivialities in a treatise on education'. He dwells at length on the other hand on the subject of physical exercise and on what we call scoutcraft. Thus, at twelve, Emile can judge distances and weights. His night games have sharpened his senses of hearing and sight. He is encouraged to draw, not for aesthetic reasons, but simply to train his perceptions. From practical experiences the boy acquires elementary notions of geometry and, in order to train his ear and teach him to enunciate clearly, is given easy music lessons. Jean-Jacques stresses the importance of sound hygiene: loose and light garments, no headgear, plenty of sleep and a generous but simple, preferably vegetarian diet. Yet, in preparation for a civilised existence, Emile must be accustomed to late hours and early rising and to being wakened unexpectedly. Moreover, he must be trained to sleep anywhere and on anything and, if need be, to sit up occasionally all night.

Why Jean-Jacques thought this 'commando' training essential for Emile's future life in society it is hard to understand. And the modern reader may be tempted to wonder whether Rousseau's negative education is really sufficient to keep an active intelligent child fully occupied from the age of five to twelve.

We are assured, however, that it made Emile self-reliant, alert and a natural leader well equipped to lead and govern his equals. But, as Rousseau candidly admits, he might strike the casual observer as a *polisson* or cheeky brat. And, indeed, he has never been taught manners so that he is perfectly frank and natural. Nor, of course, has Emile ever been consciously subjected to discipline, since the tutor's authority always cleverly simulates the natural laws of the possible and the impossible. Emile has rough notions of property, justice and liberty and even of what constitutes a pact. On the other hand, it would be idle to speak to him about his obligations or the duty of obedience. 'Our first duties are to ourselves...all our natural emotions relate primarily to our conservation and well-being.'[1]

Book III opens the next phase in Emile's education, *l'éducation positive*. Now time is short and must be fully utilised, for this brief transitory period of 'dispassionate intelligence' is unique and non-recurrent. 'At about twelve or thirteen, the child's faculties develop far more rapidly than his wants...not only can he fend for himself, but he has more energy than he needs; it is the only time in his life that he will be in this case.'[2] It will be noted that Jean-Jacques clings to the traditional psychology, inherited from Aristotle though modified by Descartes, according to which the mind has certain faculties, each of which develops at a specific period in life and gives rise to a corresponding order of psychic facts. For Rousseau and his contemporaries these successive faculties were: sensibility, intelligence, will. Therefore, we must understand by the period of 'dispassionate intelligence' that in which the boy's intellectual curiosity is now extremely active whilst he is not yet distracted by the passions that will

[1] *E.G.* 88: 'Nos premiers devoirs sont envers nous...tous nos mouvements naturels se rapportent d'abord à notre conservation et à notre bien-être.'

[2] *E.G.* 182: 'A douze ou treize ans les forces de l'enfant se développent bien plus rapidement que ses besoins...non seulement il peut se suffire à lui-même, il a de la force au-delà de ce qu'il lui en faut, c'est le seul temps de sa vie où il sera dans ce cas.'

come with puberty. His eager desire for useful knowledge must be satisfied by carefully prepared 'object lessons'. In this way, Emile obtains by personal observation a knowledge of elementary astronomy, geography, statics and dynamics. The tutor's methods are exclusively practical. The boy must discover for himself, for example, by getting lost in the forest that astronomy is of some use since it gets him home in time for dinner. The object is not to teach him the sciences but a liking for them. If Emile's knowledge is small, at least it is his own. He has received an all-round training in the methods of acquiring knowledge and realises moreover that there are many things of which he is now ignorant which he will one day know.

As speculative knowledge is still unsuitable to Emile's age, he is allowed only one book, *Robinson Crusoe*, which the tutor uses as a text-book for his experimental lessons. Re-enacting Crusoe's adventures, profiting from his mistakes, Emile learns how to form judgments. He sees, for instance, that iron is much more useful on a desert island than diamonds; that a farmer or a smith or carpenter is more valuable than a confectioner, an engraver or watchmaker. There are many ways in which an ingenious teacher can foster this psychological process and by leading Emile to compare his impressions, aid him to form ideas. Rousseau takes his pupil to dine at a grand house and, as he gazes admiringly at the sumptuous food and appointments, whispers in the boy's ear: 'Through how many hands, would you say, has all that we have seen on the table passed before it came here?' But here the tutor stops: it is too early for moral lectures. He has started Emile thinking about certain economic facts and that is a forward step. Once or twice a week, Rousseau and Emile spend a whole day in a joiner's workshop. The boy can handle all kinds of tools but he had better master one trade thoroughly, not so much for its own sake as for the principle involved. Work is an indispensable duty for social man and every idle citizen is a rascal. Besides, as Rousseau sagely remarks, 'the great secret of education is to make physical and mental exercise always serve as a relaxation to each other'.[1]

[1] *E.G.* 236: 'Le grand secret de l'éducation est de faire que les exercices du corps et de l'esprit servent toujours de délassement les uns aux autres.'

A boy of fifteen educated by Rousseau's method will have no
taste for abstract subjects like history or ethics. All his knowledge is of a practical order. He knows how man is related to
things but nothing about the moral relations between man and
man. Jean-Jacques pictures Emile at this stage as a juvenile
miller of Dee, caring for nobody and not consciously expecting
anyone to care for him. Industrious, robust, self-sufficient,
patient, this amiable young barbarian has no social virtues or
graces. However, a new phase of his psychological existence is
about to open and now Rousseau faces his most difficult task, the
moral education of Emile.

One can detect in this fourth book an echo of Rousseau's secret
regret, so poignantly expressed in the *Second Discours*, that man's
transition from his carefree savage state to his organised social
existence could not have been indefinitely postponed. But
Nature, he feels impelled to admit, intended man for a social life
and, in fact, endowed him for that purpose with an embryonic
moral and social sentiment, *la pitié*. Its function is to offset the
activity of man's primitive *amour de soi*, a passion which is, we
are again reminded, essentially good in the sense that it is always
in conformity with the 'order' or universal scheme of things.
It disposes the baby in his cot to view with benevolence, first
those who attend to his simple needs, and indirectly, through the
mother and nurse, the infant's species. Unfortunately, the
essential goodness of his *amour de soi* rapidly deteriorates with
the extension of his social contacts. Irritated by resistance to his
will, vaguely conscious that others are preferred to himself, the
infant becomes rebellious, imperious, jealous, vindictive. In
short, Rousseau implies, he begins to take a poor view of his
species. The gentle affections born of unthwarted *amour de soi*
are superseded by the hateful emotions deriving from *amour-
propre* or self-esteem. And so, thanks to an unnatural upbringing,
the young child's original goodness is perverted into badness.
Such, of course, is not the case of Emile. He has benefited from
Rousseau's experiment in 'solitary education'. Thus, at fifteen,
Emile is perfectly happy and free, never having consciously perceived any human intention to thwart the activity of his *amour
de soi*. But now, with the advent of puberty, he experiences a

profound psychological upheaval, a 'stormy revolution'. It mani-
fests itself in petulant outbursts of temper succeeded by effusions
of tenderness and uncontrollable fits of sobbing. Emile has now
entered upon his moral existence, described by Rousseau as a
'second birth': 'We are born, so to speak twice: first so as to
exist; a second time in order to live; one birth for the species,
the other for sex.'[1]

Rousseau undertakes Emile's moral instruction with a heavy
sense of responsibility. For it is so fatally easy to communicate
moral truths wrongly and thus to arouse the very ideas which
the teacher wishes to destroy. Such is the dilemma illuminated
in the following passage: 'On this earth out of which Nature
would have made the first paradise of man, beware lest, in trying
to reveal to innocence the knowledge of good and evil, you perform the function of the Tempter.'[2] As he penned these words,
I have no doubt that Jean-Jacques remembered only too vividly
the sordid history of his own initiation to the knowledge of good
and evil and resolved that every adolescent should benefit from
his own unhappy experience. Emile is now ripe for moral
instruction, since the awakening of the sexual instinct has not
only aroused the need for a female companion: he will desire
friendship even before love. It will be some time before Emile
is capable of this delicate sentiment which, Rousseau insists, must
never be confused with mere sexual appetite. The age at which
a boy becomes sex conscious varies according to individual
temperament and education. Precocious sex curiosity is the
result of a bad upbringing. It is, therefore, widespread and
Rousseau explains how it should be dealt with. His method
consists in substituting ugly or repellent images for the attractive representations of the boy's dawning imagination. So when
Emile asks how babies arrive the answer should be that they are
passed by the mother with great suffering which sometimes costs
her life. Unfortunately, the particular illustration offered by
Jean-Jacques is of little practical value since he assumes that the

[1] *E.G.* 245: 'Nous naissons, pour ainsi dire, en deux fois: l'une pour exister,
et l'autre pour vivre; l'une pour l'espèce, et l'autre pour le sexe.'
[2] *E.G.* 86: 'Sur cette terre dont la Nature eût fait le premier paradis de l'homme
craignez d'exercer l'emploi du tentateur en voulant donner à l'innocence la connaissance du bien et du mal.'

inquisitive child has recently, in urinating, passed a small stone. Still, his general approach to the problem is quite clear. Tell the facts in simple transparent words but associate them with the unpleasant impressions evoked in the child by the excretory functions. The teacher must never impose silence and never lie and, above all, never resort to mysterious euphemisms. Of course, at a later stage, the complete biological facts will be presented in objective terms.

On what basis does Rousseau proceed to build up the moral education of Emile? In the *Second Discours* we were told that man's innate passion for self was modified by an equally innate and natural principle 'anterior to reflection' which impelled him to pity other suffering fellow beings. It was described as the source of all the social virtues: generosity, clemency, humanity, benevolence, friendship. In the same *Discours*, however, Rousseau considered another interpretation of this innate disposition. Even if it were true, he argued, that our natural commiseration is only a sentiment which identifies us with a suffering fellow creature, this would not in any way affect the truth of his hypothesis but actually reinforce it. Now such, in fact, is the definition of innate human *pitié* finally adopted by Jean-Jacques in *Emile* and elaborated in three 'maxims' which considerably modify its originally irrational, unreflecting character. Here is the gist of the three maxims which might well have been conceived by La Rochefoucauld. (1) The individual cannot sympathise with others happier than himself, but only with those more deserving of pity. (2) We pity in others only the ills from which we do not believe ourselves immune. (3) The pity we feel for an unfortunate person is not to be gauged by the magnitude of his affliction but by the extent to which he pities himself. These maxims are prefaced by the general statement that if pity is sweet it is because, whilst putting ourselves in the position of the afflicted person, we have the pleasant feeling that we are not suffering like him. On the other hand, the sight of a happy person inspires envy rather than love in others.[1]

To sum up, Rousseau deduces morality from a primitive, innate disposition to sympathise, not with one's species, but only

[1] *E.G.* 370.

with those members of it who feel, like Jean-Jacques himself, that life has treated them scurvily. Moreover, this selective pity automatically ceases to operate when one personally experiences suffering. But what are we to think of a 'morality' which virtually outlaws human happiness by postulating that Nature intended us never to rejoice with those who are glad; which sees in a personal affliction only a selfish emotion? Fortunately, no-where else in *Emile* does Rousseau's moral philosophy retain this schematic character and, as we shall observe, he quietly discards his pseudo-naturalistic theory of a selective pity, notably in the admirable pages tracing Emile's social and moral progress. But Rousseau never discards the belief that morality has its genesis solely in an innate, natural sentiment of commiseration. It never occurred to him that the primitive man who resides within each of us might be just as ready to laugh with his fellows as to weep with them. Nor does he seem to have realised how much of an already existing social morality is lodged in the human tendency to sympathise with human affliction. In this respect, Jean-Jacques was slightly tarred with the same brush as his adversaries, the materialists who held that the mind at birth is a *tabula rasa* and that what we call Nature is always just the product of social habit. Their rational morality of self-interest, rightly condemned by Jean-Jacques, also predicates tacitly, the existence of an organised society whose members, in theory if not in practice, model their behaviour on a scale of moral values.

All human wisdom, in so far as it concerns the passions and their use, says Rousseau, can be summed up in two maxims. We must first of all *feel* what it is that links us to our fellow creatures and then order all our passions in accordance with these relation-ships. Essentially, this means the ability to control our imagina-tion which controls, in turn, our passions or sensibility. And who could discuss with more authority than Jean-Jacques the decisive rôle played by the imagination in shaping our moral and social existence? Encouraged by a misguided father to read, in early childhood, the romances of D'Urfé, Scudéry and La Calprenède, he had acquired from them a false image of the world, an image which he later tried to superimpose on reality with disastrous effects to his peace of mind. Indeed, it is no exaggeration to say that the whole deplorable history of Rousseau's broken friendships can be largely traced to his unfortunate upbringing. That is why Emile, at fifteen, is limited to one book, *Robinson Crusoe*. However, with puberty, the boy's imagination, which has so far been kept in a dormant state, is now thoroughly awake and its activities must be wisely controlled. The 'dangerous mysteries' so long concealed may now be revealed to him by the tutor but in words carefully selected for their aseptic quality. By contrast, the pages in which Rousseau extols the beauties of friendship glow with lyrical fire. But the passion of love, he insists, must be held at bay for as long as possible and the tutor, with donnish fussiness, keeps the adolescent segregated from feminine society lest the glimpse of a tempestuous petticoat or a whiff of perfume wreak havoc in his dawning sensibilities.

At this critical age, says Rousseau, it is vitally important to show Emile only those aspects of social life which will sober and not excite his imagination. To confront an adolescent with the hideous, extreme forms of social vice and suffering is liable to foster a cynical or callous attitude to humanity. But the method, of course, must be varied to suit the individual temperament. It might be salutary, where a youth betrays an immoderate passion for women to imitate the father who took his son round the wards of a hospital for venereal diseases. In the case of Emile no such drastic expedients are necessary. But he must be taught to love all conditions of men, even the odious governing classes who, from sheer lack of imagination rather than from deliberate cruelty, automatically equate the common man with the animal, thinking him too stupid or insensitive to feel his own hardships. And how many there are, says Rousseau, who subscribe to the damnable fallacy preached by the *philosophes* that every class has its equal dose of happiness and misery. According to their doctrine we have no need for morality or sensibility: we have only to leave things as they are and let the serf be maltreated, the sick go uncared for and the beggar starve. Fired by a noble indignation, Jean-Jacques leaps to the defence of the unprivileged masses and shatters this 'crude sophistry'. The rich man's ills are his own doing and it only depends on himself to be happy. But the poor man's misery is due to his economic position. 'No habit can remove his sensations of fatigue, physical exhaustion, or hunger: sense and wisdom are of no avail against the evils of his condition.'[1] Emile must therefore study the lower classes. He will then discover that however different may be their language from his, they have intelligence and common sense. 'Respect your species,' is the tutor's exhortation, 'remember that it is composed essentially of the masses of common people and that, if all the kings and philosophers were taken away, they would not be missed and things would go on just the same.'[2] Now, contrary to the general belief, sentiments like these are very rarely to be met with in the writings of French social reformers during the reign of Louis XV. I should like, therefore, to pay tribute to the *Dissertation sur la nature du peuple* which appeared, in 1755, from the pen of the abbé Coyer, an early champion of the common man.[3] His style, however, though sincere and eloquent, lacks the unique emotional quality of Rousseau's appeal on behalf of the underdog. It is clear that, for Jean-Jacques, social justice and equality are not just high-sounding concepts but social ideals which can and must, some day, be realised. These humanitarian sentiments could not, of course, be expected to produce an immediate or violent reaction and, indeed, the vast majority of his readers were as yet unable to grasp Rousseau's vision of a world regenerated, not by scientific progress, but by man's rediscovery of his original nature. Yet such is the vision which he tried to communicate in *Emile* to all whose task it was to educate the new generation. And the burden of his message is: 'Man, dishonour not mankind!'[4] That is why Emile must be kept from seeing the evil in his human environment before he has formed a general impression of human nature. He must believe that man is intrinsically good,

[1] *E.G.* 266: 'il n' y a point d'habitude qui lui puisse ôter le sentiment physique de la fatigue, de l'épuisement, de la faim: le bon esprit ni la sagesse ne servent à rien pour l'exempter des maux de son état.'

[2] *Ibid.*: 'Respectez donc votre espèce; songez qu'elle est composée essentielle-ment de la collection des peuples; que quand tous les rois et tous les philosophes en seraient ôtés, il n'y paraîtrait guère et que les choses n'en iraient pas plus mal.'

[3] See, for a fuller account of Coyer's views on this subject, my *Eighteenth-century France* (Dent, 1929).   [4] *E.G.* 266: 'Homme, ne déshonore point l'homme.'

however much men have been perverted by modern civilisation. Now, at last, the tutor must have recourse to the second-hand experience which is stored in books. This is the time for history. But good historians are rare, for they seldom give us an objective account of facts and these are too often distorted by the writer's ignorance or partiality. True, the eighteenth century has evolved a new and scientific approach to history yet, even so, we must still reckon with the partisan spirit, 'la fureur des systèmes'. Rousseau's shafts are clearly aimed at Voltaire whose brilliant *Essai sur les mœurs*, because of the author's prejudices, offers a somewhat distorted picture of history. Emile had better, therefore, read biography, especially Plutarch's *Lives* for their admirable panorama of the human passions, vices and virtues. He may now, also, read La Fontaine, though Jean-Jacques regrets that there is no edition which omits the moral endings since these are, or should be, superfluous. Why, he asks, by tagging on a moral to a fable, deprive the reader of the pleasure of discovering it for himself? Only thus do pupils really ever learn anything.

Emile, at eighteen, has never heard of God and that, in Rousseau's opinion, is far better than the fantastic notions of the Divinity which most boys have at his age. The psychology of the child, he repeats, is not that of the adult. It is absurd to imagine we can transform a boy into a Christian by teaching him to gabble the catechism. Young children resemble savages to some extent since they are natural idolaters or anthropomorphists. Rousseau discusses the origin of the religious sentiment very briefly and not very lucidly. He attributes it to the fear induced in primitive man by certain objects of his natural environment. To these, early man imputed unlimited powers and made gods of them: not, however, spirits but *dieux sensibles* or tangible deities. Yet, Jean-Jacques pursues: 'The stars, winds, mountains, rivers, trees, cities, even houses, each had its soul, its god, its life.'[1] This is rather vague and confusing and the reason is that Jean-Jacques approaches his subject handicapped by two illusions. The first is that primitive man could have had no idea of death. His second fallacy is that the notion of a man surviving his death

---

[1] *E.G.* 308: 'Les astres, les vents, les montagnes, les fleuves, les arbres, les villes, les maisons mêmes, tout avait son âme, son dieu, sa vie.'

in the form of a spirit could not have entered the mind of primitive man. Rousseau's sketchy treatment of this important psychological question, which he completely ignored in the *Second Discours*, suggests that, in his view, the religious sentiment ought not to be included amongst the 'innate sentiments relative to his species' with which Nature endowed man in order to fit him for a social existence. He did not apparently believe that religion is as old as our species, but rather that the religious sentiment is an acquisition from man's earliest social *milieu*. He certainly does not regard it as something responding to a permanent need of human nature. This view is explicit in the *Lettre à M. de Beaumont* where we are told that primitive man had no religious sentiment though 'the Lapps and Kaffirs living in national communities have multitudes of acquired and communicated ideas by the aid of which they acquire some crude notions of a divinity'.[1] How, why and where they formed these notions Rousseau does not try to explain. Nor does he tell us why the ideal religion for Emile must be a 'natural' religion when the religious sentiment itself does not derive from man's original nature.

By an ingenious device, Rousseau now pretends to transfer the responsibility for Emile's religious education to a representative of the Church, if one may so describe the unorthodox priest known as *le vicaire savoyard*.[2] This imaginary figure is a hybrid created by Jean-Jacques from youthful memories of the abbé Gaime and the *diacre* or acolyte, Gâtier. It was their wise and kindly intervention which, at a critical moment in his life, saved him from moral shipwreck. Now, grafting fiction on fact, Rousseau pictures an interview in which the Vicaire recounts his chequered career and his laborious progress from a state of intolerable unbelief to the religious faith he now professes. Like Julie de Wolmar, he presents a rare example of original goodness triumphant. In the eyes of the Church and Society, no doubt, the Vicaire is a sinner, having broken his vow of chastity. On the other hand, since the mother of his child is an unmarried woman,

---

[1] *H.* III, 76: 'les Lappons et les Cafres, vivant en corps de nations, ont-ils des multitudes d'idées acquises et communiquées à l'aide desquelles ils acquièrent quelques notions grossières d'une divinité.'

[2] I propose for convenience to allude to him as the Vicaire.

he had 'respected' the holy institution of marriage. Therefore, according to his curious logic, Rousseau's priest is the victim not of incontinence but of natural goodness.

We now observe, in the Vicaire's *Profession de Foi*, his gradual evolution from doubt and despair to a knowledge of the true God. In retrospect he compares his initial situation to that 'which Descartes postulates for the search of truth'.[1] It is not claimed, however, that his mode of approach to knowledge is Cartesian. The Vicaire, like Descartes, seeks, by a supreme effort of introspection, to move from a state of uncertainty and doubt to one of positive knowing. Both, also, distrust the evidence of the senses. Yet here the analogy, if it ever really existed, completely disintegrates. Doubt was not, for Descartes, as it was for Rousseau, a painful and affective state. Cartesian methodic doubt is, on the contrary, one of the processes employed by the mind in search of truth. Precisely because I doubt, I think and therefore exist. Moreover, since to know with certainty is a more perfect state than doubt, I have the idea of something more perfect than myself. This idea cannot come from nothing, nor from myself; it can only come from a nature superior to mine, possessing all the perfection of which I have an idea. That completely perfect nature is God. It is not by such a purely intellectual method that the Vicaire attains belief. His intuition, unlike that of Descartes, is not 'born of the sole light of reason': it is the 'inner light' shed by an inner sentiment which is involuntary and therefore, infallible. By these vague expressions, *sentiment intérieur*, *lumière intérieure* and *sentiment interne*, Rousseau intended, I think, to describe a kind of intuition which results in a more immediate knowledge of the self than that furnished by the purely intellectual introspection of Descartes. Of course it would be an error to identify it with that Bergsonian intuition by which the consciousness, turning inwards, perceives the inner life of the self as a 'moving, changing, coloured, living unity' and not as a juxtaposition of psychic states. Let us say, rather, that Rousseau's *sentiment intérieur*, his intuition, represents a more immediate consciousness of the self than Cartesian intuition or intellection. In this sense we

[1] *E.G.* 321: 'que Descartes exige pour la recherche de la vérité.'

must interpret the affirmations: 'To exist for us, is to feel'[1] and 'To perceive is to feel'.[2] As the Vicaire implies, there is a vast qualitative difference between the perceptions of the *sentiment intérieur* and of our five senses. The former convinces him of his existence as 'an active, intelligent being', a mind or soul capable of judging and comparing the objects of its perception. Its substance is therefore spiritual, not material. On the other hand, all that he perceives with his five senses is matter, which is naturally inert. However, since the external world is in constant and orderly movement, this can only come from an external Cause or Will similar to that which I employ when I cause my body to move. True, I only know this Will through its acts, not from its nature. But, as the Vicaire observes profoundly, since the really distinctive faculty of my active intelligence is the power to give a meaning to the verb *est*, I know that the external world is animated not only by a Will but by an Intelligence, for matter moves according to certain laws. The materialists talk grandly of 'universal force', 'necessary movement', which are empty words. They do not tell us how movement is communicated to matter or explain the cause of the physical laws defined by the physicists. Borrowing Fénelon's metaphor of the millions of characters of type which might, if tossed in the air, eventually arrange themselves fortuitously to compose the *Aeneid*, Rousseau contemptuously disposes of the materialistic theory of a universe created and conserved by blind chance. The betting against this is infinity to one.

Intuitively, therefore, the Vicaire knows that the universe is one and denotes a unique Intelligence which maintains the All in an established order.

This Being who wills and can [says the Vicaire], this Being active by itself, this Being, in short, whatever it is, which moves the universe and orders all things, I call God. I join to this name the ideas of intelligence, power, will which I have assembled and that of goodness which is a necessary consequence of these.[3]

---

[1] *E.G.* 353: 'Exister pour nous, c'est sentir.'

[2] *E.G.* 325: 'Apercevoir c'est sentir.'

[3] *E.G.* 335: 'Cet être qui veut et qui peut, cet être actif par lui-même, cet être enfin, quel qu'il soit, qui meut l'univers et ordonne toutes choses, je l'appelle Dieu. Je joins à ce nom les idées d'intelligence, de puissance, de volonté que j'ai rassemblées, et celle de bonté qui en est une suite nécessaire.'

What then accounts for the existence of evil in a universe created and ordered by a good and omnipotent God? The Vicaire, who seems to have read Leibniz's *Theodicy*, points out that since God has endowed man with free-will it is illogical to expect His providence to extend to the actions committed by men who abuse their free-will. If God were to use His power to prevent men from doing evil, He would be interfering with human liberty and reducing man, in fact, to the status of the animal, which has no free-will but only instinct. Human evil, the Vicaire affirms, is man's affair and does not disturb the universal order. Nor, he suggests, does experience show that the existence of evil has appreciably interfered with that of the human species. Humanity, he infers, must obviously think that life on the whole is good since it clings, in the mass, to life. If, as individuals, we are miserable we must blame ourselves. 'Indisputably, moral evil is our own doing and physical evil would be nothing were it not for our vices which have made us sensitive to it.'[1] It is easy to understand why Voltaire, with his robust common sense, was revolted by Rousseau's optimism. Human suffering is a terrible reality and of course there are thousands of its victims who cannot, by any stretch of the imagination be said to have forged their own misfortunes. On the other hand, is not Rousseau justified in asserting that a large measure of physical suffering is due to the fact that humanity has created for itself artificial needs or imprudently flouted the laws of Nature? Nor can one lightly reject his implication that a great deal of our moral suffering, even if it is not always our own fault, could be avoided or mitigated if we prevented our sensibility from becoming morbid through excessive reflection upon our situation. In Rousseau's view, there is no such thing as universal evil or universal disorder.

Another problem which does not exist for the Vicaire is that of survival. The soul must continue to exist after our physical demise simply because sovereign justice is inseparable from the sovereign power and goodness of God. If further proof were needed, we have it in the fact that so often in this earthly world

[1] *E.G.* 341: 'Le mal moral est incontestablement notre ouvrage, et le mal physique ne serait rien sans nos vices, qui nous l'ont rendu sensible.'

the wicked triumph over and oppress the just. Such a 'shocking discord in the universal harmony' postulates a readjustment of the universal order in another life. In reply to those who wonder how man, after the destruction of his material self, can survive, the Vicaire points out that in this world a great part of our active existence is independent of the body. Indeed, he observes, one might regard this life as a violently unhappy union of the soul and body in which each is constantly striving to reassume its natural state. Death, therefore, is a release for both:

> . . . the active and living substance regains all the force it employed in moving the passive and dead substance. Alas! I am only too well aware from my vices that man only half lives during his life and the life of the soul only begins with the death of the body.[1]

Now, at first sight, these words seem to reflect a typically Christian attitude. Did not Pascal say: 'Let us no longer consider a man as having ceased to live whatever Nature suggests; but as beginning to live, as truth assures us.'[2] Yet, as the Vicaire pursues his speculations on the after life, he does not once mention the Christian principle of the Redemption. Between God and himself there must be no intermediary, not even Jesus Christ. This is certainly implicit in his reflections on the probable nature of divine justice. Since the identity of the self is only prolonged by memory, argues the Vicaire, the self which survives death will remember its former existence on earth. The eternal happiness of the just man, therefore, will reside in the memories of his good deeds; conversely, the torment of the wicked will be the recollections of their bad actions. Whether their torment will be eternal is a matter of complete indifference to the Vicaire, but he thinks that God avenges himself on the wicked on this earth. What need to seek Hell in an-

---

[1] E.G. 344: '. . . la substance active et vivante regagne toute la force qu'elle employait à mouvoir la substance passive et morte. Hélas! je le sens trop par mes vices, l'homme ne vit qu'à moitié durant sa vie, et la vie de l'âme ne commence qu'à la mort du corps.'

[2] Pensées et opuscules, ed. Brunschvicg (Hachette), p. 101: 'Ne considérons plus un homme comme ayant cessé de vivre, quoi que la nature suggère; mais comme commençant à vivre comme la vérité l'assure.'

other life? Here and now, Hell exists in the hearts of the wicked. The good, who have not abused the free-will given them by God, shall enjoy after death 'the pure voluptuousness that comes from contentment with oneself'.[1] Freed of all the illusions bred of the senses, they shall enjoy the contemplation of the Supreme Being and the lovely vision of a divine Order where all the humiliations and injustices inflicted on them by men will be rectified. But the highest reward of the good man will be his total reintegration in his original and excellent nature, 'for what other good can an excellent being expect than to exist according to his nature?'[1] In other words, his *amour de soi*, which an unnatural social organisation had corrupted, will be restored to its original purity. For man's love of God, says Rousseau in commenting on the *Profession de Foi*, fuses with this very *amour de soi* 'so as to enjoy at last the durable happiness which the serenity of a good conscience and the contemplation of that Supreme Being promise him in the other life after having used this one well'.[2]

We have here a curious travesty of Augustinian theology as expounded by Jansenius and summarised by Pascal.[3] Man was born with two loves, one for God, the other for himself but on condition that the former should be infinite, the latter finite and relative to God. After the sin of Adam, however, man lost his love of God; and his *amour de soi* which had been previously good, deteriorated into *amour-propre* and overflowed into the vacancy produced by the disappearance of his love of God. 'That', says Pascal, 'was the origin of *amour-propre*. It was natural to Adam and, during his innocence, just; but as a result of his sin, it became criminal and immoderate.'[4] Now Rousseau, like St Augustine and Calvin, regarded human nature as fallen nature but, of course, in a very different sense, for he violently

---

[1] *E.G.* 345: 'la volupté pure qui naît du contentement de soi-même...car quel autre bien peut attendre un être excellent que d'exister selon sa nature?'

[2] *E.G.* 389: 'pour jouir enfin du bonheur durable que le repos d'une bonne conscience et la contemplation de cet Etre suprême lui promettent dans l'autre vie, après avoir bien usé de celle-ci.'

[3] *Op. cit.* p. 102.

[4] *Ibid.* 'Voilà l'origine de l'amour-propre. Il était naturel à Adam, et juste en son innocence; mais il est devenu et criminel et immodéré, ensuite de son péché.'

rejected their belief that because of Adam's original sin, man lost his primitive innocence and forfeited the divine gift of free-will. It is interesting to see how Jean-Jacques distorts their picture. According to the Vicaire, we fall from our original state of innocence when we abuse our free-will. Let us now recall, in this connection, the implications of Rousseau's *Lettre à M. Philopolis*. In perfecting his intelligence beyond the degree necessary to satisfy his natural needs, mankind inevitably sacrificed liberty and happiness. The stages of this sad process are vividly re-created in the *Second Discours*. To his opponent, Charles Bonnet, who argued that perfectibility is a natural faculty, Jean-Jacques replied that, at an early stage in his evolution, man could have avoided the temptation to develop this faculty prematurely by exercising his free-will. He failed to do so, with lamentable consequences to the human race which is now in that process of premature decay which it calls scientific or intellectual progress. The Vicaire implies that the initial error has become a habit: the vast majority of men are still abusing their free-will and, as he says, 'have eluded their destiny'[1], stepped outside their true nature. We must assume, however, that there are certain privileged souls like himself who can, by an effort of will, reorient themselves.

The Vicaire, unlike Descartes, is neither a rationalist nor a metaphysician. He acknowledges that for him the Creation and the Divine Essence are mysteries outside the scope of human reason. Indeed, the most worthy use one can make of reason is to annihilate it in the divine presence and prostrate oneself in humble adoration. 'Being of Beings,' he cries, 'I am because Thou art; to meditate upon Thee unceasingly is to uplift myself to my source.'[2] We must not, however, interpret this as the expression of a mystic *élan*. The Vicaire does not seek total identification of his will with the divine will. His happiness can only derive from the conviction that he is the 'work and instrument of the great Being who wills the Good, who does it, who will achieve mine by the co-operation of my will with His

---

[1] *E.G.* 345: 'trompé leur destination.'

[2] *E.G.* 348: 'Etre des êtres, je suis parce que tu es; c'est m'élever à ma source que de te méditer sans cesse.'

and by the good use of my liberty'.[1] The implications of this statement are clear. God, the Supreme Being, or Nature sends us into the world equipped for the happy life. We are not born sinful and, therefore, do not require Grace or divine help. But what of the moral life without which there can be no true happiness, especially in a highly organised society which tends more and more to obliterate the individual and his natural sentiments?

Confronted by this problem, the Vicaire again has recourse to the intuitive method of approach which has served him so well. The source of morality, he finds, is in man's original nature. The 'inner sentiment' if we look at it from the standpoint of morality, is really the immediate consciousness of right or wrong. Obviously, as Jean-Jacques points out, we are now considering social man, not man in the state of nature as described in the *Second Discours* and who has only one passion, *amour de soi,* which is indifferent to good or bad: 'neither hating nor loving anything, limited to mere physical instinct, he is null, he is stupid'.[2] But, if we scrutinise the deepest regions of the self, continues the Vicaire, can we honestly deny the existence of an instinctive disposition to love the good rather than the bad? Here, in our own nature, is the basic principle of all morality. It is simply man's natural goodness which, having developed and been rendered active the moment he begins to view himself in relation to his fellows, becomes Conscience, an innate, active principle of justice and virtue. By natural goodness, 'bonté originelle', Rousseau means that human nature is sound, free of any inherited tare such as original sin or perversity. Just as the tree exists in the seed, he implies, so is morality latent in man's psychological sub-structure, though if you interfere with the natural growth of the human tree, you will inevitably corrupt man's original goodness. Here we touch the very core of *Emile*. In this light, also, one must interpret the statement in the second book that what keeps man essentially good is having few needs and seldom comparing himself with others; and its

---

[1] *E.G.* 357: 'l'ouvrage et l'instrument du grand Etre qui veut le bien, qui le fait, qui fera le mien par le concours de mes volontés avec les siennes et par le bon usage de ma liberté.'

[2] *Lettre à M. de Beaumont* (*H.* III, 65): 'il ne hait ni n'aime rien; borné au seul instinct physique, il est nul, il est stupide.'

corollary that what makes him essentially bad is having many superfluous wants and attaching undue weight to the opinion of others.[1] Yet it might be objected that since Rousseau himself always insists that the basic element of man's nature is *amour de soi* it must surely be unnatural for him to love anything but his own good. Here Jean-Jacques points out that, as man is composed of two substances, his spiritual self (*l'être intelligent*) and his sensual self (*l'être sensitif*), his *amour de soi* is not a simple passion. He will always naturally seek his own good, but the well-being of his senses is different from that of his soul whose voice is Conscience. Unfortunately, it speaks a language which it is all too easy to ignore if we have been badly educated and exposed to the wrong kind of social milieu. Nevertheless, if we care to listen intently, all of us can hear it. For Conscience is timid and loves the peace and quiet of solitude.

Conscience! conscience! divine instinct, immortal and celestial voice; assured guide of a being both ignorant and limited but intelligent and free; infallible judge of good and evil, rendering man like unto God! it is thou who makest the excellence of his nature and the morality of his actions.[2]

The finest pages of the *Profession* are devoted to this theme which captures the inner melody of Rousseau's moral existence. With the same passionate intensity, the Vicaire attacks the materialists who assert that since there is nothing in the human mind which does not come from sense experience, Conscience is not a moral instinct but merely an acquired social habit. Morality, they say, is based on the principles of personal and general interest. But what, the Vicaire asks scornfully, is self-interest? Where is the sense, for example, in sacrificing one's life for self-interest? If we adopt the rationalist concept of morality, it follows that the truly just man always behaves contrary to his self-interest. And if we accept the notion of a purely utilitarian morality, we are driven to invent base motives in order

[1] *E.G.* 249.
[2] *E.G.* 354–5: 'Conscience! conscience! instinct divin, immortelle et céleste voix; guide assuré d'un être ignorant et borné, mais intelligent et libre; juge infaillible du bien et du mal, qui rends l'homme semblable à Dieu! c'est toi qui fais l'excellence de sa nature et la moralité de ses actions.'

to explain the conduct of a Socrates or a Regulus. Pure intellectualism, Rousseau means, can never discover the tap-root of
morality which lies not in reasoning but in feeling. Sensibility
precedes knowing. Our natural sentiments appeal to us on behalf of the general interest whilst our reason counsels egoism.
Whatever gave us being, endowed us with natural sentiments for
our conservation: love of self, fear of pain, horror of death, desire
for well-being. But these concern only the individual and do not
provide a basis for morality. But, since Nature clearly intended
us for a social existence, she must have given us other innate
sentiments relating to our species. She gave us, notably,
Conscience which draws its impelling force from the moral
system formed by this dual relationship of the individual to himself, on the one hand, and to his fellow men on the other. There
is no man, however depraved, who has never yielded to his
natural inclination towards well-doing or never remembered
with pleasure his good actions. But, of course, there are always
a thousand reasons for not following 'the penchant of one's
heart'. Virtue, whatever the *philosophes* say, always costs an
effort. It is always a struggle in which moral interest triumphs
over material self-interest. Moreover, the Vicaire suggests, it is
inseparable from man's eternal search for happiness. And in the
following passage we learn what he (or Rousseau) understands
by supreme happiness.

I aspire to that moment when, delivered of the fetters of the flesh,
I shall be *me* without contradiction or division and shall need only
myself in order to be happy. Meanwhile I am happy in this life because
I count all its ills for very little, because I regard it as almost foreign
to my being and because all the real goodness I can extract from it
depends on me.[1]

Christian piety, said Pascal, annihilates the human *moi*: Jean-
Jacques, on the contrary, places his ego in the centre of everything. This is a fact to keep in mind lest we might be tempted to
misinterpret the idiom now employed by the Vicaire to describe

[1] *E.G.* 358: 'J'aspire au moment où, délivré des entraves du corps, je serai *moi*
sans contradiction et sans partage, et n'aurai besoin que de moi pour être heureux;
en attendant je le suis dès cette vie parce que j'en compte pour peu tous les maux,
que je la regarde comme presque étrangère à mon être, et que tout le vrai bien que
j'en peux retirer dépend de moi.'

his 'sublimes contemplations', the devotional exercises by which he prepares his soul for the great transformation.

> I meditate upon the order of the universe, not so as to explain it by vain systems, but to admire it unceasingly, to adore the wise Author who makes his presence felt in it. I converse with Him; I allow all my faculties to be pervaded by His divine essence; His blessings fill me with tenderness; I bless Him for his gifts, but I do not pray to Him.[1]

Quite so, but always on condition that the divine essence, in permeating Rousseau's faculties, does not absorb his faculty of free-will. That is implicit in the Vicaire's rooted objections to prayers of petition which are those already formulated by Saint-Preux. What more can we ask of God than He has already given us in order to lead a righteous life: conscience whereby to love the good; reason, to know it and freedom, to choose it? If we will choose evil, says the Vicaire, that is entirely our own responsibility. It is absurd and impious to ask the Almighty to change our will and thus alter the universal order of things. Note, therefore, that in praying that God's will be done, he adds: 'In *joining* mine to it, I do what Thou dost. I acquiesce in Thy goodness; I seem to be partaking, in advance, of the supreme felicity which is its reward.'[2]

How are we to interpret these words which appear, at first sight, to reflect the emotions of a mystic soul? Here, as elsewhere in the *Profession*, the Vicaire employs a curiously ambiguous idiom which has greatly exercised Rousseau's critics and led to various interpretations of his 'natural religion'. These have been conveniently summarised by the late Albert Schinz: sentimentalist (Brunschvicg); rationalist (Beaulavon); sentimentalist in appearance but essentially rationalist (Schinz).[3] I prefer the less systematic approach to this question adopted by Masson whose comprehensive yet penetrating study, though

---

[1] *E.G.* 358–9: 'Je médite sur l'ordre de l'univers, non pour l'expliquer par de vains systèmes, mais pour l'admirer sans cesse, pour adorer le sage auteur qui s'y fait sentir. Je converse avec lui, je pénètre toutes mes facultés de sa divine essence; je m'attendris à ses bienfaits, je le bénis de ses dons: mais je ne le prie pas.'

[2] *E.G.* 359: 'En y *joignant* la mienne, je fais ce que tu fais, j'acquiesce à ta bonté; je crois partager d'avance la suprême félicité qui en est le prix.' (My italics.)

[3] *Etat présent des travaux sur Jean-Jacques Rousseau*, pp. 274–81. (Les Belles Lettres, 1941.)

first published nearly forty years ago, retains its original prestige.[1] This great scholar who viewed the *Profession de foi* in the context of Rousseau's entire life and work, describes it as 'a sentimental manifesto where we must not look for too much intellectual cohesion', a fact recognised by Jean-Jacques himself. The Vicaire, for example, opposes Christian dogma on rational grounds yet celebrates the Mass in a spirit of veneration. With the same inconsistency, observes Masson, the Savoyard priest begins his *Profession* in a vein of 'irrational logic, the logic of the heart', but later turns to Reason for an intellectual appeasement of his doubts because, 'after having dismissed her as a mistress of error and lectured us on intellectual humility, he feels, awakening within himself, an impenitent rationalist'.[2] Masson, however, can hardly have expected from the Vicaire a *Profession de foi* based either upon a rationalist or upon a purely sentimental reaction to his perceptions of the general universe. After all, why should it be surprising to encounter here a phenomenon so typical of all Rousseau's writings? I mean the agility with which he slides from one plane of his consciousness to another in response to the stimulus of memory or imagination.

For Masson, the question of mysticism scarcely arises in relation to the *Profession* though, in general, he sees Rousseau's religion as 'the mystic projection of the essential needs of his soul',[3] a phrase which really obscures the issue. There is no ambiguity, however, in Masson's final verdict. 'In the paradise of Jean-Jacques, God will discreetly efface Himself to make room for Jean-Jacques.'[4] Le Père A. Brou, an able Jesuit historian of eighteenth-century French literature, observes that Rousseau is sometimes in accord with the most orthodox and profound mystics. Yet, in conclusion, he can discover in the *Profession* only an adulterated mysticism which is really self-divinisation. Ernest Seillière, whose hostility to Rousseau is well known, thinks that

---

[1] Masson, P.-M., *La Religion de Jean-Jacques Rousseau* (Paris, 1916).

[2] *Op. cit.* I, 83: '...après l'avoir congédiée comme une maîtresse d'erreur et nous avoir prêché l'humilité intellectuelle, il sent s'éveiller en lui un rationaliste impénitent.'

[3] *Op. cit.* I, 263: 'la projection mystique des besoins essentiels de son âme.'

[4] *Op. cit.* I, 120: 'Dans le paradis de Jean-Jacques, Dieu lui-même s'effacera pour faire place à Jean-Jacques.'

Mme de Warens and the Jesuit priest Hémet converted Jean-Jacques to Quietism in 1738 and that ever afterwards he remained, subconsciously, a Quietist. However, as the late abbé Brémond remarked in his classic but uncompleted *Histoire du sentiment religieux en France*, we must not accept this statement lightly because, for M. Seillière, any manifestation of religious sensibility was mysticism. Brémond's criticism is well founded. Therefore, to avoid possible confusion, I propose in the following brief remarks on this subject to adopt Bergson's definition of the Christian mystic as a person who is convinced that, as the result of a supra-intellectual experience, his soul has been privileged to enter into direct communication with God, the transcendental principle of all life. This communication represents, not merely a contact, but a partial coincidence with what the Vicaire would call the 'divine essence'. From his unique experience, the mystic emerges with a transfigured consciousness, a sense of inner revelation. He has found a new religion and feels impelled henceforth to devote his life to the diffusion of mysticism. He must, by his example, create a divine humanity, for such is the very essence of his new faith. True mysticism is a religion of love since it originates in the love which the Christ of the Gospels gave to the world.

Rousseau's own remarks on the subject of mystics are brief and unilluminating, which is not surprising. For, although Christian mystics are as old as Christianity, the study of their psychology only really began late in the nineteenth century. Saint-Preux, it will be recalled, warns Julie against the dangers attendant upon excessive indulgence in prayer and contemplation. But, whilst condemning prayers of petition, he concedes that prayer itself is 'useful' because it is an 'act of the understanding' whereby we are uplifted to God and thus carried above and outside ourselves. However, Saint-Preux is very emphatic on one point. This spiritual transformation is produced solely by us: we change ourselves by the act of raising ourselves to God in prayer. But he warns Julie that the abuse of this exercise can easily lead to the mystic state. By 'état mystique', Rousseau obviously means the state of quietude or 'oraison mystique' familiar to Mme Guyon and other disciples of Molinos. These

Quietists claimed that once the soul was closely united with God, it should remain in a state of perfect quietude, surrendering utterly to the movement of the divine spirit; and 'whilst the higher part of the soul is in this holy repose, it must not trouble itself about what is happening to its imagination or even to its body'.[1] This is the kind of *oraison* which Saint-Preux has in mind when he warns Julie that by abusing the habit of prayer we drift into mysticism because, in seeking to uplift ourselves to God we relinquish the intellectual powers given us by Him. That Julie needed such counsel appears likely if we judge by the following effusion:

Finding, therefore, nothing to satisfy it here below, my starving soul seeks its nourishment elsewhere. By uplifting itself to the source of all feeling and being, it loses there its aridity and languor; there it is reborn, reanimated; there it finds a new motive energy; there it absorbs a new life; there it acquires another existence which does not depend on the passions of the body; or rather, it is no longer within myself; it is wholly in the immense Being which it contemplates and, momentarily freed of its bonds, consoles itself for having to reassume them by this preliminary experience of a more sublime state which, it hopes, will one day be its own.[2]

One can hardly describe this recharging of the spiritual batteries as a mystic state of quietude, particularly since Julie insists that her *séances* are of brief duration and do not interfere with her good works. Yet one can appreciate the misgivings of Saint-Preux who points out that habit may, in time, prolong her delicious ecstasies. Julie, who seems aware of the danger, vigorously dissociates herself from the Quietists. Mme Guyon, she remarks, would have been better employed in educating her children as Christians than in getting herself thrown into the Bastille for writing fantastic books which no one understands.

---

[1] See Dangeau, *Journal*, 5–6 May 1686, for a layman's résumé of the Quietist doctrines. Many of their unworthy adepts, he says, were guilty of the most scandalous behaviour.

[2] *N.H.* VI, Lettre 8: 'Ne trouvant donc rien ici-bas qui lui suffise, mon âme avide cherche ailleurs de quoi la remplir: en s'élevant à la source du sentiment et de l'être, elle y perd sa sécheresse et sa langueur; elle y renaît, elle s'y ranime, elle y trouve un nouveau ressort, elle y puise une nouvelle vie; elle y prend une autre existence qui ne tient point aux passions du corps; ou plutôt elle n'est plus en moi-même, elle est toute dans l'être immense qu'elle contemple, et, dégagée un moment de ses entraves, elle se console d'y rentrer par cet essai d'un état plus sublime qu'elle espère être un jour le sien.'

She concurs, also, with Saint-Preux in condemning the *piétistes* and their 'mystic ecstasies'. Later, when he reminds her of these protestations, Julie frankly admits that they are inconsistent with her new sentiments. But if she formerly despised the *état d'oraison* which now makes life so much less 'angular', so much lighter and gayer, it was simply because she had never experienced the joys of silent communion with God. She does not seek to justify this devotional exercise or to claim that it is wise. 'I only say it is sweet, that it makes up for the feeling that my happiness is dwindling away.'[1]

The Vicaire would not altogether condone these sentiments nor entirely condemn them. Probably, like Rousseau, he would remind us that they occur in a letter which is really Julie's swansong. Whilst ardently sharing her longing for a God capable of entering into relations with His creatures as opposed, presumably, to the metaphysical God of Plato or the avenging Deity of Calvinism, the Vicaire firmly disapproves of any form of worship which tends to diminish the majesty of God by humanising Him. It is wicked vanity, he says, to bring God down to one's own level and expect a divine illumination not vouchsafed to others. Yet, though tacitly sympathising with Julie's weakness for contemplation, he himself refuses to imitate her lest this penchant degenerate into an 'idle passion' and tempt him to neglect his pastoral duties. It can hardly be said, then, that the *Profession* resolves the question debated in the *Nouvelle Héloïse* except that the Vicaire agrees with Saint-Preux that prayers of petition are wrong, since God has given us Conscience as a guide to the good life and free-will to live it. Are we to conclude, therefore, that the Vicaire's 'natural religion' can dispense with Christ? Here Rousseau is noncommittal and perhaps disingenuous. In one of his finest pages, contrasting Socrates with Jesus, he affirms his belief in the divinity of Our Lord. 'Yes, if Socrates lived and died like a Sage, Jesus lived and died like a God.'[2] But, at the same time,

---

[1] *N.H.* vi, Lettre 8: 'je dis seulement qu'il est doux, qu'il supplée au sentiment du bonheur qui s'épuise.'

[2] *E.G.* 380: 'Oui, si la vie et la mort de Socrate sont d'un sage, la vie et la mort de Jésus sont d'un Dieu.'

the Vicaire confesses humbly to an 'involuntary scepticism' in regard to certain 'incredible things' narrated in the Gospels and considered an integral part of Christian doctrine by the Church. He finds most of the prophecies, miracles and other so-called revelations not only absurd but ignoble and often contrary to the spirit of Christianity. Yet, as a priest, he adopts the only course open to him. Subordinating reason to faith, he meticulously observes the rites of Catholicism whilst tolerating other religions which sincerely honour the majesty of the Supreme Being. After all, he thinks, prophecies, miracles and dogma have no direct bearing on human behaviour and are thus relatively unimportant. God does not reveal Himself through such agencies but in His manifold works. There is one book all men can read: the book of Nature. There, in language intelligible to all humanity we have the direct revelation of God's infinite love and power. Forms of worship vary from country to country according to local custom and tradition. All are good if they come from the heart for 'the essential worship is that of the heart'.[1]

Here we have the dominant theme of the *Profession de Foi* which, as Masson rightly suggests, must be viewed as the climax of a movement that had been long active both in France and in Switzerland. Its protagonists urged that religion should be more 'natural', more intimate and more simple, that is, less dogmatic. In Masson's illuminating phrase their belief in the possibility of a natural religion which would reflect, as it were, the spontaneous and primitive attitude of the human heart to God is a sort of theological counterpart to the dream of a Golden Age.[2] But although this movement found many sympathisers in the clergy of both Christian Churches, it attracted other supporters who were really free-thinkers like Morelly, the author of *Le Code de la nature* whose object was the destruction of Christianity. Mostly, however, they were sincere, if not always orthodox Christians. Jean-Jacques was familiar with their writings, especially with those of the Pietists Muralt and Marie Huber. He was also friendly with several of the advanced Genevan pastors who favoured a more evangelical

[1] *E.G.* 381: 'Le culte essentiel est celui du cœur.'
[2] *Op. cit.* I, 268.

approach to Christianity. Masson, indeed, thought that, but for political complications, the religion without dogma or intellectual discipline proposed by the Vicaire might eventually have been accepted by the Genevan Church. I cannot share his opinion which seems to me disproved, in fact, by Rousseau's subsequent correspondence with Moultou, Vernes, Vernet and other Genevan ministers. No enlightened Christian, wrote Moultou, would deny that Rousseau was a Christian. But the common people of Geneva believed in their religion solely because of its miracles.

If only for one reason, which appears decisive, Rousseau's natural religion is incompatible with Christian mysticism. The Vicaire's 'culte du cœur' for all its sincerity and fervour, lacks that one quality of total self-surrender which characterises all true mystics. On the contrary, Rousseau's Vicaire insists that, in conversing with God, he is simply enjoying a foretaste of that supreme moment when 'I shall be *me* without contradiction, undivided, and shall need only myself to be happy'.[1]

Again and again, in the *Dialogues* and in the *Rêveries*, we shall encounter this obsessive idea of self-sufficiency which automatically separates the 'contemplation' of Rousseau from that of the Christian mystics. The love that consumes them, as Bergson has observed, is no longer simply the love of man for God; it is God's love for all men. Through God, by God, the mystic loves all humanity with a divine love. But Rousseau's love of humanity was always simply an extension of his love of self, of that self which had retained intact the original goodness immanent in human nature. The *Third Dialogue* clearly reveals what Jean-Jacques means by loving humanity. As a result of his natural penchant for solitude and introspection, this 'historian of nature' discovered in the depths of his consciousness the image of pristine man, still fresh from the mint of Nature. From that moment his mission was clear: it was to hold up that image as an exemplar to all men and thus, eventually, achieve the regeneration of humanity.

Those traits, so new for us and so true, once traced, still found of course in the depths of men's hearts the attestation of their genuineness,

---

[1] E.G. 358: 'Je serai *moi* sans contradiction, sans partage, et n'aurai besoin que de moi pour être heureux.'

but their presence would never have been revealed if the historian of nature had not begun by removing the rust that hid them. A retired and solitary life, a love of reverie and contemplation, the habit of introspection and of seeking within himself, in the calm of the passions, those primitive traits which have disappeared in the multitude, could alone enable him to rediscover them. In a word, it was necessary that one man should depict himself in order thus to show us primitive man and if the author had not been just as singular as his books he would never have written them.[1]

The *Profession*, says Rousseau, is not a religious code: it merely shows the line of reasoning he can adopt with Emile without departing from his educational method. The pupil, at nineteen, has now the essentials of religion, of any religion, for he must later choose his own communion. But there is no fear of his being influenced by the 'mysterious dogmas' of any religious or philosophic sect. In fact, the only dogmas that interest him are concerned with practical morality on which Rousseau will have more to say. His style, however, now lacks that dynamic quality which pulsates in the first four books of *Emile*. One cannot readily dismiss the impression that Rousseau's heart is no longer in the job. Is it perhaps because, whilst insisting that the object of his natural education is to reconcile the rights of Nature with those of society, he is assailed by certain doubts as to the possibility of such a reconciliation? One feels that Emile, like his master, will always be an 'amiable stranger' in society, loving humanity yet unable to esteem men. This is implicit in Rousseau's descriptions of Emile in society. At twenty, the youth listens with indulgent contempt to the chatter of the vapid Parisians and, with a sigh of relief, bids an eternal farewell to their city, 'that famous city of noise, smoke and mud where women no longer believe in honour nor men in virtue'.[2]

[1] *H.* IX, 288: 'Ces traits, si nouveaux pour nous et si vrais, une fois tracés, trouvaient bien encore au fond des cœurs l'attestation de leur justesse, mais jamais ils ne s'y seraient remontrés d'eux-mêmes, si l'historien de la nature n'eût commencé par ôter la rouille qui les cachait. Une vie retirée et solitaire, un goût vif de rêverie et de contemplation, l'habitude de rentrer en soi et d'y rechercher dans le calme des passions ces premiers traits disparus chez la multitude, pouvaient seuls les lui faire retrouver. En un mot, il fallait qu'un homme se fût peint lui-même pour nous montrer ainsi l'homme primitif, et, si l'auteur n'eût été tout aussi singulier que ses livres, jamais il ne les eût écrits.'

[2] *E.G.* 444: 'ville célèbre, ville de bruit, de fumée et de boue, où les femmes ne croient plus à l'honneur ni les hommes à la vertu.'

Emile is no longer, it should be noted, a man of one book. He has studied the best authors, especially the Greek and Latin classics which he reads in the original—in the circumstances, as Mr Pickwick would say, an achievement of no inconsiderable magnitude. Emile has also learned one or two modern languages but not for conversational use. That, according to Rousseau, is unimportant: the real value of modern language study is to help us to understand the grammatical structure of language in general.

With the fifth book Sophie, or Woman, comes into Emile's life. So far, the tutor has managed to retard the development of the youth's sexual impulses by unceasing vigilance and strenuous physical exercises, like hunting. For Rousseau, though condemning blood sports, considers that they render their devotees immune from carnal desire. Pursuing his original policy of deceiving Emile for the latter's own good, Jean-Jacques contrives that he and his ward shall find themselves lost at nightfall in a lonely, mountainous region. A peasant directs them to the house of a gentleman renowned for his charity to footsore travellers. Picture now the welcome accorded to the weary strangers and the emotions that invade the inflammable Emile on first beholding the blushing Sophie who sees in him the miraculous incarnation of her dream-lover, Telemachus, the hero of Fénelon's celebrated prose epic.

Sophie has all the qualities of the perfect wife, the durable qualities which Rousseau associated with marriage rather than with passionate love. What these are we already know from his previous works. True love, he pointed out in the *Second Discours*, does not properly belong to the primitive natural state; but Emile, of course, is not a savage. This does not alter the fact that Nature, in establishing a fundamental biological difference between the female and the male, endowed the former with a special feminine temperament and character. Man, briefly, is active and strong: woman is passive and weak. She was made to please man and to be subjugated by him. And though Providence gave us all reason as a curb to our passions, it took care, in addition, to endow woman with modesty as a brake on her unlimited sexual desires. We must not, however, be deceived by appearances. Woman only seems to be the weaker vessel be-cause 'by an invariable law of Nature' her facility in exciting desires in man is greater than the latter's ability to satisfy them so that, in fact, he really depends upon woman. Man's greatest thrill in his relationships with her, says Jean-Jacques derives from his uncertainty as to whether she surrenders to him through involuntary weakness or of her own free will and she cleverly maintains him in a perpetual state of doubt. With great fervour Rousseau now enlarges on the sacred duties of parenthood and the importance of family love which is the nucleus of patriotism.

Sophie's education, naturally, must differ in many ways from Emile's. Her physical upbringing, however, will be much the same: cold water, fresh air and plenty of rough fare. However, as a woman, Sophie will soon have to conform to the *bienséances*, to the pattern of feminine behaviour designed by public opinion. Therefore, as Rousseau naïvely puts it, she must be accustomed at an early age to constant interference with her liberty; to being dragged away from her childish amusements in order to perform household tasks. Little is said about her programme of studies because Jean-Jacques is not interested in teaching girls to think. But, in opposition to the Genevan rigorists, he would allow them singing and dancing as a change from the domestic arts. Besides, women must entertain their men-folk as well as be useful to them. Girls, he believes, ought to be taught religion at an earlier stage than boys though in their case one need waste no time in ex-planations. Little Sophie must believe in God because she must. Yet there is no reason why her religious instruction should be made 'an object of sadness or restraint', and it should never appear to be a task or duty.

If not beautiful, Sophie is well-born and good-tempered. Her only defect, perhaps, is her excessive sensibility and imagina-tion. Whilst by no means a *dévote*, she is deeply religious and shows it in a hundred practical ways. Her father, who might have stepped out of an eighteenth-century *drame*, is an en-lightened parent who lets his daughter choose her own husband, though Sophie, until she meets Emile, has formed a very low opinion of the average eligible male. The courtship of the lovers evolves under the vigilant eye of Jean-Jacques who can always be relied upon for the word in season, the little homily, for example, on Emile's duty to respect his fiancée's reputation when the ardent youth proposes taking lodgings near her house. To their great distress, the inexorable tutor insists upon a separation of two years so that Emile may observe the various institutions, professions and classes of society and thus prepare himself for a career. But Rousseau's main purpose is to teach Emile that there is no happiness without courage and no virtue without a sacrifice.

We need not, for the moment, concern ourselves with his views on the principles of political law or on the art of good government. This section is a résumé of *Du Contrat social* and will be dealt with in the next chapter. Although this fifth book is somewhat of an anticlimax and, in places, even boring or absurd there are, on the other hand many pages which one still reads with delight. No one should miss, for example, those devoted to the art of travel, *Des Voyages*, for they crystallise a great deal of wisdom, humour and good sense besides providing Rousseau with an excuse for a really charming digression on the theme of how to be happy though wealthy. Since all journeys should end in lover's meetings, Emile returns safely and marries Sophie. But the tutor does not consider his task at an end until he has delivered a final lecture to brides on the science of preserving love in marriage, though the gist of it, one vaguely suspects, the blushing Sophie may already have heard from her grandmother. 'Do you want to see your husband constantly at your feet? Then always keep him at some distance from your person.'[1]

The most persistent of all illusions, according to Bergson, is that the new is always merely a subtle rearrangement of the old. Probably this explains why, ever since *Emile* first appeared, so much time has been spent in exploring its 'sources' or historical origins. These investigations have produced, however, one valuable result. We now know from the large number of treatises and articles on education published during the first half of the eighteenth century that, for all thoughtful Frenchmen, the subject had acquired a fresh and urgent importance. Yet, whilst these researches have brought to light many notions which,

---

[1] *E.G.* 613: 'Voulez-vous voir votre mari sans cesse à vos pieds, tenez-le toujours à quelque distance de votre personne.'

viewed in retrospect, may seem to prefigure or anticipate *Emile*, the truly basic ideas of Rousseau's doctrine are quite original. Certainly, as Jean-Jacques is the first to admit, he owed much to such predecessors as Plato, Saint Augustine, Montaigne, Locke, Fénelon, to Le Père Lamy and the Oratorians. Nevertheless, in the opinion of all modern educationists, these borrowings only serve to underline the originality of *Emile*.

Though Rousseau, in one of his letters, refers to 'my reveries on education', it would be naïve to interpret this *coquetterie* literally. His principles, as we are constantly reminded in *Emile*, have their roots in experience, not in empty concepts. Yet no one knew better than Jean-Jacques that, because of their startling novelty, his maxims and methods would inevitably seem like 'reveries' to his contemporaries. That is exactly what happened. The *philosophes*, in order to ridicule *Emile*, seized upon its most vulnerable and inessential aspects, unable to grasp its substance. Many readers, however, were converted by the irresistible appeal of the first book to a new sense of their parental obligations and tried to profit by Rousseau's advice on infant welfare. It cannot be said, on the other hand, that *Emile* substantially altered traditional methods of instruction either in the eighteenth century or during the Revolution. In this connection, it is illuminating to read the speeches addressed to the *Convention Nationale* in July 1793 on educational reform.[1] Nearly every speaker pays homage to Jean-Jacques; yet none, even his old friend Alexandre Deleyre, betrays any real understanding of *Emile*. The Rousseau they admire is the author of the two *Discours* and of the *Lettre à d'Alembert* who damned the intellectuals and advocated for all good Republicans organised games and *fêtes champêtres* in the ancient Greek and Roman style. However, Deleyre's enthusiasm for Sparta met with a cold response: those who knew about the real Sparta said they were not prepared to model the new Republic on a slave State. In short, Rousseau was of no practical assistance to these pioneers of State education though all shared his views on the importance of physical and manual training.

It was not, indeed, until the nineteenth century that educa-

[1] See Bibl. Nat. 8 L ^{38}e, 318–69 for the collected speeches and projects.

tionists like Basedow, Pestalozzi, Froebel and Montessori discerned the true significance of *Emile* and, by their intelligent application of its principles, opened a new era in education. Jean-Jacques, in his later years, maintained that his book was primarily a treatise, not on education but on the original goodness of human nature. But this view, one imagines, finds little support today. The fundamental ideas we owe to Jean-Jacques, the ideas that have revolutionised modern education may be summarised very briefly. All education must be based on an experimental knowledge of child psychology. The child's view of the external world is quite different from that of the teacher. There are various distinct phases in the development of the childish mind and these must condition the various stages of his education. The child only really learns from first-hand experience; hence the value of carefully prepared object lessons or *leçons de choses*. If the child is to learn to think, the teacher must not be in too great a hurry to cram his mind with other people's thoughts. The object of education is not primarily vocational. It is not, as Rousseau said, to produce a magistrate, a soldier or a priest, but a man. And a well educated man is he who is best equipped 'to bear the fortunes and misfortunes of life'. Was it not the Danish philosopher Höffding who remarked that *Emile* is the Magna Carta of all children? Could any man possibly wish for a more splendid epitaph?

Probably in 1762,[1] Rousseau began a sequel to the fifth book of *Emile*, an epistolary novel entitled *Emile et Sophie ou les solitaires*. He completed one *Lettre*, but never finished the second where Emile is captured by Barbary corsairs and sold into slavery. It does not bear comparison with the first which is rich in subtle psychological notations obviously inspired by the author's memories of Mme d'Houdetot and Julie de Wolmar who now coalesce in the image of a Sophie happily married to a youthful Jean-Jacques, but later, it would seem, corrupted by 'a vicious woman jealous of her virtues',[2] a transparent allusion to

---

[1] According to Courtois (*Ann.* xv, 139) Rousseau read this sequel to a young Bernese nobleman, N.-A. de Kirchberger, at Môtiers on 17 Nov. 1762. However, from the tone of certain passages, I incline to the view that this fragment may have been revised, in parts, towards the end of Rousseau's life.

[2] *H.* III, 12: 'une femme vicieuse et jalouse de ses vertus.'

Mme d'Epinay. The general plan of the novel is adumbrated in the first *Lettre*. Emile will tell his tutor and adoptive father, how 'two regenerated children' strayed from the path of virtue but eventually found their true selves again. His theme is essentially that of *La Nouvelle Héloïse* except that the heroine's lapse occurs after marriage. And we learn that, like Julie, she will reveal on her deathbed a perfection of virtue unsuspected even by her husband. But Rousseau's new novel had another object. It was to demonstrate the value of his educational system by showing what happens when his pupil is exposed to a series of misfortunes which would have crushed the spirit of a man educated in the old-fashioned way.

After eight years of ideal married happiness in their country home, the young people lose, in the space of a few months, Sophie's parents and their little daughter. These disasters befall them, moreover, after the departure of their tutor, now living in retirement. Emile, thinking that a change of scene may distract his wife's mind from her sorrows, decides to rejoin, in Paris, their former neighbours, a lady with whom Sophie had become intimate and her husband. Despite his own premonitions of evil and his wife's protests, Emile carries out this plan. Gradually, in the course of two years, Emile and Sophie drift apart, corrupted by the specious maxims of their smart friends who hold that, in marriage, husband and wife can remain good comrades whilst leading separate lives. Soon, however, Emile observes that Sophie no longer goes into society but sits brooding in her room, plunged in melancholy. She insists on breaking with her former friend to whom she refers with horror: Emile, therefore, closes his door to the husband. Once again passionately in love with Sophie, he tries to resume their marital relations, only to encounter her invincible resistance. But one day, when his wife is about to yield to his caresses, she suddenly tears herself from his arms, crying out wildly: 'Arrêtez, Emile, et sachez que je ne vous suis rien: un autre a souillé votre lit, je suis enceinte; vous ne me toucherez plus de ma vie.'[1] She then rushes into her boudoir and bolts the door.

---

[1] *H.* III, 7: 'Stop, Emile, and know that I am no longer anything to you: another man has defiled your bed and I am pregnant. You shall not touch me again as long as I live.'

The effect on the reader of Sophie's confession, for which he is totally unprepared, is like that produced by a *coup de théâtre* in a melodrama. Nor will he ever learn, of course, why and how this paragon of wifely virtue was led to break the seventh commandment. In defence of his shock tactics, Rousseau could no doubt argue that their object was to bring his reader, hitherto a mere spectator, into communion with the hero; to make him experience immediately, not only Emile's stupefaction, but the whole gamut of disarrayed and conflicting emotions so vividly portrayed in the succeeding pages. In these, as in *La Nouvelle Héloïse*, we can observe why Rousseau was only a potential novelist. The passages where Emile dissects a state of soul actually experienced by his creator reveal a delicacy of perception, a force of penetration and felicity of expression so far unknown in the French novel. But in others, where Jean-Jacques diverges from the track grooved in his consciousness by life itself, he tends to remind us of his favourite novelist, l'abbé Prévost. This is strikingly evident in his arresting impressions of Emile's tumultuous state of soul immediately after Sophie's terrible declaration and of the hero's swift instinctive flight from the spot where he suffered the deadly wound. The influence of Prévost is discernible, too, in Emile's trick of fusing, in his narrative, physical sensation and emotion. Here, one is irresistibly reminded of *Manon Lescaut*. But where Rousseau, in the character of Emile, looks into his own soul, he is a much more profound and delicate psychologist than even Prévost.

As befits a product of Rousseau's natural education, Emile must submit to the 'law of necessity'; readjust his psychological existence to conform with his new and terribly real situation. In a dozen remarkable pages which hold out the promise of an aesthetic revolution in French literature, Jean-Jacques re-creates, through the medium of Emile's inner monologue, the tragic history of his shattered dream. For he too, like Emile, had briefly experienced at Montmorency the exquisite delights of love in a rustic, Arcadian setting. And, having never really, in his heart of hearts, accepted the prior claims of Saint-Lambert he viewed the defection of Mme d'Houdetot as a betrayal comparable to that announced by the guilty Sophie. No one was better qualified, therefore, to depict Emile's desperate efforts to salvage from the ruins of his former life the elements of a new existence. The initial violence of the hero's passion soon expends itself, according to Nature's plan, in 'cries, movements, gestures'[1] and in the physical exhaustion induced by his interminable aimless walks into the open country, away from the evil, detested city.

Je sortis de la ville; et prenant le premier grand chemin, je me mis à le suivre d'une démarche lente et mal assurée qui marquait la défaillance et l'abattement. A mesure que le jour croissant éclairait les objets, je croyais voir un autre ciel, une autre terre, un autre univers; tout était changé pour moi. Je n'étais plus le même que la veille, ou plutôt je n'etais plus; c'était ma propre mort que j'avais à pleurer.[2]

But Emile cannot stem the rush of sweet and poignant memories that now flood his consciousness, all treacherously conspiring to smother the present, ugly reality and prevent him from obtaining a clear vision of his duty. That Sophie could be a typical adulterous wife is inconceivable. Emile, by his criminal folly, exposed her to the temptations of Paris and who knows how many victories preceded her one lapse? Thus, as Emile suggests, the passions simulate a moral obligation. ' . . . They assume the mask of wisdom to catch us unawares, and it is by imitating the language of reason that they make us renounce it.'[3] In short, they tell Emile that if he had been always good, Sophie would not have erred. On the other hand, do not the very qualities of her character prove that Sophie is guilty because she wanted to be guilty and because she no longer loves or respects her husband? Suddenly, Emile remembers his child and, in a fresh access of rage, Sophie's condition. He must take his son away: it is unthinkable that he should be brought up along with the child of his wife's paramour.

[1] *H.* III, 9: 'des cris, des mouvements, des gestes.'
[2] *H.* III, 10: 'I went out of the town and taking the first main road, began to follow it with a slow and faltering gait which indicated my flagging strength and dejection. As the dawning day gradually shed its light on surrounding objects, I thought I saw another sky, another earth, another universe; everything was changed for me. I was no longer the same as the evening before, or rather I no longer existed; it was my own death I had to mourn.'
[3] *H.* III, 15: ' . . . elles prennent le masque de la sagesse pour nous surprendre, et c'est en imitant le langage de la raison qu'elles nous y font renoncer.'

There emerge now from Emile's monologue the three cor-
related themes which composed the inner melody of Rousseau's
own existence: self-renewal, escape, solitude. Having cruelly
decided to deprive Sophie of their little son, Emile must now
create a new self for he proposes to shed all his former attachments. 'I had to find out if I was still that man who can fill his
place in his species when no individual is interested in him any
longer.'[1] Yet in order to know what that place is, he must have
a clear idea of his life's purpose and above all, of his duty so as
to apply its principles to his new state. The following interesting
passage reveals Emile's attempt to base a scheme of living upon
an intellectual and completely unreal concept of existence.

Délivré de l'inquiétude de l'espérance, et sûr de perdre ainsi peu à
peu celle du désir, en voyant que le passé ne m'était plus rien, je
tâchais de me mettre tout à fait dans l'état d'un homme qui commence
à vivre. Je me disais qu'en effet nous ne faisons jamais que commencer,
et qu'il n'y a point d'autre liaison dans notre existence qu'une succession de moments présents, dont le premier est toujours en acte. Nous
mourons et nous naissons chaque instant de notre vie, et quel intérêt
la mort peut-elle nous laisser? S'il n'y a rien pour nous que ce qui sera,
nous ne pouvons être heureux ou malheureux que par l'avenir; et se
tourmenter du passé c'est tirer du néant les sujets de notre misère.
Emile, sois un homme nouveau, tu n'auras pas plus à te plaindre du
sort que de la nature.[2]

What Emile has just described is the Cartesian *création con-
tinuée,* the concept of a world that dies and is reborn at every
instant: it is, therefore, the exact opposite of Bergson's *durée
concrète,* 'the continuous progress of the past eating into the

---

[1] *H.* III, 18: 'J'avais à chercher si j'étais cet homme encore qui sait remplir sa
place dans son espèce quand nul individu ne s'y intéresse plus.'

[2] *Ibid.*: 'Delivered of the anxiety of hope and sure of gradually losing thus
the anxiety of desire; seeing that the past no longer existed for me, I tried to put
myself completely in the position of a man who is beginning to live. I said to
myself that we never do anything else but begin and that there is no other liaison
in our existence than a succession of present moments, the first of which is *in actu.*
We die and we are born every moment of our lives, and what interest can death
leave to us? If there is nothing for us except what will be, we cannot be happy or
unhappy except by the future; and to torture oneself about the past is to extract
from nothingness the subjects of our misery. Emile, be a new man; you will have
no more cause to complain of fate than of nature.'

future and swelling as it advances'.[1] However, as Emile quickly discovers, we cannot shut out the past which is constantly pressing against the door of our consciousness. Whilst working as a carpenter, unobserved by Sophie, he sees her arrive one day in his workshop and overhears her agonised whisper to their child: 'Non, jamais il ne t'ôtera à ta mère.'[2] Tortured once again by bitter-sweet memories, Emile resolves to grant her prayer. But he still clings to the illusion that he can begin life again, so to speak, with a refashioned self and, as he puts it, drink the waters of forgetfulness and wipe the past from memory. There are two categories of escapists. 'Society', wrote the wise Mme de Lambert, 'is only a troop of fugitives from themselves.'[3] And during their hectic two years in Paris, Emile and Sophie were fugitives from themselves. But Emile now belongs to the second category of escapists for whom the earth, as he says, is a place of exile and who flee society in order to rediscover, in solitude, their true selves. Therefore, having settled his affairs, without money or baggage, relying on his manual skill for his livelihood, Emile sets out on a long journey that will take him into many countries. Whither it will lead him, however, he cares not. What does the physical location of an individual matter to Nature. It is sheer Romantic pride to imagine 'all Nature is interested in the little events of our life'.[4] The second *Lettre* stops abruptly at the point where Emile, because of his unique merits, is singled out as a slave to the Dey of Algiers. But we know that he will return from his wanderings after many years, to find that his son has died. The mystery of Sophie's downfall, one gathers, will be solved and in such a way as to restore Emile's faith in her virtue and natural goodness.

[1] *L'Evolution créatrice* (ed. Alcan), p. 5: 'le progrès continu du passé qui ronge l'avenir et qui gonfle en avançant.'

[2] *H.* III, 20: 'No. He will never take you from your mother.'

[3] *Oeuvres*, 1748, p. 74: 'Le monde n'est qu'une troupe de fugitifs d'eux-mêmes.'

[4] *H.* III, 22: '...toute la nature intéressée aux petits évènements de notre vie.'

CHAPTER VII

POLITICAL WRITINGS

Mettre la loi au-dessus de l'homme est un problème en politique que
je compare à celui de la quadrature du cercle en géometrie.

Considérations sur le gouvernement de Pologne

*De l' Economie politique; Jugement sur la Paix perpétuelle; Jugement
sur la Polysynodie; Du Contrat social; Projet de constitution pour
la Corse; Considérations sur le gouvernement de Pologne.*

W E learn from Rousseau himself that, in 1743, having had
occasion to note the defects of the much admired Venetian
system of government, he first conceived the idea of an extensive
work on political institutions.[1] But his interest in this subject
goes back even further and is reflected in *Le Verger de Mme de
Warens* (1739) and also in the *Epître à Parisot.* Although both
poems belong to his reactionary phase, they betray an up to date
knowledge of the Genevan political situation and Rousseau's
concern at the recent internal quarrels in which he sensed an
imminent threat to the ancient constitutional liberties of his
native city. These fears were reinforced by his study of Spon's
Histoire de Genève, a revised edition of which had appeared in
1730 copiously annotated by Rousseau's idol, Abauzit.[2] He had
been, moreover, a horrified witness of the armed conflicts of
21 August 1737 and, in a veiled allusion to the *Règlement* drawn
up by the Mediatory Powers[3] in 1738, urges Genevans to enjoy
its benefits in that spirit of concord which united their godfearing
ancestors. In fact, the *Règlement* was adopted by an overwhelming majority of the citizens largely owing to the tact and
immense popularity of the chief Mediator, comte Lautrec, to
whom Jean-Jacques had been introduced, in 1735, by *Maman.*
He himself, it is important to remember, shared the general

[1] *Conf.* 396.
[2] *Histoire de Genève rectifiée et augmentée par amples notes avec les actes et autres
pièces servant de preuves à cette Histoire* (Genève, Faber et Barrillot, 1730).
[3] France and the Cantons of Berne and Zurich.

opinion that the *Règlement*, which codified and defined the rights of the citizen-bourgeois of Geneva, had preserved their essential sovereignty for, although denying them the power to initiate legislation, its Article VII confirmed their Right of Representation or protest. He always thought, as C. E. Vaughan observes, that this Right, 'the corner-stone of the liberties of the citizens', atoned for the inevitable sacrifices required of them by the Mediators.[1] And when, in 1764, Rousseau accused the Genevan executive Council of tyranny, the chief article of his indictment was their so-called *droit négatif* which subjected the Right of Representation to an absolute veto. Ever since childhood, as he told Parisot,[2] he had cherished with pride his right to a share in the sovereignty conferred on every citizen by the Constitution of Geneva. On the other hand, it has been argued that until after his personal quarrel with the Genevan government, Rousseau neither understood the implications of the *Règlement* nor the political Constitution of Geneva and was even unaware that his *Contrat social* attacked the principles defended by the Genevan *Petit Conseil* or Executive Council.[3] For reasons which will emerge in the present chapter I am not entirely convinced by this thesis which ignores Rousseau's explicit statement that, in composing his *Contrat*, he took the Genevan Constitution as a model and takes no account of the distinction he always made between the theory of political right and actual political practice. Let us now consider, however, Rousseau's early political writings and, very briefly, the political structure of the Genevan Republic.

It is generally accepted that in 1750 or in 1751 Rousseau began to sketch out his plan of the *Institutions politiques* which he scrapped in 1759 after having extracted the part later called *Du Contrat social*. An important fragment on the question of whether the state of war derives or not from the social state was probably written about 1753–5. Such is the opinion of Vaughan who draws attention to the arguments employed by Jean-Jacques to refute Hobbes and Grotius. Man is not by nature belligerent

<hr />

[1] *V.* ii, 180–1.
[2] *C.G.* i, 164 (*Epître à Parisot*): 'Tout petit que j'étais, faible obscur Citoyen/Je faisais cependant membre du souverain.'
[3] J. S. Spink, in his able thesis, *Jean-Jacques Rousseau à Genève* (1934).

and the state of war is really a conflict, not between men but between States in order to assert their equality and vindicate their national rights. But the strength of Rousseau's essay, Vaughan points out, resides in his championship of the noble idea that war is a baleful and irrational tradition, to abolish which we must go back to the first principles of reason and conscience. Right, as Jean-Jacques insists, has not to be established from the facts. The facts must be judged by Right.[1] One other point, however, deserves mention. For Rousseau, what is commonly called international Right is an empty concept and, 'in the absence of any sanction, its laws are mere chimeras weaker still than the law of nature'.[2] This view derives from his conviction that whereas the members of a political society are all subject to law, each nation in regard to another nation is still in the state of nature and, therefore, still enjoys its primitive or natural liberty. 'International Right having no other guarantee than the utility of the individual who submits to it, its decisions are only respected to the extent that they are confirmed by interest.'[3]

As we have observed, the *Dédicace* of Rousseau's *Second Discours* is essentially a 'message' addressed to his fellow citizens exhorting them to preserve a Constitution which embodies, in his opinion, all the conditions of political freedom and happiness. It would be a great mistake, however, to conclude that he misunderstood the nature of the Genevan Constitution or was ignorant of the political situation that had developed in his native city since the beginning of the century. For one thing, as we learn from the *Confessions*, he found amongst his uncle Bernard's papers 'several curious documents', including the pamphlet addressed by the celebrated Genevan patriot, Micheli Ducrest, in November 1728, to fifty selected members of the General Council.[4] Now, in this document which was suppressed by the *Petit Conseil*, Ducrest not only criticised, as a technician,

---

[1] *V*. 1, 289.

[2] *V*. 1, 304: '...faute de sanction, ses lois ne sont que des chimères plus faibles encore que la loi de nature.'

[3] *V*. 1, 304–5: 'le droit des gens n'ayant d'autre garant que l'utilité de celui qui s'y soumet, ses décisions ne sont respectées qu'autant que l'intérêt les confirme.'

[4] *Conf.* 213: 'beaucoup de pièces curieuses.'

the new plan for the fortifications of Geneva but also the uncon-
stitutional behaviour of the government in extending the project
originally approved by the General Council without having
obtained the authority of that sovereign body. Ducrest, on a
trumped up charge of *lèse-majesté*, was summoned before an
illegally constituted tribunal and, on his failure to appear,
deprived of his citizen's rights and exiled. Rousseau also discovered and removed five or six manuscript pamphlets, obviously
also of a political character. He was certainly aware, therefore,
of the situation which led to the Mediation of 1738.

Dupan grasped the real purpose of the *Dédicace* when he wrote
to Jean-Jacques: 'You represent us as we ought to be, not as we
are.'[1] In short, Rousseau knew very well that the Constitution
was interpreted in one sense by the conservative members of the
two chief executive councils (*Conseil des XXV* and *Conseil des
CC*) and in another by the 'left-wing' citizens and bourgeois who
supported Ducrest whom he considered 'too turbulent' though
'a man of great talent and an enlightened scientist'.[2] In the
Dédicace, unwilling to offend either party, Rousseau enlarges on
the spirit of the Constitution which is based, he says, on the
common-sense maxim that the Sovereign and the People have
the same interests and are, in fact, one and the same person.
Consequently, the Genevan régime is a democratic government,
'wisely tempered', an important qualification. A Genevan
citizen, therefore, lives and dies a free man. He is free because
by the Constitution no one is above the Law: the individual
citizen is so bound by the Law that no one can shake off this
'honourable yoke'. Moreover, in a tiny State like Geneva the
people, in their annual elections, are able to entrust the functions
of government to citizens of whose integrity they have personal
knowledge. This is of capital importance since the smooth
working of the constitutional machine depends, in practice, on
such mutual esteem. And the government are fortunate in having
as their electors men who are, by education and birth, their
equals. The latter enjoy, in turn, the unique advantage of being

[1] *C.G.* ii, no. 236 (20 June 1755): 'vous nous représentez tels que nous devrions
être et non pas tels que nous sommes.'
[2] *Conf.* 213: 'homme d'un grand talent, savant éclairé, mais trop remuant.'

governed by administrators of exceptional wisdom and humanity whose ideals coincide with their own. Moreover, by an equally happy and unique state of things, Geneva is blessed with a Church whose members take a practical interest in public affairs. We should be naïve, however, to imagine that in Rousseau's private view, everything was quite so lovely in the Genevan political garden.

It seems necessary at this point to outline, rapidly, the structure of the Genevan Constitution and to define the political situation as it was in 1754. It was, in fact, relatively calm and had been so since the Mediation. Geneva had a population of about 26,000 of whom, however, only a small percentage, the citizens and bourgeois over 25 years of age, enjoyed political rights. Their numbers fluctuated, but 1500 would be a fair average. The others consisted of *natifs* and *habitants*. The citizens and bourgeois composed the electorate and were convened annually, as the sovereign body called the *Conseil Général* or *Assemblée du Peuple*, in order to elect the four chief government officers, the Syndics who functioned for one year. There were always, in fact, four Syndics in office and twelve former Syndics, functioning as chief *conseillers*. The first Syndic presided over all the Conseils: *Le Conseil des CC* or *Grand Conseil*; *Le Conseil des XXV* or *Petit Conseil* and *Le Conseil des LX*.[1] The *Grand Conseil* was, so to speak, the custodian of the sovereignty of the People and its members were elected by the *Petit Conseil* in periodic batches of forty. These, however, had to be approved by the *Grand Conseil* after an investigation of their character and competence known as *le grabeau*. The *Petit Conseil*, properly speaking, the *Conseil des Syndics* had, therefore, considerable privileges and authority and dealt, finally, with urgent current affairs: others were passed to the *Grand Conseil* which handled all business except that which was important enough to be submitted to the *Conseil Général*. The *Conseil des LX* was composed of the *Petit Conseil* and thirty-five members of the *Grand Conseil*. It dealt with matters too big for the *Petit Conseil* yet too secret

---

[1] Nat. Lib. Scotland, MS. Hist. 341/29. 6. 1, *Réponse aux questions de Milord Townsend sur l'Histoire et Gouvernement de Genève par M. Chouet, Conseiller et Secrétaire d'Etat. Etat présent du Gouvernement de Genève en 1734.*

to be discussed by the Two Hundred. When the need for secrecy was over, they were handled, in the ordinary way, by the other two councils. The *Conseil Général* also elected the *Lieutenant de Police*, the *Trésorier Général* and the *Procureur Général*, an important officer elected for six years and responsible for the observance of the Laws and Edicts, either in the *Conseils* or outside them. He was the channel through which the People could communicate requests and complaints to the governing Councils.

Now, from the sixteenth to the beginning of the eighteenth century, despite the constitutional articles designed to prevent family cliques in the *Conseils*, their members had gradually formed a patriciate by virtue of their bureaucratic and legal experience. It was they who discussed and initiated legislation which was then submitted for acceptance or rejection by the *Conseil Général*. And, whilst not disputing the principle that all sovereignty resided in that body, the two smaller *Conseils* came to regard themselves as separate political orders or classes, co-operating with the *Conseil Général* and sharing its sovereign powers. This interpretation of the Constitution was very clearly expressed, as follows, by Jacob de Chapeaurouge: 'The *Conseil Général* is a body embracing, on the one hand, the Syndics and *Conseillers* of the XXV and CC who compose its head and, on the other, all the Citizens and Bourgeois who are heads of families and over twenty-five.'[1] His critics, the 'innovateurs', argued that there were not two separate orders in the *Conseil Général* and that the citizens and bourgeois, being more numerous, could at any time revoke the authority entrusted by them to the *Conseils* and enforce any changes they liked in the laws. From 1707 until the Mediation of 1738, these conflicting interpretations of the Constitution gave rise to various *Représentations* by a minority group. The latter, in 1725, was led by Micheli

[1] Nat. Lib. Scotland, MSS. 29. 6. 8, *Mémoire servant de Réponse à la Représentation remise par 24 Citoyens le 4 mars, 1734 à MM. les 4 Sindics*. 'C'est un Corps composé, d'un côté, des Syndics des Conseillers des XXV et des CC, qui en font la tête, et de l'autre, de tous les Citoyens et Bourgeois, chefs de famille qui ont passé 25 ans.' A manuscript note on this document by the Genevan bookseller, Bardin, states that De Chapeaurouge was assisted in drawing up this memoir by his father-in-law, Burlamaqui.

Ducrest a dissenting member of the *Conseil des CC*, and Geneva hovered on the brink of civil war. An *Edit de Pacification* (1734) pacified nobody; economic depression set in; the exiled Ducrest returned to the Genevan frontier and negotiated with the *Représentants*. Further disturbances led to the *Règlement de la médiation*, the effect of which was to deprive the *Conseil Général* of the power to initiate legislation but, as we have seen, it established their Right of Representation. Measures were taken, besides, to admit more families into the *Grand Conseil*. Finally, the bourgeois companies of militia were forbidden under pain of death to muster and arm without the consent of the Syndics. But Ducrest, whose motives were questioned because he was embroiled with his family over landed property, devoted himself to an intensive study of the origins and history of the Genevan Constitution. In 1745 he published an exhaustive criticism of the *Règlement* based on his researches, arguing that it had stripped the *Conseil Général* of most of the rights granted to them by the original Constitution of January 1543: i.e. the sole power to make laws and change them; to interpret the laws and remedy any contraventions; to elect government officers; call them to account and, if necessary, punish them; to constrain the Syndics to submit to the *Conseils* any proposal or request made by one or several citizens; to pronounce, in the last instance, on all judicial matters affecting the life, death, honour and property of the citizens. Ducrest maintained also that no court of justice not presided over by a Syndic was legal.

Such is the gist of Ducrest's *Supplication*[1] which I mention because, in 1768, the celebrated Jacob Vernet, Professor of Theology at Geneva, links it up with Rousseau's *Contrat social*. He writes:

It has been a great misfortune for us that M. Rousseau, too friendly with the Sieur Lenieps in Paris, adopted all these ideas and invested them with the brilliance of his style. His *Contrat social* is merely a general theory to serve as a basis for this system and his *Lettres écrites de la montagne* are a direct application of this very system to our Republic;

[1] SUPPLICATION/*avec Supplément*/*présentée aux Louables Cantons*/DE ZURICH ET DE BERNE/ *en Juillet & Décembre 1744*/ *par*/ *Noble Jacques Barthelemi Micheli Citoyen de Genève et Seigneur du Crest*/ *au sujet du Règlement fait en 1738*/ *par*/ L'ILLUSTRE MEDIATION DE GENEVE. M. DCC. XLV, pp. 135.

even to the point of using all the reasonings and all the arguments of M. Micheli. The only difference I see is that M. Rousseau, wishing to treat the Mediatory Powers with consideration and not daring to attack their work openly, employs the same subterfuges, the same disguises as in the *Profession de Foi*. He treats this Règlement de la Médiation as he did the Gospels. He pretends to respect it whilst sapping its foundations.[1]

Now, though Jean-Jacques did not, for obvious reasons, discuss politics in his letters to Lenieps who was closely watched by the Genevan Resident in Paris and the French authorities, it would be astonishing if they never talked of Micheli Ducrest and Genevan affairs. Yet, it does not follow that Rousseau, at that period or any other, completely endorsed Ducrest's concept of popular sovereignty. We have noted that, in 1767, he thought Ducrest too revolutionary or 'turbulent'. On the other hand, Vernet was a fine scholar and much-travelled man whose opinions merit serious attention. In fact, whether by accident or not, the *Contrat* does rest on principles identical with some of those enunciated by Ducrest. But they might very well have been induced by Rousseau himself from his researches whilst preparing *De l'Economie politique*, the article he contributed to the *Encyclopédie* in 1755, and whilst documenting himself for the *Contrat*. Indeed, he tells us in his article that he was studying the political system of Geneva: 'In order to expound here the economic system of a good Government, I have often turned my eyes towards that of this Republic [Geneva].'[2] And, with reference

---

[1] *Lettre d'un Citoyen de Genève à un autre Citoyen* (15 Feb. 1768): 'C'a été un grand malheur pour nous que M. Rousseau, trop ami du Sieur Lenieps à Paris ait adopté toutes ces idées et les ait revêtues de l'éclat de son style. Son *Contrat social* n'est qu'une théorie générale pour servir de base à ce système, et ses *Lettres écrites de la montagne* sont une application directe de ce même système à notre République, jusque là où il se sert de tous les raisonnements et de tous les arguments de M. Micheli. La seule différence que j'y vois, c'est que M. Rousseau, voulant garder des ménagements pour les Puissances Médiatrices et n'osant pas heurter de front leur ouvrage, emploie les mêmes subterfuges et les mêmes déguisements que dans sa *Profession de Foi*. Il traite ce Règlement de la Médiation comme il a traité l'Evangile. Il fait semblant de le respecter et le sape réellement.' E. Ritter mentions this *Lettre* in *Ann.* xi, 146-9, but, though regarding it as important, passes on to other matters.

[2] *V.* i, 263: 'Pour exposer ici le système économique d'un bon gouvernement, j'ai souvent tourné les yeux sur celui de cette République.'

to his documentation for the *Contrat*, we note the following *Fragment* published by Vaughan: 'On examining the constitutions of the States which compose Europe, I have seen that some were too big to admit of good government, the others too small to be able to maintain themselves in independence.'[1] We may safely credit Rousseau, therefore, with a sound knowledge of the Genevan constitution long before he undertook, in 1764, the onerous task of refuting, by opposing edict to edict, the interpretations of Tronchin, the *Procureur-Général*. In approaching this whole question we must not identify our twentieth-century idea of democracy with that of the Genevan reformers who, as Jacob Vernet remarks wickedly, were scarcely qualified to advocate 'equality and pure democracy' seeing that they composed a privileged aristocracy in relation to the 90 per cent of Genevans who had no electoral rights at all.

Rousseau's article *De l'Economie politique* is loose in texture and consists really of tentative reflections on various aspects of political society: the relation between the Family and the State; between the Individual and the State; the essential nature of political law; civic education; the right of property and, finally, the problem of taxation which occupies over a third of the essay. Rousseau does not accept the view that political society derives from the family group since there is no real analogy, he asserts, between paternal and political government. No ruler could afford to imitate the natural sentiments which link a father to his children. Besides, paternal authority lasts only so long as the children need their parents, after which they break away from the family group. In short, though Nature created in the Family an embryonic but impermanent society, the larger family called political society can only have been founded on various conventions of mutual advantage to the individuals composing the State.

In defining the State or the Political Body, Rousseau establishes a clear-cut distinction between Sovereign and Government, between the right to legislate and the power to execute

---

[1] *V.* I, 321 (*Further Fragments relating to the 'Contrat social'*): 'En examinant la constitution des Etats qui composent l'Europe, j'ai vu que les uns étaient trop grands pour pouvoir être bien gouvernés, les autres trop petits pour pouvoir se maintenir dans l'indépendance.'

the will of the Sovereign. Viewing the Political Body as a living organism, he compares the Sovereign to the head, the laws and customs to the brain, the nervous centre and seat of the understanding whose organs are the executive officers of the government. The mouth and stomach are represented by commerce, industry and agriculture; the economy of the State by the heart. But the life of the State resides in the existence of *le moi commun*, the corporate self to which the individual subordinates his human self or *moi humain* by which Rousseau means, really, the individual's *amour-propre*. The Political Body is a moral entity which has a general will tending always (like the *amour de soi* of primitive man) to the conservation and well-being of every part. This general will is the source of the laws, the supreme rule of justice for all members of the State. The general will of the sovereign State is always right, even when, as for example in Sparta, it educated its children to steal their food, a practice which unenlightened historians call theft. Such an accusation would be valid only if we were considering the State in relation to other States, each one of which has its own general will. The moment we envisage human society as a whole, says Rousseau, this general will is the natural law. But in the *Contrat social* he will deny the existence of a 'natural law'.

'The first and most important maxim of legitimate or popular government i.e. that which has for its object the good of the people, is...to follow in everything the general will.'[1] This at once raises a problem. How has it come to pass that individuals ever united to form political societies, that is to say, conceived the obligation to protect the life and property of each without prejudice to the others? After all, it is a fact that if anyone can constrain my will, I am no longer free. The key to this enigma, says Rousseau vaguely, must be sought in Law, the most sublime of all human institutions which must have derived from a 'celestial inspiration'.

It is to Law alone that men owe justice and liberty; it is that salutary organ of the will of all which re-establishes in Right the natural equality

---

[1] *V.* I, 244: 'La première et plus importante maxime du Gouvernement légitime ou populaire, c'est à dire de celui qui a pour objet le bien du peuple est...de suivre en tout la volonté générale.'

between men; it is that celestial voice which dictates to each citizen the precepts of public reason and teaches him to act according to the maxims of his own judgment and not to be in contradiction with himself.[1]

It is because of the Law that all can obey and no one command; serve and have no master so that when the individual is apparently a subject, he is really freer, because no one relinquishes any part of his liberty save that which would harm others. Here already we have the essence of the *Contrat social*, though indeed, the social pact itself is not explicitly defined. But I cannot agree with Vaughan that it is 'hurriedly slurred over' for it is implicit in everything Rousseau has said about the 'prodigies' which are 'the work of Law'. However, neither here nor in the *Contrat* does he explain the mysterious power which transfigures his primitive man living in the pure state of nature into man living in the political state. But he remarks significantly that the moment one citizen, independently of the laws, claims to subject another to his will he reverts automatically to the pure state of nature 'where obedience is never prescribed save by necessity'.[2]

The chief function and obligation of government is to inculcate and maintain respect for the Law. And just as it is the duty of the legislator to frame laws that conform to the general will of the State, the government must organise its administrative system in the same sense. But how can the citizen know what is the general will in doubtful cases since it is obviously impracticable to assemble the people on all such occasions? , Jean-Jacques evades the problem. A well-intentioned government knows that the general will is always on the side of the party most favourable to the public interest, that is, the most equitable party, so that one has only to be just in order to be sure of following the general will. Besides, he adds rather naïvely, in any dispute between the people and its officials, the former is always on the side of justice. His real solution, however, is a

---

[1] *V.* 1, 245: 'C'est à la Loi seule que les hommes doivent la justice et la liberté; c'est cet organe salutaire de la volonté de tous qui rétablit dans le droit l'égalité naturelle entre les hommes; c'est cette voix céleste qui dicte à chaque citoyen les préceptes de la raison publique, et lui apprend à agir selon les maximes de son propre jugement, et à n'être pas en contradiction avec lui-même.'

[2] *Ibid.*: 'où l'obéissance n'est jamais prescrite que par la nécessité.'

State education in citizenship beginning at childhood, and his models are, of course, the governments of classical antiquity which taught civic virtue, or in other words, how the private will of the individual citizen should conform to the general will. From infancy the individual must learn to identify himself with the fatherland, 'to love it with that exquisite sentiment which every man living in isolation has only for himself'.[1] This important function should not be entrusted to the parents, whose authority over their children will be thereby reinforced, however, not weakened. Rousseau does not appear to mean that this will be the child's only education for he observes regretfully that such a system is no longer practicable in large modern States and indeed was not employed by the ancient Romans since the absolute authority of the father made State education in citizenship unnecessary. Vaughan, who ignores this important reservation, concludes that Rousseau, despite *Emile*, never wavered in his preference for a public to a private education. I think that Vaughan is in error here and, indeed, Rousseau bluntly states in *La Nouvelle Héloïse* that children who are destined for manual labour need no education: 'their buried talents are like the gold mines of Le Valais which the public interest forbids anyone to exploit'.[2]

Rousseau's views on taxation betray the influence of Locke, Pufendorf, Bodin and, above all, his experience of the widely different French and Genevan systems. Inevitably, the republics of classical antiquity receive great praise though no mention is made of the slave labour which solved their economic problems. All taxation, for Jean-Jacques, is an infringement, necessitated by modern progress, of the right of property, 'the most sacred of all the citizen's rights, more important in some respects than liberty itself'.[3] The ideal Republic, at its institution, ought to be richly endowed so as to be able to dispense with taxation. However, since taxes are inevitable, they must be established legitimately, that is, by the public or their representatives. Commenting on this alternative, Vaughan remarks: 'It may be

[1] *V*. i, 256: 'ce sentiment exquis que tout homme isolé n'a que pour soi-même.'
[2] *N.H.* v, 3: 'leurs talents enfouis sont comme les mines d'or du Valais que le bien public ne permet pas qu'on exploite.'
[3] *V*. i, 259: 'le plus sacré de tous les droits des citoyens et plus important à certains égards que la liberté même.'

observed that Rousseau, still under the influence of Locke, does not here reject the representative system as he does in the *Contrat social.*[1] More probably, Rousseau had in mind the violent protests of the Genevan minority party when, in 1714–15, the Government, obliged to levy taxes for the new fortifications, did not consult the *Conseil Général.* The blunder was repaired in July 1734 when that Assembly gave its consent to the project and authorised further expenditure. Possibly, too, it was this affair which prompted Rousseau to observe that the people are inclined to see in any proposal for increased taxation merely the extravagance of the administration rather than the needs of the State; implying that in such matters the government may be the more reliable judge. The secret of a healthy national economy, he says, is economy in the narrowest sense of the term; the reduction to an essential minimum of the nation's requirements and, as in Geneva, the exercise of intelligent foresight. As to methods of taxation, he personally favours a capitation tax, based not only on the taxpayer's income but on his real needs. Here Rousseau's language becomes tinged with the bitterness of class hatred, bred of his unhappy experiences in Paris. Needless to say, he advocates swingeing taxes on every conceivable article of luxury, on all entertainments and on idle professions. Such taxes he regards 'as a kind of fine, the product of which compensates for the abuse which it punishes'.[2]

We have already referred to the *Extraits*, accompanied by *Jugements*, which are the sole relics of Rousseau's attempt to edit the abbé de Saint-Pierre. The splendid vision displayed in the *Projet de Paix perpétuelle* captivated Jean-Jacques, but after a realistic and penetrating appreciation of this essay he concluded, reluctantly, that its author's noble project of a Federal European Government was quite unrealisable in the eighteenth century. The logical Saint-Pierre thought, naïvely, that he had only to submit his Articles to a European Congress in order to secure their enthusiastic adoption. He forgot, says Rousseau, that a Congress is composed of men swayed, not by principles, but by

---

[1] *V.* 1, 266.
[2] *V.* 1, 273: 'une espèce d'amende dont le produit dédommage de l'abus qu'elle punit.'

their individual passions, interests and vanities. History teaches us, moreover, that such federative leagues are never established save by revolutions and that, Jean-Jacques suggests, would be a queer way of initiating a project for perpetual peace. His *Jugement* on *La Polysynodie* was also composed in 1743. Here Saint-Pierre, he thought, was again far in advance of his age. His idea of government by councils, or as we should say, by ministries, under the direction of a co-ordinating body similar to our Cabinet had no place, as Rousseau saw, in an absolute monarchy but only in a régime where the Head of the State is simply a President.

Rousseau, in the original draft of the *Contrat social*, makes it clear that he is concerned solely with principles, not with historical facts. 'I am seeking Right and reason; I am not arguing about facts.'[1] This caveat was not embodied in the final version, so that the reader, surrendering to the appeal of Rousseau's style, is apt to be hypnotised into believing that, at some stage in human evolution, men actually entered into the association so minutely defined in his treatise. In fact, like Emile, the Social Contract is a fiction, stylising the author's political ideas or principles. Rousseau's object was not to discover empirically the original political association which led to any known civil order. It was to visualise the type of civil or political organisation which could have justified the abandonment, by uncivilised man, of his natural liberty and primitive happiness. This point is illuminated by the chapter entitled *De la société générale du genre humain* in the first draft of *Du Contrat social*. It was probably composed between 1756 and 1759 and, as Vaughan has shown, is a reply to Diderot's article, *Droit naturel* (Natural Right), published in the *Encyclopédie* in 1755.

Diderot, in one of his typical, histrionic moments, invents a dialogue between himself and a 'violent interlocuteur' who is obviously a malicious parody of Rousseau's natural man of the *Second Discours*. This fictitious being, enraged because he has been forced to exchange his solitary, independent existence for the social state, obstinately refuses to subordinate his individual

---

[1] *V.* I, 462: 'Mais je cherche le droit et la raison et ne dispute pas des faits.'

will to the general will of universal society, thus cynically
flouting the natural law. Diderot's verdict is that the brutish
fellow must be 'smothered' in the interests of mankind. Though
secretly irritated, Jean-Jacques urbanely pointed out that
Diderot's 'universal society' and 'natural law' were empty concepts since they tacitly postulated the existence of an already
civilised political society. It was naïve, therefore, to imagine
that Rousseau's 'independent man' could understand Diderot's
rational exhortations. In this skirmish, Jean-Jacques let fly a
Parthian shaft which hit a vital spot. It was odd, he remarked, to
hear Diderot pleading with 'independent man' to listen to the
'inner voice' of the general will when, according to the *philosophes*, the so-called 'inner voice' of moral conscience is a mere
product of education and social habit. It would have required a
very different kind of appeal, Rousseau concluded, to convert
savage man into a law-abiding citizen. Unfortunately, neither
here nor in the final version of his *Contrat social* does Rousseau
bridge this gap in human evolution. He observes vaguely that
'independent man' would have to be convinced somehow that
his unregulated liberty was a spurious liberty, hampering the
development of his most excellent human faculties. But we are
left in the dark as to how the process of enlightenment was
achieved. The discarded second chapter of the *Contrat social* closes,
therefore, with an unsolved problem. The origins of political
society are not to be found in man's original psychological
constitution; not in any innate disposition to obey the dictates of
a 'natural law' nor, Rousseau infers, in any natural religious
sentiment which could have played a moral or social role in the
genesis of a primitive society.

A question arises here which we must try to answer before
examining the details of Rousseau's social contract. How did he
envisage the relationship of the individual to society, that is, to
a community whose members are linked by the conviction that
their group is superior to any other and are prepared, if necessary,
to defend it against other groups? It is doubtful whether Jean-
Jacques would endorse the modern view that a social self is
immanent in our individual self. 'Do not forget, please,' he
wrote to Charles Bonnet in 1755, 'that, according to me, society

is natural to the human species in the way that decrepitude is natural to the individual.'[1] The context of his letter makes Rousseau's attitude quite clear. The period in the life-history of man where men prematurely formed large, organised societies is that which foreshadowed the inevitable demise of the human species. In other words, unless human consciousness can be reoriented in a more natural direction, our cult for scientific social progress will result in the global extinction of humanity. On the other hand, might we not be justified in concluding from Rousseau's *Second Discours* that in man's natural pity we have the nucleus of a social self and thus, of society? Not necessarily, because that fount of the social virtues practically dried up when the primitive individual was prematurely obliged, for his self-conservation, to become dependent on other humans and to associate with them. We read in *Emile* that 'Men were not made to live in crowded ant-heaps, but scattered over the earth which they must till. The more gregarious they become, the more they corrupt each other.'[2] But surely Emile, the natural man, is enabled as a result of Rousseau's 'natural' education, to live happily in modern society? Do not let ourselves be deceived by words. In the first place, all education is unnatural, says Jean-Jacques, since it gives us something we were not born with.[3] And Emile, he reminds us, is not natural man living in the state of nature but natural man destined to live in modern society: there is a great difference between the two.[4] We cannot, therefore, identify him with that desolate, bewildered creature, primitive man, at the stage so vividly portrayed at the close of the *Discours sur l'inégalité*.

My final impression is that Rousseau, whilst reluctantly granting that Nature intended man to lead a social existence, always privately believed that, in creating our species, she was primarily concerned with the individual, not the group. On one point he was quite certain: political society was never comprised

---

[1] *V.* 1, 223 (*Lettre à M. Philopolis*): 'n'oubliez pas, je vous prie, que, selon moi, la société est naturelle à l'espèce humaine comme la décrepitude à l'individu.'

[2] *E.G.* 37: 'Les hommes ne sont pas faits pour être entassés en fourmilières mais épars sur la terre qu'ils doivent cultiver. Plus ils se rassemblent, plus ils se corrompent.'

[3] *E.G.* 7.   [4] *E.G.* 239–40.

in Nature's plan. For Rousseau, that is ruled out by the fact that she endowed primitive man with the faculty of choice so that he had no instinctive urge, like the ant, to form 'ant-heaps' or highly organised political associations. How he came to do so was always a mystery to Jean-Jacques. Civilised society as we know it, he thinks, originated in a series of terrible accidents which forced men to choose between extinction and an association based on a pact which seemed equitable but was really a cunning trick to enslave them, invented by a clever minority who exploited the simplicity of the ignorant masses. Now, this hypothesis, which is contained in the *Second Discours* does not reappear in the *Contrat social* where Rousseau merely states: 'Man was born free and everywhere he is in fetters....How did this change occur? I do not know.'[1] He means, apparently, that the processus described in his *Second Discours* must be regarded as conjecture, not historic fact. It is, however, a painfully evident fact that our primitive ancestors somehow took the wrong turning. Yet they might just as easily have taken the right one leading to a very different kind of political association. Rousseau now takes us back to that crucial bifurcation and speculates on what might have occurred had there been no clever, rich and guileful minority, but only a mass of simple, bewildered and desperate individuals like the 'independent man' in the original version of the *Contrat social*. Given such a situation, what kind of association would have been most likely to appeal to the individual and best calculated to ensure his future happiness? Rousseau's treatise will answer that question clearly. But there is another to which he can find no satisfactory answer. Is it psychologically credible that man, just emerged from the state of nature, would have possessed the intelligence to realise the advantages of Rousseau's social contract? My own view is that Jean-Jacques, brooding over his vision of man's terrible plight in this life or death crisis, felt that the 'very remarkable change' might well have been effected by a sudden expansion of human intelligence such as does in fact occur in the case of individuals whose existence is suddenly threatened.

[1] *V*. ii, 23: 'L'homme est né libre, et partout il est dans les fers....Comment ce changement s'est-il fait? Je l'ignore.'

Rousseau now makes good the promise he made to 'independent man' in his reply to Diderot and which he expressed in these words: 'Montrons-lui, dans l'art perfectionné, la réparation des maux que l'art commencé fit à sa nature.'[1] And indeed the political system he devises in the *Contrat* is a work of art, a *tour de force* of deductive reasoning. But first he deals with certain classic theories on the origins of political society which strike him as obsolete. Elaborating the opinions already expressed in his *Second Discours*, he argues that the Family was too fluid and impermanent to have developed naturally into a political organism. And it is sheer humbug to describe the king as father of his people: there is no real analogy between the king-subject and father-child relationship. Rousseau disagrees also with Aristotle's view that man is a 'political animal' and that certain men are born with a talent for leadership and the masses with the disposition to obey such natural leaders. Rousseau bluntly denies that sovereignty can be traced to any so-called natural authority innate in certain remarkable individuals. Nor, he objects, is humanity divided as Grotius and Hobbes believed, into groups comparable to flocks, each with its own chief or shepherd since the latter, Rousseau observes dryly, only guards his flock in order to devour it. Hobbes and his school held that, in the state of nature, man waged continuous war against man and lived in constant fear of death. Therefore, brute force, the 'natural right' of the strong to dominate the weak, must have formed the basis of sovereignty. This Rousseau indignantly rejects as nonsense. Might is a reality, but nothing can ever transform it into Right. The weak may yield to superior human force through fear or prudence, never of their own free will. Equally absurd and revolting is the notion that the mass of human beings are by nature slavish. They may have been born into slavery, but only because their ancestors were once enslaved by force. The State, concludes Rousseau, must have originated in a pact or convention. But no pact based on force could have originally induced man to relinquish the independence of his natural condition.

In the chapter *Du pacte social* the speculative conditional tense

---

[1] *V*. i, 454: 'Let us show him, in art perfected, the remedy for the evils inflicted on his nature by art in its rudimentary state.'

is replaced by the arresting historic present when Rousseau, dominated by his faculty of self-hallucination, as if re-creating historic fact, describes the genesis and nature of his ideal State. Based on a social contract, it is 'a form of association which defends and protects, with all the force of the community, the person and goods of each associate and by which each, in uniting himself with all would, however, obey only himself and remain as free as before.'[1] The concluding phrase reveals an explicit intention and should be firmly kept in mind because many critics, following on Vaughan, interpret the *Contrat social* as a manual of *étatisme*. By Rousseau's system, they maintain, the individual would be completely absorbed by the State. Yet there is no mistaking his purpose which is clearly stated at the outset. It was to indicate the constituent elements of a State in which the individual, whilst obeying the laws framed so as to reflect the general will and interest, should yet remain as free as before. Previously, in his natural condition, the individual's liberty was not really complete. It was limited by the extent of his individual strength and, above all, by the laws governing inorganic nature. Yet man, in submitting to these, felt no loss of liberty because he knew subconsciously that they were impersonal and necessary. We can now discern the true object of the *Contrat*, which is to imitate by art what Nature has done so well. In the State based on Rousseau's social pact, man will accept the human laws which he himself has willed because they are impersonal and necessary. Seeing only the organ of the Law and never a particular human individual, he will accept the laws of the State just as cheerfully as he obeyed the universal physical laws.

In trying to picture the genesis of this new association, Rousseau visualises it as a spontaneous act of communion and mutual trust out of which, in a flash, something completely new and original emerges: a moral and collective body, 'une personne publique'. But we must not think of it simply as the arithmetical sum of the individual wills that made its existence possible. The new entity is of quite a different order since its essence is the

---

[1] *V*. I, 32: 'une forme d'association qui défende et protège de toute la force commune la personne et les biens de chaque associé, et par laquelle chacun, s'unissant à tous, n'obéisse pourtant qu'à lui-même, et reste aussi libre qu'auparavant.'

general will, the supreme rule, binding on all the members of
the community yet, precisely because it is the will of all, in no
way affecting their individual liberty. We may describe this
abstract and collective being, when it is passive, as the State;
when it is active, as the Sovereign. Viewed in the mass, the
members of this political body are known as the People. As
individuals, each of whom participates in the sovereign authority,
they are citizens. But if we look at them from another angle
they are subjects, having freely contracted to obey the laws of
the State which is really just another way of saying that they
obey themselves, since nothing that does not express the general
will is a law. Here, roughly, is Rousseau's argument. An
individual is free not because he can do what he wills, but because
he is not subject to the will of another. We must not confuse
independence, which may involve doing harm to others, with
true liberty. Now, by the social contract, each, in giving himself
to all, gives himself to nobody so that no member is subject to
the will of another. He obeys instead, Rousseau means, an
impersonal entity, the State which incorporates the general will.
And, because it is as impersonal as the physical laws to which
savage man submitted without any sense of constraint or loss of
liberty, the individual subscriber to the social compact will obey
the State in a like spirit. On balance, he gains far more than he
loses. In the natural state, the individual was 'a stupid and
limited animal': now he is 'an intelligent being and a man'.[1]
True, he has abdicated his natural freedom but of what did that
consist? It was really the capacity to satisfy his physical
appetites with no regard for other men and often, though un-
wittingly, to their harm. Indeed, one can hardly call it freedom
since primitive man was a slave to his animal impulses. We must
never, Rousseau insists, confuse independence with true liberty.
Now, in place of his natural independence, the individual enjoys
a higher freedom: civil or moral liberty, which involves a profound change in his whole being, for he is now master of himself.
He is a rational creature whose actions are determined by justice,
not brute instinct. His intelligence has become active; his
sentiments are nobler; his spirit has been liberated. All this is the

[1] *V*. i, 36: 'un animal stupide et borné'...'un être intelligent et un homme.'

result of one momentous, inspired, collective act by which a number of individuals decided to unite in a spirit of mutual confidence, each freely devoting himself and all he had, to the common good.

Yet surely, as Vaughan and others have argued, the practical effect of this 'total alienation' will be to deprive the individual of his former material possessions. No, replies Jean-Jacques, because man in the natural state had no real possessions since, at any moment, they could be taken from him by superior force. It is only by the social contract that such a precarious tenure is transformed into property, that is to say, into possession approved and guaranteed by the community. Moreover, although in principle the State is the sole master of all the goods of its members, it is the latter who, as the sovereign people, will fix the régime under which property is held. It may be their general will that all property shall be owned by private individuals and that is Rousseau's strong preference. For it must not be thought, he remarks emphatically, that the members of the State, viewed as a plurality of individuals, have alienated by the social contract absolutely everything they had in the way of power, goods and liberty in the state of nature. They give up only that part which is necessary to the State for its own conservation. Anything else is retained by the individual citizen though here, of course, the State is the sole judge.

The twentieth-century reader must be forgiven if he views the last statement with some distrust, seeing in it the very idiom of Nazism, Communism, Fascism or of every totalitarian régime which places the citizen at the complete mercy of what is called the State, obliterating him, in fact, as an individual. To this scepticism Rousseau would react by pointing out that in a good State, based that is to say on a proper social contract, the citizen has only himself to blame if he allows such an iniquitous system ever to materialise. And he would add that in these despotic or totalitarian States, the social contract has been dissolved because the people were so stupid and apathetic as to transfer their sovereignty into the hands of an individual or clique. The inhabitants of such countries have really lapsed back into the state of pure nature and each is therefore free to follow his own caprice regardless of his neighbours. For sovereignty is the exercise of the general will and is, by its nature, inalienable and indivisible. The will of an individual might, no doubt, occasionally happen to coincide with the general will but not necessarily or permanently. The general will is unerringly oriented towards the public weal, but the deliberations of the members composing the political body do not, unfortunately, possess the same unswerving rectitude. Whilst the people as a mass cannot be corrupted, says Rousseau, they can be misled and thus often appear to will what is bad or unjust. In practice, however, we are bound to assume that a majority vote reflects the general will since it is the algebraic sum of the differences arising from the psychological fact that, in any assembly, the individual voter is influenced, in turn, by considerations of private and of public interest. Do not let us forget, however, that the original pact of association has to be voted *unanimously*. In accepting, thereafter, a majority vote as the probable expression of the general will, Rousseau makes an important reservation. The majority vote is valid only if we assume that the members are free and independent voters who have not previously been exposed to the interested propaganda of cliques or parties. In that case, the law of probability ceases to operate.

The social contract brings into existence the political entity called the State which acts through laws. Since these must express the general will, they can never have a particular or individual object. The application of the laws is a different matter which Jean-Jacques examines in his chapters on government. Note, meanwhile, that he defines a law as a declaration of the general will made by the sovereign people assembled as a legislative body in conditions of absolute freedom. But how can a 'blind multitude' legislate with foresight and wisdom, since they do not know the nature of Law? 'De lui-même le peuple veut toujours le bien, mais de lui-même il ne le voit pas toujours.'[1] They must have enlightened and, above all, disinterested guidance. At this point, that enigmatic personage, the Lawgiver enters the scene.[2]

[1] *V.* I, 50: 'Of itself the People always desires the Good, but does not of itself always discern it.'

[2] *V.* I, 29. Vaughan describes him as 'a highly idealised version of Moses, Solon, Lycurgus; a Social Contract incarnate'.

The Lawgiver, Rousseau always insists, does not in any way encroach on the sovereignty of the assembled people. His role is that of consultant who merely submits for their approval or rejection a system of legislation. Yet, from Rousseau's description of the almost godlike qualifications which the Lawgiver must possess, it is hard to see how he could fail to shape the general will of the legislative assembly since his function is to persuade them to follow what he, with his divinatory powers, knows to be the real interest of the community. He tries, in short, to arouse their civic conscience by emphasising the sacred character and semi-divine origin of the laws. His function, says Rousseau explicitly, is 'a special and superior function which has nothing in common with human dominion'.[1] The Lawgiver is faced, indeed, with a task of almost superhuman difficulty, particularly since he is armed with no executive powers. He cannot employ force, precisely because his mission is to educate the legislators politically, to persuade them that just laws are based on right and reason. That is why, observes Rousseau, all the early Lawgivers were obliged to attribute their own wisdom to the gods and thus induce their peoples to accept the laws of the State as they accepted the laws of physical nature, as emanations of the divine will. It is evident here, as in *Emile*, that the master really deceives the pupil for the latter's good and such is the essential function of the Lawgiver. 'The great soul of the Lawgiver is the true miracle which must prove his mission.'[2] Nevertheless, it is hard to follow Rousseau when he insists that the Lawgiver does not interfere with the sovereignty of the people whilst maintaining simultaneously that his function is to enlighten them in regard to what really is their own general will. Nor is it clear why Jean-Jacques assumes that the Lawgiver is addressing a body that has no 'esprit social', that is to say, no notion of a common interest when surely that is implicit in the original act which produced the social contract. Apparently, however, we are meant to understand that the mysterious *élan*

---

[1] *V*. I, 52: 'une fonction particulière et supérieure qui n'a rien de commun avec l'empire humain.'
[2] *V*. I, 54: 'La grande âme du Législateur est le vrai miracle qui doit prouver sa mission.'

that brought men together originally into the political association based on the contract, has lost its original virtue; that the
enthusiasm which generated the Act of the Covenant is destined,
inevitably, to evaporate in the very different atmosphere of the
legislative chamber. It is, after all, one thing to agree in
principle to follow only the public interest: it is quite another to
carry this resolve into practice when one may quite honestly find
it hard to distinguish between private interest and that of the
community. Therefore, the fundamental laws of the State must
be framed by a completely disinterested outsider, by a Lawgiver
who knows what the members of the political body would vote
for if they were able to see clearly into the depths of their consciousness. But why does Jean-Jacques confuse us by saying that
the Lawgiver must be able ' . . . to change, so to speak, human
nature; to transform each individual who is by himself a perfect
and solitary All into part of a greater All from which the
individual receives, in a sense, his life and being'?[1] Surely, as
we were given to understand in the chapters *Du pacte social* and
De l'état civil that transformation was already achieved, not by
any individual agency, but by a collective and spontaneous act.

With the chapter *Du peuple*, Rousseau's approach to his subject becomes definitely more empirical. It is not enough for the
Lawgiver to frame a good code of laws. The vital question is
whether the people for whom they are intended is able to
assimilate them. That, Rousseau infers, really depends on the
nature of the common interests which combine to weld them into
a political association. In *Emile*, he stressed the point that there
is a certain phase in the life of a child when he is ripe for certain
instruction. So it is with the political education of a people.
Rousseau thinks it is the phase where they have attained a sense
of solidarity and of common obligation sufficient to promote the
welfare of the State but have not yet ' . . . borne the true yoke of
the laws'.[2] He means that they are ripe to accept good laws with
docility, unlike, for example, a people that has been long wedded

---

[1] *V.* I, 51: ' . . . changer pour ainsi dire la nature humaine, de transformer chaque
individu, qui par lui-même est un tout parfait et solitaire, en partie d'un plus grand
tout, dont cet individu reçoive en quelque sorte sa vie et son être.'
[2] *V.* I, 60: ' . . . porté le vrai joug des lois.'

to traditional, deeply rooted customs or superstitions. Ideally, too, it should be a society able to support itself and free from the continual threat of invasion. Need one say that the model Jean-Jacques always had before his eyes was the Republic of Geneva at the moment of its institution? This fact should always be in our minds as we read the *Contrat social*. And because Geneva, when he wrote his treatise, seemed to be in danger of losing the spirit which presided at the inception of her Republic, Jean-Jacques now defines the meaning of government and establishes the relationship that must always exist between a government and a sovereign people if the latter is to retain its sovereignty.

The object of all legislation must be liberty and equality. That is true whether we view the State as passive or active; from the standpoint of the individual citizen who is subject to the laws or from that of the sovereign people whose general will is expressed in the laws. The social contract, we have seen, endows the citizen with civic liberty and, whilst obliging all indiscriminately to obey the laws, gives to all, equally, the protection of the State. But equality of wealth in the literal sense does not come into Rousseau's scheme. It is sufficient that '...no citizen shall be rich enough to buy another or so poor as to be obliged to sell himself'.[1] In short, there must be no extremes of wealth or poverty. The paramount consideration, always, is to maintain the strength and unity of the State which cannot obviously be done if rich individuals are able to impose their will on their poor neighbours. The object of all legislation must be to achieve a state of things whereby '... each citizen is perfectly independent of all the others and excessively dependent upon the State'.[2] This applies to the political laws governing the relations between the Sovereign and the State; to the civil laws that govern the relations between individual citizens. It applies also to the criminal laws fixing the relations between the citizen-subject and the State viewed as a judge who punishes breaches of the social contract. Yet the most important laws of all are not recorded in the

---

[1] *V*. I, 61: '...que nul citoyen soit assez opulent pour en pouvoir acheter un autre et nul assez pauvre pour être contraint de se vendre.'

[2] *Ibid.*: '...que chaque citoyen soit dans une parfaite indépendance de tous les autres et dans une excessive indépendance de la Cité.'

statute-book, but engraved in the hearts of the citizens: 'I am speaking of *mœurs*, customs and, above all, of public opinion'.[1]

The third book treats of government in general and of various forms of government. But what most interests Rousseau is the peculiar dual role played by this organism in relation to the State. Government he defines as the legitimate exercise of the executive power which the State can only delegate, never actually relinquish. In the eyes of the latter the members of the Government are merely officials paid to execute the general will of the sovereign people and to see to it that the same people, in their role of citizen-subjects, obey the laws of the State. A government, whether it consists of few or many members, is always 'An intermediary body established between the subjects and the Sovereign for their mutual correspondence, charged with the execution of the laws as well as with the maintenance of liberty, both civil and political.'[2] We should take it as axiomatic, Rousseau thinks, that in any State, just as sovereignty will always tend to relax, so the government will inevitably tend to strengthen itself. There is no hidden cynicism in his remark: he merely wishes to stress a psychological fact. In defence of their sovereignty, therefore, the people must use their legislative power to control or, if necessary, replace their appointed executive officers. They must never forget that the government is an intermediary body situated between themselves viewed, on the one hand, as legislators and on the other, as subjects of the State. The pattern of this relationship must be rigorously maintained: otherwise there will be anarchy or despotism. That occurs, for example, if the sovereign people insists on governing; if the government seizes the legislative power or, finally, if under a weak government, the citizens refuse to obey the laws. The government, Rousseau demonstrates mathematically, is the geometric mean between the Sovereign (the State viewed as an assembly of the sovereign people) and the State (the people regarded as an aggregate of subjects) viz. Sovereign : Govern-

---

[1] *V*. I, 64: 'Je parle des mœurs, des coutumes et surtout de l'opinion publique.'
[2] *V*. I, 65: 'Un corps intermédiaire établi entre les sujets et le souverain pour leur mutuelle correspondance, chargé de l'exécution des lois et du maintien de la liberté tant civile que politique.'

ment = Government : State. This proportional relationship must always be maintained whatever the population of the State or the size or form—which is essentially the same thing—of the government. A populous State, according to Rousseau, needs a strong, that is to say, a small government the force of which is condensed in a few members. Otherwise, he means, its executive power will be dissipated in the constant efforts of the higher government officers to maintain the *esprit de corps*, the unity of the corporate will of their governing body.

We have, generally speaking, three classic forms or types of government: democratic, aristocratic and monarchical. The second is favoured by Rousseau as least likely to threaten the sovereignty of the people. He detests, on the other hand, the aristocratic *State* where the sovereignty is, of course, in the hands of a privileged caste. But here he is dealing solely with forms of government: the only State Jean-Jacques recognises, obviously, is that of the social contract. In a democratic government, the executive power is in the hands of all or of a majority of the citizens. Not only is this impracticable, and conceivable only in very small States: it is also fundamentally bad since sovereignty cannot be identified with government. It is wrong that he who makes the laws should execute them. Laws are the expression of the general will and bear only on matters of general interest to the State. It is clearly dangerous that the legislators should be concerned with particular interests, for that could only lead to corruption. Strictly speaking, no really democratic government has ever existed nor ever can exist, says Rousseau, because one cannot imagine the people constantly assembled for public business. On the other hand, the moment the legislators delegate public business to others, they cease to hold the executive power themselves. ' If there was a nation of gods, they would govern themselves democratically. A government so perfect is not suitable for men.'[1] It will be observed that Rousseau's idea of democracy has, naturally, little resemblance to that of our age.

Early societies, according to Jean-Jacques, must have had aristocratic or patriarchal governments where public affairs were

[1] *V.* 1, 74: 'S'il y avait un peuple de Dieux, il se gouvernerait démocratiquement. Un Gouvernement si parfait ne convient pas à des hommes.'

managed by heads of families with the tacit assent of the younger men who bowed to the authority of experience. Soon, however, considerations of wealth and power became more important than age and wisdom. Membership of the government ceased to be a question of selection and became hereditary, the worst of all forms of government. In advocating the aristocratic form of government Rousseau, with Geneva in mind, admits that it implies 'a certain inequality of fortune', offset, however, by the fact that the management of public business is entrusted to men who have the requisite experience and leisure. And it need not follow that such government officers are immoderately wealthy: the sovereign people, after all, elects them.

Aristocratic government is best suited to small, and monarchical government to large States. In the latter, the executive power is delegated to one person, the king, who will be assisted, it is implied, by ministers and councils. Nevertheless, it is the king, inside the cadre of the government, whose will is supreme though only, of course, in relation to his subordinate government officers. Otherwise, despite his royal title, he is simply an executive official appointed and revocable by the sovereign people. The obvious objection to monarchical government is that all kings are not good governors and, in a hereditary régime, a man of sense may be succeeded by an imbecile, or a scoundrel.

The best form of government, says Rousseau after Montesquieu, is that best suited to the particular country for which it is instituted and here the deciding factors are climate and soil. In general, in countries where there is a small surplus of production over consumption, government will tend to be democratic or aristocratic; where much is produced by little labour, the government will be monarchical. In sparsely populated States, the government inclines to tyranny because the inhabitants cannot easily concentrate to defend their sovereignty. For Rousseau, therefore, the infallible sign of good government is a well populated State. On the other hand, a government begins to deteriorate when it becomes too small and when the executive power which, under a democratic system is delegated to the many, is centred in one man or a clique. Such, he warns us, is the natural, inevitable trend of every government. If it is not checked, the social pact dissolves and the people revert to their natural state of lawless independence or, more probably, forfeit their civil and political liberty entirely. For they have lost their legislative power which Rousseau compares to the heart of the political body, its brain being the executive power. Only when the heart fails can the State be considered dead. 'The brain may be stricken with paralysis and the individual may still live.'[1] It is more important, he means, for the legislative authority to survive than even the laws themselves: no particular type of executive organism can be eternal. The State, in order to defend its sovereignty, may find it necessary to legislate for another form of government. 'It is not by the laws that the State subsists, it is by the legislative power.'[2] On the other hand, in a well constituted State there should be no 'dead-letter' laws. When ancient laws have lost their force, it is a sure sign that the legislative power and thus the State, has ceased to exist.

Again and again we are reminded that the legislative power and the executive power are two separate things and must be kept separate. That is only possible, however, if the individual citizen honestly performs his civic and political duties. His vigilance alone can avert the dissolution of the free State. Only by frequent assemblies of the legislative body of the sovereign people can the process be checked by which the government inevitably tends to annex the legislative authority. Haunted by childhood memories of Plutarch's *Lives*, Jean-Jacques gazes lovingly at those stalwart little republics of classical antiquity where no laws were made except in the presence of all the citizens. At this point his enthusiasm for the grand old Greeks and Romans leads him into an awkward dilemma. The Spartans, he is obliged to admit, had plenty of time for politics because, while they crowded the public place, their wretched slaves, who were protected by no social contract, toiled in the fields and quarries. Even so, he cannot bring himself to condemn his beloved Sparta:

Everything which is not in nature has its inconveniences, and civil society more than anything else. There are such unhappy situations

[1] *V*. I, 91: 'Le cerveau peut tomber en paralysie, et l'individu vivre encore.'
[2] *Ibid.*: 'Ce n'est point par les lois que l'Etat subsiste, c'est par le pouvoir législatif.'

where one can only preserve one's liberty at the expense of that of others and where the citizen can only be perfectly free if the slave is extremely a slave. Such was the position of Sparta.[1]

An interesting point now arises which needs clarification. The sovereign or legislative body makes laws which are concerned only with objects of general interest to the State. Matters deriving from the application of such laws are of a particular nature and cannot be dealt with by the legislature. They are, in fact, the business of the government. But, as Rousseau points out, it is difficult to understand '...how one can have an act of government before the government exists'.[2] He means that whilst it is quite clear that the legislative body, in willing that there shall be a particular form of government is acting like a legislative body, there has to be another act concerning the appointment of the particular individuals who are to compose this government. Strictly speaking, we are now outside the legislative domain and in that of the executive because, in practice, the choice of government officers will rest with a group of persons qualified by their special knowledge to arrive at a wise decision which must, however, reflect the general will of the sovereign people. Obviously, Rousseau implies, we are no longer in the atmosphere which must reign in the legislative assembly where only general questions are deliberated. He was thinking, no doubt, of the annual elections by the Genevan *Conseil Général* of the four Syndics who presided over the governing councils. The solution derives from 'one of those astonishing properties of the political body by which it reconciles operations that are apparently contradictory'.[3] What happens is that the sovereign or legislative body is suddenly converted, provisionally, into a democratic government of which every citizen is a member. As such, they decide who shall be the

---

[1] *V.* i, 97: 'Tout ce qui n'est point dans la nature a ses inconvénients, et la société civile plus que tout le reste. Il y a telles positions malheureuses où l'on ne peut conserver sa liberté qu'aux dépens de celle d'autrui, et où le citoyen ne peut être parfaitement libre que l'esclave ne soit extrêmement esclave. Telle était la position de Sparte.'

[2] *V.* i, 100: '...comment on peut avoir un acte de gouvernement avant que le gouvernement existe.'

[3] *Ibid.*: 'une de ces étonnantes propriétés du corps politique, par lesquelles il concilie des opérations contradictoires en apparence...'.

officers of the particular kind of government set up by themselves previously when they met in their sovereign capacity.
Then they did not have to think of A, B or C as potential
governors, but only of the *form* of government. Now, temporarily
acting as a governing body, they bridge the awkward gap and
create a specific government, lapsing afterwards into their true
role of legislators.

In the fourth and last book of his *Contrat social*, Rousseau deals
with the general working of the political machine. For, although
the general will, in theory, is always oriented towards the
general good of the community, it is idle to deny that, in practice, the majority decisions of the assembled sovereign people
often do not reflect their real common interest. Nevertheless,
the general will remains intact at the core. Rousseau implies
that it is indestructible by virtue of the fact that the political
association still exists. Its members may be induced by their
private interests or by the propaganda of interested persons or
cliques to elude the general will. But even so, in their inmost
soul, they continue to respect it. What happens, says Jean-
Jacques indulgently, is that the voter fails to discern the nature
of the question to which his vote shall be the answer. 'So that
instead of saying by his vote: "It is to the advantage of the
State", he says: "It is to the advantage of such and such a man
or party that this or that opinion shall prevail".'[1] Yet it does not
follow, according to Rousseau, that the common people are
easily deceived, or because of their limited intelligence, incapable of knowing what is to their common interest. 'Upright
and simple men are hard to deceive, because of their simplicity.
Enticements, clever pretexts do not impose on them; they are
not even subtle enough to be dupes.'[2] Witness, for example, the
political behaviour of the Swiss people in the early days of their
Republic. One must not judge of the political sagacity of the
common man from what happens in our modern States, all of
which betray the vices of their original, unjust constitution.

[1] *V.* i, 104: 'en sorte qu'au lieu de dire par son suffrage: *Il est avantageux à
l'Etat*, il dit: *Il est avantageux à tel homme ou à tel parti que tel ou tel avis passe.*'
[2] *V.* i, 102: 'Les hommes droits et simples sont difficiles à tromper, à cause de
leur simplicité; les leurres, les prétextes raffinés ne leur en imposent point; ils ne
sont pas même assez fins pour être dupes.'

What aids, then, are we to adopt in order to preserve the integrity of the free State based on the social contract? In the first place, Rousseau would, as far as possible, create an atmosphere of freedom in the legislative Chamber by suppressing all organised parties whose activities must always be hostile to the general will and general good. But it is not enough for the voter to be able to exercise his right to vote in freedom: he must understand what voting really means. By the original social contract, the individual tacitly consents, once the political body has been unanimously established, to accept henceforth the vote of the majority as an expression of the general will. But we may ask how the minority of opposing voters can be obliged to accept what they have just disapproved of. The question, Rousseau explains, is wrongly posed. As a voter, I am not really being asked to say whether I approve or disapprove of a given proposition, but to say whether I think it conforms or not to the general will. Therefore, if the majority decides against me, I have merely been mistaken in my opinion of what was the general will. 'If my particular opinion had prevailed, I should have done something different from what I had wanted and it is then that I should not have been free.'[1] As to what percentage of the total votes ought to constitute a majority opinion, Rousseau offers two general directives. If the matters under deliberation are very grave, the requisite majority should be as near unanimity as is practicable. Where a speedy decision is imperative, a majority of even one vote must be accepted as reflecting the general will.

The chapters on the Roman *comitia*, tribunate, dictatorship and censorship require no comment since they are brought in merely to illustrate Rousseau's own theories. But the last chapter, *De la religion civile*, is extremely important. Yet it is not an integral part of his treatise to which it was hurriedly tagged on just before the final draft went to press, for reasons that are worth exploring. In his *Lettre sur la providence* (1756), Rousseau had already outlined a profession of civic faith which every State, he told Voltaire, should exact from its citizens. This is the

[1] *V*. I, 106: 'Si mon avis particulier l'eût emporté, j'aurais fait autre chose que ce que j'avais voulu; c'est alors que je n'aurais pas été libre.'

scheme now elaborated in his closing chapter. Its general aim is to fortify and conserve the spirit of the social contract by giving every citizen a religion calculated to make him love his duties to the State. On reviewing his completed treatise, especially the chapter, *Du pacte social*, Rousseau suddenly realised, I think, that he had forgotten to safeguard his pact by adequate sanctions. In the rough draft, on the other hand, we read that since the oath of association is a notoriously unreliable guarantee, the State reserves the power, implicit in the contract, to constrain any recalcitrant individual to obey the general will. But Rousseau seems to have realised also that, in order to conserve the original spirit of the pact, something in the nature of a religious sanction was required.

We can observe the general trend of Rousseau's thoughts in the opening words of his last chapter. He was evidently much impressed by the fact that history recorded no example of a State without a religion. Yet, it will be remembered, he would never admit that man was a religious animal, and was, therefore, unable to conceive the vital role played by religion in the formation of primitive society. As a result, Rousseau wrongly concluded from his reflections on theocratic government in the early Greek and Roman communities, that primitive society began with a king-god, an old belief entirely disproved by M. Davy who has shown that, on the contrary, sovereignty was diffused throughout the group. Concentrated in the totemic clan—the primitive element of political society—were all the social functions and these were of a mystic or religious nature. However, though Rousseau's analytic intelligence led him astray, he felt intuitively that if the spirit of the social contract was to survive, it must acquire a mystic or religious quality in the mind of the citizen, who must be made to feel that in violating the pact he had sinned against the civic Holy Ghost.

Jean-Jacques makes it clear that the opinions of the citizen do not concern the State except in so far as they interest the community. His religious beliefs are his own affair provided they conform to the maxims of the civil code. The State must, of course, ban religious fanatics because of their intolerance and, for the same reason, atheists or materialists. To those who might object that a Christian State has no need for a purely civil religion, Jean-Jacques replies that Christianity, because of its very perfections, is essentially incompatible with the principles of the *Contrat social* whose object is to ensure the happiness of men as they are, not as they might be if the kingdom of Heaven existed on earth. Christianity, which Rousseau is careful to define as the 'Christianity of the Gospels', has, or should have, no particular connection with any political body. Christ's ideal is a universal society detached from earthly matters and solely preoccupied with the life to come. The true Christian is not really interested in the State though no doubt he fulfils his civic duties. But it does not matter to him whether things go well or badly in the country he happens to inhabit. In short, from Rousseau's point of view, he is a bad citizen and, in times of national danger, a definite liability. It is nonsense to say Christians are good soldiers. The expression 'Christian soldiers' is a contradiction in terms and the Crusaders were not Christians, but citizens of the Church, a very different thing. True Christianity, i.e. Rousseau's theism, excludes the idea of the State as a political body with its own sovereignty and government. But in a Christian State there are always two powers and two sovereigns: the Church and the State: no one has ever joined the two heads of the eagle.

Whilst it is true that Christianity, like most religions, teaches its adherents to respect their obligations and to lead a moral life, Christian morality inculcates meekness and resignation, admirable qualities but of no help to the State when the liberty of the sovereign people is threatened by tyrants. Rousseau now establishes the articles of a civil code to which every citizen must solemnly subscribe if he wishes to enjoy the benefits of the social contract. He must profess his faith in the existence of an all-powerful, beneficent and provident Deity, of a life after death where the just shall be happy and the wicked punished. He must also profess his belief in the holiness of the social contract and of the laws. No one can be forced to believe in these articles, but any dissenter shall be banished, not for impiety but for being antisocial, '. . . incapable of sincerely loving the laws, justice, and of sacrificing his life to his duty if necessary'.[1] Quite suddenly,

---

[1] *V*.1, 132: '. . .comme incapable d'aimer sincèrement les lois, la justice, et d'immoler au besoin sa vie à son devoir.'

with no perceptible change in the rythm or quality of his style, Rousseau announces impassively: 'If anyone, after having publicly recognised these same dogmas, behaves as if he did not believe them, let him be punished by death; he has committed the greatest of all crimes; he has lied in the face of the laws.'[1]

Vaughan, who remarks that it is right to condemn Rousseau for this cruel doctrine, thinks that his real mind is probably better shown in a Note to *La Nouvelle Héloïse*[2] where Jean-Jacques says that if atheism were a capital offence and he a magistrate his first judicial act would be to send to the stake as an atheist anyone who denounced another for atheism. For once, I confess myself unable to follow Vaughan's reasoning. Surely, in the hypothetical case just mentioned, it is Rousseau who would be the criminal since, in accepting office he had presumably sworn to respect and enforce respect of the existing laws. Therefore, in substituting his own code of justice for that of the State he would be guilty of having 'lied in the face of the laws'. What really emerges from the Note and the passage in the *Contrat* is that a ruthless inquisitor is immanent in every fanatic. Rousseau, in his fanatical zeal to preserve the sanctity of his social pact, was prepared to go to any extreme, at least on paper and in the heat of literary composition. Recklessly, in that fatal article of his civic profession of faith, he conceived the formula for a process of judicial mass murder which, with various refinements, was destined to form the basis of the twentieth-century totalitarian State. That a noble creation like the *Contrat social* should have been disfigured by such a monstrous appendage is one of the most baffling enigmas recorded in literature. But we should not allow it to blind us to the enduring truths enshrined in Rousseau's treatise. Of these the greatest and, today, the most precious, is that sovereignty belongs to the people and must never, under any pretext, be transferred to any individual or group of individuals. What happens when Rousseau's teachings are ignored is written large on the map of the World.

---

[1] *V.* i, 132: 'Que si quelqu'un, après avoir reconnu publiquement ces mêmes dogmes, se conduit comme ne les croyant pas, qu'il soit puni de mort; il a commis le plus grand des crimes; il a menti devant les lois.'

[2] *N.H.* v, 5.

Without warning, Rousseau was called upon to translate his theory into practice by Corsica which he had described in the *Contrat* as the only European country still open to the Legislator. A request for a complete plan of institution was submitted to him in August 1764 by Buttafoco, a Corsican officer who enjoyed, apparently, the confidence of General Pasquale Paoli, the valiant leader of the Corsicans in the revolt against their Genoese masters. Whilst eager to undertake such a noble mission, Rousseau fully realised that it bristled with difficulties because, since the general rising of 1752, the political and military position of the island had remained fluid and indeed precarious. As a first step, therefore, he asked for a detailed, factual report on everything relating to the history and actual situation of Corsica and her people: their *mœurs*, religious habits and social conditions; the physical configuration, natural resources and industries of the island; the fiscal and judicial systems. He adopted, in short, the empirical method outlined by Montesquieu in *L'Esprit des Lois*. This, as Vaughan has remarked, is the really novel feature of Rousseau's *Projet de Constitution pour la Corse* which was unfortunately never completed owing to the train of events that drove Jean-Jacques from the Ile de Saint-Pierre where he composed the first part of the *Projet*: the second consists only of miscellaneous yet illuminating notes.

In framing the act of inauguration, Rousseau adheres closely to the *Contrat social*. Vaughan errs, somewhat, in affirming that the religious basis of the new Corsican State is proclaimed 'at least as unequivocally' in the *Projet* as in the *Contrat*. Mindful of the traditional Catholicism of the islanders, Rousseau does not base their constitution on a purely civil profession of faith. The contracting members take their oath of allegiance with '...their hand on the Bible' and swear 'in the name of Almighty God and on the Holy Gospels'.[1] In fact, their profession of faith resembles that of the Vicaire Savoyard.

It is not easy to form a clear idea of the form of government Rousseau intended for Corsica. His allusions to a *gouvernement mixte*, to the *Grand Podestat*, the *Sénat* and the *Conseil d'Etat*

[1] *V*. II, 350: '...la main sur la Bible...Au nom de Dieu tout-puissant et sur les saints Evangiles.'

suggest a representative government on the Genevan model but with 'Gardes des lois' whose function is to preserve the sovereignty of the people. Apparently, these officers whose person is 'sacred and inviolable', are empowered to convoke the *Etats généraux* at any time and from that moment until the assembly of the sovereign people, the authority of the *Grand Podestat* and of the *Conseil d'Etat* is suspended. In Rousseau's preface occurs 'the riddling passage' which disconcerts Vaughan. The gist of Rousseau's statement is that whilst the wisest legislators shape the government for the nation in order to ensure that the two bodies shall compose one, it would be wiser still, for the same reason, to shape the nation for the government.[1] Very ingeniously, Vaughan interprets this passage as meaning 'almost the reverse of that for which it might be taken at first'.[2] He argues that Jean-Jacques, anxious to maintain the harmony between nation and government which existed at the institution of the State, thought that the original form of government should not be framed to suit the character of the nation at that particular moment but with a view to 'training and strengthening the character of the nation'. That could be, yet my own impression is that Rousseau meant exactly what he has written. He remarks that '. . . the Corsican nation has prejudices very contrary to my principles'.[3] And in general, the spirit of his *Projet* is empirical, not speculative. He knew that the Corsicans had a long history of lawlessness which was a virtue so long as it sprang from patriotic ardour. But, in the new Corsica this habit of lawlessness had to be stamped out. 'One must not count on the intense but always brief enthusiasm which follows the recovery of liberty.'[4] The chief function of government is to inculcate a religious veneration for the Law and that is probably what Rousseau meant by his statement that the nation must be shaped for the government.

The salvation of Corsica, he insists, depends entirely on a return to the rustic, laborious existence of their distant ancestors;

[1] *V*. ii, 307.   [2] *V*. ii, 299.
[3] *V*. ii, 353: '. . .la nation corse a des préjugés très contraires à mes principes.'
[4] *V*. ii, 352: 'Il ne faut point compter sur un enthousiasme vif, mais toujours court, à la suite de la liberté recouvrée.'

to their spirit of equity and humanity. 'The Corsicans', he remarks, 'are still almost in the sound, natural state: but it will require much art to keep them in it.'[1] All Rousseau's schemes for the financial and economic administration of the island reflect this retrospective vision. The use of money must be eliminated as far as possible; Corsica must become self-sufficing because commerce and trade are corrupting agencies; communications must be few in order to scatter the inhabitants and attach them to their native soil; taxes should be paid, where feasible, in kind. Ideally, the State should have everything and each citizen possess only that part of the common domain to which his services entitle him. But it is impossible, Rousseau admits, to abolish private ownership completely. The State must not, therefore, deprive anyone of his property but merely keep him from acquiring more. Consequently he would not touch the Church lands but impose a civic tithe for the benefit of the State.

The whole art of government, according to Jean-Jacques, lies in persuading men, who are by nature lazy, that labour is an honourable occupation. The State must accordingly offer incentives calculated to flatter the vanity of the individual, especially his desire for esteem and power. Therefore, in the new Corsica, authority and consideration shall be placed within reach of every laborious citizen since 'Fear and hope are the two instruments with which men are governed'.[2] Even if Rousseau's project had been completed, as he intended, in 1769, it would have been of little use to Corsica which was purchased from Genoa by France in 1768 for two million francs.

On reflection, I do not think that the *Lettres écrites de la montagne* belong, properly, to this chapter. True, four of these *Lettres* deal with Genevan party politics and echo, inevitably, the themes orchestrated in the *Contrat social*. Their general tone and intention, however, is polemical and it would be a mistake, in my judgment, to isolate these *Lettres* from their natural context. The *Considérations sur le gouvernement de Pologne* are in

---

[1] *V.* II, 355: 'Les Corses sont presque encore dans l'état naturel et sain; mais il faut beaucoup d'art pour les y maintenir.'

[2] *V.* II, 344: 'La crainte et l'espoir sont les deux instruments avec lesquels on gouverne les hommes.'

a different case. First published in 1790, they were written probably at the beginning of 1771 at the request of Count Wielhorski during a brief moment of relative calm in Poland's tragic and convulsive struggle for liberty. At the Convention of 1769 organised by the Confederates of Bar, it was resolved to consult the leading political theorists of France on the problem of a Constitution for the new Poland and in this connection, Wielhorski was instructed to approach Mably and Rousseau.

In his concise and penetrating study of this work, Vaughan disposes of the legend that Jean-Jacques had moved into a political cloud-cuckoo land. He stresses, also, that rooted distrust for revolutionary methods which explains the conservatism of Rousseau's plan for Poland. His ruling maxim is concisely stated: 'to change nothing, either for retrenchment or addition, unless it is necessary'.[1] Vaughan has admirably summarised, as follows, the positive changes proposed by Jean-Jacques:

A guarantee that the Crown should be in fact, as well as in name, elective; the appointment of the Senate, or a majority of its members, by the Diet instead of by the king; a limitation of the *liberum veto*; a provision for casting all taxation, in equitable proportion, upon the produce of the land; a reform in the whole educational system of the country; an elaborate gradation of social service and promotion, from the bottom to the top of the ladder.[2]

Rousseau proposes for the new Poland a confederation of States comparable, indeed, to what obtains in Switzerland today. This is, of course, in line with his unswerving conviction that the ideal political society is that of the small, compact State.

Nearly all the little States, Republics and Monarchies indiscriminately, prosper from the very fact that they are small; that all the citizens know and watch each other; that the Heads can see for themselves what is going wrong and what good they have to do; and that their orders are being carried out before their eyes. All the great nations, crushed by their own weight either groan, like you, in anarchy

---

[1] *V.* II, 456: 'ne rien changer sans necessité, ni pour retrancher ni pour ajouter.'

[2] *V.* II, 376–7.

or under subordinate oppressors whom a necessary, gradual process obliges kings to place over them. Only God can govern the universe and it would require superhuman faculties to govern great nations.[1]

The retrospective character of Rousseau's political thought, which stands out so vividly against the background of eighteenth-century scientific progress, is reflected also in his educational plan for Poland. Here again, Jean-Jacques surveys the future through the mirage of his early Plutarchian memories. In general, he advocates a system of national education but Vaughan was, perhaps, mistaken when he wrote: 'All that may be said in favour of private, individual training is at once thrown to the winds.'[2] As we shall see, Rousseau makes it quite clear that his plan does not exclude private or domestic educa-tion. The primary object of his State-controlled education is to produce tough, patriotic citizens able to defend their country in time of need, by means of organised games and instruction designed to inculcate a spirit of nationalism. The children shall be taught the history, geography and traditions of their country, not by professional pedagogues, but by married Polish citizens who are ear-marked for higher administrative posts in the State. They must not be 'foreigners and priests'. The programme of these civic studies is to be drawn up and administered by the government which will also found State bursaries, on the French model, for the benefit of 'the children of poor gentlemen who have deserved well of their fatherland'.[3] Rousseau does not explicitly say whether his national instruction is to be given in special State schools or within the walls of the existing *collèges*. Probably the latter, for he insists that a gymnasium must be installed in every *collège*.

---

[1] *V*. II, 442: 'Presque tous les petits Etats, Républiques et Monarchies in-différemment, prospèrent par cela seul qu'ils sont petits; que tous les citoyens s'y connaissent mutuellement et s'entre-gardent; que les chefs peuvent voir par eux-mêmes le mal qui se fait, le bien qu'ils ont à faire; et que leurs ordres s'exécutent sous leurs yeux. Tous les grands peuples, écrasés par leurs propres masses, gémissent, ou comme vous dans l'anarchie, ou sous les oppresseurs subalternes qu'une gradation nécessaire force les rois de leur donner. Il n'y a que Dieu qui puisse gouverner le monde; et il faudrait des facultés plus qu'humaines pour gouverner de grandes nations.'   [2] *V*. II, 380.
[3] *V*. II, 439: 'aux enfants des pauvres gentilshommes qui auraient bien mérité de la patrie.'

This matter, so greatly neglected, is, according to me, the most important part of education, not only as forming robust and healthy temperaments but still more for its moral aim, which is ignored or implemented only by a mass of vain, pedantic precepts which amount to so many empty words. I can never repeat often enough that good education must be negative. Prevent the birth of vices and you will have done enough for virtue.[1]

However, Rousseau clearly defines the limits of his national system of education when he states that parents who prefer to have their children educated privately must, nevertheless, send them to these exercises:

Their instruction can be domestic and private, but their games must always be public and common to all; for here it is not only a question of occupying them, of giving them a robust constitution, of making them agile and muscular, but of accustoming them at an early stage to discipline, equality, fraternity, competition, to live under the eyes of their fellow citizens and to desire public approbation.[2]

For the same reason, Jean-Jacques warmly recommends the introduction of Boys' Parliaments on the model of the Bernese *Etat extérieur*, as nurseries of future politicians and administrators. But his ideas on State education, he concludes, are 'undeveloped' and intended simply to indicate the avenues, unknown to the Moderns, by which the Ancients led their people to 'that spiritual energy and patriotic zeal'[3] no longer to be found in the eighteenth century. Yet their seeds lie dormant in every human heart, ready to germinate and blossom in the climate of political freedom.

[1] *V.* ii, 439: 'Cet article si négligé est, selon moi, la partie la plus importante de l'éducation, non seulement pour former des tempéraments robustes et sains, mais encore plus pour l'objet moral, qu'on néglige ou qu'on ne remplit que par un tas de préceptes pédantesques et vains, qui sont autant de paroles perdues. Je ne redirai jamais assez que la bonne éducation doit être négative. Empêchez les vices de naître, vous aurez assez fait pour la vertu.'

[2] *V.* ii, 439–40: 'Leur instruction peut être domestique et particulière, mais leurs jeux doivent toujours être publics et communs à tous; car il ne s'agit pas seulement ici de les occuper, de leur former une constitution robuste, de les rendre agiles et découplés, mais de les accoutumer de bonne heure à la règle, à l'égalité, à la fraternité, aux concurrences, à vivre sous les yeux de leurs concitoyens et à désirer l'approbation publique.'

[3] *V.* ii, 441: 'à cette vigueur d'âme, à ce zèle patriotique.'

CHAPTER VIII

THE FUGITIVE
1762–1778

Un jour viendra, j'en ai la juste confiance, que les honnêtes
gens béniront ma mémoire, et pleureront sur mon sort.
Troisième Dialogue

*Lettre à Christophe de Beaumont; Lettres écrites de la montagne;
Rousseau Juge de Jean-Jacques. Dialogues; Les Rêveries du promeneur solitaire.*

O N 14 June 1762 Rousseau crossed the Bernese frontier, alighting
at Yverdun where he was warmly received by his dear old friend,
Papa or Daniel Roguin and by the latter's niece Mme Pierre
Boy de la Tour. Let us salute in her a great-hearted lady, the
incarnation of practical kindness, who mothered Jean-Jacques
simply for himself and not because he was a famous man. At
Yverdun, where he stayed for over three weeks, he learned from
his admirer, the Genevan pastor Moultou, that the *Petit Conseil*
had followed the example of the Parlement de Paris. Moreover,
a request by his relatives to examine the decree against him had
been refused. Holland also had banned *Emile*. Forestalling an
order of eviction from Berne, Rousseau left on 9 July for Môtiers
in the Val-de-Travers, a Prussian enclave governed by that
illustrious Jacobite exile, George Keith, Earl Marischal of
Scotland, better known on the Continent as *milord maréchal*.
To him and to his royal employer, Frederick, the fugitive
announced his arrival at Môtiers where, unfortunately for
his subsequent peace of mind, he was joined by Thérèse on
20 July.

Rousseau maintains in the *Confessions* that the only worry he
ever had about *Emile* was lest Conti might apply to himself the
passage condemning those *grands seigneurs* who abuse their
hunting rights at the expense of their wretched tenants. Yet he
admits that Duclos, Moultou and other friends had voiced their

alarm at the probable effect on the Church of the *Profession de foi*. These forebodings, however, Rousseau could not share. *Emile* had the blessing of Malesherbes, the prince de Conti and the Luxembourgs, and besides it was always the publisher, he said, whom the law punished in such cases, forgetting that it was most exceptional for the author to put his name on the title-page. Yet the *Correspondance* shows that Jean-Jacques was sufficiently impressed by these warnings to suggest, on 18 February, that the second half of *Emile* should be printed in Holland, for his own safety and that of Duchesne.[1] In April he told Moultou that the book would probably not be published in France, an arrangement to which he had always been opposed. On the other hand, nothing would convince him that the special brand of religion advocated in *Emile* could give offence to the French or Genevan clergy. And only four days before the Parlement launched its *décret*, he wrote soothingly to the scared Néaulme: 'je ne pense point qu'un corps si sage et si éclairé fasse une pareille sottise.'[2]

It is tempting, with our superior knowledge of the general political situation, to exclaim at Rousseau's obtuseness. It would be more pertinent to inquire why Malesherbes, as he admits himself, consistently ignored the author's objections to a French edition. What of Rousseau's confident belief, reiterated in the *Correspondance*, that the Parlement had no quarrel with him personally but, having dealt harshly with the Jesuits, dared not risk a charge of religious indifference? That might well be true. For example, when Jean-Jacques in November 1765 appeared publicly in Paris, the police made no attempt to seize him. Indeed, in April of that year, one of his admirers, Séguier, marquis de Saint-Brisson, assured him that he could quite safely return to the capital. The Parlement, said this correspondent, had deliberately committed an error of procedure in the matter of the warrant

so that this procedure should become null and that you should not have to fear its consequences. They had to condemn you for fear that tolerance

[1] *C.G.* vii, no. 1284 (to Mme de Luxembourg).
[2] *C.G.* vii, no. 1395 (5 June 1762): 'I do not think for a moment that such a wise and enlightened body will be guilty of such a stupidity.'

in your case might indicate animosity directed against the Jesuits whose books were being burnt, but nobody had any wish to ruin you.[1]

Even the most pious people, Saint-Brisson continues, including the well-known *dévote*, Mme de Gisors, were Rousseau's ardent supporters. Of course, these are the views of a friend writing nearly three years after the catastrophe of June 1762 which probably startled Malesherbes as much as Jean-Jacques. Technically, however, the former had broken no regulation. Officially, he had never sanctioned the publication of *Emile*: in case of trouble with the Parlement, the *permission tacite* granted by him to Duchesne afforded no protection whatsoever either to the publisher or author.

But we need not picture Jean-Jacques during his flight from Montmorency as a crushed and terrified fugitive. With his child-like and enviable capacity for shutting out unpleasant realities, he whiled away the tedium of the three days' journey to Yverdun in literary composition. Inspired by memories of Gessner's *Idylls* and by the gory incident recorded in Judges xix–xxi, he almost completed *Le Lévite d'Ephraïm*, a prose-poem on his favourite theme of the golden age, when man's primitive simplicity rendered law superfluous. Jean-Jacques, who was saturated in Bible lore, experiments here with an idiom which Chateaubriand later brought to perfection in *Atala*. In other respects, *Le Lévite* is quite negligible.

Happily, we can observe in the voluminous *Correspondance* the evolving pattern of Rousseau's existence during the critical years 1762–70. For the twelfth and last book of the *Confessions* stops at the point where Jean-Jacques, on 29 October 1765, left Bienne, as he confidently imagined, for Berlin. On the other hand, we need not bewail Rousseau's failure to continue his autobiography since the projected Third Part was to have exposed, he says, the intrigues by which his old friends Mme de Boufflers and Mme de Verdelin diverted him from Berlin to London at the instiga-

---

[1] Neufchâtel MS. Ancien fonds 7902, t. v, fol. 130 (unpublished, I believe): 'afin que cette procédure devînt nulle et que vous n'eussiez pas à en craindre les suites. Il fallait vous condamner de peur que la tolérance envers vous ne marquât une animosité dirigée contre les Jésuites dont on brûlait les livres, mais aucun n'avait envie de vous perdre.'

tion of David Hume and the latter's French accomplices. As the *Correspondance* discloses, it was not until February 1770 that this particular delusion crystallised in Rousseau's tormented mind.[1]

We may now consider the salient features of the picture unfolded in the *Correspondance*. What really shook Rousseau was the reaction of Geneva to *Emile* and the *Contrat social*, a matter on which he was kept well informed by his devoted friends, Du Peyrou and Moultou. He was alarmed and displeased by the zeal of the faithful J.-F. De Luc, that stormy petrel of Genevan politics whose intervention in the *affaire Rousseau* was merely part of his general campaign against the government. On 18 June 1763 De Luc headed a group of forty *Représentants* who protested to the First Syndic against three illegalities committed by the *Magnifique Conseil* one of which was the decree condemning Jean-Jacques and his two latest books. The *Conseil*, they argued, should have given the author an opportunity to defend his works. Moreover, in condemning *Emile*, the government had usurped a prerogative of the Consistory which, by Article 88 of the Ecclesiastical Ordinances was alone competent to pronounce on religious matters. The *Conseil* replied that, on assuming office, they had sworn to defend the Republic against any citizen who violated his burgess's oath by attacking the Constitution and that Article 88 only concerned a person who 'dogmatises orally'. Moreover, the *Conseil* added, the resolution they had passed on the author was not a judgment or a sentence, but merely a summons which would in no way have prejudiced Rousseau's right to defend himself if it had resulted in a formal prosecution. The *Conseil*, by this lame and equivocal reply, naturally exposed itself to further *représentations*. But Rousseau, in January 1766, complained to De Luc that his intervention was belated though what really annoyed him was the general apathy evinced by the *imbéciles bourgeois* of Geneva who, instead of rushing immediately to his defence, felt that the condemnation of Jean-Jacques was a

---

[1] *C.G.* XIX, no. 3884 (26 Feb. 1770). In this important letter to Saint-Germain, the detailed history of the 'conspiracy' is re-created by Jean-Jacques. It originated, he asserts, with Diderot and Grimm but was later organised and directed by the duc de Choiseul in collusion with D'Alembert and the *ligue holbachique*. Why Choiseul? Because he interpreted as an insult a remark in the *Confessions* intended as a eulogy. Needless to say, this was a pure delusion.

matter that hardly concerned them.[1] And, indeed, to appreciate the justice of Rousseau's complaint, one has only to observe how seldom his case figures in the masses of polemical writings thrown up by the Genevan political controversies of the period 1763–70.[2] However, that was not the only cause of Rousseau's chagrin. The letters of his Genevan friends made it plain that his reputation as a great Christian writer had been seriously damaged by *Emile*. Moultou, he now remembered, had warned him that the effect of his two books would be to unite Genevans of every class in defence of their religion and country. The position was indeed critical, but it occurred to Rousseau that chance had just provided him with an admirable opportunity for vindicating his orthodoxy.

At the end of August 1762 the Sorbonne concluded its examination of *Emile* which was denounced in a *Mandement* circulated in the name of the Archbishop of Paris, Christophe de Beaumont. This pastoral letter closes with a brief and pungent commentary on Rousseau's life as opposed to his maxims which the latter could scarcely ignore because of its wicked resemblance to the truth. According to Saint-Brisson, the Archbishop himself was annoyed when he saw the 'horribles épithètes' which had been applied to Jean-Jacques in his own *Mandement*.[3] The polemics aroused by his two *Discours* had profoundly disgusted Rousseau with literary controversy, but now his sincerity was questioned. By November 1762 his *Lettre à Christophe de Beaumont* was completed though it did not appear in print until March 1763. Its object, he explains, was not so much to defend *Emile* as his personal honour; to examine the *Mandement*, not the *Profession de foi*. And, in refuting the calumnies of De Beaumont, he was firmly determined not to imitate the brutal methods employed on such occasions by Voltaire. 'Je ne sais me battre qu'avec dignité.'[4]

---

[1] *C.G.* IX, no. 1706 (26 Feb. 1763).

[2] *Vide Mémoires et documents publiés par la Société d'Histoire et d'Archéologie de Genève*, 2e série, t. I and II, for a complete list of titles. The National Library of Scotland possesses an interesting collection of these pamphlets, Cat. 'Geneva', D. 19 d.

[3] It was by no means unusual for bishops not to see the pastoral letters issued in their name.

[4] *Conf.* 597. 'I can only fight in a dignified manner.'

In fact, the *Lettre* betrays a tense and prolonged conflict between the writer's resolve to behave with dignity and his rankling sense of injustice and persecution. As a result, the style reflects a strange confusion of emotional states: vituperation, bitter irony, megalomania, evangelical mansuetude, righteous indignation and prophetic solemnity. In opposing his doctrine of natural human goodness to the Catholic dogma of original sin, Jean-Jacques briefly traces the evolution of his ideas, clarifying or amplifying certain pages of *Emile*. Passing now to the attack, Rousseau boldly asserts that his natural religion, which contains the substance of Christianity, is the only religion suited to mankind since it is rooted in a true knowledge of human nature. It offers a morality 'made for humanity' whereas that taught by the Catholic Church is founded on the blasphemous lie that our vices derive from original sin. The truth which no priest or prelate will squarely face up to is that the majority of Catholics have no real faith. No one genuinely believes the absurd dogmas of Catholicism:

> However, the form of worship is regulated, the ritual is prescribed, the laws established and transgressors are punished. Will any single individual go and protest against all that; challenge the laws of his country and renounce his father's religion? Who would dare? One submits in silence; self-interest prescribes deference to the opinions of him from whom one inherits. Therefore, one behaves like the others, reserving the right to laugh heartily in private at what one pretends to respect in public.[1]

The civic religion of the *Contrat social* is summarised in the *Lettre à Christophe de Beaumont* as a universal religion, 'the humane and social religion which every man living in society is obliged to admit'. Significantly, Rousseau does not mention the ferocious article consigning all recusants to the scaffold. Instead, borrowing the language of the Genevan Ecclesiastical Ordinances, he merely proclaims that anyone who 'dogmatises'

---

[1] *H.* III, 91: 'Cependant, le culte est réglé, les formes sont prescrites, les lois sont établies, les transgresseurs sont punis. Ira-t-on protester seul contre tout cela, récuser les lois de son pays et renier la religion de son père? Qui l'oserait? On se soumet en silence; l'intérêt veut qu'on soit de l'avis de celui dont on hérite. On fait donc comme les autres, sauf à rire à son aise en particulier de ce qu'on feint de respecter en public.'

against his social religion shall be banished from the State. And, indeed, Jean-Jacques could hardly have maintained an attitude reminiscent of the Inquisition in a book in which he asserts that if France had professed, instead of Catholicism, the religion of the Vicaire Savoyard her history would not be drenched in blood.

It would be otiose to follow Rousseau in his clause-by-clause dissection of the *Mandement*. In defending his views on revelation and the miracles, he merely embroiders on the Vicaire's theme: 'Que d'hommes entre Dieu et moi!' The Catholic Church tells us that Christ's divinity is proved by His miracles. But the only evidence of these comes to us from human testimony and Jesus Himself denies that He performed miracles. Rousseau's faith rests on the more solid basis of his own intuition. How then can De Beaumont be so cruelly unjust as to question the sincerity of his belief in revelation? What really infuriated Jean-Jacques was that section of the *Mandement* which, by stressing the contrast between his life and his writings, virtually depicted him as a humbug, if not a hypocrite. Hence, no doubt, the unusual truculence and bad taste of Rousseau's attacks on Catholic dogma: his jeers at the 'grands enfants' who meet in solemn conclave to argue about hypostasis, and the blasphemous syllogism by which he refutes the doctrine of transubstantiation. In composing these pleasantries, Jean-Jacques kept a hopeful eye cocked on the Genevan pastors who were not, however, amused or impressed. His *Lettre à Christophe de Beaumont* was banned by the *Petit Conseil* at the request of the French Resident. On 12 May 1763 Rousseau wrote to the First Syndic, formally renouncing his Genevan citizenship.

From this point until his death, one must always bear in mind the insidious and progressive toxic effects produced by Rousseau's chronic malady. It is clear from his letters to Duclos and Moultou that in August 1763 he seriously contemplated suicide as an escape from his intense physical sufferings.[1] He did not

---

[1] *C.G.* x, nos. 1878–9 (1 Aug. 1763). In both letters Rousseau states that he is in the exceptional situation mentioned by Lord Edouard Bomston who claimed that suicide was justifiable only as an escape from the physical torment of an incurable disease.

expect, in any case, to survive the winter and made arrangements for the future of Thérèse. For some time they had been
subjected to petty annoyances and insults by the villagers of
Môtiers instigated, Rousseau claimed later, by their pastor
Montmollin. But all the available facts point to Thérèse as the
sole cause and object of this animosity which eventually drove
Jean-Jacques from Môtiers to the little island of Saint-Pierre on
the Lac de Bienne.[1] As I see it, the quarrel with Montmollin
arose from an initial misunderstanding due largely to the
pastor's eagerness to have as his parishioner the illustrious
Rousseau, the intimate friend of *milord maréchal*, Governor of
Neuchâtel. In August 1762 he decided, apparently as the result
of his talks with Jean-Jacques, to admit him to Holy Communion.
The latter, before partaking of this sacrament, wrote to the
pastor declaring his sincere attachment to the Protestant faith.
His letter, couched in very general terms, does not explicitly
retract the unorthodox sentiments expressed in *Emile* which
he 'neither desires to defend or disavow'.[2] Yet it was clearly
interpreted as at least a virtual retractation by Rousseau's lay
and clerical friends of Geneva who were so elated that they had
200 copies printed and circulated. But Jean-Jacques, who regarded his *Déclaration* simply as a reaffirmation of the *Profession
de foi*, persuaded himself that, because he had been readmitted
as a communicant, Montmollin and probably the majority of the
Vénérable Classe of Neuchâtel tacitly endorsed, therefore, the
Vicaire's religious tenets. In October, whilst admitting that he
had been wrong about Montmollin's colleagues, Jean-Jacques
wrote to Mme de Boufflers: 'Voilà pour ainsi dire, la *Profession
de foi* approuvée dans tous ses points par un de leurs confrères:
ils ne peuvent digérer cela.'[3] It is difficult to understand what
grounds Rousseau had for believing that the pastor approved of

---

[1] See *Voyage en Suisse en 1777*, by L.-F. Ch. Dejobert, who learned from various
inhabitants of Môtiers that Thérèse was an inveterate trouble-maker and liar whom
Rousseau always, however, implicitly believed. Montmollin told Dejobert that
before the arrival of Thérèse, Jean-Jacques was quite different and blamed her
entirely for their quarrel.

[2] *C.G.* viii, no. 1501 (24 Aug. 1762): 'sans vouloir le défendre ni le désavouer.'

[3] *C.G.* viii, no. 1574 (30 Oct. 1762): 'There you have, so to speak, the *Profession
de foi* approved on every point by one of their *confrères*: they cannot stomach that.'

the Vicaire's theism. Mlle Rosselet, in an excellent study of *L'affaire Rousseau-Montmollin,* points out sensibly that the ecclesiastical discipline of the Swiss Protestant Churches demanded from its communicants, as Jean-Jacques must have known, 'absolute adhesion to the established faith with no exception whatever'.[1] But it seems probable that Montmollin, in the unusual circumstances and under the insidious spell of Rousseau's dialectic, felt it would be unchristian not to accede to his urgent plea. That is implicit everywhere in Montmollin's letter to F.-H. d'Ivernois of Geneva which repeats, incidentally, what he had already told his colleague, the pastor, Sarasin.[2] And it is virtually certain, as Mlle Rosselet observes, that Montmollin, in his private conversations with Rousseau, was greatly impressed by the latter's argument that the *Profession de foi* was exclusively aimed at the Catholic Church. Undoubtedly, too, after listening to his parishioner's violently expressed disgust for the craft of letters, Montmollin interpreted it as a pledge never again to write on religion. Rousseau subsequently admitted that he might have made such a promise to himself but certainly gave no such undertaking to the pastor. One can readily imagine, therefore, Montmollin's distress and consternation when, early in November 1764, Jean-Jacques published *Les Lettres écrites de la montagne* which open with a lengthy defence of *Emile* and a reasoned, merciless indictment of the Genevan Church. Passing, in the sixth *Lettre,* to politics, he refutes the charge that his *Contrat social* tends to undermine the authority of all established government. In the remaining three *Lettres,* Rousseau locks horns with the Procureur-Général, Tronchin. The latter, in an effort to allay the growing unrest caused by the activities of the De Luc party, had published anonymously in September 1763 a defence, based on constitutional grounds, of the recent decisions and general policy of the Genevan executive councils. Smoothly written, moderate in tone, Tronchin's *Lettres écrites de la campagne* made a profound and favourable impression on Genevan and foreign readers. The

---

[1] *Musée Neuchâtelois* (1934): 'une adhésion absolue à la foi établie sans aucune exception.'
[2] *C.G.* viii, no. 1610 (27 Nov. 1762).

author, wrote Lenieps to Rousseau in February 1764, was widely compared to Cicero who had saved Rome from Catilina.[1] Lenieps did not know that the Genevan Catilina was secretly preparing his reply to Tronchin which was ready for the press early in June. It is evident from a letter written to De Luc in October 1763 that he had undertaken this work with the greatest reluctance.[2] No one knew better than Rousseau the hazards of the polemical game where the attacker invariably starts off with an advantage. For, in a few seconds, he can make a false, erroneous or misleading statement which often can only be refuted at the expense of much laborious documentation and tiresome explanation. That is why, in 1753, Rousseau had resolved never, in future, to reply to his critics. But, once again, his personal honour was involved. Nevertheless, Jean-Jacques was determined not to engage in this 'great enterprise' unless he was absolutely sure of victory. In this mood he told De Luc that he had never studied the Genevan Constitution, meaning, as the context reveals, that he had never studied the practical application of the constitutional laws to situations like his own. He cites, for example, the procedure followed at the trial of one Morelli, prosecuted in the sixteenth century under Article 88 of the Ecclesiastical Ordinances. In a controversy with an Attorney General who exploited the fact that many Genevan institutions were founded merely on usage consecrated by time, Rousseau intended to take no chances. He insisted, therefore, on being properly briefed by the *Représentants*. Fortunately, De Luc and his friend Vieusseux had been working like terriers in the dusty Genevan archives for their own purposes. Indeed, their *Réponse* to Tronchin's *Lettres*, published shortly after Rousseau's, was considered even more dangerous to the government in well informed quarters.[3]

In presenting Montmollin with a copy of his book, Rousseau obviously felt that he owed the pastor some explanation. He affirms, therefore, that the sole object of the opening *Lettres* is to

---

[1] *C.G.* x, no. 2025 (25 Feb. 1764).   [2] *C.G.* x, no. 1953 (25 Feb. 1763).

[3] Sir Francis d'Ivernois, *Tableau des Révolutions de Genève* (1782). English translation (Cadell, 1784), p. 177. Born in 1757, he was the son of one of Rousseau's warmest supporters.

settle his personal quarrel with the Genevan ministers, not to attack the Protestant religion which he brings in only in order to defend it against certain theologians who seek to overthrow Protestantism. From the outset, however, Rousseau's defence of *Emile* and the *Contrat* is, in effect, a powerful offensive. The arguments employed to refute De Beaumont's charges are refurbished here in order to attack the Church of Geneva. The Vicaire's disciples are Christians despite their indifference to ritual and theological niceties for, instead of arguing about Christ's teachings, they practise them. Simple in their worship as in their belief, they are Christians, not in the manner of the persecutor Paul, but of James, the true confidant of Jesus. Defending the allusions to Christianity contained in the *Contrat*, Rousseau explains that the chapter on civic religion implies no slight on Christianity which, he repeats, cannot be a national religion without betraying its principles and its spirit. Humanity and patriotism are necessarily incompatible. Reverting to the Genevan decree, Jean-Jacques demands to know in what essential respects *Emile* deviates from the Bible. The truth is, surely, that no Genevan pastor can answer that question since no one can tell him what are the fundamental articles of the Reformed Church. As a result, when the ministers wish to charge an author with irreligion, they are always obliged to resort to an ingenious technique. They draw up a list of his opinions and set down their opposites, adopting these as articles of faith. The fact is that no other course is open to them, for the essence of Protestantism is tolerance. The Reformers broke with Rome because they defended the right of any individual to interpret the Gospels according to his lights and honest belief. Rousseau's *Profession de foi* is, therefore, just one more Protestant profession of faith. Jean-Jacques is charged with rejecting the miracles. But Christ never proclaimed His divinity by miracles. A miracle is a real and visible exception to the natural laws. Yet what was yesterday a reversal of the physical order is today shown by science to be nothing of the kind.

In the fifth *Lettre*, pressing home his attack, Rousseau accuses the *Petit Conseil* of usurping the functions of the Consistory since *Emile* could only be legally condemned by that body under

Article 88. His reasoning is subtle, but less impressive than in the remaining *Lettres* where greater and less personal issues are in question. Now, concentrating his fire on Tronchin and the *Petit Conseil*, he observes that no other government has proscribed the *Contrat social*. Why, then, Geneva whose Constitution he took as his model of a political institution though not in the servile condition to which it has been reduced by the executive Councils? Here Rousseau brilliantly reviews the long process by which the sovereignty of the *Conseil Général* was gradually usurped by the aristocratic governing class until, in order to avert civil war, the Mediatory Powers were asked to define the respective constitutional rights of the citizens and their governing bodies. As the dimensions of this study rule out a detailed analysis of Rousseau's exegesis, I will present only its salient features. The abuses of the original Constitution by the patriciate are starkly exposed: the *Conseil Général* practically stripped of its legislative powers; the virtual absorption of the Syndics by the smaller Councils which they are supposed to control; the ban on periodic meetings of the *Conseil Général*; the illegal refusal by the *Petit Conseil* to bring accused persons before the Syndics prior to their commitment to prison; its cynical attempt to nullify the citizens' Right of Representation by a so-called *droit négatif* or Right of Veto.

On the last two points, Rousseau fights the government tooth and nail, yet approves of the Act of Mediation. It was, he maintains, the salvation of the State and, if observed, would conserve the national sovereignty. Unlike Ducrest who demanded total sovereign powers for the *Conseil Général*, Rousseau is content, for example, to leave the initiation of legislation to the other Councils thus, according to Vaughan, contradicting the spirit if not the letter of his *Contrat social*. That is to overlook, however, an important safeguard underlined by Rousseau when he observes that the Edict of Mediation is not a law. Any of its articles, including such as limit their sovereign rights, can be amended by the people at will. Again, Rousseau always insisted that the legislative and executive were distinct and separate functions, regretting even that the Mediators had given the General Council the right to deliberate on such matters as declarations of war, peace treaties and alliances. These *Lettres*, indeed, disclose the realistic aspect of Rousseau's political thought. After all, the *Conseil Général* had freely accepted the *Règlement* by a huge majority in 1738 and in Rousseau's view their sovereignty was completely guaranteed by their Right of Representation. It was the attempts of the *Négatifs* to destroy this Right, just as much as personal interest, which had brought him into the fray. The effect of his *Lettres de la montagne* was to give fresh courage to the *Représentants* and to increase their numbers. That the unjust decree was not rescinded did not unduly depress Jean-Jacques since all Europe now knew why he had been so scurvily treated by the Genevan oligarchs. As a rule, nothing dies so quickly as a work of polemics. And if these *Lettres* still pulse with vitality it is because the genius of Rousseau perceived and isolated the radioactive truths lurking in the dust and débris of Genevan party politics.

It was Voltaire who opened the campaign against the *Lettres de la montagne*. On 27 December 1764 he published, anonymously, his *Sentiment des citoyens*, written ostensibly by a pious Genevan who protested indignantly at the blasphemies of *Emile* and the *Lettres* and concluded a virulent, personal attack on Rousseau with the words: 'Mais il faut lui apprendre que si on châtie légèrement un romancier impie, on punit capitalement un vil séditieux.'[1] The reason for this hymn of hate is to be found in Rousseau's fifth *Lettre*. Convinced that all his persecutions in Switzerland originated in Ferney, he avenged himself by a clever, satiric *pastiche* of Voltaire's style, openly naming him as the author of *Le Sermon des cinquante*, a typically Voltairian 'fusée volante' which its author, however, had always strenuously disavowed. Infuriated by what he regarded as an inexcusable and cowardly act, Voltaire resolved henceforth to show Rousseau no mercy. In fact, he followed up the *Sentiment des citoyens* with the *Lettre au Docteur Pansophe* and his *Lettre à Hume* (1766). And not content with having vilified his enemy in England, he awaited his return in order to conspue him in the burlesque, scurrilous poem entitled *La Guerre civile de Genève* (1767). Yet,

---

[1] 'But he must be taught that if an impious novelist gets off lightly, a vile fomenter of sedition is punished by death.'

so completely was Jean-Jacques deceived by the style of the *Sentiment des citoyens* that he attributed it to the Genevan pastor Vernes, and branded him publicly as the author in a reprint of the pamphlet which he circulated in January 1765. And though Rousseau, in response to the frenzied denials of Vernes, suppressed a second edition, he could never bring himself to admit that he had been guilty of a flagrant injustice.

Publicly burnt at The Hague in January 1765, Rousseau's *Lettres de la montagne* naturally scandalised also the Genevan clergy, and in February were condemned by the *Petit Conseil*. Vigorously attacked by the Neuchâtel ministers, the book was defended, however, by the *Conseil d'Etat* on the intervention of Rousseau's friends, Meuron, Chaillet, C.-G. d'Ivernois and Colonel de Pury. But that did not protect him from the reproaches of Montmollin, now an unwilling instrument of the *Vénérable Classe*. In order, no doubt, to avert possible incidents at Môtiers, he requested Jean-Jacques not to attend communion and procured a declaration that there would be no more writings on religion. Unimpressed by Rousseau's assurances and no longer able to regard him as a genuine member of their Church, the Neuchâtel clergy instructed Montmollin to summon the culprit before the Consistory of Môtiers. Jean-Jacques, who had no intention of listening to the reprimands of these village wiseacres, quite unreasonably denied the authority of the *Classe* to bring him before the Consistory and went off on a visit to Neuchâtel but had to turn back because of illness. As it happened, no decision was reached at the meeting, four Elders being opposed to his excommunication though apparently for reasons connected with local politics. At the end of March 1765 Frederick issued, at Keith's suggestion, a Rescript placing Jean-Jacques under the protection of the Neuchâtel *Conseil d'Etat* to whom the harassed invalid, on 6 April, gave a written pledge not to engage in further polemics. On 1 May the *Conseil* informed the people of Môtiers that Rousseau was under royal protection and, by June, it looked as if the whole affair had blown over.

As Rousseau's health had somewhat improved, he was able during the summer of 1765, to indulge his passion for botanising in the wild and lovely Jura region. One of these excursions took him to the enchanting Ile de Saint-Pierre which he was shortly to revisit in less happy mood. The clergy of Neuchâtel or, as Keith humorously dubbed them, the *Sacrogorgons* had not finished with Rousseau and, on Sunday, 1 September, whilst Mme de Verdelin was his guest at Môtiers, a sermon preached by Montmollin fanned the smouldering animosity of the villagers. According to Jean-Jacques, stones were thrown at his window the following night and he was subjected to other insults and annoyances. On 6 September, after the local fair, occurred the incident which Rousseau describes as the 'lapidation' of Môtiers. From more objective accounts, however, it seems that a few village drunks bombarded the cottage with pebbles and not, as Jean-Jacques claims, with huge and murderous rocks. It is also highly probable that Thérèse and not he was the object of this typical rustic *charivari*. Since a royal protégé was involved, however, the *Conseil d'Etat* exaggerated the importance of the affair and offered a reward for information, whilst the neighbouring village of Couvet offered the victim a sanctuary. But Rousseau, thoroughly scared, decamped on 8 September for Neuchâtel en route for the Ile de Saint-Pierre where, three weeks later, he was rejoined by Thérèse. Frederick, in a second Rescript, again ordered the *Conseil d'Etat* to protect Rousseau and, inspired no doubt by the loyal but prejudiced Keith, blamed Montmollin for the disturbance. Soon the *Petit Conseil* of Berne, which had reluctantly granted asylum to Jean-Jacques, was anxious to get rid of their unwelcome guest. On 10 October, during the autumn recess, a sparsely attended meeting resolved that he must be given notice to quit the Ile de Saint-Pierre within twenty-four hours. It was not, however, until 25 October that Rousseau sorrowfully departed for Bienne, leaving Thérèse on the island.

It is necessary, at this point, to view the absurd Montmollin episode in its proper perspective. As we shall now observe, in briefly surveying Rousseau's chequered existence from 1762 until his death in 1778, this muddled affair constitutes merely one element of a crazy design and should be regarded as one symptom of a complex psychological disturbance which flashes intermittently throughout the *Correspondance*, attaining its climax about

1770. *Emile* had profoundly altered public opinion in regard to Jean-Jacques, for it was this book and not, as is so often stated, *La Nouvelle Héloïse* which created a moral revolution in Europe. And though we are constantly assured by Rousseau that he had long ceased to live in the opinion of others it is painfully evident from the *Correspondance* that he was appalled and disoriented by the transformed attitude of his French and Swiss public. Refusing, as always, to accept responsibility for his actions, Jean-Jacques now searched the horizon for scapegoats. His chief object in writing the *Profession de foi*, he told De Luc and Sarasin, had been to combat not only Catholicism but the doctrines of the *philosophes*. He was obviously, therefore, the victim of a campaign, organised in Geneva by the 'jongleurs' Voltaire and Dr Tronchin, abetted in Paris by D'Alembert. From his friends, at this stage, Rousseau wanted only consolation and a categoric expression of faith in his innocence. Moultou, for daring to suggest that he might do well to clarify his views on religion and to adopt a less arrogant tone, incurred Rousseau's suspicion and grave displeasure, for which the latter afterwards begged forgiveness and indulgence:

Mais, cher Ami, pardonnez les inquiétudes d'un pauvre solitaire qui ne sait rien de ce qui se passe, dont tant de cruels souvenirs attristent l'imagination, qui ne connaît d'autre bonheur dans la vie que l'amitié, et qui n'aima jamais personne autant que vous.[1]

Yet this 'solitaire' was besieged with visitors at Môtiers and they arrived from all quarters, mostly from idle curiosity though some hoped to convert him. Most of them, says Jean-Jacques, got what they deserved. Yet there were exceptions like the Hungarian 'baron' later unmasked as an adventurer. His real name was Sauttersheim but, as the 'baron de Sauttern', he completely infatuated Jean-Jacques who had originally suspected him of being a spy hired by the French government to abduct him. And even after Sauttersheim's sordid record was exposed, Jean-

---

[1] *C.G.* VIII, no. 1589 (13 Nov. 1762):'But, my dear friend, pardon the anxieties of a poor lonely man who knows nothing about what is going on, whose imagination is saddened by so many cruel memories, who knows no other happiness in life but friendship, and who never loved anyone so much as you.'

Jacques could not find it in his heart to condemn him.[1] Boswell, in his own inimitable manner, has related the astonishing story of how he 'gate-crashed' Rousseau's house early in December 1764. Yet, if Boswell owed his initial success to unlimited effrontery, it was largely because he was a friend of *milord maréchal* that 'the genteel black man in the dress of an Armenian' indulgently humoured this transparent lion-hunter and replied to his impudent questions. Boswell made a favourable impression on Thérèse, 'a little, lively, neat French girl' and Jean-Jacques was quite disarmed by the Scotsman's frank yet amusing egotism: 'Oui, vous êtes un malin mais c'est une malignité agréable.'[2]

Still, the only friend whom Rousseau implicitly trusted during this period was George Keith whom he loved and deferred to like an obedient son. To Jean-Jacques he was always 'mon père' whilst Keith addressed him affectionately as 'mon fils'. They took to each other from the first and were soon inseparable friends. Every fortnight Jean-Jacques walked six leagues to the Governor's residence, the château de Colombier where he spent twenty-four hours and Keith, under the pretext of shooting quail, would wander over in the direction of Môtiers. After a few months, they arranged to spend the rest of their lives together at Keith Hall in Aberdeenshire with David Hume, 'le bon David'. *Milord maréchal* did, in fact, revisit his ancestral home in the autumn of 1763 but their dream of a 'château d'Ecosse' never materialised. By October 1764 Keith was disgusted with Aberdeenshire society and with his native climate. Realising that the Scotland he had known as a youth existed only in memory, the old Jacobite accepted, to Rousseau's dismay, Frederick's pressing invitation to return to Berlin. Through *milord maréchal* and Mme de Boufflers, Jean-Jacques had entered into correspondence with Hume for whom he conceived a deep admiration cordially reciprocated by the Scottish philosopher and historian. But it was not until 4 December 1765 that

---

[1] The *C.G.* does not print all Rousseau's correspondence with this strange character whose letters are in the Library of Neuchâtel. They have been reproduced, however, by L. Rácz, *Rousseau és Sauttersheim* (Budapest, 1913).

[2] *Private Papers of Boswell*. Privately printed (1928), vol. 4, p. 110. 'Yes, you are a knowing rascal but a nice one.'

Rousseau accepted Hume's offer of a sanctuary in England. Now it is clear from Keith's letters[1] to Rousseau in 1765 that, already in June, the latter was anxious to leave Môtiers and, in July, was attracted by an invitation from the Duchess of Saxe-Gotha to visit her on the way to Berlin. At this time, also, to the delight of Keith, his adoptive son, 'Jean-Jacques le bon enfant', accepted an annuity of £50. With touching gratitude, the old man thanked Rousseau for this signal 'distinction and preference'.[2] It transpires, moreover, that whilst Rousseau, in November, was trying to make up his mind whether to seek a refuge in Germany, Holland, Venice or England his constant mentor and guide was George Keith who strongly recommended the south-west of England, preferably Falmouth. And it is interesting to note, in view of the quarrel which later estranged Jean-Jacques and Hume, the following suggestive passage from a letter written by Keith on 19 November 1765. With remarkable prescience, he begs Rousseau not to confuse Hume with the 'Yahoos' who were persecuting him:

You do not shun mankind, you only avoid, and rightly, the Yahoos. David is not one; he is a man. And when one has found one (a man), one must recognise him as such, distinguish him from the Yahoos and treat him well. I am counting on your behaving thus towards David to whom I send my kindest wishes. You have always treated me well. David is even more deserving: he is a Government official and you will be safe with him. He is the Houyhnhnm who will protect you from the Yahoos.[3]

The wise Keith, evidently, anticipated trouble and was, I suspect, more distressed than surprised by Rousseau's behaviour in England.

---

[1] First published by Streckeisen-Moultou, *J.-J. Rousseau, ses amis et ses ennemis* (1865). I find, however, on collating these with the manuscript originals at Neuchâtel that the editor has omitted many passages. Some of these published letters have been reproduced in the *C.G.* but with the omissions of Streckeisen-Moultou. See, for the amended version, my article in *French Studies*, IX, 54–9.

[2] Neuchâtel MSS. Ancien fonds 7902, t. XXI, ff. 144–5.

[3] *Ibid.* ff. 158–9: 'Vous ne fuyez pas les hommes, vous évitez seulement et avec raison les Yahoos. David ne l'est pas: il est homme. Quand on en a trouvé un il faut le reconnaître et le distinguer des Yahoos et le bien traiter. Je compte que vous en userez ainsi avec David à qui mille choses de ma part. Vous m'avez toujours bien traité. David le mérite encore plus: il est ministre publique [sic]. Vous serez en sûreté chez lui. C'est le Houyhnhnm qui vous protégera des Yahoos.'

It is difficult to resist the impression—so strong is the force of intellectual habit—that the whole Rousseau-Hume affair is 'prefigured' in the *Correspondance* for the period 1762–5. Grievously wounded in his *amour-propre* by the defection of his public, tormented by a lacerated urethra, Jean-Jacques was, for three years, a prey to the various states of soul reflected in his letters. At times, he derived consolation from the image of Rousseau the Mediator whose career, with the completion of his mission, was now at an end. All that now remained was to suffer and die. But for the malevolence of his enemies, he would now be living in retirement, esteemed by the country which he had intended to honour by his choice.[1] More often, however, Rousseau's prevailing mood was one of childish self-pity characterised by outbursts of petulance. Read, for instance, the cruel letters to Mme de Luxembourg when, on the death of her husband, she recalled his great friendship for Jean-Jacques. 'Je suis plus à plaindre que vous',[2] he wrote to the sorrowing widow, begging her to interest herself rather in his misfortunes. And, in answer to her reproaches, he observes calmly: 'I dare say that he owed me that sincere friendship which you assure me he always had for me; for my heart never had a truer, more lively or more tender attachment than that which he had inspired in me.'[3] More justifiable, yet equally symptomatic, is Rousseau's treatment of Mme La Tour de Franqueville, or as she archly signed herself, 'Julie'. The classic type of feminine limpet who, from motives of self-glorification, fastens inexorably on distinguished men, this lady bombarded Jean-Jacques with her letters from September 1761 until his death. Impervious to rebuffs, convinced that she was Rousseau's spiritual mate, she wore down his resistance and, during the Môtiers phase, her admiration soothed his bruised self-esteem. But 'Julie' or as she later christened herself, 'Marianne', foolishly tried to imitate the Master's candour, a blunder which earned for her a brutal *congé*. During his prosperity, said Jean-Jacques unjustly, she had

---

[1] *C.G.* VIII, no. 1477 (to B. Tscharner, 27 July 1762).

[2] *C.G.* XI, no. 2105 (5 June 1762): 'I am more to be pitied than you.'

[3] *C.G.* XI, no. 2121: 'J'ose dire qu'il me la devait cette amitié que vous m'assurez qu'il eut toujours pour moi; car mon cœur n'eut jamais d'attachement plus vrai, plus vif, plus tendre que celui qu'il m'avait inspiré.'

flattered him but now, in his adversity, she indulges in 'frankness'. In such a case, he himself would rather lie than not pronounce words of consolation.[1]

The *Correspondance* discloses two interesting facts relating to Rousseau's fears and suspicions at this stage. They were, quite clearly, intermittent and synchronised with the crises of his physical malady which, in turn, became especially acute at critical periods in his affairs. Again, they were often due to the suggestions of well-meaning friends like D'Ivernois and Lenieps. Finally, without injustice to Thérèse, it is virtually certain that, in this matter, she exercised a deplorable influence on her companion. In calmer mood, however, he would apologise for his unjust suspicions. To Watelet, for instance, he wrote during a painful attack of his illness: '. . . mais j'avoue que des malheurs sans exemple et sans nombre et des noirceurs d'où j'en craignais le moins, m'ont rendu défiant et crédule sur le mal.'[2]

Early on the morning of 25 October 1765 Rousseau set out alone from Bienne for Berlin, hoping to find there a congenial milieu where he might forget the humiliations inflicted on him by Geneva, Neuchâtel and Paris. For only one thing could bring quiet to his turbulent spirit: the positive assurance that he had been reintegrated in public opinion as a moral legislator. The reception accorded to him by Strasbourg acted, therefore, as a tonic to his morale. So here Jean-Jacques lingered for a month, fêted and caressed by all, including the *lieutenant du roi* who introduced him to the *Intendant*, Blair de Boisemont. His comedy *Narcisse* was being rehearsed at a private theatre and he attended a concert where Mlle de Barbesan sang the theme song from *Le Devin du village*. The Cossack Count Razoumovsky offered him a refuge in the Ukraine; his publisher, Rey, sent a clerk to escort him to Holland but, on 30 November, Jean-Jacques finally chose England. Mme de Verdelin had procured him a French passport and on 9 December he left for Paris where, as the protégé of the

---

[1] *C.G.* xiii, no. 2505 (10 March 1765).

[2] *C.G.* xii, no. 2289 (18 Nov. 1764). Rousseau admits that he has been unjust to D'Alembert and continues: '. . . but I confess that unparalleled and countless misfortunes and villainies coming from the most unexpected quarters have made me distrustful and prone to suspect evil.'

prince de Conti, he put up at a hotel in the Temple.[1] Despite a warning from the police to lie low, the fugitive received numerous visitors one of whom, to his annoyance, was the enterprising 'Marianne' who was determined to see the idol of her heart. With David Hume and the *banneret*, De Luze, he set out on 4 January 1766 for London via Roye, Arras, Aire and Calais, reaching Dover on the eleventh after a rough crossing during which, to Hume's amazement, his invalid companion stayed on deck.

Rousseau's sojourn in England lasted eighteen months and proved even more disastrous for his peace of mind than the Venetian adventure. Since the detailed story of his experiences has been admirably narrated by Courtois,[2] we may confine ourselves here to the Rousseau-Hume Affair over which so much ink has been shed. And to judge from the most recent works on the subject, it looks as if what was essentially a personal quarrel is beginning to acquire, in retrospect, the character and significance of an ideological conflict.[3] Whether the facts, as recorded in the correspondence of Hume and Rousseau, will bear such an interpretation seems to me very doubtful.

The two men, who had conceived a strong mutual liking, met for the first time in Paris almost on the eve of their journey to England. Hume shared Rousseau's views on revealed religion and, like him, had fallen foul of the *Llamas*, as Keith called them. Besides, *milord maréchal* to whom Jean-Jacques listened with filial respect, praised 'le bon David' to the skies. So did Mme de Boufflers who had a secret *tendresse* for Hume which he passionately reciprocated though with great discreetness since she was the *maîtresse en titre* of the powerful Conti. Mme de Verdelin, originally prejudiced against Hume as against all Anglo-Saxons,[4]

[1] This was a district in Paris owned by the Order of Knights Templar under whose protection lived numbers of servants, certain privileged merchants and sometimes persons convicted of various crimes.

[2] 'Le Séjour de J.-J. Rousseau en Angleterre,' *Ann.* VI (1911). For a shorter account see H. Roddier, *J.-J. Rousseau en Angleterre*, ch. vii (1950). This is an authoritative study of Rousseau's influence in England.

[3] H. Roddier, 'La Querelle Rousseau-Hume', *Revue de Littérature comparée*, no. 71 (1938). H. Guillemin, *Cette Affaire infernale*, etc. (1942).

[4] *C.G.* XI, no. 2101 (1 June 1764). Having mentioned the interesting fact that Mme d'Houdetot had given a dinner in honour of Hume, and that he was all the rage with the women, Mme de Verdelin attributes his success to his lack of frankness.

became, on closer acquaintance, one of his warmest admirers and, on her visit to Môtiers strongly urged Rousseau to seek refuge in England. Now it is important to note that for two years David Hume, who was private secretary to our ambassador Lord Hertford, had been the idol of the Parisian *salons* and a frequent guest of the *coterie holbachique*, who warned him that he would never get his companion to England without a quarrel.[1]

Thérèse did not join Rousseau in London until 10 February and Hume, on learning that her escort was Boswell, confided to Mme de Boufflers that he dreaded an event 'fatal to our friend's honour'. We have it, one might say, straight from the stallion's mouth that Hume's fears were amply justified.[2] Meanwhile, Jean-Jacques lodged for a fortnight at the house of John Stewart in Buckingham Street, a friend not only of Hume but, it should be noted, of Keith who had recommended the Stewarts, father and son to Rousseau early in November 1765.[3] All fashionable London was eager to see the famous Jean-Jacques who received many distinguished visitors including even royalty, for the Hereditary Prince of Brunswick called incognito at York Buildings. Garrick invited him to a command performance at Drury Lane where the man in Armenian costume attracted more attention than the King and Queen. The latest Rousseau anecdotes went the round of the clubs and the Press treated him with marked respect. Jean-Jacques, a connoisseur in such matters, was surprised and delighted. 'A good lesson for the others', he wrote to Du Peyrou with bitter memories of the Genevans and Bernese, 'who deserve indeed to be dragged through the mud.'[4] To humiliate them he decided to publish in London all the documents relating to his persecution in Switzerland. Yet Rous-

---

[1] The *Letters of David Hume* (ed. Greig, 1932), no. 303 (to H. Blair, Feb. 1766).
[2] *Journal of James Boswell* (1765–1768), pp. 66–7 (privately printed, 1930). Boswell suggests that he was seduced by Thérèse who was an experienced amorist. It is obvious from a sarcastic note in which Jean-Jacques advised Boswell to have himself bled from time to time that Thérèse had blabbed (*C.G.* xv, no. 3089 (2 Aug. 1766)).
[3] See Neuchâtel MS. f. 155 (7 Nov. 1765). Passage omitted by Streckeisen-Moultou. 'Mr Penneck at the Museum. Je l'écris en anglais pour qu'on vous entende. Il vous fera connaître Mrs Stuart [sic] Père et fils.'
[4] *C.G.* xv, no. 2917 (27 Jan. 1766): 'c'est une bonne leçon pour les autres...ils méritent en vérité d'être trainés par les boues.'

seau's overwhelming need was to get out of London to some lonely, romantic spot where he could forget the present and relive the golden days of his youth. Impatiently, therefore, he awaited the material for his *Confessions* whilst his friends tried to find him a house. In the meantime, he had moved to Chiswick and there Thérèse rejoined him. Her arrival created an awkward social problem though General Conway gallantly invited Jean-Jacques with his *gouvernante* to meet Lady Aylesbury. Hume, in his letters to Paris, laughed at the absurd forebodings of the *philosophes*. No shadow could ever darken the perfect friendship which linked him with the gentle, disinterested and childlike Rousseau. True, at times, he was a little hasty with those who displeased him and apt, it was said, to entertain groundless suspicions of his friends though David, personally, had never observed this trait. He was soon to be brutally disillusioned.

Meanwhile, Rousseau botanised in the Thames valley or went sightseeing with a Professor Walker who had been unofficially deputed by Lord Bute to escort the distinguished visitor. Daniel Malthus begged Jean-Jacques to settle down as his guest at Dorking but the latter, for the moment, had set his heart on Wales. Finally, having strained even David Hume's patience, he accepted the offer of Wootton Hall, in Dovedale, Derbyshire. Its owner was a wealthy Cheshire gentleman called Davenport, a jewel of a man who had been introduced whilst Rousseau was being painted by Allan Ramsay.[1] Jean-Jacques insisted, of course, on paying rent and Davenport unwillingly agreed to take £30 though he placed his staff at the disposal of his tenants.

There are few, I imagine, who have not had occasion to observe, in a general way, the psychology of 'persecution mania'. The person thus afflicted, whilst retaining intact his reasoning faculty, can no longer interpret the actions of others correctly. For him there are no contingencies in life. Every incident reveals an intention which is hostile to himself. To the most casual events, words, gestures and glances, he attributes a malicious

---

[1] The famous picture now in the National Gallery of Scotland. Jean-Jacques later regarded it as part of the 'conspiracy' to blacken his character in the eyes of the English. He called it Ramsay's 'terrible portrait' and was very annoyed with Moultou for admiring 'cette mine farouche qui n'est pas la mienne assurément' (*C.G.* XIX, no. 3912 (28 March 1770)).

purpose and then, with dreadful logic, assembles these into a pattern conforming to his delusion of persecution. That is precisely how Rousseau, brooding in the solitude of Wootton Hall and having traced all his recent calamities to the *philosophes* of Paris and Geneva, now became convinced that David Hume was one of their emissaries. In a series of quite disconnected incidents he discovered the explanation of the following enigma. Why did the English Press, hitherto so deferential, now treat him with levity and veiled contempt? All the 'evidence' pointed to one conclusion. It was the work of Hume who had deliberately, in collusion with Rousseau's enemies, lured him to London so as to ruin his prestige in England. We may now review the incidents in question.

Hume, before leaving Paris, heard at Lord Ossory's dinner-table of a practical joke invented by the egregious Horace Walpole who was afflicted, like many otherwise intelligent Englishmen of the period, with an oafish sense of humour. Aided by his friends he concocted a bogus letter from the King of Prussia to Jean-Jacques, offering him a refuge, but only if he discarded his eccentricities. If, however, he persisted in racking his brains to discover fresh misfortunes, Frederick could supply him with some real ones. But these persecutions would cease when Jean-Jacques ceased to glory in being a victim of persecution. This killingly funny elucubration was loudly applauded by all, including Hume though there is no proof that he assisted in its composition.[1] Late in January, Rousseau heard it was circulating in Paris. It was, he wrote to Du Peyrou, obviously of 'Genevan manufacture', and even when informed that the author was Walpole refused to believe it. At the end of February, when lodging with Hume at a Miss Elliot's in Lisle Street, he asked him if he had heard of a bogus letter which was being disseminated by Walpole. Foolishly, Hume evaded the question, no doubt because of an uneasy conscience. It so happened, also,

---

[1] Hume admitted having made a joke about it at Lord Ossory's (Letter no. 304 to Mme de Barbentane (16 Feb. 1766)). This admission is not incompatible with Mme de Verdelin's statement to Rousseau that Walpole, on giving it to a certain lady to read, warned her not to show it to Hume because: 'il raffole de son cher petit homme, vous nous brouilleriez' (He's crazy about his dear little man, you would set us against each other'). (*C.G.* xvi, no. 3147 (9 Oct. 1766).)

that Rousseau became greatly agitated on hearing in the next room the voice of young François Tronchin, the son of the detested 'jongleur' of Geneva, Dr Tronchin. His incipient distrust of Hume was increased, moreover, by the latter's inquisitiveness about his private affairs. In fact, David who was already rather sceptical about Rousseau's much-advertised ill-health and wondering whether his vaunted poverty might not be just another harmless affectation, was now, 'out of mere curiosity', secretly investigating his friend's financial position.[1] Of this Rousseau was fortunately unaware but Hume's interest in his correspondence struck him as excessive. A new and horrible image of his friend now began to take shape in his consciousness. And, on the eve of his departure for Wootton a dramatic scene occurred at Lisle Street where he and Thérèse put up for the night. Brooding by the fire, Rousseau furtively observed Hume and was appalled when he intercepted 'a long, searching, burning and mocking look'. Then, filled with remorse and indignation at his unworthy suspicions, Jean-Jacques leapt up, embraced his friend and in a voice choking with sobs, cried out: 'Non, non, David Hume n'est pas un traître. Cela n'est pas possible. S'il n'était pas le meilleur homme du monde, il faudrait qu'il en fût le plus noir!'[2] But Hume remained unmoved by this explosion of sensibility. Now Hume describes this scene two weeks later in a letter to Mme de Boufflers, but attributes Rousseau's outburst, rather oddly, to the following incident. Davenport, in order to save his guest the whole cost of the journey to Wootton, pretended that by good luck there happened to be a coach returning empty to Derbyshire with seats at a reduced fare. But it is evident from the *Correspondance* that Jean-Jacques did not find out about this kindly plot until *after* he left London. It is, of course, possible that Hume's memory was at fault. On the other hand, the explanation he gave to Mme de Boufflers of Rousseau's agitation placed David in a very favourable light, as the friend whose connivance in Davenport's innocent stratagem was

---

[1] *Letters of Hume*, no. 314 (to Blair, 25 March 1766).
[2] *C.G.* xv, no. 2990 (to Mme de Verdelin, 9 April 1766): 'No, no, David Hume is not a traitor. That is not possible. If he were not the best man in the world, he would have to be the blackest!' This letter, it is worth noting, already contains all the charges set forth afterwards in Rousseau's reply to Hume of 10 July.

entirely to his credit. Besides, Hume could hardly have forgotten the letter sent from Wootton on 22 March in which, alluding to the coach incident, Jean-Jacques wrote:

> Si vous y avez trempé, je vous conseille de quitter, une fois pour toutes, ces petites ruses qui ne peuvent avoir un bon principe, quand elles se tournent en pièges contre la simplicité. Je vous embrasse, mon cher patron, avec le même cœur que j'espère trouver en vous.[1]

Having apparently failed to grasp the significance of this letter, Hume merely apologised for his share in the friendly little plot: all he had done was to conceal it from Rousseau. He was now actively engaged in trying to procure for the latter a royal pension of £100 a year through General Conway, the brother of Lord Hertford. Meanwhile, Jean-Jacques was morally certain that David was hand in glove with the 'jongleurs', keeping them *au fait* with the contents of his letters and insidiously undermining his reputation in England. He could not yet fathom Hume's motives but thought they were undoubtedly sinister. All this he communicated to his friend D'Ivernois on 31 March. Three days later the *St James's Chronicle* published French and English versions of Walpole's Prussian letter which elicited from Jean-Jacques a protest in which he remarked that the author of the forgery had accomplices in London. At the same time, he wrote sharply to the publishers Becket and De Hondt saying that he now understood why they had not yet printed the letters by Du Peyrou on the Swiss persecutions. By 9 April Rousseau's *dossier* on Hume was complete, though his long letter to Mme de Verdelin reveals two additional 'proofs' of David's guilt. On the journey from Paris to the coast they had shared, at Roye, the same bedroom. In the night, his companion uttered several times the strange words: 'Je tiens Jean-Jacques Rousseau'[2] which, at the time, he interpreted in a favourable sense. Now, in retrospect, their sinister import was all too clear. Now, too, he understood the reason for the 'infamous reception' accorded to Thérèse by Miss Elliot; the hatred and disdain shown to himself

---

[1] *C.G.* xv, no. 2966: 'If you had a hand in it, I advise you to drop, once and for all, these little ruses which cannot derive from a good principle when they become snares set to trap simple people. I embrace you, my dear patron, with the same cordiality I hope to find in you.'

[2] *C.G.* xv, no. 2990 (9 April 1766): 'I've got Jean-Jacques Rousseau.'

by her servants; the 'smear campaign' of the Press; the changed attitude of the Court and public; the broken seals on his letters; the behaviour of Becket and De Hondt and the aloofness of Hume's friends. Everything fitted beautifully into the general design. Jean-Jacques resolved, therefore, to cease all correspondence with Hume, who received no reply to his letters. That, of course, struck him as odd; but, as his correspondence shows, he was beginning to regard Jean-Jacques as a very odd person indeed: subject to fits of melancholy and spleen, sometimes apparently queer, even violent in his conduct, rather fond of posing as a confirmed invalid but at heart, a man of feeling. Though Wootton seemed to offer Rousseau all the conditions he had always desired to make him happy, Hume thought he would soon leave and be forced to admit that man was never meant for solitude.[1] In fact, having solved in a manner flattering to his *amour-propre* the enigma of his diminished prestige in England, Rousseau found life at Wootton very pleasant though, in early May, he had not entirely recovered from an attack of his old malady.[2] Davenport paid him a visit and he had other friends amongst his neighbours, especially Bernard Granville whose niece, Mary Dewes, was a great favourite. So far, apparently, Thérèse had not quarrelled with the Wootton Hall staff.

The matter of the pension began to trouble Rousseau who had been informed by Conway, through Hume, that the king desired to award him a private grant of £100 a year. Rousseau was in a quandary. He could not offend the king and the amiable general yet he could not, on the other hand, dishonour himself by accepting a pension really obtained for him by David Hume. The latter, clearly, had played his cards with diabolic cunning. Jean-Jacques wrote, therefore, to Conway on 12 May a vague, equivocal letter. Having just been overwhelmed by fresh and unexpected misfortunes, he begged leave to postpone acceptance of His Majesty's gracious bounty until such time as he should be able to enjoy it with an untroubled mind. 'Far from refusing the King's benefactions with the arrogance which is imputed to me, I should be proud to glory in them and what really

[1] *Letters of Hume*, no. 319 (to Malesherbes, 2 May 1766).
[2] *C.G.* xv, no. 3013 (to B. Granville, 3 May 1766).

distresses me is not being able to express publicly the personal pride I feel at being honoured thus.'[1] As Rousseau had intended, Hume was furious, since Conway, quite bewildered, urged him to find out whether his protégé meant that he would now accept the award only if it were conferred publicly, to which the king had no objection. Hume, at his wits end, tried to establish contact through Davenport. What was the deep affliction mentioned in Rousseau's letter to Conway? To his amazement, he learned that Jean-Jacques was as happy as a sand-boy. Finally, on 23 June, Rousseau wrote to Hume accusing him of collusion with his enemies and rejecting his further services in regard to the pension. Hume's rage and stupefaction at this 'ingratitude, ferocity and frenzy' is adequately expressed in his letter of 26 June to Davenport. At the same time, he summoned Jean-Jacques to name his unknown calumniator, recalling their previous affectionate correspondence. Rousseau, who had inadvertently opened and read Hume's letter to Davenport, remained silent until 10 July when he sent him an elaborate version of the *dossier* already communicated, in April, to Mme de Verdelin. Here is a typical extract:

> En achevant cette lettre, je suis surpris de la force que j'ai eue à l'écrire. Si l'on mourait de douleur, j'en serais mort à chaque ligne.... Je suis le plus malheureux des humains si vous êtes coupable; j'en suis le plus vil si vous êtes innocent....Si vous êtes innocent, daignez vous justifier....Encore un coup, si vous êtes innocent, daignez vous justifier: si vous ne l'êtes pas, adieu pour jamais.[2]

What are the implications of this final, reiterated appeal which has the urgency of a *cri du cœur*? Was Rousseau no longer absolutely certain of Hume's duplicity? That is not impossible. On 25 May he confessed to Mme de Verdelin:

> Vingt démonstrations de sa trahison devraient me suffire pour oser l'en accuser, et telle est la déplorable situation de mon âme que sans

---

[1] *C.G.* xv, no. 3027: 'Loin de me refuser aux bienfaits du Roi par l'orgueil qu'on m'impute, je le mettrais à m'en glorifier, et tout ce que j'y vois de pénible est de ne pouvoir m'en honorer aux yeux du public comme aux miens propres.'

[2] *C.G.* xv, no. 3068: 'On finishing this letter, I am surprised I had the strength to write it. If one died of grief, I should have died at every line....I am the most miserable of human beings if you are guilty; I am the most vile if you are innocent. ...If you are innocent, deign to justify yourself....Once again, if you are innocent, deign to justify yourself: if you are not, farewell for ever.'

être absolument convaincu, je suis tous les jours plus persuadé. Dans cette horrible perplexité que puis-je faire sinon me taire et attendre?[1]

But for Hume's persistence, it is doubtful whether Jean-Jacques would ever have accused him directly, for no fresh 'evidence' cropped up between the end of May and 19 June when the former, in cold, formal terms requested Monsieur Rousseau to indicate whether he intended to accept or refuse the pension. Indignant at what he regarded as Hume's cynical hypocrisy, Jean-Jacques launched his first direct accusation, with the inevitable consequences. Hume, who knew about the *Confessions* and was rightly jealous of his good name, denounced Rousseau to all his friends as a dangerous liar and a monster of ingratitude. That was, of course, pure nectar to the *coterie holbachique*. Others, like Mme de Boufflers, whilst condemning Jean-Jacques were surprised at Hume's talent for vituperation. A philosopher, they politely inferred, should set an example of philosophic moderation. They discounted also Hume's charge that Rousseau's letter was no sudden outburst but the culmination of a plan that had been maturing for several months. Hume, meanwhile, assembled the documents in the case and began to write a *Concise Account* of the quarrel. Copies were to be sent to Mme de Boufflers, Keith, Conway, Davenport and a few other interested parties, including one to Jean-Jacques with a list of the addressees, for information. The latter, to the amazement of his disciple, Daniel Malthus, seemed to have dismissed the whole affair from his mind.[2] 'Tout est dit désormais entre lui et moi', he wrote to Keith[3] and, despite what he heard to the contrary, openly stated that Hume would not dare to publish the correspondence relating to their quarrel. Irritated by this challenge, ignoring the advice of Turgot, Malesherbes, Mme de Boufflers and other wise friends, Hume decided to publish his *Concise Account* in Paris and London. It was translated by Suard and prepared for the press by

[1] *C.G.* xv, no. 3032: 'Twenty demonstrations of his treachery should be sufficient for daring to accuse him of it, and such is the deplorable state of my soul that without being absolutely convinced, I am daily more persuaded. In this horrible perplexity what can I do but remain silent and wait?'

[2] *C.G.* xv, no. 3073 (18 July 1766).

[3] *C.G.* xv, no. 3075 (20 July 1766): 'Everything has been said henceforth between him and me.'

D'Alembert whom Rousseau had quite wrongly designated as
the author of the Walpole forgery. The *Exposé succinct de la
contestation qui s'est élevée entre M. Hume et M. Rousseau* and its
English original produced a shower of letters and pamphlets on
both sides of the Channel. However, as the issue was purely
personal, involving no dispute about ideas, it would be misleading to speak of a polemic. Many of Rousseau's admirers
were disconcerted by his strange and nebulous 'proofs' but
ardent disciples like 'Marianne' rallied to his side. In England,
he found some support amongst the Scotophobes. Hume's active
partisans were not numerous, no doubt because Rousseau's
charges seemed to them too absurd to merit discussion and such
was the general view of his French friends. Others, however,
welcomed the opportunity for another smack at Jean-Jacques.
By February 1767 the whole affair was virtually forgotten. On
the whole, its effect had been to diminish Hume's prestige in
Paris where many impartial observers felt that his behaviour
revealed a lack of charity and, above all, of discernment since he
ought to have realised that Rousseau's distressing experiences
had disturbed his mental balance. One most unfortunate result
of the quarrel was to detach George Keith from Jean-Jacques.
Gently but firmly refusing to take sides with his 'bon fils'
against 'le bon David', *milord maréchal* regretfully intimated
that, henceforth, his letters would be less frequent. His decision
was a crushing blow to Rousseau[1] and, in conjunction with his
domestic troubles, produced a fresh attack of nerves. Thérèse,
that 'imbécile femelle' as Mme de Verdelin calls her, was now
heartily sick of Wootton. Adopting her usual technique, she
picked quarrels with the servants and made life a torment for
Jean-Jacques, persuading him that Davenport's staff resented their
presence. According to that truly angelic man, her poisonous
tongue was responsible for all her master's suspicions and so
thought Mme de Verdelin.[2] The *Correspondance* shows that
Rousseau dreaded a repetition of the Môtiers scenes. Winter
had set in and there were few visitors to Wootton. Driven

---

[1] *C.G.* xvi, no. 3193 (11 Dec. 1766). In this despairing letter Jean-Jacques
wrote that he would die of grief if Keith adhered to his 'cruel decision'.

[2] *C.G.* xvii, no. 3430 (July or August 1767).

almost frantic by the incessant naggings of Thérèse, he, in turn, pestered Davenport, bedridden with gout in Cheshire. The latter succeeded, however, in settling the matter of the pension which Jean-Jacques finally accepted on the assurance that it was offered by the king himself. At the end of March 1767 he told his host that on account of Thérèse's 'health' they intended vacating Wootton Hall. But he privately informed Louis Dutens who was buying his library that he would rather be at the mercy of all the devils in Hell than of Davenport's servants.[1] From other letters it is clear that he was once more tormented by his former delusions. Everywhere in England he suffered ignominy and humiliation, even at Wootton. Lashing out at poor Davenport, he accused him of inexcusable neglect, for surely it was his duty as a host to know what was going on in his own house. 'Demain, Monsieur, je quitte votre maison.'[2] But would he be allowed to slip so easily out of the net? Hume, who had held a government post had powerful friends and perhaps they had already closed the road to London and the coast. Having disposed of his library and, through Lord Nuneham, of his prints, Jean-Jacques decamped with Thérèse on 1 May for Spaulding probably en route for Louth where lived an old friend of Du Peyrou called De Cerjeat. But was it safe to continue his journey? In a panic, he wrote to the Lord Chancellor, Camden, asking for protection[3] and, a few days later, to Davenport, asking to be taken back, for although he preferred freedom to life at Wootton, the latter was infinitely preferable to his present horrible captivity. In point of fact, Rousseau spent much of his time at Spaulding botanising with the local parson. On 14 May, he left for Dover and remained there for three days obviously still terrified lest, at the eleventh hour, he might be prevented from sailing. His letter to Conway, written at Dover, makes painful reading, betraying that strange

---

[1] *C.G.* xvii, no. 3316 (26 March 1767).

[2] *C.G.* xvii, no. 3340 (30 April 1767): 'Tomorrow, Sir, I leave your house.'

[3] *C.G.* xvii, no. 3344 (5 May 1767). The editor, P.-P. Plan, casts doubts on the authenticity of this letter transcribed in 1879 from a copy with no indication of the addressee and preserved at the Library of the Institut de France in the manuscripts of Condorcet and D'Alembert. Plan even suggests that it may have been fabricated by Hume but gives no valid reasons for this remarkable statement. The letter was mentioned in the *St James's Chronicle* of 20 May 1767.

confusion of tragedy and farce which occurs when a luminous intelligence is temporarily clouded by delusions:

> Ma diffamation est telle en Angleterre que rien ne l'y peut relever de mon vivant.... Mais on ne veut pas que j'en sorte; je le sens, j'en ai mille preuves et cet arrangement est très naturel; on ne doit pas me laisser aller publier au-dehors les outrages que j'ai reçus dans l'île ni la captivité dans laquelle j'ai vécu....Je veux sortir, Monsieur, de L'Angleterre ou de la vie; et je sens bien que je n'ai pas le choix. Les manœuvres sinistres que je vois m'annoncent le sort qui m'attend si je feins seulement de vouloir m'embarquer...[1]

Yet a man of Rousseau's fame, he continues, cannot disappear without a trace and if Conway will only let him go, he will promise to abandon the idea of writing his memoirs and will never utter a word of complaint about his misfortunes in England.

Rousseau crossed the Channel on 21 May, proceeding by way of Abbeville to Amiens where he spent ten days, fêted by the town and receiving many visitors. Alarmed by this publicity, Conti warned him to slip away quietly before the police took action. But Rousseau, now 'M. Jacques', had already left via Saint Denis for Fleury-sous-Meudon where he remained for two weeks as the guest of that astonishing character, the marquis de Mirabeau, whose outspoken yet kindly letters had brought him much comfort during the winter months at Wootton. Mirabeau, whilst stoutly defending Hume, airily dismissed the quarrel as the clash of two diametrically opposed temperaments and 'le beau roman des machinations' as the product of an 'imagination echauffée par un foyer inextinguible'.[2] These letters, far from annoying Rousseau, delighted him because their writer was so genuinely interested in the psychology of Jean-Jacques. Mirabeau was, in fact, an extremely wise and perceptive man who was very careful, when Rousseau visited Fleury, to avoid any

---

[1] C.G. xvii, no. 3350 (approx. 18 May 1767): 'My disrepute is such in England that nothing can remove it in my lifetime.... But they do not want me to get out; I feel it; I have a thousand proofs of it and this scheme is very natural; they dare not let me publish abroad the insults I have received on the Island or the captivity in which I have lived.... Sir, I want to depart from England or from this life. I know intuitively that I have no choice. The sinister manœuvres I perceive announce the fate that awaits me if I even pretend to try to embark...'

[2] C.G. xvi, no. 3237 (27 Oct. 1766): 'the wonderful story of the machinations'... 'imagination glowing with an inextinguishable fire.'

subject which might release the pent-up agitation he observed
in his guest. The latter, he remarked tactfully, had allowed his
excessive sensibility to get the better of his reason. In these
circumstances, Rousseau's move to Conti's château at Trye was
a disastrous mistake, especially since he went there under an
alias. To the prince's servants he was a 'M. Renou' accompanied
by his 'sister'. Possibly, as Rousseau suggests, their modest
attire led the staff to treat them with veiled insolence. On the
other hand, it is clear that Thérèse lost no time in getting into
action because only a week after their arrival, Jean-Jacques began
to wonder what would happen if Conti's domestics raised the
village against him. His prize suspects were the prince's
steward, Manoury, and the *concierge*, Deschamps.

The sojourn at Trye lasted almost a year and the *Correspondance*
offers the piteous spectacle of a brilliant imagination crashing
the barrier of reason in a sheer descent into hallucination.
Transparent in all Rousseau's letters is the now familiar design
of his acute persecution mania. Hume, determined to drive him
from Trye, has somehow contrived to win over Manoury. Evil,
subterranean forces are at work in the château; the very walls
have ears; vigilant, malevolent eyes spy upon Rousseau's every
movement. Two trivial incidents convinced him that his enemies
had invented a new and horrible scheme to encompass his ruin.
Du Peyrou, though in very bad health, came to Trye in response
to his friend's urgent pleadings and whilst there had a serious
illness. In a semi-delirious state, the sick man muttered some
words which persuaded the horrified Jean-Jacques that he was
being accused by Du Peyrou of an attempt to poison him. In a
panic, he wrote a memoir for Conti minutely describing everything that had happened before, after and during the 'fatal
night' of 5 November. Du Peyrou, it appears, sank into a coma
after taking the Hoffman's drops prescribed by his doctor.
Thinking the patient was dying, Rousseau completely lost his
head and clasped Du Peyrou in his arms, weeping and uttering
stifled cries. But what was the effect produced by this effusion of
sensibility on the selfish and callous Du Peyrou? 'The barbarian
dared', writes Jean-Jacques, 'to reproach me with having chosen
the moment of his greatest weakness to give him a shock which

might finish him off.'[1] From that moment all his affection and esteem for Du Peyrou was extinguished and on the following day he cancelled the agreement by which, in return for an annuity of 1600 francs, his friend had taken over, for the *Société typographique de Neuchâtel*, all Rousseau's manuscripts and the right to produce a complete edition of his works. Eventually this pathetic but crazy imbroglio was disentangled when Du Peyrou explained that, owing to his extreme deafness, he had only partially understood Jean-Jacques. As to the delirious utterances, they had probably been suggested by two incidents: a hemlock salad recommended by his valet and what Rousseau had once told him about having been poisoned by hemlock at Wootton.

By the early spring of 1768, Rousseau's physical and mental health had greatly improved and on 28 March he confided to D'Ivernois: 'je commence à craindre après tant de malheurs réels d'en voir quelquefois d'imaginaires qui peuvent agir sur mon cerveau.'[2] But his old fears were revived by the death, two days later, of Deschamps, the *concierge*. Terrified lest he be accused of poisoning this man, one of his chief suspects, Rousseau insisted upon an autopsy.[3] He now resolved to leave Trye for Lyons despite Conti's warning that this city was in the juridical area of the Parlement de Paris. Rousseau's sudden decision gives us the measure of his grief and despair for, during all these months he had been treated with exemplary kindness, tact and patience by the prince who knew from Rousseau's disciple, Coindet, about the domestic troubles at Trye which the latter ascribed largely to the baneful influence of Thérèse. Poor Coindet's dog-like fidelity was scurvily rewarded. Jean-Jacques, whilst accepting his services now privately noted him down as one of Hume's emissaries.[4]

---

[1] C.G. xvii, no. 3526 (to Conti, 19 Nov. 1767): 'Le barbare osa me reprocher que je choisissais l'instant de sa plus grande faiblesse pour lui donner une commotion qui l'achevât.'

[2] *C.G.* xviii, no. 3638: 'I am beginning to fear, after so many real misfortunes, that I sometimes see imaginary ones which possibly affect my brain.'

[3] See his *Note mémorative sur la maladie et la mort de M. Deschamps* based on the results of the autopsy.

[4] *C.G.* xvii, no. 3468 (to Du Peyrou, 8 Sept. 1767).

Perhaps, though it is by no means certain, Rousseau stayed for two days at the Temple before leaving, on 14 June, for Lyons where he remained nearly three weeks. Accompanied by Claret de La Tourette, an official of the Lyons Mint and three ecclesiastics, he set out on a botanising excursion in the region of La Grande Chartreuse, proceeding, a few days afterwards, to Grenoble. Here, amongst many other admirers he met J.-M.-A. de Servan, *avocat-général* at the Parlement de Grenoble whose enlightened views on crime and punishment owe much to Rousseau. The latter, during his month's holiday, explored the environs of Grenoble, walking and botanising. He paid a brief visit to Chambéry not only to see the grave of Mme de Warens but also, as he told Thérèse, to give his enemies the opportunity for 'a final fling'.[1] A prey once again to delusions of persecution, revived apparently by a sharp attack of his physical malady, Rousseau suddenly departed, on 11 August, for Bourgoin where, a fortnight later, he was rejoined by his *gouvernante* who had been living at Trye. On 30 August they went through a form of marriage at the local inn, *La Fontaine d'or*. Meanwhile, an incident had occurred at Grenoble which confirmed and aggravated Rousseau's darkest suspicions. A leather-dresser called Thévenin who, it transpired, had already served a term in the galleys for forgery, publicly declared that for ten years Jean-Jacques had been owing him nine francs. Deeply agitated, Rousseau wrote to the comte de Clermont-Tonnerre, G.O.C. of the Grenoble area, demanding and obtaining an investigation which unmasked the impostor. Indeed, when confronted by his victim, Thévenin admitted they had never met before. But Rousseau, firmly convinced that the whole affair had been inspired and directed by his enemies, applied to the duc de Choiseul for a permit to leave the country, secretly hoping that the Minister would invite him to remain in France. Now we may observe the genesis of a fresh delusion. Rousseau, in the *Contrat social*, had referred admiringly to Choiseul's administration in a passage which, he wrongly imagined, had given grave offence. Obsessed by this absurd notion he wrote to Choiseul, in March 1768, urgently protesting his innocence. Now, therefore, on receiving from the

[1] *C.G.* xviii, no. 3683: 'jouir de leur reste.'

Minister for Foreign Affairs only a formal reply to his request for a passport, Rousseau was filled with mortification and despair. From that moment, the seeds of a new delusion began to germinate in his tormented brain though they took over a year to fructify. In the meantime, at the close of 1768, Rousseau found himself in a dilemma, saddled with an unwanted exit permit and at a loss to know how to use it. Perhaps in Cyprus or on some little island in the Greek archipelago, he might be able to indulge his passion for botanising, the one pursuit that soothed his frayed nerves and induced forgetfulness.[1] But on closer examination, the Cyprus scheme proved materially impossible. Remembering his kind Wootton friends, Davenport, Granville and Mary Dewes with whom he had never lost touch, Rousseau decided impulsively to spend his remaining days with them and wrote to the English Embassy for a visa. Yet, once committed to the English journey, he confessed to Moultou that the prospect filled him with horror. Minorca, he now felt, would be a better refuge. However, on receiving the English visa accompanied by a courteous note, Rousseau could not decently back out. But these scruples vanished when he learned that the ambassador's secretary was none other than the 'honnête Walpole'. On the strength of this completely false rumour, Jean-Jacques immediately abandoned the Derbyshire project and turned his eyes towards Pézenas near Montpellier, the birthplace of Moultou whose father had just died there.

In November Rousseau contracted a new malady, an inflammation of the bowels accompanied by feverish headaches. But it seems to have temporarily banished his irrational fears of which there is no trace, for example, in the closely reasoned letter to M. de Franquières, a gentleman whose belief in the existence of God had been undermined by the teachings of the *philosophes*.[2] Reaffirming his faith in the validity of intuitive knowledge, Rousseau points out that rationalist philosophy has always been obliged in the last resort to fall back on the 'inner judgment' which it professes to deride and he cites as a recent example its reply to the idealism of Berkeley. Transferring the

[1] *C.G.* xviii, no. 3728 (to Laliaud, 2 Nov. 1768).
[2] *C.G.* xix, no. 3781 (15 Nov. 1769).

onus of proof to the materialists, he asks them to demonstrate by their own empirical methods 'the purely material generation of the first intelligent being'.[1] The truth is that their atheism is rooted in a fallacy, in an *a priori* concept of the Divinity. And, Rousseau implies, because the universe does not resemble that which the ideal God of the materialist ought to have created, we are informed that God, therefore, does not exist. Equally false, for the same reason, is the familiar argument of the atheist that the existence of God is incompatible with that of Evil.

The *Lettre à M. de Franquières* closes on a very different note. Commenting on his correspondent's parallel between Socrates and Christ and on his statement that the Greek sage is superior to Our Lord, Rousseau suggests that De Franquières has failed to grasp the real personality of Jesus. And in simple words, charged with emotion, he communicates a vision of Christ's life and mission which is transparently inspired by his own experience. Christ was born amongst the vilest men who ever lived and His noble purpose was to uplift them, making them once again a free people worthy of freedom. But His base and cowardly fellow countrymen hated Him for his genius and virtue which was a reproach to their own unworthiness. And, a month later, Jean-Jacques wrote to Moultou:

Jésus, que ce siècle a méconnu...ne mourut point tout entier sur la croix; et moi qui ne suis qu'un chétif homme plein de faiblesses, mais qui me sens un cœur dont un sentiment coupable n'approcha jamais, c'en est assez pour qu'en sentant approcher la dissolution de mon corps je sente en même temps la certitude de vivre.[2]

We need not, however, picture a Jean-Jacques lost in dreams of Elysian Fields. Thérèse saw to that. She was now 48 and, as Rousseau's wife, no longer considered it necessary to indulge his caprices. Jean-Jacques had become, in short, a typical henpecked husband. In August 1769, goaded to desperation by her

---

[1] *C.G.* xix, no. 3781, p. 55.

[2] *C.G.* xix, no. 3795 (14 Feb. 1769): 'Jesus, whom this century has disowned... did not die completely on the Cross; and I who am only a sickly man full of weaknesses but who feel within me a heart which no guilty feeling ever approached, I am certain that I shall live even as I perceive the imminent dissolution of my body.'

ill-temper and threats to leave him, Rousseau took Thérèse at her word. In a long, temperately phrased letter he begged her to consider seriously the question of a separation though, of course, without her care he would soon be a dead man. On the other hand, better die a thousand deaths than continue on their present intolerable footing and witness the extinction of their former mutual confidence and friendship. And it would be shameful and dishonourable if Thérèse, as she threatened, were to leave without telling him where she was going. Meanwhile he was about to set out on a journey and had made arrangements for her future. That, he emphasised, was ordinary prudence in view of his state of health. She need not fear that he would ever take his own life. Leaving his wife to ponder over his ultimatum, Jean-Jacques departed in mid-August on a botanising excursion to Mont Pilate in the Cévennes accompanied by some friends. He returned to his home at Monquin a week later disgruntled by the rainy weather, the flea-infested beds and his companions who found him as surly as he did them. Moreover, the botanical results of the expedition had been negligible so that Rousseau was unable to send to the Duchess of Portland certain plants he had promised her. But these trifling annoyances were not the real cause of his growing depression.

Rousseau, ever since his return to France, had been longing for Paris, the forbidden city. He wanted, also, to discard his hated alias, Renou, unable or rather unwilling to recognise that if he wandered about the country under his true name, the authorities would have no option but to arrest him. In June Conti had tried in vain to drive that fact into his head.[1] Jean-Jacques pleaded for an interview which took place near Nevers. What elapsed is not clear except that the prince reluctantly agreed to undertake a certain 'preposterous and distressing commission',[2] the result of which he duly reported in September though in cryptic language. I surmise that he approached the king without success. However, Conti warned Jean-Jacques that if he carried out his idea of moving to Paris, he would do himself no good and make it impossible for the prince and other friends

---

[1] *C.G.* xix, no. 3822 (16 June 1769).
[2] *C.G.* xix, no. 3840 (2 Sept. 1769).

to assist him. Conti's letter plunged Rousseau into a state of morbid gloom which a freezing winter and the illness of Thérèse did nothing to dispel. Prolonged brooding reanimated the dark butterflies, the painful memories sleeping in Rousseau's unconscious. The 'conspiracy' now assumed terrifying dimensions, involving Mme de Boufflers, Mme de Luxembourg and Choiseul, now identified as the master mind operating behind the scenes. In Rousseau's voluminous letter to a friend, Saint-Germain, the intricate system of his delusions is fully exposed.[1] It is perhaps significant that about this time, a letter from a young married woman, Mme de Berthier, wrung from Jean-Jacques the following cry of anguish: 'Mais moi qui parle de famille, d'enfants . . . Madame, plaignez ceux qu'un sort de fer prive d'un pareil bonheur; plaignez-les s'ils ne sont que malheureux; plaignez-les beaucoup plus s'ils sont coupables.'[2] Yet, concludes Rousseau, he would rather a hundred times be the unfortunate father who neglected his duty than the perfidious friend (Diderot) who divulged a friend's secret in order to defame him.

Ignoring the urgent appeals of Saint-Germain to remain in seclusion, Rousseau decided to leave for Lyons but was held up by bad weather until early in April 1770. The delay had a disastrous effect on his nerves already frayed by the ill-temper of Thérèse who quarrelled violently with the servants at Monquin.[3] Du Peyrou, too, had annoyed him by observing humorously that, in his dealings with Jean-Jacques, he had long been resigned to a role of passive acquiescence. His little joke produced a typical reaction. Fréron had published in his *Année littéraire*[4] Rousseau's *Discours sur la vertu du héros,* an old work which the author preferred to forget. As he well knew, the manuscript copy printed by Fréron had never been deposited with Du Peyrou. Yet Rousseau now accused his old friend, in a letter to Saint-Germain, of having allowed the manuscript to be stolen and of having said nothing about the theft until further concealment was

---

[1] *C.G.* xix, no. 3884, pp. 233–62 (26 Feb. 1770).

[2] *C.G.* xix, no. 3875 (17 Jan. 1770): 'But I who speak of family, of children . . . Madame, pity those whom an iron fate deprives of such a happiness; pity them if they are merely unhappy; pity them much more if they are guilty.'

[3] *C.G.* xix, no. 3887 (Feb. 1770).

[4] T. vii, 1768.

impossible. But all his friends were now suspect, even the devoted Mme Pierre Boy de la Tour and her daughter, Mme Etienne Delessert.[1]

Jean-Jacques remained nearly two months in Lyons where the Boy de la Tour family had many relatives. A composer named Coignet set his *Pygmalion* to music and this mediocre piece was performed on 19 April, along with the famous *Devin du village*, in honour of the Intendant des Finances, Trudaine de Montigny. Little is known, however, of Rousseau's other activities in Lyons which he left on 8 June for Paris, by way of Dijon. Here, two days later, he was welcomed by the botanist Robinet who introduced him to the Président de Brosses. Robinet was besieged with visitors, mostly strangers, all eager to see the famous man in whom to his surprise, he did not notice 'the slightest singularity'.[2] And indeed, the *Correspondance* shows that the Lyons sojourn had produced a bracing effect on his morale. One incident, however, betrays the instability of Rousseau's mental state. Just before leaving for Paris, he received from the Monquin farmer and his wife a bill he had already paid. Suspecting at once another Thévenin affair, Rousseau became violently agitated. Fortunately, Saint-Germain interviewed the couple, extorted a tearful confession and procured their instant dismissal. Jean-Jacques magnanimously pronounced absolution, adding a little homily on the virtue of resignation in adversity.[3] From Dijon he made an excursion to Montbard and was received by Buffon. Travelling by way of Chablis and Auxerre he arrived in Paris on 24 June and settled down in his old haunt, the Hôtel du Saint-Esprit in the rue Plâtrière.[4]

For the first time, numerous gaps begin to appear in the vast and detailed fresco of the *Correspondance générale*. In fact, the twentieth and final tome, published in 1934, easily takes in the

---

[1] *C.G.* xix, no. 3897 (March 1770). Rousseau wrote to Mme Delessert that undoubtedly they were the dupes of wicked and cunning people so that if they deceived him, he would understand and forgive.

[2] MS. Neuchâtel, Fonds 7924 (Robinet to La Tourette, 16 June 1770). (Unpublished, I believe.)

[3] *C.G.* xix, no. 3929 (undated, to M. 'Granger', i.e. to the tenant-farmer).

[4] Since 1791 rue Jean-Jacques Rousseau. He moved in the autumn to a two-roomed flat on the fifth floor of another house in the same street and stayed there four years, afterwards occupying a house a few doors down.

last eight years of Rousseau's history. With admirable foresight, however, L. Courtois had already garnered from other
sources much interesting material which can be found in his
indispensable *Chronique*. And during the last twenty years
additional fragments of information have been unearthed in the
form of sundry letters or allusions to Jean-Jacques discovered in
obscure publications. Yet, in the last analysis, except for what
Jean-Jacques has told us, almost everything we know about his
life is due to the laborious and intelligent researches of a now
vanished generation: to Dufour, Plan, Jansen, Mrs Macdonald,
Streckeisen-Moultou. *Sit eis terra levis.*

The change of environment distracted Rousseau temporarily
from his morbid introspections which were liable to be revived,
however, at any moment by a chance word or incident remotely
connected with his delusional system. Meanwhile, delighted to
find himself the most sought-after man in Paris, he completely
forgot that he was a fugitive from justice.[1] But Sartine, the
Lieutenant-Général de Police took no action. Unmolested,
therefore, Jean-Jacques played chess at the Café de la Régence,
visited the Keeper of the Jardin des Plantes, saw his *Devin* performed at the Opéra, supped with his leading lady, Sophie
Arnould, called on old friends and dined with the Archbishop of
Embrun, uncle of his former landlady at Monquin. He received,
in his miserable lodging, a swarm of inquisitive visitors, anxious
to boast they had conversed with the most celebrated man in
Paris. At first, as he told La Tourette, his 'wounded soul'[2] was
glad of these distractions but too many dinners out soon played
havoc with his digestion. Besides, it was imperative to supplement by music copying, his meagre income of 1100 francs.
Soon, too, in order to escape the importunities of these 'terrible
people', and to breathe fresh air, Rousseau began to take long
solitary walks. His passion for botanising revived and it was,
therefore, a pleasure to welcome, in August, a pupil of the great

---

[1] See *Mémoires secrets* of Bachaumont and others, t. v (1 July 1770) for a comment on Rousseau's situation. The writer observes that even if it were true, as
people said, that the *procureur-général* had promised not to have him arrested, that
immunity would cease if anyone denounced him.

[2] *C.G.* xix, no. 3933 (4 July 1770): 'mon âme navrée.'

Linnaeus. He was a professor from Upsala called Bjoernstael who has left us the following impression of Jean-Jacques at 59:

> I should never have thought him so old, if he had not told me himself: he seems infinitely younger. He is of medium height, rather small and thickset than tall: his eyes are dark and full of fire. He keeps his head inclined to one side always and usually looks down but sometimes darts quick, furtive glances. His face is full, handsome and pleasant. His manners are amiable and gracious though his voice is loud and his speech vehement.[1]

Bjoernstael makes the interesting remark that Rousseau married Thérèse as a reward for the care she had taken of him during his illnesses. It was obvious, the professor adds, that he had not taken her for her beauty though she was not ill-favoured and was devoted to her husband.

In June 1772 Rousseau informed Lord Nuneham that, except for absolutely essential letters, he had discontinued all correspondence.[2] Extreme poverty, also, obliged him to refuse a great quantity of unfranked communications and it was his fixed policy to ignore all English letters unless he recognised the handwriting. Much of the *Correspondance générale* is taken up with his letters on botany to Malesherbes, to the Duchess of Portland and to Mme Delessert for her little daughter.[3] To this lady, her mother, Mme Pierre Boy de la Tour and Mme Guyenet (Isabelle) née D'Ivernois he wrote his most intimate letters. Through Mme Delessert, indeed, Jean-Jacques kept in touch with the very last surviving member of his family, his father's sister, Mme Goncerut (Tante Suzanne). In more affluent days he had allowed her 100 francs a year which he was resolved to continue though hardly able to do so as he tactfully informed the old lady and Mme Delessert. The undefeatable 'Marianne' was on Rousseau's track soon after his arrival in

---

[1] *C.G.* xix, Appendice, *Extraits de la traduction italienne des lettres de Bjoernstael, professeur à Upsal*, p. 375: 'Je ne l'aurais jamais cru si âgé s'il ne me l'avait dit lui-même: il semble infiniment plus jeune. Sa taille est moyenne, et plutôt petite et trapue que grande: ses yeux sont noirs et pleins de feu. Il tient toujours sa tête penchée d'un côté, et en général, il baisse la vue; mais quelquefois il lance à la dérobée de vifs regards. Il a le visage plein, bien fait et avenant. Ses manières sont aimables et gracieuses, quoique sa voix soit forte et son parler véhément.'
[2] *C.G.* xx, no. 4044.
[3] *Lettres sur la Botanique.* Six in all, written between August 1771 and May 1773.

Paris, furious because he had been there a month without in-forming her. Having failed to bring him to heel by a threat to publish their lengthy correspondence, she wormed her way into his lodgings under the pretext that she wanted some music copied. Jean-Jacques, whilst grateful for her defence of him during the Hume quarrel, firmly intimated that their liaison was at an end. Undaunted, she tried to wear down his resistance, but finally retired from the battle in March 1776 hopefully informing Rousseau of her new address, for she had remarried. Mme La Tour de Franqueville was one of those female literary snobs who are exasperating precisely because their vanity and snobbery are nearly always wedded to loyalty and goodness of heart.

One can form only a sketchy picture of Rousseau's social and domestic life during these last eight years. In the winter months he was 'nailed' to his chair, busily copying music and mounting portable herbaria for Malesherbes and other amateur naturalists. The rest of the year he botanised, usually alone, in the Parisian countryside round Ménilmontant, Gentilly or in the Bois de Boulogne. Once, with Bernard de Jussieu, he went as far afield as Montmorency. But, in August 1773, Rousseau stopped making and selling his *herbiers* and, a year later, abandoned botany. At the end of July 1772 the marquise de Mesmes was informed that he no longer paid visits either in town or country though, in fact, he still called on old friends like Mme de Créqui. From various sources one gathers that some of his callers were great noblemen: the prince de Croÿ-Solre, the comte de Crillon, the prince de Ligne, prince Galitzin and the duke of Alba with whom he maintained, at least until 1774, a sympathetic cor-respondence. They had a mutual friend in George Keith whom Jean-Jacques describes as 'l'homme que j'honore, respecte et chéris le plus au monde'.[1] Crillon talked with Rousseau on several occasions, regretting always that the hours sped like minutes. 'Cet homme a une chaleur qui est ravissante: il me semblait qu'il m'électrisait'.[2] The capricious spotlight of history

---

[1] *C.G.* xx, no. 4052 (21 July 1772): 'the man I honour, respect and cherish most in the world.'

[2] *C.G.* xx, no. 4042 (to Prince Emmanuel de Salm-Salm): 'That man has a warmth which is delightful: he seemed to electrify me.'

illuminates briefly other figures in this motley cavalcade: the Neuchâtelois, Pourtalès and Dr Levade of Vevey; J.-A. De Luc explaining that the *représentants* had done all they could for Jean-Jacques; Bernardin de Saint-Pierre with whom he attended a rehearsal of Gluck's *Iphigenia*;[1] Brooke Boothby, to whom he entrusted the manuscript of the *Premier Dialogue*; Pierre Prévost who found him, in April 1777, in great fettle, reading Tasso and composing an opera not to be given to the public;[2] the dramatist and translator of Shakespeare, Ducis with Alexandre Deleyre; Paul Moultou, to whom Rousseau entrusted several manuscripts including the *Confessions*; the Norman chevalier de Flamenville who offered him a retreat near Cherbourg; François de Chambrier who introduced Galitzin and Baron Stroganoff, and finally, the vain and obtuse Dusaulx who helped Jean-Jacques with his housing problems, received an invitation to dinner which rendered him almost delirious with pride but found himself, shortly afterwards, accused of treachery[3] and thrust into the outer darkness.

What the luckless Dusaulx could not know is that Rousseau, who had finished the *Confessions* in the autumn of 1770, had entered that phase of his mania described by psychiatrists as the 'delirium of revindication'. Obsessed with the idea of rehabilitating himself in the eyes of the French public he gave readings of his *Confessions* in February 1771 at the residence of the marquis de Pezay in the presence of the Crown Prince of Sweden and in May, at the salon of the comtesse d'Egmont. Mme d'Epinay, in a panic, asked Sartine to intervene and the readings were discontinued. For some time Grimm and Diderot had foreseen something of this kind and now awaited, with great apprehension, the publication of the *Confessions*. Esteeming that in defence of their reputation the end justified the means, they persuaded Mme d'Epinay who had written her memoirs in the form of a romanced biography, that her work could be in-

---

[1] See his *La Vie et les ouvrages de Jean-Jacques Rousseau* (ed. Souriau, 1907).

[2] *C.G.* xx, no. 4133 (13 April 1771, to G. Le Sage).

[3] Dusaulx unwisely read out to Jean-Jacques an extract from a story he was writing about a hypocrite who deluded his victims by employing the virtuous language and sentiments of Rousseau. The latter, after brooding on this peculiar situation, calmly informed Dusaulx that he was a false friend.

geniously 'doctored' so as to dishonour Jean-Jacques in the eyes of posterity. But this was only the final step in a process of systematic vilification which began in 1762 with Grimm's *Correspondance littéraire*, where Jean-Jacques was portrayed as a 'hypocrite infernal' and with Diderot's *Essai sur Claude et Néron* (ed. 1778, note 191), where he figured as 'un maniaque atrabiliaire et fou d'orgueil'.[1] The 'editing' of Mme d'Epinay's pseudo-memoirs was so expertly carried out that for over eighty years their appalling portrait of Jean-Jacques was accepted as genuine by most historians and critics. In 1905, whilst examining the original manuscripts of the pseudo-memoirs, Mrs Frederika Macdonald discovered the falsifications and exposed the plot. But unfortunately, in her passionate zeal to defend the reputation of Jean-Jacques, she made several gratuitous statements which compromised her thesis. As we have noted, however, the objective and detailed edition of Mme d'Epinay's pseudo-memoirs recently published by M. G. Roth has definitely established the authenticity of the unpleasant facts revealed by Mrs Macdonald.

Grievously disappointed at the lukewarm reaction of his private audiences to the *Confessions* and resolved, once and for all, to vindicate his innocence at the bar of public opinion, Rousseau began to compose, in 1772, his *Rousseau, Juge de Jean-Jacques. Dialogues* at which he worked for about a quarter of an hour every day during four years. Apparently this occupation acted as a safety-valve, for there were no serious manifestations of his psychosis until the beginning of 1776. On 24 February, as the result of a chance incident, his delusional state reached its climax. Terrified lest the manuscript of his *Dialogues* might be abstracted and destroyed by his enemies, Jean-Jacques decided to place it on the High Altar of Notre-Dame, thus entrusting his destiny to Almighty God. But on that particular day it so happened that the iron screen between the aisle and the choir was closed. Shattered at first by what he interpreted as a sign that God had deserted to the camp of his enemies, Jean-Jacques rushed from the Cathedral and wandered blindly through the streets. He returned to his home at nightfall in a state of physical

[1] 'A melancholy maniac crazy with pride.'

collapse. Reflection and his urgent need for consolation suggested a new interpretation of what had occurred. Far from deserting him, God had averted a disaster. His *Dialogues* would never, as he had foolishly supposed, have reached the king: they would have been intercepted and altered by his persecutors to serve their devilish purpose. Rousseau, therefore, left one of the manuscripts in the charge of the famous philosopher, the abbé Etienne Bonnot de Condillac, but not entirely trusting him, gave a copy of the first *Dialogue* to a former Wootton acquaintance, Brooke Boothby, who happened to be passing through Paris. In April Rousseau composed a circular letter *A tout Français aimant encore la justice et la vérité*, copies of which he distributed to passers-by or sent to various correspondents, pathetically reproaching the French public with having helped to defame the victim of a diabolic conspiracy and imploring the right to prove his innocence. In May Jean-Jacques read his *Confessions* to Mme de Créqui but shortly afterwards broke with her abruptly, deeply offended because she could not receive him one day, being otherwise engaged. But that, as she told a friend[1] some years later was a mere pretext. In fact, Rousseau was ashamed because, when he read out the passage about the theft of the ribbon and the fate of his children, she had burst into tears. This is highly probable for, in his *Rêveries*, which were begun either in the late summer or early autumn of 1776, Jean-Jacques returns to these distressing events.

That Rousseau's domestic situation had now become intolerable is evident from the *Mémoire* he wrote in February 1777 and circulated among a few chosen admirers. It reveals a pathetically human picture of Jean-Jacques reduced, by the successive defections of eleven servants in ten months, to the role of household drudge and sick-nurse to Thérèse. Only sheer desperation could have impelled Rousseau, normally so proud and independent, to issue this moving appeal for assistance. It appears from a letter to comte Duprat who was trying to find Rousseau a retreat near Clermont, that Thérèse was in low

---

[1] *C.G.* xx, no. 4084 (7 Aug. 1783). Plan could not identify her correspondent. But from her references to his writings, he was clearly J.-M.-A. Servan, *avocat-général* at the Parlement of Grenoble.

spirits, wailing that she would rather die in the rue Plâtrière than be exposed again to the humiliations she had suffered in the other houses they had inhabited during their travels. She was, however, not at death's door for she survived Jean-Jacques by 22 years and died at 80, in 1801.

Rather suddenly, on 20 May 1778, Rousseau left for Ermenonville where the marquis de Girardin had prepared a house for him in the charming park of his château. Oddly enough, Jean-Jacques, who told Alba that he had long ceased to have any truck with the Faculty, was accompanied by the famous physician, Le Bègue de Presle. Yet there is no evidence that his physical health had deteriorated. On 16 June we find him with Girardin at Senlis where he received the mayor and gave an audience to the *notables*. Next day he tramped to Dammartin, putting up at the Hôtel des deux Anges. The last summer of his life was very happy. At Ermenonville, his chief recreations were chamber-music, botanising with his host's small son, boating on the little lake or, seated on a grassy knoll, telling amusing stories to the Girardins. Rousseau died at eleven on the morning of 2 July in circumstances that gave rise to the kind of sinister rumours— in his case of suicide and murder—which are spawned on such occasions by malevolent or disordered imaginations. Indeed, the only *canard* lacking was that Jean-Jacques had not died at all. Housed in the Archives at Neuchâtel is a collection of forty manuscript letters from Girardin to Du Peyrou. One of them relates very simply how Rousseau died.[1] On the previous afternoon, he had complained of intestinal pains but was apparently quite well next morning. However, on returning from an errand, Thérèse became alarmed at his condition and, unobtrusively, sent for Mme de Girardin who invented some excuse for her unusual visit. Smiling gently, Rousseau said he was very touched by her fairy-tales and asked to be left alone with his wife who managed, with difficulty, to get him to bed. Rousseau then asked her to open the window so that he might look once again at the green trees and when she began to weep told her that this was the death he had always prayed for: no long illness and no doctors. He reminded Thérèse that his

---

[1] Pub. by J. S. Spink, *Ann.* xxiv, 155–9.

friends had promised not to dispose of his papers without her consent. His last requests were that he might be buried somewhere in the château grounds and that an autopsy should be performed, with an exact description of the state of his organs. Seized with violent pains, he tried to get out of bed, crying: 'Etre des Etres...Dieu! Voyez comme le ciel est pur, il n'y a pas un seul nuage. Ne voyez-vous pas que la porte m'en est ouverte et que Dieu m'attend.'[1] At these words, he fell head downwards on to the tiled floor. Attracted by the screams of Thérèse, the marquis and others rushed in and lifted Rousseau on to his bed. There was still some movement but he was dead before the doctor arrived. The famous sculptor, Houdon moulded the death-mask which is now in the Musée Jean-Jacques Rousseau at Geneva. It bears the imprint of the bruise on the forehead caused by the fall. The autopsy was carried out by Dr Le Bègue de Presle and disclosed bloody, serous matter in the brain. It is generally agreed now that Rousseau died of uraemia and that the rumours of suicide and assassination can be dismissed as pure inventions.

Girardin's correspondence with Du Peyrou makes sad reading.[2] As Rousseau's trustees, they were responsible for his manuscripts some of which were in the possession of Moultou. As Du Peyrou was at Neuchâtel and in poor health, the task of assembling the material and disposing of it so as to provide for Thérèse fell on Girardin whose loyalty to his dead friend is above praise. As a result of his tireless labours, the widow now enjoyed a life-rent of 3000 francs and lived in a fine house provided by her benefactor. We shall now observe how she repaid his disinterested kindness.

In August 1779 the marquis visited Du Peyrou at Neuchâtel to discuss the publication of Rousseau's manuscripts. Du Peyrou was worried about the fate of the *Confessions* and the *Dialogues*. Now Girardin found himself in a moral dilemma, for he had found autograph copies of these in Rousseau's desk. Thérèse, however, swore that Jean-Jacques, before his death, had given

---

[1] Bibl. de Neuchâtel, MSS. 7923. *Lettres à M. Du Peyrou*, etc. fol. 2–11 (2 July 1778): 'Being of Beings...God! See how pure the sky is, there is not a single cloud. Don't you see that its gate is open for me and that God awaits me?'
[2] *Ibid*. fol. 2–108.

explicit instructions that their existence should be kept secret
even from Du Peyrou. The latter, during Girardin's visit enlightened him as to the true character of Thérèse: 'the most
odious and vilest of women', the sole cause of his calamities and
the unworthy heiress of a man whose name she dishonoured
during his life.[1] On his return to Ermenonville, the marquis
found that, if anything, Du Peyrou was guilty of understatement.
Thérèse, now 58, became enamoured of Girardin's English valet,
John Bally, whom she determined to marry. Anticipating objections, she took the offensive and demanded a statement of
accounts from the marquis which he at once supplied, only to
learn a few days later of the projected marriage. Bally, when
interviewed, said he would be failing in his duty to himself if he
refused such a windfall. Girardin sacked him out of hand and
ordered Thérèse to leave. She settled down close by, at Plessis-
Belleville, uttering threats and insults. Her revenge was to
write to Du Peyrou accusing Girardin of having stolen her money
and various manuscripts, including the *Confessions* and part of the
Dialogues. The wretched marquis tried to explain his position
but in vain. The two executors became completely estranged.

Posterity has been unkind to Rousseau's *Dialogues* which his
critics either completely ignore or else deposit, with a sigh of
relief, on the doorstep of the psychiatrist. This is unfortunate
and seems to me inadmissible. True, rather more than one-half
of this lengthy book is a detailed account of the 'conspiracy' and,
as such, matter for the alienist. But the remainder forms an
indispensable prelude to the *Rêveries* which also reflect, in many
places, the author's delusional system though no one has ever
suggested that they lie outside the province of literature.

A striking feature of the *Dialogues* is the supreme role attributed by Rousseau to the imagination in shaping man's destiny.

---

[1] Quoted by Mlle Rosselet in her interesting article 'Thérèse Levasseur' (*Musée
Neuchâtelois*, 1939) which gives a full account of the latter's behaviour at Ermenonville. We catch a final glimpse of her in the letter of a tourist, J.-C. Grancher,
who saw her at Plessis-Belleville in June 1798. Though she had sworn to Du
Peyrou that she had no intention of remarrying after her 'irreparable loss' she
became Mrs Bally. She revolted Grancher and everyone at Ermenonville by
her horrible and stupid remarks about Jean-Jacques. Having squandered her
pension, she seems to have lived on tips from visitors for she told Grancher she had
recently got 25 louis from an English tourist. (See *C.G.* xx, p. 358.)

In a new and musical idiom he constantly glorifies 'the beneficent imagination', stressing its blessed, consolatory function:

> Enfin tel est en nous l'empire de l'imagination, et telle en est l'influence, que d'elle naissent non seulement les vertus et les vices, mais les biens et les maux de la vie humaine, et que c'est principalement la manière dont on s'y livre qui rend les hommes bons ou méchants, heureux ou malheureux ici-bas.[1]

Of course, before the arrival of Jean-Jacques, French literature reveals many symptoms of incipient revolt against the hegemony of reason, but no one hitherto had openly proclaimed that the secret of man's happiness depends entirely on how he cultivates his *faculté consolatrice*, imagination. Nowhere else in his writings does Rousseau so clearly define the line of cleavage which separates him not only from the materialists of his century but also from the humanism of a Montaigne or from the asceticism of a Pascal for whom the imagination, that 'enemy of reason', was also man's worst enemy since it had established in him a 'second nature'.[2]

The *Dialogues* establish Jean-Jacques as one of the most practical and most delicate psychologists in French literature and, in his century, *hors concours*. One may still read with profit as well as with delight the pages where he subtly distinguishes the various nuances of *rêverie*. Here is a typical example of their quality: the day-dreamer is Rousseau:

> Cependant il est vif, laborieux à sa manière. Il ne peut souffrir une oisiveté absolue: il faut que ses mains, que ses pieds, que ses doigts agissent, que son corps soit en exercice et que sa tête reste en repos. Voilà d'ou vient sa passion pour la promenade; il y est en mouvement sans être obligé de penser. Dans la rêverie on n'est point actif. Les images se tracent dans le cerveau, s'y combinent comme dans le sommeil, sans le concours de la volonté; on laisse à tout cela suivre sa marche, et l'on jouit sans agir. Mais quand on veut arrêter, fixer les objets, les ordonner, les arranger, c'est autre chose; on y met du sien.

---

[1] *H.* IX, 204, *Second Dialogue*: 'In short, such is in us the sway of imagination and such its influence that from it arise not only the virtues and vices, but the good and evil of human life and it is chiefly the manner in which we surrender to it that makes men good or wicked, happy or unhappy in this world.'

[2] *Pensées*, no. 82.

Sitôt que le raisonnement et la réflexion s'en mêlent, la méditation n'est plus un repos, elle est une action très pénible; et voilà la peine qui fait l'effroi de Jean-Jacques.[1]

Rousseau, without doubt, meant the *Dialogues* to be his last work. It is the *summa* of his sentimental, moral and intellectual experience from boyhood to old age. Here, too, Jean-Jacques resolves in a masterly synthesis the apparently contradictory elements which, in their ensemble, compose the personality of one regarded by his contemporaries as 'un homme nouveau'. This, he protests, is a profound error. The truth is that he represents a very old, but rapidly vanishing species: the man of Nature. The 'new man' is the product of materialism, of so-called progress. In the *philosophes*, those 'cadaverous souls', Rousseau discerns a much greater threat to human freedom than the Society of Jesus whose propaganda methods they have adopted; packing the Académie Française with their nominees; insinuating their teachings into the seminaries and colleges; placing their disciples in private houses as tutors or as secretaries to influential administrators. There is nothing delusional in this indictment.

Probably in the late summer of 1776, Rousseau began to write his last book, *Les Rêveries du promeneur solitaire* and worked on it until April 1778. He never completed the tenth and final *Promenade*. Crushed by the Notre-Dame fiasco and by subsequent events, Rousseau imagined that with the 'unanimous consent'[2] of society he was now branded as a moral leper. In this illusion, so terribly real to Jean-Jacques, lies our only clue to the purpose, meaning and essential unity of his 'shapeless journal',[3] the record of his survival from an ordeal which would have

[1] *H.* IX, 224: 'However, he is lively and in his own way, hard-working. He cannot stand absolute idleness: his hands, feet and fingers must be active, his body exercised, his mind at rest. Hence his passion for walking; then he is in motion without being obliged to think. In reverie, one is not active, The images trace themselves on the brain and there combine, as in sleep, without the help of the will; one lets all that go its own way, enjoying without acting. But it is a very different thing when one wants to arrest and fix objects, to arrange and order them; one cooperates. As soon as reasoning and reflection come in, meditation is no longer repose, it is very painful action and that is what terrifies Jean-Jacques.'

[2] *R.* 7: 'un accord unanime.'

[3] *R.* 14: 'un informe journal de mes rêveries.'

annihilated the spirit of an ordinary man. Viewed in perspective, the *Rêveries* illuminate the final phase of Rousseau's life-long struggle to preserve the integrity of his fundamental self in an age dedicated to the cult of material progress, the 'new doctrine' which might ultimately destroy mankind by eliminating what is specifically natural and human in the individual. That is the real 'conspiracy' so grotesquely stylised in the delusions of Jean-Jacques. The 'secte philosophique' had wreaked a terrible revenge on their former colleague by hounding him from society with every circumstance of ignominy. But, if they had succeeded in discrediting his writings they had failed to kill the spirit from which his philosophy emanated: the self inured so long to neglect, misunderstanding and contempt, and indestructible by virtue of its unique inner resources. What these were and how they delivered Jean-Jacques from the suffering and despair generated by his proscription is the story recorded in the *Rêveries*.

Rousseau, it should be noted, constantly insists that this state of isolation was alien to his nature and imposed on him by duress. We need not, therefore, identify him with those unhappy souls who seek, in some form of mystic contemplation, a refuge from the cruelty of life.[1] Nor, of course, was he capable of that effort once described as 'the mysterious and total gift of oneself' which results in a joyful fusion of the troubled soul with God's love. True, in a first violent access of despair, Rousseau made a futile attempt at escape to the plane of a godlike impassivity. But he knew, like his own Emile, that such an attitude can only be ephemeral; that no mortal can find deliverance in the total extinction of his sensibility. 'Mais quel être sensible peut vivre toujours sans passions, sans attachements? Ce n'est pas un homme; c'est une brute, ou c'est un dieu.'[2] Brute or god? The following passage suggests the instinctive 'freezing' of the tracked beast rather than the majestic remoteness of a divinity: '...m'y voilà tranquille au fond de l'abîme, pauvre mortel

---

[1] M. Osmont, for instance (*Ann.* xxiii, 99), describes the state of somnolence which Jean-Jacques sought in his reveries or day-dreams as 'a sort of nirvana'. But I can find nothing in the *Rêveries* or elsewhere to suggest that Rousseau was capable of the elaborate mystic discipline which is a prelude to nirvana.

[2] *H.* iii, 2: 'But what sentient being can live always without passions or attachments. It is not a man. It is a brute or it is a god.' (*Emile et Sophie.*)

infortuné, mais impassible comme Dieu même.'[1] In fact, the theme of religion scarcely enters into the *Rêveries* and this is one aspect of their originality. Precisely because, in his great loneliness, Jean-Jacques found other avenues of escape than the way to God, the *Rêveries* initiated a new literary genre: the literature of contemplation and introspection.

Twice in the *Rêveries*, in the third and sixth *Promenades*, we read that Jean-Jacques was never made for society, yet every page betrays the anguish caused by his illusion of social isolation. The book is, indeed, a journal of escape and of spiritual survival. A passage in the sixth *Promenade*, however, explains the apparent contradiction: 'The wrong they [his persecutors] did me was not in brushing me aside as a useless member of society, but in proscribing me as a pernicious member.'[2] It is one thing, Rousseau implies, to be treated as an idle dreamer, a social misfit, a fellow with a bee in his bonnet on the subject of personal liberty. It is quite another to be branded as an evil man, an enemy of the human race. And in the same context, obviously tormented by memories of his conduct towards Mme d'Epinay, he dwells once again on the interconnected themes of friendship, obligation and natural goodness. Since virtue always involves the conquest of our natural inclinations, Rousseau cannot honestly claim that his good actions were virtuous. To find pleasure in well-doing he had to feel free: the moment a good action presented itself as a duty, well-doing was robbed for him of its sweetness. The implication is clear. What passes for virtue is simply another habit imposed on the individual by society: in no way does it reflect his real personality. Jean-Jacques, evidently, did not believe that moral habits may, in time, induce a moral and happy state of soul. Yet in what other sense must we interpret the Gospel teachings of which Rousseau claimed such a profound and unique knowledge?

How then did Jean-Jacques, cut off from society, excluded from the social effort, recover 'serenity, tranquility, peace, even

---

[1] *Op. cit.* 13: '...behold me then, lying quietly in the depths of the abyss, a poor unfortunate mortal, but impassive like God Himself.'

[2] *R.* 103: 'Leur tort n'a donc pas été de m'écarter de la société comme un membre inutile, mais de m'en proscrire comme un membre pernicieux.'

happiness'[1] and, what is more important, how did he maintain this state of inner harmony and equilibrium? Quite simply, by following the contours of his character. Ever since childhood, he had practised the art of evading unpleasant realities by various methods. These he now co-ordinated into a system or technique of escape based on what might be described as the principle of selective or pragmatic introspection. Rousseau tells us that during his long and solitary walks in the rustic suburbs of Paris, he left his mind to wander at its sweet will, exercising no control over its thoughts or representations: 'These hours of solitude and meditation are the only ones of the day when I am completely myself and occupied with myself without distraction or hindrance and when I can truly say I am what Nature intended.'[2] But, in fact, this was an artificially induced state of soul because, as Jean-Jacques admits in the first *Promenade*, he began by excluding from his consciousness 'all the disagreeable objects which it would be painful as well as useless for me to think about'.[3] These things, in short, were thrust into his unconscious, eluding therefore the exploring beam of his introspection. This psychological fact must be kept in mind if we would interpret correctly such expressions as: 'm'étudier moi-même'; 'l'habitude de rentrer en moi-même'; 'Réduit à moi seul, je me nourris de ma propre substance'.[4]

At times, however, Rousseau's technique of escape failed him. Read, for example, in the fourth *Promenade* his discourse on lying which is a fascinating yet repellent exercise in casuistry prompted by involuntary memories of the purloined ribbon and poor Marion. Or again, turn to the ninth *Promenade* where Jean-Jacques communicates, in simple words charged with sincere remorse, the poignant emotions that rent his soul when, on one of his lonely walks, a playful child clasped his knees and smiled up into his face. In these moments of unguarded introspection,

---

[1] *R.* 129: '...la sérénite, la tranquillité, la paix, le bonheur même.'

[2] *R.* 18: 'Ces heures de solitude et de méditation sont les seules de la journée où je sois pleinement moi et à moi, sans diversion, sans obstacle et où je puisse véritablement dire être ce que la nature a voulu.'

[3] *R.* 13: 'tous les pénibles objets dont je m'occuperais aussi douloureusement qu'inutilement'.

[4] 'To study myself'; 'the habit of getting back inside myself'; 'Reduced to myself alone, I feed on my own substance'.

Rousseau observes with astonishing lucidity the reactions of his deepest self to its impressions of the external world. Of this we have a remarkable illustration in the second *Promenade*:

> La nuit s'avançait. J'aperçus le ciel, quelques étoiles, et un peu de verdure. Cette première sensation fut un moment délicieux. Je ne me sentais encore que par là. Je naissais dans cet instant à la vie, et il me semblait que je remplissais de ma légère existence tous les objets que j'apercevais. Tout entier au moment présent je ne me souvenais de rien; je n'avais nulle notion distincte de mon individu, pas la moindre idée de ce qui venait de m'arriver; je ne savais ni qui j'étais ni où j'étais; je ne sentais ni mal, ni crainte, ni inquiétude. Je voyais couler mon sang comme j'aurais vu couler un ruisseau, sans songer seulement que ce sang m'appartînt en aucune sorte. Je sentais dans tout mon être un calme ravissant, auquel chaque fois que je me le rappelle, je ne trouve rien de comparable dans toute l'activité des plaisirs connus.[1]

In the above passage Rousseau is describing his return to consciousness after having been knocked down and stunned by a large dog which ran into him.

When the meandering stream of Rousseau's consciousness follows its predefined channels of escape, the *Rêveries* display a range of emotional nuances and qualities of style which come as a surprise and delight even after the *Confessions* and the *Dialogues*. Perhaps that is because Rousseau in the *Rêveries*, is no longer the apologist or the 'judge' but rather the anxious, reassuring elder brother of Jean-Jacques. We read in the first *Promenade* that, unlike Montaigne, he is writing only for himself; for the sheer pleasure of 'conversing' with his soul.

> If in my extreme old age, when the hour of departure approaches, I remain, as I hope, in my present disposition, to read them [the *Rêveries*] will recall the delight I experience in writing them and by resurrecting past time for me, will, as it were, double my existence.

---

[1] R. 23: 'Night was falling. I perceived the sky, a few stars and a little verdure. That first sensation was a delicious moment. It was still only through it that I could feel myself. In that moment I was born to life and it seemed to me that I filled with my whole slight existence all the objects I perceived. Wholly in the present moment, I remembered nothing; I had no distinct notion of my individuality, not the least idea of what had just happened to me; I did not know who I was or where I was; I felt neither hurt, nor fear nor anxiety. I saw my blood flowing as I would have seen a brook flowing without even dreaming that this blood belonged to me in any way. I felt in all my being a delightful calm with which, every time I recall it, I can find nothing comparable in all the activity of known pleasures.'

Despite men, I shall enjoy once again the charm of society and I shall live, decrepit, with myself in another age, as I should live with a friend less old.[1]

Perhaps one might best describe the *Rêveries* as an anthology of the emotional, philosophic and aesthetic moods induced by a past-master in the art of spiritual self-preservation. Rousseau's most constant and most durable state of soul in affliction was the liminary state he calls *rêverie* or *extase* where the self, hovering on the brink of sleep, is conscious only of its actual existence and would fain seal off for ever the future and the past, eternalising a precious fragment of its consciousness. Man cannot arrest the rhythmic and inexorable flow of life but his art can create the illusion of such a miracle. That Rousseau achieved in the fifth *Promenade*, when he relived his brief, enchanting sojourn on the Ile de Saint-Pierre. For nowhere else did he experience more completely the delights of *far niente*, the ecstasies of reverie.

Quand le soir approchait, je descendais des cimes de l'île et j'allais volontiers m'asseoir au bord du lac, sur la grève, dans quelque asile caché: là le bruit des vagues et l'agitation de l'eau, fixant mes sens et chassant de mon âme toute autre agitation, la plongeaient dans une rêverie délicieuse où la nuit me surprenait souvent sans que je m'en fusse aperçu. Le flux et le reflux de cette eau, son bruit continu mais renflé par intervalles, frappant sans relâche mon oreille et mes yeux, suppléaient aux mouvements internes que la rêverie éteignait en moi, et suffisaient pour me faire sentir avec plaisir mon existence, sans prendre la peine de penser. De temps à autre naissait quelque faible et courte réflexion sur l'instabilité des choses de ce monde dont la surface des eaux m'offrait l'image: mais bientôt ces impressions légères s'effaçaient dans l'uniformité du mouvement continu qui me berçait, et qui sans aucun concours actif de mon âme ne laissait pas de m'attacher au point qu'appelé par l'heure et par le signal convenu, je ne pouvais m'arracher de là sans efforts.[2]

---

[1] *R.* 15–16: 'Si dans mes plus vieux jours, aux approches du départ, je reste, comme je l'espère, dans la même disposition où je suis, leur lecture me rappellera la douceur que je goûte à les écrire, et faisant renaître ainsi pour moi le temps passé, doublera pour ainsi dire mon existence. En dépit des hommes je saurai goûter encore le charme de la société et je vivrai décrépit avec moi dans un autre âge, comme je vivrais avec un moins vieux ami.'

[2] *R.* 81–2: 'When evening drew near, I came down from the crest of the island and I used to love to sit at the lakeside, on the strand, in some hidden sanctuary. There, the sound of the waves and the rippling of the water, fixing the attention of my senses and purging my soul of all other agitation, plunged it into a delicious

Here, in his musical, rythmic prose, Jean-Jacques communicates a purely sensuous experience, an *extase* quite different in quality from a mystic ecstasy. Nor is there anything truly mystic in the intoxicating sensation he sometimes procured of a fusion with the physical universe.[1] We have only to read his practical hints to beginners on the art of inducing reverie to realise that he is describing a state of self-hypnosis. The subject must remain calm; the indispensable external movement must be uniform and smooth; if it is too violent or jerky, the subject will be painfully recalled to a consciousness of the external world and of his misfortunes.[2]

On the topic of his reawakened interest in botany, Jean-Jacques mentions in the seventh *Promenade* an illuminating psychological fact which profoundly affected his passion for reverie and produced a new perception of Nature:

> In this state, an instinct natural to me, causing me to shun any depressing idea, imposed silence on my imagination and, fixing my attention on the objects surrounding me, made me for the first time observe in detail the spectacle of Nature which I had hitherto scarcely ever contemplated save in the mass and in its ensemble.[3]

In fact, as the *Rêveries* disclose, Rousseau's 'feeling for Nature' presents a curious variety of conscious states. Whilst studying the delicate structural perfection of plants and, above all, their ingenious reproductive mechanism, he experienced a satisfaction at once aesthetic and intellectual. More intense were

---

reverie in which I was often surprised by nightfall without my having noticed. The ebb and flow of the water, its continuous sound, but swelling at intervals, ceaselessly falling on my ears and arresting my eyes, took the place of the deep emotions extinguished by reverie and were just sufficient to leave me with a pleasurable sensation of my existence without my having to take the trouble to think. From time to time there glimmered a brief reflection on the instability of wordly things whose image was adumbrated on the surface of the waters: but soon these faint impressions vánished in the continuous motion which lulled me and which, entirely without my conscious or active participation, never failed to engross me so completely that, when recalled by the lateness of the hour and by the pre-arranged signal, I could not tear myself away without an effort.'

[1] *R.* 112.   [2] *R.* 85–6.

[3] *R.* 107: 'Dans cet état, un instinct qui m'est naturel, me faisant fuir toute idée attristante, imposa silence à mon imagination, et fixant mon attention sur les objets qui m'environnaient me fit pour la première fois détailler le spectacle de la nature, que je n'avais guère contemplé jusqu'alors qu'en masse et dans son ensemble.'

the impressions made on his senses by the colours, scents and harmonies of Nature especially, says Jean-Jacques, in his old age when pleasure came to him almost exclusively through his sensations. But Nature was now, *par excellence*, a refuge from the cruelty of her children, a theme which constantly recurs in the *Rêveries*. In the cool, green depths of the forest or on some lonely mountain side he enjoyed a blissful feeling of security, 'forgotten, free and at peace as if I had no enemies'.[1] On the other hand, he always retained that 'horror' of uninhabited Nature so typical of the eighteenth century, a paradox charmingly illustrated in the seventh *Promenade*. Botanising in the Jura, he found himself on the desolate upper slopes of Mount Robaila in a solitude broken only by the screams of eagle and osprey. To escape his sense of awe and fear, Rousseau pictured himself as a new Columbus, the first ever to penetrate a 'sanctuary unknown to the whole universe'.[2] But suddenly a familiar clacking noise struck his ear. Carefully parting the undergrowth, he beheld, about twenty yards away, a stocking-factory in full operation. Even more remarkable was the emotional conflict which followed this discovery: the instinctive *élan* of joy at finding himself once more among his fellow men and then, the painful recollection of his isolation.

The *Rêveries* fade out in the afterglow of a remembered happiness tinged with regret for the paradise that Jean-Jacques lost when Mme de Warens ceased to love him. Such is the mood reflected in the lovely opening phrase of the tenth *Promenade*: 'Aujourd'hui jour de Pâques fleuries.'[3] For the ageing Rousseau, these words possessed the quality of a benediction, evoking visions of innocence, beauty and youth. And so, on the last of his solitary walks, we catch our final glimpse of him, travelling fast along familiar roads, homeward bound for Les Charmettes, Chambéry, Annecy and the golden, radiant past.

[1] *R.* 118: 'oublié, libre et paisible, comme si je n'avais plus d'ennemis.'
[2] *R.* 119: 'un refuge ignoré de tout l'univers.'
[3] 'Today, Palm Sunday.' It was, therefore, the fiftieth anniversary of Rousseau's first meeting with Mme de Warens.

INDEX

(*Note.* Principal references are given in italics)

24   G R

DATE DUE